INTERNATIONAL LAW
AND ARMED CONFLICT

INTERNATIONAL LAW
AND ARMED CONFLICT

FUNDAMENTAL PRINCIPLES AND CONTEMPORARY CHALLENGES IN THE LAW OF WAR

CONCISE SECOND EDITION

LAURIE R. BLANK
CLINICAL PROFESSOR OF LAW
DIRECTOR, INTERNATIONAL HUMANITARIAN LAW CLINIC
EMORY UNIVERSITY SCHOOL OF LAW

GREGORY P. NOONE
CAPT, JAGC, USN (RET.)
DIRECTOR, NATIONAL SECURITY AND INTELLIGENCE PROGRAM
PROFESSOR OF POLITICAL SCIENCE AND LAW
FAIRMONT STATE UNIVERSITY

ASPEN
PUBLISHING

To contact Customer Service, e-mail customer.service@aspenpublishing.com, call 1-800-950-5259, or mail correspondence to:

Aspen Publishing
Attn: Order Department
PO Box 990
Frederick, MD 21705

Cover: U.S. Army Soldiers transport a trauma victim to a U.S. Army medical helicopter in Tarmiyah, Iraq, Sept. 30, 2007. The Soldiers are working with local Iraqi hospital personnel in administering aid to trauma victims following an explosion caused by insurgents, which wounded several civilians. The Soldiers are from Charlie Company, 4th Battalion, 9th Infantry Regiment, 4th Stryker Brigade Combat Team, 2nd Infantry Division out of Ft. Lewis, Washington. (U.S. Navy photo by Mass Communication Specialist 2nd Class Summer M. Anderson).

Printed in the United States of America.

2 3 4 5 6 7 8 9 0

ISBN 978-1-5438-3553-3

Library of Congress Cataloging-in-Publication Data

Names: Blank, Laurie R., author. | Noone, Gregory P., author.
Title: International law and armed conflict : fundamental principles and
    contemporary challenges in the law of war / Laurie Blank, Gregory P.
    Noone.
Description: Concise second edition. | Frederick, MD: Aspen Publishing, 2021. | Includes
    bibliographical references and index. | Summary: "Textbook for courses
    on law and war"– Provided by publisher.
Identifiers: LCCN 2021030544 (print) | LCCN 2021030545 (ebook) | ISBN
    9781543835533 (paperback) | ISBN 9781543835540 (ebook)
Subjects: LCSH: War (International law) | LCGFT: Casebooks (Law)
Classification: LCC KZ6385 .B53 2021 (print) | LCC KZ6385 (ebook) | DDC
    341.6–dc23
LC record available at https://lccn.loc.gov/2021030544
LC ebook record available at https://lccn.loc.gov/2021030545

About Aspen Publishing

Aspen Publishing is a leading provider of educational content and digital learning solutions to law schools in the U.S. and around the world. Aspen provides best-in-class solutions for legal education through authoritative textbooks, written by renowned authors, and break-through products such as Connected eBooks, Connected Quizzing, and PracticePerfect.

The Aspen Casebook Series (famously known among law faculty and students as the "red and black" casebooks) encompasses hundreds of highly regarded textbooks in more than eighty disciplines, from large enrollment courses, such as Torts and Contracts to emerging electives such as Sustainability and the Law of Policing. Study aids such as the *Examples & Explanations* and the *Emanuel Law Outlines* series, both highly popular collections, help law students master complex subject matter.

Major products, programs, and initiatives include:

- **Connected eBooks** are enhanced digital textbooks and study aids that come with a suite of online content and learning tools designed to maximize student success. Designed in collaboration with hundreds of faculty and students, the Connected eBook is a significant leap forward in the legal education learning tools available to students.
- **Connected Quizzing** is an easy-to-use formative assessment tool that tests law students' understanding and provides timely feedback to improve learning outcomes. Delivered through CasebookConnect.com, the learning platform already used by students to access their Aspen casebooks, Connected Quizzing is simple to implement and integrates seamlessly with law school course curricula.
- **PracticePerfect** is a visually engaging, interactive study aid to explain commonly encountered legal doctrines through easy-to-understand animated videos, illustrative examples, and numerous practice questions. Developed by a team of experts, PracticePerfect is the ideal study companion for today's law students.
- The **Aspen Learning Library** enables law schools to provide their students with access to the most popular study aids on the market across all of their courses. Available through an annual subscription, the online library consists of study aids in e-book, audio, and video formats with full text search, note-taking, and highlighting capabilities.
- Aspen's **Digital Bookshelf** is an institutional-level online education bookshelf, consolidating everything students and professors need to ensure success. This program ensures that every student has access to affordable course materials from day one.
- **Leading Edge** is a community centered on thinking differently about legal education and putting those thoughts into actionable strategies. At the core of the program is the Leading Edge Conference, an annual gathering of legal education thought leaders looking to pool ideas and identify promising directions of exploration.

Summary of Contents

CONTENTS

The law of armed conflict governs the conduct of states, individuals, and non-state actors during armed conflict and is a dynamic field replete with constantly changing questions and challenges. It is based on treaty law, customary international law, domestic law, and international and domestic jurisprudence, all of which must be woven together along with policy and operational considerations. Studying and applying the law of armed conflict (LOAC) requires a grasp of the fundamental principles of the law and how they interact with each other and with related legal frameworks in a complicated and ever-changing world. Also called international humanitarian law (IHL) or the law of war, LOAC dates back thousands of years and has served as an essential guide for military commanders and lawyers, particularly, throughout modern history.

In the 1990s, genocide, war crimes, mass atrocities, and international criminal justice became part of the public discourse in the aftermath of the conflicts in the former Yugoslavia, Rwanda, Sierra Leone, and ongoing conflicts in the Democratic Republic of the Congo, Sudan, and elsewhere. The attacks of September 11, 2001, then brought LOAC onto the front page—we have engaged now for two decades in an ongoing national and international conversation about detention, the nature of conflicts with terrorist groups, interrogation, targeted killing, asymmetrical warfare, military commissions, cyber and other new technologies, hybrid or grey zone warfare, and a host of other complex conflict-related topics. Understanding how the law regulates behavior during conflict and in the aftermath of conflict is fundamental to the study of not only LOAC, but also international law, international relations, national security, conflict resolution, post-conflict justice systems, war and conflict, and other related topics.

On the macro level, therefore, the instruction, materials, and discussions in this book prepare you to (1) understand and apply the law applicable in times of conflict; (2) understand the role of international law in conflict, counterterrorism operations, stability operations, and other complex situations; (3) analyze the obligations of the United States and other countries when engaged in various types of military operations, including traditional interstate war, asymmetrical warfare, counterterrorism, counterinsurgency, and more; and (4) develop a more nuanced understanding of the current world situation and modern conflicts. The key issues in the law of armed conflict—protection of civilians, distinguishing between combatants and civilians, humane treatment, accountability for atrocities—are not only relevant and important for lawyers, but for policy makers and ordinary citizens alike. Whether you are—or are on your way to becoming—a lawyer, an advocate, a military officer, a policy maker, or other public actor, you can and should grapple with the moral issues that arise in conflict, such as targeted killing, torture, human shields, proportionality, and self-defense, and understand how the moral questions relate to the legal paradigms and influence policy.

This second concise edition of *International Law and Armed Conflict* provides condensed instruction and analysis of the key topics in the law of armed conflict. Like the original edition and the first concise edition, this book addresses three main components: the fundamental principles and history of the law of armed conflict; the applicable law and sources of that law; and the application, implementation, and enforcement of the law. The information is organized in a functional manner to provide a clear and concise framework for understanding and analyzing the information: *why* do we have a law of armed conflict; *what* is armed conflict, and *when* does it occur; *who* are the relevant persons in armed conflict; and *how* must states and individuals conduct themselves during armed conflict. Throughout, this structure mirrors the analytical approach that militaries take to the application of the law of armed conflict, often termed the "right kind of conflict, right kind of person" approach. That is, one must first understand what type of conflict is taking place and then what category of person or persons are involved before analyzing the relevant conduct. After a preliminary section setting forth the *why*—the historical underpinnings of the law of armed conflict and the justifications and purposes for a law governing what might otherwise appear to be a state of lawlessness and violence—the book tackles the major components of the law: *what* and *when* (i.e., what triggers the application of the law and for how long), *who* (i.e., to whom does the law, or particular provisions, apply in a given circumstance and for what reason), and *how* (i.e., how are states and individuals obligated to conduct themselves while in armed conflict). The final section then examines enforcement of the law and accountability for violations of the law—the natural next step once students have a foundational understanding of the relevant legal obligations. To provide this same instructional value in this concise edition, we eliminated most of the primary source excerpts, offering instead a tailored summary of the key points of each case, and condensed several sections to achieve an efficient and agile volume for use in a wide variety of educational and training settings.

Finally, a word about bringing LOAC to life in the classroom. One of the main challenges in teaching the law of armed conflict is conveying a sense of the real world of conflict and on-the-ground issues that arise. Most students studying this subject will not have served in the military and will have little or no experience in conflict or post-conflict environments. It is essential, therefore, to use materials that go beyond treaty law and domestic and international jurisprudence, materials that bring the complex and complicated world of armed conflict to life, such as after-action reports and other operational materials, newspaper articles, movie scenes, biographical accounts of war, and other diverse materials. Alongside these more conventional materials, woven throughout the book you will find short first-person vignettes, real stories written by practitioners with operational experience and expertise in the specific topic. These vignettes pose interesting questions from a wide range of past and present conflict situations and offer an extraordinary opportunity to bring the relevant issues and questions to life for students and faculty alike. In essence, the pages of this book bring military lawyers, commanders, human rights advocates, international officials and others into the classroom directly to tell their stories and challenge you to seek answers to difficult questions.

LOAC has always been a living, breathing body of law rather than a static set of concepts, repeatedly adapting to changing and uncertain circumstances. The key principles of LOAC—introduced at the start of the book and used as the foundational analytical structure throughout—are critical to the ability of militaries around the world to carry out effective military operations. Use them as your own tools, whether in the classroom, in a career in operational law or advocacy for international criminal justice, or as an informed citizen of the world.

Laurie R. Blank
Gregory P. Noone

July 2021

ACKNOWLEDGMENTS

Throughout the process of writing this book, we have benefitted from the generous support, wise counsel, and tireless efforts of many friends, colleagues, and students. Contributions came in all manner and form—from brief conversations and written contributions to research, proofreading, and editing. We have the great good fortune—and great pleasure—to be part of a remarkable community of people working and teaching in the field of the law of armed conflict: military lawyers, academics, government officials, and attorneys at nongovernmental organizations. Above all, we want to express our deepest thanks and affection for all of these friends and colleagues, who make the study and teaching of the law of armed conflict engaging, fun, and dynamic every day. Many of you contributed vignettes and stories from your personal experiences—some by name and some anonymously; your willingness to share your first-person stories and accounts of interesting legal issues and challenges truly brings the law to life for students and faculty alike. Others offered equally helpful insights, suggestions, and questions. We are thus grateful for the assistance, support, and contributions from so many, including Michael Schmitt, Geoffrey Corn, Dick Jackson, Eric Jensen, Daphné Richemond-Barak, Anne Quintin, Adam Oler, Emanuela Gillard, Amos Guiora, Thomas Ayres, Chad Brooks, Diana Noone, Sandra Hodgkinson, Chris Jenks, Kurt Larson, Russ Verby, Dan Rice, Ben May, Jonathan Shapiro, Uncle Hank Zabierek, Karl Farris, Ken Magee, Michael Scharf, Paul Williams, Rick Sinnott, Robert Ault, Richard Whitaker, Charles Garraway, Bonnie Docherty, Mark Silverman, Charles Dunlap, Sean Watts, Gregory Gordon, David Green, Aniela Szymanski, Jamie Williamson, Paul Kong, Amelia Griffith, Bret Swaim, John-Paul Wheatcroft, Jason Morris, Kurt Sanger, Patricia Viseur Sellers, Cyanne Loyle, Pete "Pene" Hayes, Phil Fluhr, Chris Fleming, John Danner, Kevin Brew, John Marley, and Tim Manning. In many ways, this book itself is an expression of our gratitude for your friendship, expertise, and advice over many years.

In our effort to recognize everyone who graciously and enthusiastically provided assistance throughout this process, we realize that we run the risk of omitting someone—for that we apologize in advance.

No one carried more weight than Emory University School of Law 2011 graduate Ben Farley. Through his constant efforts in providing real-time research and top-quality analysis and insights, as well as his invaluable editing and citation assistance, he made truly immeasurable contributions to the book, and we are extraordinarily grateful not only for his fantastic work but also for his enthusiasm and devotion to the project.

We also want to single out Audrey Patten, Emory University School of Law 2012 graduate, for whom no historical research was too buried in the archives, and the efforts of Fairmont State University and University of Chicago Law School graduate Nick Oliveto. Both were instrumental in tracking all things large and small. No task was too great, no needle too lost in a haystack. We also thank Emory Law School Deans Jim Hughes and Mary Anne Bobinski for their support, both financial support for research assistance and encouragement.

Numerous law students at Emory University School of Law, Case Western Reserve University School of Law, and Roger Williams University School of Law School stepped up to provide research and assistance on countless areas throughout the book. They include, but are not limited to: Emory—Jade Gaudet, Elise Foreman, Hana Shatila, Bradley Gershel, Aalia Maan, Mithuna Sivaraman, Tariq Mohideen, Martin Bunt, Nick Aliotta, Christina Zeidan, Kayla Polonsky, Kyle Hunter, Sai Santosh Kolloru, and all the students in the 2011 and 2012 International Humanitarian Law Clinic at Emory Law School; Case Western—Jacob Lipp, Thomas Au, Brett O'Brien, Sarah Pierce, Zachary Smigiel, Andrew November, LaVonne Pulliam, Brin Anderson, Rebecca Clayton Smith, Nathan Quick, Elisabeth Herron, Ruth Dickey, Anna Blum, Christian Greco, Stephanie Corley, Effy Folberg, Tyler Talbert, Anna Hoelzel, Drew Dennis, Melinda Robinson, Sarah Ashley Cotterell, Russell Caskey, Kyle Johnson, Sarah Nasta, Ted Parran, Stuart Sparker, Brittany Pizor, LeAnne Dao, Cameron MacLeod, and all the students in the 2011, 2012, and 2013 International Humanitarian Law course at Case Western; Roger Williams—Tunde T. Adepegba and Alisha Perry.

We would also like to thank the many National Security and Intelligence students at Fairmont State University for their support in this project: Joe McCarty, Dennis Burke, Bruce Lane, Ben McClain, Valbona Palco, Tyler Hawkins, Travis Brown, Olivia Bowen, Gregory Stockinger, Dustin Hotsinpiller, Meagan Gibson, Kait Yohe, Sarah Heppner, Troy Heaney, Robert Bolton, Timothy Holmes, Dominick Pellegrin, Darren Freme, Tyler Rodriguez, Sherry Feather, Lukas Griffith, Mary Ford, Tito Cantalamessa, D'Ondre Stockman, and Tehron Jacobs. We also want to thank the faculty at Fairmont State University for their support, specifically: Professors Donna Long, Elizabeth Savage, Ken Millen-Penn, and Nenad Radulovich. We also appreciate the contributions of West Virginia University students Destiny Harrison, Dillon Muhly-Alexander, and Emily Neely as well as Stanford University student Alexandra Koch, and The Ohio State University Moritz College of Law student Sarah M. Pribe.

We also want to thank our editors, John Devins, Jeff Slutzky, and Justin Billing, for their steady, invaluable, and cheerfully provided advice, and many others at Aspen Publishing for their guidance and support in the completion of the book. In addition, we wish to thank the many colleagues who reviewed the book for their extraordinarily thoughtful and useful comments, including, among others: David Kaye, Clinical Professor of Law, University of California Irvine School of Law; Beth Van Schaack, Visiting Professor in Human Rights, Stanford Law School, along with the students in her spring 2012 class at Santa Clara University School of Law; Lesley Wexler, Professor of Law, University of Illinois College of Law, along with the students in her spring 2013 class; Lieutenant Colonel Carroll Connelley, U.S. Marine Corps (ret.); and anonymous reviewers.

We also thank the following copyright holders for permission to excerpt their materials:

Rick Beyer, Freddy Fox Goes to War, Princeton Alumni Weekly, March 21, 2012. Copyright © by the Princeton Alumni Weekly.

Geoffrey S. Corn, *Hamdan*, Lebanon, and the Regulation of Hostilities: The Need to Recognize a Hybrid Category of Armed Conflict, 40 Vanderbilt Journal of Transnational Law 295 (2007). Copyright © 2007 by Vanderbilt University. Reprinted with permission.

Geoffrey S. Corn, Mixing Apples and Hand Grenades: The Logical Limit of Applying Human Rights Norms to Armed Conflict, 1 Journal of International Humanitarian Legal Studies 52 (2010).

Yoram Dinstein, The Conduct of Hostilities Under the Law of International Armed Conflict (2010). Copyright © by Cambridge University Press.

Bonnie Lynn Docherty and Marc E. Garlasco, Off Target: The Conduct of the War and Civilian Casualties in Iraq (2003). Human Rights Watch. Licensed under CC BY-NC_ND 3.0. https://creativecommons.org/licenses/by-nc-nd/3.0/us/.

Steven Erlanger, A Gaza War Full of Traps and Trickery, The New York Times, Jan. 10, 2009.

Hans-Peter Gasser, The U.S. Decision Not to Ratify Protocol I to the Geneva Conventions on the Protection of War Victims: An Appeal for Ratification by the United States, 81 American Journal of International Law 912 (1987). Copyright © 1987 by the American Journal of International Law. Reprinted with permission.

International Committee of the Red Cross, Commentary on the Geneva Convention (III) Relative to the Treatment of Prisoners of War (1958). Copyright © 1958 by the International Committee of the Red Cross.

International Committee of the Red Cross, Commentary on the Geneva Convention (IV) Relative to the Protection of Civilian Persons in Time of War (1958). Copyright © 1958 by the International Committee of the Red Cross.

Raphael Lemkin, Axis Rule in Occupied Europe, d. 1959, published 1944 Carnegie Endowment for International Peace.

Theodor Meron, The Humanization of Humanitarian Law, 94 American Journal of International Law 239 (2000).

Photograph of markings on a Syrian hospital in the summer of 2012. Licensed under CC BY-NC_ND 3.0. https://creativecommons.org/licenses/by-nc-nd/3.0/us/.

Jean Pictet, Development and Principles of International Humanitarian Law (1985).

Claude Pilloud, Yves Sandoz, Christophe Swinarski, Bruno Zimmerman, Commentary on the Additional Protocols of 8 June 1977 to the Geneva Conventions of 12 August 1949 (1987). Copyright © by the International Committee of the Red Cross.

David Rohde, Perfidy and Treachery, in Crimes of War (1999).

Kenneth Roth, The Law of War in the War on Terror: Washington's Abuse of "Enemy Combatants," Foreign Affairs (Jan./Feb 2004). Copyright © 2004 by Foreign Affairs. Reprinted with permission.

Marco Sassòli, Antoine A. Bouvier & Anne Quintin, How Does Law Protect in War? Cases, Documents and Teaching Materials on Contemporary Practice in International Humanitarian Law (2011). Copyright © by the International Committee of the Red Cross.

Ann Scott Tyson, A Deadly Clash at Donkey Island, Washington Post, Aug. 19, 2007. Copyright © 2007 by the Washington Post. Reprinted with permission.

James J. Weingartner, Crossroads of Death: The Story of the Malmedy Massacre and Trial (1979). Copyright © by University of California Press.

Henry C. Zabierek, Beyond Pearl Harbor, I Company in the Pacific of WWII (2010).

Finally, our families' support every day truly made this project possible. Without their love, patience, support and feedback, this book would be just a glint in our eyes.

Of course, all errors and omissions are ours alone. The content of this book does not represent the official positions of any government agency or nongovernmental organization.

For the past two decades, the law of armed conflict has occupied the attention of the global community to an extent not seen since the war crimes tribunals at Nuremberg and Tokyo following World War II. Many factors have contributed to this reality. Globalized commercial and social media provide unfiltered "real time" battlefield commentary and imagery that sometimes appears to depict violations of the law. Transnational terrorism places individuals who would otherwise be far distant from the violence of war at ever-greater risk, thereby commanding their attention. Asymmetrical warfare raises questions as to the fairness of applying the law of armed conflict equally to both parties, whereas the propensity of certain organized armed groups to disregard the law excites the emotions of potential victims and onlookers alike. And new weaponry, such as cyber, nano, and autonomous systems, captures the imagination of a technologically sophisticated public, while sometimes appearing to test norms governing the conduct of hostilities that were responsive to twentieth century conflicts. There is no denying that the law of armed conflict "moment" is at hand.

But is this development positive or negative? On the one hand, there is much about which to be pleased. Funding flows into the coffers of non-governmental organizations dedicated to alleviating the human suffering of warfare, the international community has created tribunals to prosecute war criminals, States are actively training their military forces in the law, and many universities now offer sophisticated courses on the law of armed conflict. The result is a better-educated, highly committed, and more capable community of law of armed conflict academics, practitioners, and activists.

On the other hand, much of the discourse regarding the nature and applicability of the law of armed conflict has been ill-informed and decidedly emotive. To some extent, this is because the law of armed conflict has become a topic du jour. Commentators lacking the practical or legal background to provide analysis are nevertheless anxious to do so irrespective of their own limitations. The resulting flawed pronouncements have a propensity to replicate in an environment in which packaging and means of dissem- ination often play a greater role in the proliferation of ideas than does substance. So the good news is that today attention is being devoted to the law of armed conflict to an unprecedented degree. The bad news is that much of the material being produced is of substandard quality.

I am delighted, therefore, at the publication of this excellent text by Professors Laurie Blank and Greg Noone. Professor Blank has extensive experience at the United States Institute of Peace where, with Professor Noone, she directed an important and influential study of law of armed conflict programs and teaching methodologies. Professor Noone is a distinguished US Navy Reserve senior Judge Advocate. Both authors are dedicated teachers and serious scholars. Professor Blank directs Emory University Law School's International Humanitarian Law Clinic, while Professor Noone leads Fairmont State University's National Security and Intelligence Program. They are uniquely situated to translate their experience and knowledge into an effective, accurate, and comprehensive textbook for students of the subject.

Several qualities distinguish *International Law and Armed Conflict* from other books on the same subject. It is organized in a creative and practical manner. Rather than simply dealing with the various law of armed conflict topics based on their appearance in key treaty instruments, as is usually the case, Professors Blank and Noone present the material in a building block fashion. Thus, the book begins by examining the "why" (or purpose) of the law of armed conflict, before turning to the "what" (definition) and "when" (scope of application). The authors then deal serially with the "who" (participants) and "how" (conduct of hostilities) of the law of armed conflict before concluding with an examination of the ways in which this body of law is implemented and enforced. The result is a book that is uniquely accessible to non-experts, while remaining useful to those who have spent years immersed in the subject.

Equally innovative is the inclusion of extracts from primary source material — case law, historical documents, and firsthand accounts by those who have applied the law of armed conflict on the battlefield. The result is much more than a standard casebook. It is a learning-teaching tool that empowers students to move beyond a purely intellectual grasp of the law of armed conflict to a point where they can comprehend the law in its unique context.

Perhaps the greatest strength of this book is its balance. In a field that deals with human suffering and destruction on one hand and the pursuit of national security objectives on the other, it is commonplace for those dealing with the law of armed conflict to overemphasize considerations of either humanity or military necessity. Nongovernmental organizations tend to be guilty of the former error, whereas the military has a propensity to offend by engaging in the latter. What one sees depends, after all, on where one stands.

However, as noted in the 1868 St. Petersburg Declaration, the purpose of the law of armed conflict is to "fix[] the technical limits at which the necessities of war ought to yield to the requirements of humanity. . . ." *International Law and Armed Conflict* is particularly well-balanced in this regard. It neither suggests unrealistic limitations on how warfare may be conducted, nor affords military forces a carte blanche. Rather, it adopts a mature and reasoned approach to the topic that is all too rare.

I congratulate Professors Blank and Noone on their impressive accomplishment. This fine book makes a valuable contribution to the literature in the field, one that not only is sensitive to the needs of students but also returns objectivity to study of the law of armed conflict.

Michael N. Schmitt
Professor of International Law
University of Reading School of Law
Francis Lieber Distinguished Scholar
United States Military Academy at West Point
Charles H. Stockton Distinguished Scholar-in-Residence
United States Naval War College

PART I

WHY

CHAPTER 1

FOUNDATIONS

"War is hell" and "the fog of war" may well be two of the most common colloquial expressions about war. While they remain eminently true, the law of war—the central focus of this book—has developed over thousands of years to counter and address those challenges. Some argue that "in times of war, the law falls silent,"[1] but as these pages demonstrate, the law in fact speaks loudly and with great purpose during wartime.

The law of armed conflict (LOAC)—otherwise known as international humanitarian law (IHL) or the law of war—governs the conduct of both states and individuals during armed conflict and seeks to minimize suffering in war by protecting persons not participating in hostilities and by restricting the means and methods of warfare. The extensive, comprehensive, and in-depth nature of this body of law may come as a surprise; after all, war is, if nothing else, messy, bloody, and full of destruction. One might naturally wonder what role the law can play in such an environment. Indeed, it is a critical role. In short, the law is designed *to protect those who cannot protect themselves.* Civilians have protection from attack—and those who attack civilians face criminal prosecution—because of the law. Mosques, synagogues, churches, hospitals, schools, and other essential civilian objects are protected from attack and destruction because of the law. Prisoners of war are detained with dignity and security because of the law of war.

One key aspect of the law of armed conflict is that it is not designed to outlaw war—a worthy, yet unrealistic cause. Nor does it seek to impose rules on the conduct of war that make it impossible to fight. As unfortunate as it is, armed conflicts exist and we see few signs that military force will disappear as a tool for nations and non-state actors.

> An examination of the rules applicable to the conduct of fighting cannot be based on a desire to make conflict unfightable. That would, in fact, be counter-productive. If the rules were such as to make lawful fighting impossible, the result would not be no fighting. It would be fighting conducted unlawfully. In order for there to be any chance of the rules being respected, it must be possible to fight according to the rules. That said, it is still the case that LOAC deals with the killing of people and the

---

1. THE OXFORD DICTIONARY OF QUOTATIONS 204 (Angela Partington ed., 4th ed. 1992) (translating Cicero's quotation, "*silent enim leges inter arma*").

destruction of things. The subject matter gives rise to the responsibility to treat the subject seriously. It also requires an understanding of the situation in which all the participants find themselves. They are all, in a sense, victims. . . . Since humans started to organise themselves in communities, they have contemplated resorting to the use of armed force against their neighbours, whilst also crafting limits to the force that may be used. In effect, they have wanted to drive in top gear with the handbrake on. This statement is true irrespective of the period in time, region or religion.[2]

The law of armed conflict therefore regulates the conduct of hostilities and mandates rules for the protection of those who are fighting, and those who are not, in an attempt to minimize suffering during wartime.

The "paradox of war . . . is that there are legal limits upon the conduct of warring nations and their armed forces," and yet "the law acknowledges the historical reality: War is inevitable and legal."[3] Many, including legal scholars, military practitioners, statesmen, and humanitarian organizations, debate whether and to what extent LOAC is effective. The different points of view range from one end of the spectrum to the other. Some say it will never work as intended, but others counter that it is the best solution available. Laws are never perfect either in their creation or their enforcement. Certainly, the laws that are intended to regulate something as drastic as war will fall prey to the same pitfalls as simpler and more pedestrian laws. "There are going to be violations," stated a Pentagon official during Operation Desert Storm in 1991, "but it's better to have the rules than not have the rules, because most nations of the world are going to say that they follow the rules, and there's enormous pressure to observe the rules."[4]

A. PURPOSES

The law of armed conflict has multiple purposes that all stem from or contribute to the regulation of the conduct of hostilities and the protection of persons and objects affected by conflict. The most obvious, perhaps, is the humanitarian purpose, the focus on protecting persons who are caught up in the horrors of war. Equally important, however, is the regulation of the means and methods of warfare for the direct purpose of protecting those who are fighting—soldiers and others—from unnecessary suffering during conflict. Finally, it is crucial to recognize that the law of war does not exist to inhibit military operations or prevent war; rather, the goal of this body of law is to enable effective, moral and lawful military operations within the parameters

---

2. Françoise Hampson, *Teaching the Law of Armed Conflict*, ESSEX HUM. RTS. REV. 7-8, July 2008.

3. Eric L. Chase, *To Punish and Deter Grievous Misconduct in War*, WASH. POST, Sept. 3, 1995, at C7.

4. Martha Sherrill & Joel Achenbach, *Killing by the Rules*, WASH. POST, Jan. 23, 1991, at B1.

of the aforementioned two protective purposes. Some might think that war—a situation marked by chaos, bloodshed, and violence—could not possibly be susceptible to legal regulation and legal parameters. And yet, there have been legal frameworks for war and the use of military force for thousands of years and across multiple continents and different cultures.

1. *Protection of Civilians and Others* Hors de Combat

Innocent civilians have always suffered during wartime—from "rape, pillage and plunder" to mass deportations, internment and killings. The urbanization of warfare, in which parties fight in and among the civilian population, compounds the suffering and carnage. A look at any of the numerous conflicts of the twentieth century and the first two decades of the twenty-first century clearly demonstrates the death, destruction, depredation, and other harms civilians suffer during wartime: barrel bombs launched by the Assad regime against civilians throughout Syria, sexual slavery of Yazidi women and girls in Iraq, bombing of hospitals and other essential civilian facilities, and unfortunately many more dangers to the civilian populations in conflicts around the world. As the International Committee of the Red Cross (ICRC) summarized:

> Today, civilians still bear the brunt of armed conflicts. Civilians have remained the primary victims of violations of IHL [LOAC] committed by both State parties and non-State armed groups. Deliberate attacks against civilians, forced displacement of civilian populations, the destruction of infrastructure vital to the civilian population and of civilian property are just some examples of prohibited acts that have been perpetrated on a regular basis. Individual civilians have also been the victims of violations of the law such as murder, forced disappearance, torture, cruel treatment and outrages upon personal dignity, and rape and other forms of sexual violence. They have been used as human shields. Persons detained in relation to armed conflicts have been deprived of their basic rights, including adequate conditions and treatment while in detention, procedural safeguards aimed at preventing arbitrary detention and the right to a fair trial. Medical personnel and humanitarian workers have also been the targets of IHL violations. In many instances, humanitarian organizations have been prevented from carrying out their activities or hampered in their efforts to do so effectively. This has further aggravated the plight of those whom they are meant to assist and protect. Attacks on journalists and other members of the media are a source of increasing concern as well.[5]

One of LOAC's central goals is to protect civilians from the horrors of war and reduce suffering during conflict. It does so through rules that

5. Int'l Comm. Red Cross, *International Humanitarian Law and the Challenges of Contemporary Armed Conflicts* 3 (Nov. 2007), http://www.icrc.org/eng/assets/files/other/ihl-challenges-30th-international-conference-eng.pdf.

prohibit attacks on civilians, torture, and other violence; that set standards for detention and treatment; and that, in general, seek to minimize the effects of war on civilian populations. As the signatories to the St. Petersburg Declaration in 1868 stated, one of the law's goals is that "the progress of civilization should have the effect of alleviating as much as possible the calamities of war."[6] Although the St. Petersburg Declaration focused on minimizing suffering for those engaged in combat, the broader import of this appeal remains at the forefront of LOAC. Indeed, nearly 150 years later, core provisions of LOAC continue to place the protection of civilians at the very heart of the law's framework. This essential purpose can be seen not only in specific treaty provisions, but in analyses and interpretations of the law. As the Constitutional Court of Colombia stated: "The distinctive feature of this law is therefore that its rules constitute inalienable guarantees that are unique in that they impose obligations on armed individuals not for their own benefit but for that of third parties, namely the non-combatant population and the victims of the conflict."[7]

The obligation to protect civilians is therefore not dependent on the other side's comparable behavior or on any other reciprocal conditions. It is a fundamental principle and purpose of LOAC: the obligation to protect civilians is for the sake of the civilian populations caught up in combat zones; it is not a tool or bargaining chip to accomplish alternative purposes.

2.   *Minimize Unnecessary Suffering*

The law also seeks to protect those who are fighting from unnecessary suffering. Thus, wounded soldiers must be cared for, protected from danger, and treated with dignity. The modern infrastructure of the law of war was born directly out of this concern. Henri Dunant, who would become the founder of the International Red Cross movement, launched the drive for protection of war wounded after witnessing the horrors of the Battle of Solferino, the decisive battle in the struggle for Italian unification in 1859, about which he wrote *A Memory of Solferino*. In 1864, the first Geneva Convention was signed, obligating countries to provide protection to wounded soldiers from both sides. The First and Second Geneva Conventions of 1949 are devoted to the protection of wounded and sick soldiers, and wounded, sick and shipwrecked sailors during armed conflict.

---

6. Declaration Renouncing the Use, in Time of War, of Explosive Projectiles Under 400 Grammes Weight, pmbl., Nov. 29, 1868, *reprinted in Official Documents*, 1 Am. J. Int'l L. Supp. 87, 95 (1907).

7. Constitutional Review of Additional Protocol I, Colombian Constitutional Court, Ruling C-225/95 Re: File No. LAT-040, unofficial translation from Spanish reprinted in Marco Sassòli et al., How Does Law Protect in War? Cases, Documents and Teaching Materials on Contemporary Practice in International Humanitarian Law 2240 (3d ed., 2011).

The goal of minimizing unnecessary suffering goes far beyond treatment of wounded soldiers, however. It extends to the limitations on the means and methods of warfare, prohibiting the use of weapons that cause unnecessary suffering, such as poisonous gases. As the International Court of Justice (ICJ) declared in its *Advisory Opinion on the Legality of the Threat or Use of Nuclear Weapons*:

> The cardinal principles contained in the texts constituting the fabric of humanitarian law are the following. The first is aimed at the protection of the civilian population and civilian objects and establishes the distinction between combatants and non-combatants; States must never make civilians the object of attack and must consequently never use weapons that are incapable of distinguishing between civilian and military targets. According to the second principle, it is prohibited to cause unnecessary suffering to combatants: it is accordingly prohibited to use weapons causing them such harm or uselessly aggravating their suffering. In application of that second principle, States do not have unlimited freedom of choice of means in the weapons they use. . . .
>
> It has been maintained in these proceedings that these principles and rules of humanitarian law are part of *jus cogens* as defined in Article 53 of the Vienna Convention on the Law of Treaties of 23 May 1969.[8]

Similarly, the 1899 Hague Declaration prohibits "the use of bullets which expand or flatten easily in the human body, such as bullets with a hard envelope which does not entirely cover the core or is pierced with incisions."[9]

In contrast to the fundamental goal of protecting civilians, this equally central purpose of LOAC focuses on protections for combatants. However, the notion of unnecessary suffering is not an absolute one, but rather is considered in light of the circumstances of war. Another term often used in partnership with unnecessary suffering is "superfluous injury." Thus, the modern incarnation of this principle, appearing in Article 35(1) of Additional Protocol I, states that "it is prohibited to employ weapons, projectiles and material and methods of warfare of a nature to cause superfluous injury or unnecessary suffering." Combat inherently involves suffering, including horrendous injury and death. The principle of unnecessary suffering in LOAC prohibits the use of weapons or methods of warfare that increase suffering but do not increase military advantage. The fact that a weapon is lethal does not mean it causes unnecessary suffering, nor does the fact that a soldier intends to kill his enemy mean that he seeks to cause unnecessary

---

8. Legality of the Threat or Use of Nuclear Weapons, 1996 I.C.J. 226, ¶¶ 78, 83 (July 8). *Jus cogens* refers to peremptory norms of international law from which no derogation is permitted (such as the prohibitions against slavery, piracy, and genocide).

9. Declaration (II) To Prohibit the Use of Bullets Which Expand or Flatten Easily in the Human Body, July 29, 1899, 187 Consol. T.S. 459.

suffering. Thus, unnecessary suffering must be understood within the context of war itself:

> Warfare obviously justifies subjecting an enemy to massive and decisive force, and the suffering that it brings. Military necessity justifies the infliction of suffering upon an enemy combatant. Since 1868, however, it has been explicitly recognized that military necessity only justifies the infliction of as much suffering as is necessary to bring about the submission of an enemy. Prohibiting the infliction of suffering upon enemy combatants, beyond what is necessary, [thus acts as a "brake" on acts otherwise justified as military necessity].[10]

3.   Mission Fulfillment

Beyond its critical protective purposes, the law of armed conflict is an essential component of good military discipline and effective military operations. This linkage between law, discipline, and military success is an ancient one:

> If laws and orders are not clear and rewards and punishments not reliable, troops will not stop at the sound of the bells nor advance at the roll of the drums and though there be a million of this sort, of what use are they? What is called discipline is that when encamped their conduct is proper; that when on the move the army is awe-inspiring. . . .[11]

A unit that does not adhere to the law is not going to focus its energies on the mission at hand, but will be distracted by disciplinary problems and incidents. Such incidents are counterproductive and may even include "friendly fire" casualties to one's own troops. Adherence to the law is fundamental to the notion of the professional soldier. As the U.S. Chief Prosecutor at the Nuremberg Tribunals later wrote:

> [An] even more important basis of the laws of war is that they are necessary to diminish the corrosive effect of mortal combat on the participants. War does not confer a license to kill for personal reasons — to gratify perverse impulses, or to put out of the way anyone who appears obnoxious, or to whose welfare the soldier is indifferent. War is not a license at all, but an obligation to kill for reasons of state; it does not countenance the infliction of suffering for its own sake or for revenge.
>
> Unless troops are trained and required to draw the distinction between military and nonmilitary killings, and to retain such respect for

---

10. Geoffrey S. Corn, *International & Operational Note: Principle 4: Preventing Unnecessary Suffering*, ARMY LAW., Nov. 1998, 50.

11. Wu Ch'i, *Art of War, reprinted in* Samuel B. Griffith, *Appendix, in* SUN TZU, THE ART OF WAR 159 (Samuel B. Griffith trans., Oxford U. Press 1971) (220 B.C.).

the value of life that unnecessary death and destruction will continue to repel them, they may lose the sense for that distinction for the rest of their lives. The consequence would be that many returning soldiers would be potential murderers.[12]

In addition, history includes countless examples of military operations in which violations of the law compromised mission success by bolstering enemy morale—whether because of the killing of prisoners of war, abuses against civilians, or other violations: the Alamo, Malmedy, Hue, Kohima and, in recent years, Abu Ghraib. The goal of military operations is the complete submission of the enemy forces as quickly as possible, using all means and methods of force not prohibited by the law. Abuses that reinforce the enemy's desire to "fight to the last man" undermine that goal by prolonging the conflict and result in more casualties to *both* sides. Compliance with the law and adherence to basic notions of humanity also provide greater potential for success in the post-conflict stage. In the aftermath of conflict, society needs to rebuild, and atrocities and other violations of the law hinder that process dramatically by undermining efforts at a sustainable and durable peace and leaving only distrust, destruction, and horror in the place of a functioning society.

B. KEY SOURCES OF LOAC

1. Treaties

The main sources of LOAC are treaties and customary law. Early rules regulating the conduct of war can be found throughout history in bilateral treaties on the treatment and exchange of prisoners, treatment of wounded soldiers, and other similar issues. Since the mid-nineteenth century, countries began to codify LOAC in multilateral treaties, such as the 1864 Geneva Convention for the Amelioration of the Condition of the Wounded in Armies in the Field and the Hague Conventions of 1899 and 1907. In the twentieth century, codification of LOAC continued apace with developments in warfare and in the capacity of warring parties to inflict greater death and destruction. The Geneva Conventions of 1949 are the primary example of how LOAC has developed in response to major wars: the horrors of World War II demonstrated beyond a doubt not only that existing protections for wounded, prisoners of war, and others needed to be reinforced, but also that the law needed to protect civilians directly—the group most devastatingly affected by war.

---

12. TELFORD TAYLOR, NUREMBERG AND VIETNAM: AN AMERICAN TRAGEDY 40-41 (1971).

LOAC: THE KEY TREATY SOURCES

The four Geneva Conventions of 1949 are the centerpiece of LOAC and are ratified by every country in the world. The two Additional Protocols of 1977 supplement the 1949 Conventions.[13]

- Geneva Convention (I) for the Amelioration of the Condition of the Wounded and Sick in Armed Forces in the Field of August 12, 1949
- Geneva Convention (II) for the Amelioration of the Condition of the Wounded, Sick and Shipwrecked Members of Armed Forces at Sea of August 12, 1949
- Geneva Convention (III) Relative to the Treatment of Prisoners of War of August 12, 1949
- Geneva Convention (IV) Relative to the Protection of Civilian Persons in Time of War of August 12, 1949
- Protocol Additional to the Geneva Conventions of August 12, 1949, and Relating to the Protection of Victims of International Armed Conflicts (Protocol I), June 8, 1977
- Protocol Additional to the Geneva Conventions of August 12, 1949, and Relating to the Protection of Victims of Non-International Armed Conflicts (Protocol II), June 8, 1977

Numerous other multilateral treaties also form the body of positive law governing the conduct of hostilities and protection of persons during conflict. These treaties form a comprehensive framework, ranging from treatment of persons to prohibitions on certain weapons, making LOAC one of the most codified branches of international law. Although international law does not establish a hierarchy of sources of law, it is generally understood that "[t]he rights and duties of states are determined in the first instance, by their agreement as expressed in treaties—just as in the case of individuals their rights are specifically determined by any contract which is binding upon them."[14] In analyzing the conduct of states, individuals, or other parties during armed conflict, therefore, the first inquiry will always be to see which treaties bind those relevant states. Note, however, that treaties do not override custom. Rather, standard canons of construction give priority to the more specific provision (*lex specialis derogat generali*—literally translated as "specific law prevails over general law") or to the later in time provision. Throughout this book, we rely predominantly on the four

13. Additional Protocol I has been ratified by 174 countries; Additional Protocol II by 169 countries. As of this writing, the United States has not ratified either Additional Protocol, although President Obama announced in March 2011 that he would seek Senate advice and consent to ratification of Additional Protocol II.

14. 1 LAUTERPACHT, INTERNATIONAL LAW: COLLECTED PAPERS 86-87 (1970).

Geneva Conventions of 1949—universally ratified and thus binding on all states—as well as on the numerous provisions of Additional Protocol I that are recognized as binding customary international law.

2.   *Customary International Law*

Customary international law develops from the general practice of states, practice that is "accepted and observed as law, i.e. from a sense of legal obligation."[15] The formation of customary international law rests on two factors: state practice and *opinio juris sive necessitates* (or more simply *opinio juris*), the belief that the action was taken out of a sense of legal obligation. The first factor is an objective inquiry looking at whether international actors follow the relevant rule, whether it is followed consistently, and for how long. The second factor looks at why a state or other international actor undertakes such practice—it is a subjective inquiry aimed at determining whether "a practice is observed out of a sense of legal obligation or necessity, or, rather, merely out of courtesy, neighborliness, or expediency."[16]

The nature of customary law raises some interesting issues with regard to the formation of customary LOAC. First, only some states are actively engaged in armed conflict, adding complications to the obligation of state practice as a component of the formation of customary international law. Think about the consequences of having the practice of only a few states exert disproportionate influence on the formation of customary LOAC. On the contrary, however, consider the ramifications of having state practice determined by states not engaged in conflict and therefore not forced to wrestle with the complicated issues of new developments in the conduct of warfare. Second, LOAC is often described as being "honored in the breach," meaning that the response to violations will often be a key factor in the customary law analysis.

KEY ACTOR: THE ROLE AND FUNCTION OF THE INTERNATIONAL COMMITTEE OF THE RED CROSS[17]

Since it was founded in 1863, the ICRC has been working to protect and assist the victims of armed conflict and other situations of violence. It initially focused on wounded soldiers but over time it extended its activities to cover all victims of these events. . . .

15.   THEODOR MERON, HUMAN RIGHTS AND HUMANITARIAN NORMS AS CUSTOMARY LAW 3 (1989).

16.   DAVID J. BEDERMAN, INTERNATIONAL LAW FRAMEWORKS 19 (2006).

17.   Excerpted from INT'L COMM. RED CROSS, THE ICRC: ITS MISSION AND WORK 3, 6-7, 21-23 (2009), https://www.icrc.org/eng/assets/files/other/icrc_002_0963.pdf.

The ICRC's work developed along two lines. The first of these is operational, i.e. helping victims of armed conflict and other situations of violence. The second involves developing and promoting international humanitarian law and humanitarian principles. . . .

A key characteristic of the ICRC is that it was given a mandate (or rather mandates) by the States party to the Geneva Conventions to help victims of armed conflict. Its work is therefore firmly rooted in public international law. . . . States gave the ICRC the responsibility of monitoring the faithful application of international humanitarian law. As the guardian of humanitarian law, the ICRC takes measures to ensure respect for, to promote, to reaffirm and even to clarify and develop this body of law. The organization is particularly concerned about possible erosion of international humanitarian law and takes bilateral, multilateral or public steps to promote respect for and development of the law. . . .

The ICRC's humanitarian work is *impartial, neutral and independent*. Experience has taught it that this approach offers the best chance of being accepted during an armed conflict or other situation of violence, in particular given the risk that actors at a local, regional or international level may become polarized or radicalized. The integration of political, military and humanitarian means as recommended by some States is therefore a major source of difficulty for the ICRC. The organization insists on the need to avoid a blurring of lines while still allowing for the possibility of complementary action.

Many of the ICRC's tasks are carried out *close to the people concerned*—in the field, in other words, where the organization has better access to them. The individuals and communities concerned must be consulted in order to better establish their needs and interests, and they should be associated with the action taken. Their value systems, their specific vulnerabilities and the way they perceive their needs must all be taken into consideration. The ICRC favours a participatory approach aimed at building local capacities.

The ICRC has a *universal* vocation. Its work is not limited to certain places, or to certain types of people (such as children or refugees). With a presence in numerous regions of the world, the ICRC has an overall vision that enables it to undertake comprehensive analysis. The organization must have a coherent approach everywhere it works if it is to appear transparent and predictable. However, this does not mean that ICRC activities are uniform. Taking the context into consideration is still a key aspect of analysis and strategy.

The ICRC gets involved during the emergency phase and stays for *as long as is necessary*. However, the organization is careful to ensure that its involvement does not dissuade the authorities from fully assuming their responsibilities or the communities affected from relying on their usual coping mechanisms. It also takes care not to get in the way of other organizations and actors who are building up civil society's resources. Measures are taken so that the ICRC is able to leave the scene in an appropriate manner when the time comes.

The ICRC engages in *dialogue* with all those involved in an armed conflict or other situation of violence who may have some influence on its course, whether they are recognized by the community of States or not. No one is excluded, not only because engaging in dialogue does not equate to formal recognition but also because multiple and varied contacts are essential for assessing a situation and for guaranteeing the safety of ICRC activities and personnel. The ICRC maintains a network of contacts locally, regionally and internationally. In the event of violations of international humanitarian law or other bodies of law or other fundamental rules protecting people in situations of violence, the ICRC attempts to influence the perpetrators. In the first instance, it will take bilateral confidential action. When it comes to confidential action and to communication with the public, the ICRC wants to promote transparency and present itself as an organization acting in a credible and predictable manner. Moreover, reflecting the interest that States have in the unique status and role of the ICRC, the organization's right to abstain from giving evidence has been recognized by several sources of international law.

C. JUS AD BELLUM *VS.* JUS IN BELLO

Jus in bello is the Latin term for the law of armed conflict, the law governing the conduct of hostilities and the protection of persons in times of conflict. *Jus ad bellum* is the Latin term for the law governing the resort to force; that is, when a state may lawfully use force on the territory of another state. Both bodies of law apply to the use of force, but in separate and very different ways. More importantly, the effectiveness of each body of law depends on a strict separation between and independent application of the two legal frameworks.

1. Jus ad Bellum

Just war theory—legal and moral parameters for resorting to war—is centuries old.[18] The modern incarnation of *jus ad bellum* has its origins in the 1919 Covenant of the League of Nations, the 1928 Kellogg-Briand Pact

18. *See* Ian Brownlie, International Law and the Use of Force by States 4-5 (1963).

and the United Nations Charter in 1945. In particular, the U.N. Charter prohibits the use of force by one state against another in Article 2(4): "All members shall refrain in their international relations from the threat or use of force against the territorial integrity or political independence of any state, or in any other manner inconsistent with the Purposes of the United Nations." This article, in many ways, is the foundation of the U.N.'s goal of "sav[ing] succeeding generations from the scourge of war, which twice in our lifetime has brought untold sorrow to mankind."[19] International law provides only three justifications (consent, U.N. Security Council Chapter VII authorization, and self-defense, as discussed below) that rebut this presumption against the use of force; therefore, any use of force not falling within one of these three justifications violates Article 2(4) and the fundamental prohibition of the use of force by one state against another. These exceptions to the prohibition of the use of force balance two key international law principles: first, the respect for state sovereignty and second, the collective interests of the international community, including the right to use force in self-defense. Thus, a state's right to protect its sovereignty and territorial integrity is foundational to international law and the international system. At the same time, however, states have an inherent right to protect their legally recognized individual and collective interests and their nationals from attack.

First, a state may use force in the territory of another state with the consent of that state. A state engaged in an internal conflict with a rebel group may seek assistance from other states in defeating the rebels and restoring order and security. U.S. and international coalition operations in Afghanistan through the International Security Assistance Force (ISAF) fall within this category of consent, as do individual interventions like the U.S. role in support of the Republic of Vietnam. In a different variation, a state may also consent to another state using force in counterterrorism operations, such as Yemen's consent to United States drone strikes against al Qaeda and al Qaeda in the Arabian Peninsula (AQAP) operatives in that country. In such cases, however, the territorial state can only consent to such assistance and uses of force in which it could legally engage—no state can consent to actions by another state that would violate international law if undertaken on its own. This means the intervening state may not use the request as the means for engaging in an act of aggression against a neighboring state.

The U.N. Charter provides the second and third exceptions to the prohibition of the use of force: the multinational use of force authorized by the Security Council under Chapter VII (Article 42) and the inherent right of self-defense in response to an armed attack (Article 51). Chapter VII of the U.N. Charter covers "action with respect to threats to the peace, breaches of the peace, and acts of aggression." First, Article 39 empowers the U.N. Security Council to determine that a particular situation constitutes a threat

---

19. U.N. Charter, pmbl.

to international peace and security and to decide what measures shall be taken under Articles 41 and 42 to maintain or restore peace and security. If non-forceful measures recommended under Article 41 have failed or are not adequate to deter or end the crisis, Article 42 authorizes the Security Council to "take such action by air, sea, or land forces as may be necessary to maintain or restore international peace and security . . . [including] operations by air, sea, or land forces of Members of the United Nations." The multinational military operation to protect civilians in Libya in the spring and summer of 2011 is an example of the Security Council authorizing the use of force in accordance with Chapter VII's Article 42.

States may use force as an act of individual or collective self-defense in response to an armed attack in accordance with Article 51 of the U.N. Charter. This latter exception—the most commonly relied upon justification for the use of force—builds on and establishes the basic framework of *jus ad bellum*. Article 51 states:

> Nothing in the present Charter shall impair the inherent right of individual or collective self-defence if an armed attack occurs against a Member of the United Nations, until the Security Council has taken measures necessary to maintain international peace and security.

This provision recognizes the pre-existing right of states to use force—and to use force in response to another state's request for assistance—in self-defense against an attack.

The prerequisite for any use of force in self-defense is the existence of an armed attack. The ICJ has considered the scale and effects of any particular hostile action directed at a state to see if it rises to the level of an armed attack.[20] For example, deployment of a state's regular armed forces across a border will generally constitute an armed attack, as will a state's sending irregular militias or other armed groups to accomplish the same purposes. In contrast, providing assistance—such as weapons or other support—to rebels or other armed groups across state borders will not reach the threshold of an armed attack.

The question of who can launch an armed attack—that is, must an attack be launched by a state to qualify as an armed attack—continues to be debated. In its jurisprudence, the ICJ has consistently held that only attacks by states can trigger the right of self-defense.[21] Article 51 does not specify, however, that the right of self-defense is only available in response to a threat or use of force by another state. In fact, state practice in the

---

20. Military and Paramilitary Activities in and against Nicaragua (Nicar. v. U.S.), 1986 I.C.J. 14, ¶ 195 (June 27).

21. *See id.*; Case Concerning Oil Platforms (Iran v. U.S.), 2003 I.C.J. 161 (Nov. 6); Armed Activities on the Territory of the Congo (Dem. Rep. Congo v. Uganda), 2005 I.C.J. 116 (Dec. 19); Legal Consequences of the Construction of a Wall in the Occupied Palestinian Territory, Advisory Opinion, 2004 I.C.J. 136 (July 9).

aftermath of 9/11 provides firm and increasing support for the existence of a right of self-defense against non-state actors, even if unrelated to any state. For example, in response to the September 11th attacks on the United States, both the U.N. Security Council and the North Atlantic Treaty Organization (NATO) issued resolutions characterizing the attacks as an armed attack triggering the inherent right of self-defense. Other acts of self-defense against armed attacks by non-state actors have been generally accepted as well, such as Israel's response to Hezbollah's attack on an Israeli army unit and capture of two Israeli soldiers in the summer of 2006, Colombia's raid into Ecuador to attack guerrillas of the Revolutionary Armed Forces of Colombia (FARC), or Turkey's repeated cross-border raids against Kurdistan Workers' Party (PKK) forces in Iraq. Although still disputed, there is now general acceptance that attacks by non-state actors can amount to armed attacks triggering the right of self-defense.

The classic formulation of the parameters of self-defense stems from the Caroline Incident in 1837. British troops crossed the Niagara River to the American side and attacked the steamer *Caroline*, which had been running arms and matériel to insurgents on the Canadian side. The British justified the attack, which killed one American and sent the burning *Caroline* over the Niagara Falls, as an act of self-defense. In an exchange of letters with his British counterpart, U.S. Secretary of State Daniel Webster set forth what are now the parameters of the right of self-defense in response to an armed attack:

> It will be for [Her Majesty's] Government to show a necessity of self-defence, instant, overwhelming, leaving no choice of means, and no moment for deliberation. It will be for it to show, also, that the local authorities of Canada, — even supposing the necessity of the moment authorized them to enter the territories of the United States at all — did nothing unreasonable or excessive; since the act justified by the necessity of self-defence, must be limited by that necessity, and kept clearly within it. . . . Undoubtedly it is just, that while it is admitted that exceptions growing out of the great law of self-defence do exist, those exceptions should be confined to cases in which the "necessity of that self-defence is instant, overwhelming, and leaving no choice of means, and no moment for deliberation."[22]

Under Article 51 and the historical right of self-defense, therefore, a state can use force in self-defense in response to an armed attack as long as the force used comports with the requirements of necessity, proportionality, and immediacy in repelling the attack or ending the grievance.[23] The law focuses on whether the defensive act is appropriate in relation to the

---

22. Letter from Daniel Webster, U.S. Secretary of State, to Lord Ashburton, Special British Minister (Aug. 6, 1842), *reprinted in* 2 J. Moore, Digest of Int'l Law § 217 at 409 (1906).

23. Legality of the Threat or Use of Nuclear Weapons, 1996 I.C.J. 226, ¶ 41 (July 8); Military and Paramilitary Activities in and against Nicaragua (Nicar. v. U.S.), 1986 I.C.J. 14, ¶ 194 (June 27); Eri. — Eth. Cl. Comm'n., Diplomatic Claim — Ethiopia's Claim 8, (2005).

ends sought. The requirement of necessity addresses whether there are adequate non-forceful options to deter or defeat the attack, such as diplomatic avenues to halt any further attacks or reparations for injuries caused. To this end, "acts done in self-defense must not exceed in manner or aim the necessity provoking them."[24] In the case of attacks by non-state actors, states seeking to act in self-defense must first explore whether the territorial state can take action to stop the non-state actors from launching further attacks and, potentially, to detain those responsible. For example, as the then-U.S. Department of State Legal Advisor explained with respect to the U.S. exercise of self-defense in 2001,

> if [the United States] did not have the right to use force against al Qaida and the Taliban, then we would have had no acceptable way to defend our citizens after the most devastating attack against the United States in history. Given the Taliban's unwillingness to cooperate with the international community to bring the perpetrators of the September 11th attack to justice, it cannot be reasonably argued that the only recourse the United States had was to file diplomatic protests or extradition requests with Mullah Omar.[25]

Furthermore, necessity not only justifies action taken to halt and defeat an initial attack, but can also include broader action to eliminate a continuing threat.

The requirement of proportionality in *jus ad bellum* measures the extent of the use of force against the overall military goals, such as fending off an attack or subordinating the enemy. This proportionality focuses not on some measure of symmetry between the original attack and the use of force in response, but on whether the measure of counterforce used is proportionate to the needs and goals of *repelling* or *deterring* the original attack.[26] In other words, the defending party is not limited to using the same means or same amount of force as the original attacker. As a report to the International Law Commission explains,

> it would be mistaken . . . to think that there must be proportionality between the conduct constituting the armed attack and the opposing conduct. The action needed to halt and repulse the attack may well have to assume dimensions disproportionate to those of the attack suffered. What matters in this respect is the result to be achieved by the "defensive action" and not the forms, substance and strength of the action itself.[27]

24. Oscar Schachter, *In Defense of International Rules on the Use of Force*, 53 U. Chi. L. Rev. 113, 132 (1986).

25. John B. Bellinger III, *Address at the London School of Economics: Legal Issues in the War on Terrorism* (Oct. 31, 2006), https://www.state.gov/s/l/2006/98861.htm.

26. Yoram Dinstein, War, Aggression and Self-Defense 225 (2005).

27. Robert Ago, *Addendum to Eighth Report on State Responsibility*, [1980] 2 Y.B. Int'l L. Comm'n 13, 69, U.N. Doc. A/CN.4/318/ADD.5-7.

The ICJ has repeatedly reaffirmed that proportionality focuses on the degree of force needed to eliminate the danger or repel the attack.[28] Thus, a violation of *jus ad bellum* proportionality only occurs when "the defender [does] more than reasonably required in the circumstances to deter a threatened attack or defeat an ongoing one."[29]

Immediacy, the final requirement for lawful self-defense, will generally not be relevant in the case of a response to an ongoing attack, given the need to repel or deter the attack. Immediacy considerations do arise when a state uses force in self-defense in advance of an attack or long after an attack is over. In the latter case, a forceful response long after an attack will no longer serve defensive purposes, but will be retaliatory, and therefore unlawful. The first scenario is often termed "anticipatory self-defense"—the use of force to prevent an imminent attack and the death and damage it will cause. A state need not wait until it is the victim of aggression to act in self-defense. Although the precise contours of the delineation between an imminent threat triggering the lawful use of force in self-defense and actions not so justified are not entirely clear, the *Caroline* requirement that an imminent attack be "instant, overwhelming, [and] leaving no moment for deliberation" continues to provide the basic framework.

2.   Jus ad Bellum *in an Age of Counterterrorism*

State use of military force against terrorist groups has been a defining feature of the post-9/11 world since the United States began bombing al Qaeda and Taliban forces in Afghanistan in October 2001. It is now axiomatic that a terrorist group based thousands of miles away in the remote reaches of a developing nation can pose a significant threat to a powerful industrialized nation. As the United Nations has repeatedly characterized international terrorist attacks as a threat to international peace and security in the years since 2001[30] and states have responded with force to terrorist threats and attacks, the international community has seen a corresponding evolution in the application of international law. Indeed, "the acceptability

28. Military and Paramilitary Activities in and against Nicaragua (Nicar. v. U.S.), 1986 I.C.J. 14, ¶ 237 (June 27); Armed Activities on the Territory of the Congo (Dem. Rep. Congo v. Uganda), 2005 I.C.J. 116, ¶ 147 (Dec. 19) (declaring that "the taking of airports and towns many hundreds of kilometres from Uganda's border would not seem proportionate to the series of transborder attacks it claimed had given rise to the right of self-defence").

29. Michael N. Schmitt, *"Change Direction" 2006: Israeli Operations in Lebanon and the International Law of Self-Defense*, 29 MICH. J. INT'L L. 127, 154 (2008).

30. *See* S.C. Res. 1368 (Sept. 12, 2001) (responding to the 9/11 attacks); S.C. Res. 1373 (Sept. 28, 2001) (same); *see also* S.C. Res. 1438 (Oct. 14, 2002); S.C. Res. 1440 (Oct. 24, 2002); S.C. Res. 1450 (Dec. 13, 2002); S.C. Res. 1530 (Mar. 11, 2004); S.C. Res. 1611 (Jul. 7, 2005).

of resorting to military force in response to transnational terrorism [has] crystallized in the aftermath of 9/11."[31]

The United States and coalition operations against the Islamic State of Iraq and Syria (ISIS or ISIL), as well as the conflict in Syria, have brought extensive attention to the question of when a state can use force in self-defense against a terrorist group. Consider the following communications from states in response to ISIS's attacks on and capture of Iraqi territory and attacks in multiple European cities:

- Iraq's letter to the Secretary-General of the United Nations, September 22, 2014:

  As we noted in our earlier letter, ISIL has established a safe haven out-side Iraq's borders that is a direct threat to the security of our people and territory. By establishing this safe haven, ISIL has secured for itself the ability to train for, plan, finance and carry out terrorist operations across our borders. The presence of this safe haven has made our bor-ders impossible to defend and exposed our citizens to the threat of terrorist attacks.

  It is for these reasons that we, in accordance with international law and the relevant bilateral and multilateral agreements, and with due regard for complete national sovereignty and the Constitution, have requested the United States of America to lead international efforts to strike ISIL sites and military strongholds, with our express consent. The aim of such strikes is to end the constant threat to Iraq, protect Iraq's citizens and, ultimately, arm Iraqi forces and enable them to regain control of Iraq's borders.[32]

- The United States letter to the Secretary-General of the United Nations, September 23, 2014:

  [T]he United States has initiated necessary and proportionate mili-tary actions in Syria in order to eliminate the ongoing ISIL threat to Iraq, including by protecting Iraqi citizens from further attacks and by enabling Iraqi forces to regain control of Iraq's borders. In addition, the United States has initiated military actions in Syria against al-Qaida elements in Syria known as the Khorasan Group to address terrorist threats that they pose to the United States and our partners and allies.[33]

---

31. Michael N. Schmitt, *Responding to Transnational Terrorism Under the* Jus ad Bellum*: A Normative Framework*, *in* ESSAYS ON LAW AND WAR AT THE FAULT LINES 49, 57 (Michael N. Schmitt, ed. 2012).

32. Permanent Rep. of Iraq to the U.N., Letter dated Sept. 20, 2014, from the Permanent Rep. of Iraq to the United Nations addressed to the Secretary-General, U.N. Doc. S/2014/691 (Sept. 22, 2014).

33. Permanent Rep. of the United States of America to the U.N., Letter dated Sept. 23, 2014, from the Permanent Rep. of the United States of America to the United Nations addressed to the Secretary-General, U.N. Doc. S/2014/695 (Sept. 23, 2014).

- The United Kingdom letter to the Secretary-General of the United Nations, November 25, 2014:

  [T]he United Kingdom of Great Britain and Northern Ireland is taking measures in support of the collective self-defence of Iraq as part of international efforts led by the United States.

  These measures are in response to the request by the Government of Iraq for assistance in confronting the attack by the Islamic State in Iraq and the Levant (ISIL) on Iraq. . . . The United Kingdom fully supports these international efforts, whose purpose is to end the continuing attack on Iraq, to protect Iraqi citizens and to enable Iraqi forces to regain control of the borders of Iraq by striking ISIL sites and military strongholds in Syria, as necessary and proportionate measures.[34]

- The United Kingdom letter to the President of the United Nations Security Council, September 7, 2015:

  I am writing to report to the Security Council that the United Kingdom of Great Britain and Northern Ireland has undertaken military action in Syria against the so-called Islamic State in Iraq and the Levant (ISIL) in exercise of the inherent right of individual and collective self-defence.

  On 21 August 2015, armed forces of the United Kingdom of Great Britain and Northern Ireland carried out a precision air strike against an ISIL vehicle in which a target known to be actively engaged in planning and directing imminent armed attacks against the United Kingdom was travelling. This air strike was a necessary and proportionate exercise of the individual right of self-defence of the United Kingdom.

  As reported in our letter of 25 November 2014, ISIL is engaged in an ongoing armed attack against Iraq, and therefore action against ISIL in Syria is lawful in the collective self-defence of Iraq.[35]

- Germany's letter to the President of the United Nations Security Council, December 10, 2015:

  [T]he Federal Republic of Germany, in the exercise of the right of collective self-defence, has initiated military measures against the terrorist organization Islamic State in Iraq and the Levant (ISIL). These measures are directed against ISIL, not against the Syrian Arab Republic. . . .

---

34. Permanent Rep. of the United Kingdom of Great Britain and Northern Ireland to the U.N., Identical Letters dated Nov. 25, 2014 from the Permanent Rep. of the United Kingdom of Great Britain and Northern Ireland to the United Nations addressed to the Secretary-General and the President of the Security Council, U.N. Doc. S/2014/851 (Nov. 26, 2014).

35. Permanent Rep. of the United Kingdom of Great Britain and Northern Ireland to the U.N., Letter dated Sept. 7, 2015 from the Permanent Rep. of the United Kingdom of Great Britain and Northern Ireland to the United Nations addressed to the President of the Security Council, U.N. Doc. S/2015/688 (Sept. 8, 2015).

ISIL has carried out, and continues to carry out, armed attacks against Iraq, France, and other States. These States have acted, and continue to act, by taking measures of self-defence.

ISIL has occupied a certain part of Syrian territory over which the Government of the Syrian Arab Republic does not at this time exercise effective control. States that have been subjected to armed attack by ISIL originating in this part of Syrian territory, are therefore justified under Article 51 of the Charter of the United Nations to take necessary measures of self-defence, even without the consent of the Government of the Syrian Arab Republic. Exercising the right of collective self-defence, Germany will now support the military measures of those States that have been subjected to attacks by ISIL.[36]

How have these states characterized the legal justification for the use of force? What is the triggering event and justification and what is the goal of the use of force? Do the different formulations affect the legality of the use of force? Do they affect the extent of force the state can use?

3. *Separation of* Jus ad Bellum *and* Jus in Bello

Jus ad bellum is not concerned with the conduct of hostilities, the targeting of persons or objects, or the extent of civilian casualties. These issues remain at the forefront of *jus in bello*, which relies at the most basic level on the equal application of the law to all parties to conflict. This principle of equal application can be found as far back as late medieval writings on the laws of war. Major treatises emphasized that certain restraints in war must apply equally to all combatants; that "whatever is permitted to the one in virtue of the state of war, is also permitted to the other."[37] Although international law applies both *jus ad bellum* and *jus in bello* to all situations of armed conflict, therefore, the two legal frameworks serve different purposes and produce different results. Violation of *jus ad bellum*—an unlawful use of force—constitutes the crime of aggression; a violation of *jus in bello*, depending on the seriousness of the violation, is a war crime.

Since at least the seventeenth century, therefore, international law has reinforced a strict separation between the two bodies of law. This separation mandates that all parties have the same obligations and the same rights during armed conflict to ensure that all persons and property benefit from

---

36. Chargé d'affaires a.i. of the Permanent Mission of Germany to the U.N., Letter dated Dec. 10, 2015 from the Chargé d'affaires a.i. of the Permanent Mission of Germany to the United Nations addressed to the President of the Security Council, U.N. Doc. S/2015/946 (Dec. 10, 2015).

37. EMMERICH DE VATTEL, THE LAW OF NATIONS, Book III, Ch. XII, §§ 190-191, p. 591 (Kapossy & Whatmore eds. 2008)

the protection of the laws of war. Common Article 2 to the Geneva Conventions and the preamble to Additional Protocol I contain the modern incarnation of this distinction:

> The provisions of the Geneva Conventions [and] this Protocol must be fully applied in all circumstances . . . without any adverse distinction based on the nature or origin of the armed conflict or on the causes espoused by or attributed to the Parties to the conflict.

Jus in bello does not rely on, nor is it limited by, *jus ad bellum*. In other words, it does not matter how or why a conflict started; once it begins, *jus in bello* is in effect without regard to any *jus ad bellum* considerations. In essence, *jus ad bellum* addresses why states go to war (the purview of heads of state), and *jus in bello* governs how parties fight on the battlefield.

For example, after World War II, German leaders were prosecuted before the International Military Tribunals at Nuremberg. The London Charter, the treaty establishing the tribunals, provided authority to try the crime of aggression as well as war crimes, crimes against humanity and other violations of the laws of war (the legal term genocide had not yet been created and was therefore not charged—crimes of the Holocaust were charged under crimes against humanity). Notably, the tribunal consistently reinforced the separation between *jus in bello* and *jus ad bellum*, even while convicting defendants of crimes under both bodies of law. Thus, in the *Hostages Trial*, German leaders faced prosecution for crimes committed during the occupation of, and campaigns in, Greece and Yugoslavia. Rejecting the argument that the illegal use of force prevented Germany from invoking the law of belligerent occupation, the Tribunal emphasized that "whatever may be the cause of a war that has broken out, and whether or not the cause be a so-called just cause, the same rules of international law are valid as to what must not be done, may be done, and must be done by the belligerents themselves in making war against each other."[38] Similarly, in the *Justice Trial*, the Tribunal declared:

> [i]f we should adopt the view that by reason of the fact that the war was a criminal war of aggression every act which would have been legal in a defensive war was illegal in this one, we would be forced to the conclusion that every soldier who marched under orders into occupied territory or who fought in the homeland was a criminal and a murderer.[39]

More recently, the Special Court for Sierra Leone refused to reduce the sentences of Civil Defense Forces fighters on the grounds that they fought in a "legitimate war" to protect the government against the rebels. The

---

38. USA v. Wilhelm List and Others (The Hostages Trial), Case No. 47, Judgment (U.S. Mil. Trib., Nuremberg, Feb. 19, 1948) *in* VIII LAW REPORTS ON THE TRIALS OF WAR CRIMINALS 60 (1949).

39. USA v. Altstötter et al., *in* VI LAW REPORTS ON THE TRIALS OF WAR CRIMINALS 52 (1947-1949).

Court declared that "[a]llowing mitigation for a convicted person's political motives, even where they are considered . . . meritorious . . . provides implicit legitimacy to conduct that unequivocally violates the law—the precise conduct this Special Court was established to punish."[40]

QUESTIONS FOR DISCUSSION

1. LOAC does not take into account whether the resort to force was lawful. What might be the arguments for doing otherwise—that is, for taking *jus ad bellum* into account in assessing *jus in bello* adherence? What are the arguments against?

2. In many situations, both *jus ad bellum* and *jus in bello* may operate concurrently with regard to regulation of the use of force. In 1999, NATO launched a bombing campaign against the former Yugoslavia to force the regime of Slobodan Miloŝević to end its repression in Kosovo and bring an end to the conflict there. After the military operation was over, the Office of the Prosecutor of the International Criminal Tribunal for the former Yugoslavia (ICTY) received numerous requests to investigate allegations of violations of the law of war during the NATO bombing campaign. The investigating committee issued its *Final Report to the Prosecutor by the Committee Established to Review the NATO Bombing Campaign Against the Federal Republic of Yugoslavia* in June 2000. The report first explained that if the "fundamental legality of the use of force by NATO members against the FRY . . . was unlawful, it could constitute a crime against peace and the ICTY has no jurisdiction over this offence"[41] and noted that the legitimacy of the operation was the subject of a case brought by the Federal Republic of Yugoslavia (the name at the time for what remained of the former Yugoslavia—Serbia and Montenegro) against NATO at the ICJ. The report focused only on *jus in bello* issues, as required by the Statute of the ICTY, and rejected any attempts to link *jus ad bellum* with *jus in bello*: "[a]n argument that the 'bad' side had to comply with the law while the 'good' side could violate it at will would be most unlikely to reduce human suffering in conflict."[42] How effective can this separation be in practice? Is it likely that evidence of war crimes could sway perceptions of the legality of the use of force? Or that aggression by one side could influence the process of investigating war crimes by both sides?

---

40. Prosecutor v. Fofana & Kondewa, Case No. SCSL-04-14-A, Appeal Judgment, ¶ 534 (May 28, 2008).

41. OFFICE OF THE PROSECUTOR, INTERNATIONAL CRIMINAL TRIBUNAL FOR THE FORMER YUGOSLAVIA, FINAL REPORT TO THE PROSECUTOR BY THE COMMITTEE ESTABLISHED TO REVIEW THE NATO BOMBING CAMPAIGN AGAINST THE FEDERAL REPUBLIC OF YUGOSLAVIA (13 June 2000) ¶ 4, *reprinted in* (2000) 39 ILM 1257.

42. *Id.* at ¶ 32.

D.   *INTERSECTION WITH AND DISTINCTION FROM HUMAN RIGHTS LAW*

International human rights law governs the relations between a state and individuals within its territory and jurisdiction, guaranteeing certain protections to individuals from state encroachment on their rights. Although it developed primarily in the mid-twentieth century, human rights law has many national, cultural, and religious antecedents. In addition, LOAC served as an important historical foundation for the development of human rights law, resting on the notions of protection of human dignity inherent in LOAC. Throughout the first half of the twentieth century, the growing list of major international human rights concerns included protection of minorities, labor rights, political rights, and social and cultural rights. By the time of the founding of the United Nations, human rights were a central concern, particularly in the aftermath of the horrors of World War II. Thus, the U.N. Charter contains over a dozen references to human rights, including the statement in the preamble that one of the four key purposes of the United Nations is "to reaffirm faith in fundamental human rights, in the dignity and worth of the human person, in the equal rights of men and women and of nations large and small."

The Universal Declaration of Human Rights, proclaimed by the General Assembly as a "common standard of achievement for all peoples and all nations," the International Covenant on Civil and Political Rights (ICCPR), and the International Covenant on Economic, Social, and Cultural Rights (ICESCR) form the central foundation for modern human rights law. Many of the rights in the ICCPR, such as the right to life, the right to be free from torture and inhuman treatment, the right to be free from arbitrary detention, the right to a fair trial and others, are highly relevant during times of conflict and civil strife. Over the past few decades, there has been an increasing conversation—and debate—about the similarities and differences between LOAC and human rights law and what the interplay means in practice.

> Not surprisingly, it has become common in some quarters to conflate human rights and the law of war/international humanitarian law. Nevertheless, despite the growing convergence of various protective trends, significant differences remain. Unlike human rights law, the law of war allows, or at least tolerates, the killing and wounding of innocent human beings not directly participating in an armed conflict, such as civilian victims of lawful collateral damage. It also permits certain deprivations of personal freedom without convictions in a court of law. It allows an occupying power to resort to internment and limits the appeal rights of detained persons. It permits far-reaching limitations of freedoms of expression and assembly.

The law of armed conflict regulates aspects of a struggle for life and death between contestants who operate on the basis of formal equality. Derived as it is from the medieval tradition of chivalry, it guarantees a modicum of fair play. As in a boxing match, pummeling the opponent's upper body is fine; hitting below the belt is proscribed. As long as the rules of the game are observed, it is permissible to cause suffering, deprivations of freedom, and death. This is a narrow, technical vision of legality.

Human rights laws protect physical integrity and human dignity in all circumstances. They apply to relationships between unequal parties, protecting the governed from their governments. Under human rights law, no one may be deprived of life except in pursuance of a judgment by a competent court. The two systems, human rights and humanitarian norms, are thus distinct and, in many respects, different.[43]

The role and relevance of human rights law during armed conflict, the interrelationship between human rights law and LOAC, and the primacy of one body of law over the other are key questions that inform the applicable law during armed conflict. For starters, LOAC applies only during times of armed conflict while international human rights law applies at all times, in peace and in war. But that does not provide the full answer to the question of how the two bodies of law relate to each other, when one overrides the other, and when they could apply concurrently. At perhaps the most fundamental level, human rights law and LOAC share common themes and goals: protection of persons and of basic human dignity. In some situations, they may each provide rights and protections with regard to the same or similar conduct. However, key conceptual differences are critical to understanding the two bodies of law and how they apply during armed conflict. The following chart highlights some of these differences.[44]

Human Rights: Law of Peace	IHL: Law of War
Developed to prohibit arbitrary treatment of citizens by state	Developed to regulate the conduct of hostilities between states
Presumption that individuals act on their own volition	Presumption that hostile groups act pursuant to leaders' will
Presumes individuals normally comply with state authority and are therefore inoffensive	Presumes members of hostile groups intend to inflict harm on opponent and are therefore presumed offensive
Requires state actor to make individualized judgment to support deprivations of life or liberty	Authorizes deprivations of life and liberty based on presumption of offensiveness

43. Theodor Meron, *The Humanization of Humanitarian Law*, 94 Am. J. Int'l. L. 239, 240 (2000).

44. Extracted from Geoffrey S. Corn, *Mixing Apples and Hand Grenades: The Logical Limit of Applying Human Rights Norms to Armed Conflict*, 1 J. Int'l Hum. Legal Studies 52, 93 (2010).

Human Rights: Law of Peace	IHL: Law of War
Allows only that force necessary to restore the status quo: deadly force is a measure of last resort	Allows for application of overwhelming force: deadly force as a measure of first resort
Protects the object of state violence from excessive application of force	Protects collateral victims from excessive effects of lawful attack

These differences — perhaps at their starkest with regard to the use of force — mean that it is essential to have a guiding framework for understanding which body of law to apply in which circumstances and in which manner. Uncertainty can have consequences for training, implementation, and accountability. To start with, courts and commentators look to a principle of legal interpretation known as *lex specialis*, a Latin phrase meaning "law governing a specific subject matter." The doctrine states that a law governing a specific subject matter overrides a law that only governs general matters. In this context, LOAC is the more specific law — applying only during and specifically to armed conflict — while human rights law is the more general body of law. However, resolving the relationship between LOAC and human rights law has proved to be more complicated.

Although the ICJ has addressed the relationship between LOAC and human rights law in several cases, it has not reached a definitive conclusion regarding the precise delineation between the application of LOAC and the application of human rights law.[45] There is no firm agreement among states at present either: the United States — and Israel — believe that LOAC prevails during armed conflict to the exclusion (in most situations) of human rights law; most European countries and scholars hold the view that human rights law always applies in conjunction with LOAC. One way to view the relationship between LOAC and human rights law is to envision a role for human rights law as a "gap-filler" of sorts. Thus, where LOAC does not apply or does not provide specific guidance, such as in non-international armed

45. For example, in the *Advisory Opinion on the Legality of the Threat or Use of Nuclear Weapons*, the ICJ stated that LOAC is the applicable *lex specialis*, meaning that "whether a particular loss of life, through the use of a certain weapon in warfare, is to be considered an arbitrary deprivation of life contrary to Article 6 of the [ICCPR], can only be decided by reference to the law applicable in armed conflict and not deduced from the terms of the [ICCPR] itself." Legality of the Threat or Use of Nuclear Weapons, 1996 I.C.J. 226, ¶ 25 (July 8). In contrast, in the *Advisory Opinion on the Legal Consequences of the Construction of a Wall in the Occupied Palestinian Territory*, the ICJ took a different approach, stating that "there are thus three possible situations: some rights may be exclusively matters of international humanitarian law; others may be exclusively matters of human rights law; yet others may be matters of both these branches of international law." Legal Consequences of the Construction of a Wall in the Occupied Palestinian Territory, Advisory Opinion, 24 I.C.J. 136, ¶ 106 (July 9).

conflict, where the content of LOAC is significantly more limited than in international armed conflict, human rights law can be a relevant framework. For example, LOAC applicable in non-international armed conflict contemplates detention of persons during conflict but does not provide any parameters or guidelines for such detention. Human rights law can thus help offer an understanding of the basic protections due to such detained persons. Another view of the intersection between LOAC and human rights law is to see the latter as a reference point for certain norms and rights set forth in LOAC, such as the right to a fair trial or, as provided for in Common Article 3 of the Geneva Conventions, the right to a judicial proceeding "affording all the judicial guarantees which are recognized as indispensable by civilized peoples."[46] Human rights law can help flesh out the content of such judicial guarantees.

QUESTIONS FOR DISCUSSION

1. What are the ramifications of different interpretations of the relationship between LOAC and human rights law? Which offers greater protection for persons in a conflict area: the view that LOAC applies exclusively in times of conflict or the view that the two legal frameworks apply simultaneously?

2. What about clarity? Which approach offers greater clarity for military and civilian actors alike?

3. Should the nature of the activity affect how we view the interplay between LOAC and human rights law, such that use of force issues naturally place LOAC at the forefront but detention and other issues stemming from the state's custody of the individual would give primacy to human rights law?

4. As the former Judge Advocate General of the Canadian Armed Forces explained,

> In meeting its goal of limiting the effects and suffering of armed conflict[,] international humanitarian law shares many of the same principles and concepts as human rights. However, international humanitarian law differs from human rights law in its requirement to interface with "military necessity." At the heart of military necessity is the goal of the submission of the enemy at the earliest possible moment with the least possible expenditure of personnel and resources. It justifies the application of force not prohibited by international law.[47]

46. The four Geneva Conventions have several "common" articles, meaning articles that appear in the same form in each of the four conventions, most notably Common Article 2 and Common Article 3.

47. K.W. Watkin, Combatants, Unprivileged Belligerents and Conflicts in the 21st Century 6 (2003), http://www.hpcrresearch.org/sites/default/files/publications/Session2.pdf.

CHAPTER 2

BASIC PRINCIPLES

Four fundamental principles lie at the heart of the law of armed conflict: military necessity, humanity, distinction, and proportionality. Each of these principles is critical for achieving the law's goals of protection of civilians and regulation of the conduct of hostilities. Together the four principles create a framework that can guide examination of the obligations and actions of parties to conflicts and the rights and privileges of individuals in the conflict zone. No less, when viewed as a whole, these principles clearly underline the delicate balance the law strikes between military necessity and humanity.

Jean Pictet

Development and Principles of International Humanitarian Law

(1985)

The International Conventions contain a multitude of rules which specify the obligations of states in very precise terms, but this is not the whole story. Behind these rules are a number of principles which inspire the entire substance of the documents. Sometimes we find them expressly stated in the Conventions, some of them are clearly implied and some derive from customary law.

We are acquainted with the famous Martens clause in the preamble to the Hague Regulations, referring to the "principles of the law of nations, as they result from usages established among civilized peoples." A number of articles in the Geneva Conventions of 1949 also refer to such principles, which are as vitally important in humanitarian law as they are in all other legal domains. They serve in a sense as the bone structure in a living body, providing guidelines in unforeseen cases and constituting a complete summary of the whole, easy to understand and indispensable for the purposes of dissemination . . . .

The principles do not in any sense take the place of the rules set forth in the Conventions. It is to these rules that jurists must refer when the detailed application of the Conventions has to be considered.

A. *MILITARY NECESSITY*

This principle recognizes that a military has the right to use any measures not forbidden by the law of war "which are indispensable for securing the complete submission of the enemy as soon as possible."[1] In essence, military necessity is a principle of authority: the authority to use force to accomplish strategic and national security goals. The Lieber Code, the first codification of the law of war, drafted during the U.S. Civil War, provides the earliest statement of military necessity: "those measures which are indispensable for securing the ends of the war, and which are lawful according to the modern law and usages of war."[2] In addition,

> military necessity does not admit of cruelty—that is, the infliction of suffering for the sake of suffering or for revenge, nor of maiming or wounding except in fight, nor of torture to extort confessions. It does not admit of the use of poison in any way, nor of the wanton devastation of a district.[3]

The framing of military necessity as a principle of authority, but limited in scope, is considered in many ways the Lieber Code's greatest contribution, "the final product of the eighteenth-century movement to humanize war through the application of reason."[4] At the time, the introduction of the principle of military necessity represented a substantial shift in military theory:

> Although not readily apparent today, recognition of military necessity as a legal precondition for destruction represented an enlightened advance in the laws of war in the nineteenth century. In the first half of that century, the law of nations permitted the capture or destruction of any and all property belonging to any person owing allegiance to an enemy government, whether or not these measures were linked to military needs.[5]

Critically, military necessity does not justify departures from the law of armed conflict. A doctrine popular among German theorists at the turn of the twentieth century, called *Kriegsraison*, suggested that military necessity should override the law and that one could abandon the laws of war in situations of extreme danger.[6] At Nuremberg, for example, several German

---

1. DEPARTMENT OF THE ARMY, FM 27-10, THE LAW OF LAND WARFARE art. 3 (1956).

2. FRANCIS LIEBER, WAR DEPARTMENT, INSTRUCTIONS FOR THE GOVERNMENT OF ARMIES OF THE UNITED STATES IN THE FIELD art. 14 (1863).

3. *Id.* art. 16.

4. Burrus M. Carnahan, *Lincoln, Lieber and the Laws of War: The Origins and Limits of the Principle of Military Necessity*, 92 AM. J. INT'L L. 213 (1998).

5. *Id.* at 217.

6. CLAUDE PILLOUD, YVES SANDOZ, CHRISTOPHE SWINARSKI, BRUNO ZIMMERMAN, COMMENTARY ON THE ADDITIONAL PROTOCOLS OF 8 JUNE 1977 TO THE GENEVA CONVENTIONS OF 12 AUGUST 1949 391 (1987).

generals invoked "[m]ilitary necessity . . . as justifying the killing of innocent members of the population and the destruction of villages and towns
in the occupied territory."[7] The Tribunal firmly rejected this notion, declaring that "[m]ilitary necessity or expediency do not justify a violation of positive rules,"[8] and this doctrine remains simply in the archives of legal history.

According to the United Kingdom's *Manual of the Law of Armed Conflict*,
military necessity has four basic elements:

- The force used can be and is being controlled;
- Necessity cannot excuse a departure from the law;
- The use of force in ways which are not otherwise prohibited is legitimate if it is necessary to achieve, as quickly as possible, the complete
  or partial submission of the enemy;
- Conversely, the use of force which is not necessary is unlawful, since
  it involves wanton killing or destruction.[9]

Most important, military necessity is inherent in existing LOAC norms and
incorporated into numerous provisions. It does not exist as a norm separate from existing black letter law that can be presented as an alternative
approach. Indeed, in this way, military necessity exists in a delicate balance
with the second core principle of LOAC, the principle of humanity.

SCREEN SHOT!

In *Saving Private Ryan*, the American unit charges a German machine
gun position, and the medic is shot in the course of the assault. The
medic dies, and one German soldier survives and surrenders. The U.S.
soldiers, who are very emotional over the death of their friend, argue
about whether they should kill the German captive. They cannot take
him along on their mission, and they cannot afford to spare a single
man to escort the German soldier back to Allied lines. Ultimately, Captain Miller (played by Tom Hanks) ends the debate: he says that they
cannot kill him and so tells the soldier to walk toward the Allied lines
and surrender to the first unit he encounters. Near the end of the
movie, during the penultimate battle scene, the very same German soldier shoots and kills Captain Miller. With nowhere to go, the German

---

7. USA v. Wilhelm List and Others (The Hostages Trial), Case No. 47, Judgment (U.S.
Mil. Trib., Nuremberg, Feb. 19, 1948) *in* VIII Law Reports on the Trials of War Criminals 66 (1949).

8. *Id.*

9. UK Ministry of Defence, JSP 383: The Joint Service Manual of the Law of
Armed Conflict ¶ 2.2.1 (2004).

soldier drops his weapon and puts his arms up, but this time one of the American soldiers shoots him.

1. This small unit was on an important mission — could they argue that "military necessity" allows them to kill a prisoner because they had no other option? Did they have other options — was Captain Miller's solution reasonable in light of the law and operational considerations?
2. Does the end result (i.e., the German soldier went back into combat and killed an American soldier) alter your analysis or conclusions?

QUESTIONS FOR DISCUSSION

1. In the *Hostages Trial*, the Nuremberg decision mentioned above, the United States Military Tribunal stated, "the rules of International Law must be followed even if it results in the loss of a battle or even a war."[10] Is this realistic? In his 1832 book *On War*, Carl von Clausewitz stated, "Violence arms itself with the inventions of Art and Science in order to contend against violence. Self-imposed restrictions, almost imperceptible and hardly worth mentioning, termed usages of International Law, accompany it without essentially impairing its power."[11] German Chancellor Otto von Bismarck famously asked, "What leader would allow his country to be destroyed because of international law?"[12] Is the Tribunal correct or are Clausewitz and Bismarck correct?

2. In the past few decades, the question of limiting one's own casualties has entered the public debate about military operations in a much

---

10. USA v. Wilhelm List and Others (The Hostages Trial), Case No. 47, Judgment (U.S. Mil. Trib., Nuremberg, Feb. 19, 1948) *in* VIII Law Reports on the Trials of War Criminals 67 (1949).

11. Carl von Clausewitz, On War 101 (Anatol Rapoport ed., J.J. Graham trans., 1968) (1832).

> That Clausewitz was not alone in his condemnation of the idea that international law had any effective role in the humanization of war may be seen in the comment of Lord Fisher: "The humanizing of War! You might as well talk of the humanizing of Hell. When a silly ass at The Hague got up and talked about the amenities of civilized warfare and putting your prisoners' feet in hot water and giving them gruel, my reply, I regret to say, was considered totally unfit for publication. As if war could be civilized! If I'm in command when war breaks out I shall issue my order — 'The essence of war is violence. Moderation in war is imbecility. Hit first, hit hard, and hit everywhere.'"

L.C. Green, *Cicero and Clausewitz or Quincy Wright: The Interplay of Law and War*, 9 A.F. Acad. J. Leg. Stud. 59, 60 (1998).

12. Chris Jochnick & Roger Normand, *The Legitimation of Violence: A Critical History of the Laws of War*, 35 Harv. Int'l L.J. 49, 64 (1994).

more direct way. How much should the need to protect one's own troops impact a commander's decision-making in wartime? Should this obviously important goal of limiting one's casualties justify a greater use of force or firepower?

B. HUMANITY

The principle of humanity—also referred to as the principle of unnecessary suffering—aims to minimize suffering in armed conflict. To that end, the infliction of suffering or destruction not necessary for legitimate military purposes is forbidden. Once a military purpose has been achieved, the infliction of further suffering is unnecessary. For example, if an enemy soldier is "out of the fight" by dint of being wounded or captured, continuing to attack him serves no military purpose. Another facet of this core principle is that weapons causing unnecessary suffering, such as dum-dum bullets or asphyxiating gases, are outlawed. Similarly, direct attacks on civilians serve no military purpose; the principle of humanity affirms the immunity of civilians from attack. Humanity is therefore LOAC's essential counterbalance to the principle of military necessity and serves as a central principle of constraint.

Numerous specific provisions in treaty and customary LOAC demonstrate the comprehensive role that humanity plays in this body of law: the prohibition against using any type of coercion or torture against a prisoner of war or civilian internee; the obligation to search for and collect the wounded and sick, friend and foe alike, and ensure that priority of medical care is based solely on medical considerations; the obligation to search for and collect the shipwrecked at sea; the obligation to provide notice of capture of enemy personnel to the enemy state through a neutral intermediary; the obligation to facilitate the efforts of neutral relief agencies; the extensive immunities from attack afforded to places engaged in medical functions; and even the obligation to maintain and record the location of interment of the enemy dead.

THE MARTENS CLAUSE

Found in the preamble to the Hague Convention II of 1899, the Martens Clause is the primary codification or incarnation of the principle of humanity:

> Until a more complete code of the laws of war has been issued, the High Contracting Parties deem it expedient to declare that, in cases not included in the Regulations adopted by them, the inhabitants and the belligerents remain under the protection and rule of the

principles of the law of nations, as they result from the usages established among civilized peoples, from the laws of humanity, and the
dictates of public conscience.

*Article 1(2) of Additional Protocol I to the Geneva Conventions provides a
modern formulation:*

In cases not covered by this Protocol or by other international agreements, civilians and combatants remain under the protection and
authority of the principles of international law derived from established custom, from the principles of humanity and from the dictates
of public conscience.

Humanity, as set forth in the Martens Clause, is a direct outgrowth of the
code of chivalry, itself an early manifestation of the laws of war. Chivalry was a
code of conduct for knights during medieval times and included specific rules
for fighting, treatment of other combatants, quarter, and mercy—all based
on loyalty, honor, justice, and courage. Indeed, "the idea that chivalry requires
soldiers to act in a civilized manner is one of its most enduring legacies."[13]
Hundreds of years later, "commands to spare the enemy who asks for mercy,
to aid women in distress, to keep one's promise, to act charitably and to be
magnanimous transcend any one particular historical period or socio-political
context."[14] Although in 1899, the Martens Clause was the first direct iteration
of the principle of humanity as a fundamental incident of LOAC, it linked
directly to earlier notions of natural law. In this way, "the Martens Clause establishes an objective means of determining natural law: the dictates of the public
conscience. This makes the laws of armed conflict much richer, and permits
the participation of all States in its development."[15]

The principle of humanity, through the Martens Clause, provides a
means to fill potential gaps in LOAC stemming from an erroneous belief
that anything not prohibited is permitted in conflict. It is thus

much more than a pious declaration. It is a general clause, making the
usages established among civilized nations, the laws of humanity, and
the dictates of public conscience into the legal yardstick to be applied if
and when the specific provisions of the Convention and the Regulations
annexed to it do not cover specific cases occurring in warfare, or concomitant to warfare.[16]

---

13. Theodor Meron, Bloody Constraint: War and Chivalry in Shakespeare 118
(2000)

14. *Id.* at 108.

15. Rupert Ticehurst, *The Martens Clause and the Laws of Armed Conflict,* 317 Int'l Rev.
Red Cross 125, 133 (1997).

16. United States v. Krupp, 15 Ann. Dig. 620, 622 (U.S. Mil. Trib. 1948).

The Martens Clause also serves as a constant reminder that the principle of humanity remains relevant and retains its primacy even as new developments, whether in the types of conflicts, technology, or weapons, outpace codification. As the ICJ stated in the *Nuclear Weapons* Advisory Opinion, "the Martens Clause . . . has proved to be an effective means of addressing the rapid evolution of military technology."[17]

QUESTIONS FOR DISCUSSION

1. Does the concept of humanity make sense during wartime? Think about the examples offered above of specific provisions incorporating the principle of humanity—why are such obligations important?

2. Consider these quotes from U.S. military leaders, past and present:

- "The soldier, be he friend or foe, is charged with the protection of the weak and unarmed. If he violates this sacred trust, he profanes his entire culture . . ."
  — General Douglas MacArthur, General of the Army

- "To a Marine, honor is more than just honesty. It means having uncompromising personal integrity and being accountable for all actions. It is the moral courage to do the 'right thing' in the face of danger or pressure from other Marines."
  —General Michael Hagee, Commandant of the Marine Corps

- "We are, have been and will remain a values-based institution. Our values will not change, and they are non-negotiable. Our Soldiers are warriors of character. They exemplify these values every day."
  —General Peter Schoomaker, Army Chief of Staff

- "Quite contrary to trivial opinion, all professional military men do not walk blind and brutal."
  —General Curtis LeMay, United States Air Force

How does the notion of character or values coincide with the principle of humanity?

C. DISTINCTION

One of the most fundamental issues during conflict is identifying who or what can be targeted. The principle of distinction—sometimes referred to as discrimination—requires that any party to a conflict distinguish

---

17. Legality of the Threat of Use of Nuclear Weapons, 1996 I.C.J. 226, ¶ 78 (July 8).

between those who are fighting and those who are not, and direct attacks solely at the former. Similarly, parties must distinguish between civilian objects and military objects, and target only the latter.

Distinction has a long pedigree, forming a central tenet of warfare for thousands of years. Many ancient codes of conduct during wartime differentiated in some way between those who could be killed and those who must be spared. For example, in his orders to his commanders, the first Caliph, Abu Bakr, stated, "[t]he blood of women, children and old people shall not stain your victory."[18] The Greeks considered the temples, embassies, priests, and envoys of the opposing side inviolable.[19] Beginning with St. Augustine and St. Thomas Aquinas, early legal theorists began to set forth a framework for who could be killed during armed conflict—the early underpinnings of today's principle of distinction. Thus, St. Thomas Aquinas declared that "it is in no way lawful to slay the innocent."[20] During the Enlightenment, Jean-Jacques Rousseau advanced the analysis significantly in his seminal work, *The Social Contract*, focusing primarily on distinguishing between those who bore arms and those who did not. In this way, Rousseau formulated the principle of noncombatant immunity in terms that remain vital and recognizable today:

> Since the purpose of war is to destroy the enemy State, it is legitimate to kill the latter's defenders *so long as they are carrying arms*; but as soon as they lay them down and surrender, they cease to be enemies or agents of the enemy, and again become mere men, and it is no longer legitimate to take their lives.[21]

Although early wars were often uncompromising in their brutality, these early moral, religious, and legal precepts and teachings established a firm foundation for the modern law of war and the notion of discrimination between and among persons on the battlefield.

In the modern law of war, distinction was first set forth in Article 22 of the Lieber Code:

> Nevertheless, as civilization has advanced during the last centuries, so has likewise steadily advanced, especially in war on land, the distinction between the private individual belonging to a hostile country and the hostile country itself, with its men in arms. The principle has been more and more acknowledged that the unarmed citizen is to be spared in person, property, and honor as much as the exigencies of war will admit.

A few short years later, the international community reinforced the rule in the St. Petersburg Declaration, which stated that "the only legitimate object which States should endeavour to accomplish during war is to weaken the

---

18. Christopher Greenwood, *Historical Development and Legal Basis, in* The Handbook of Humanitarian Law in Armed Conflict 1, 14 (Dieter Fleck ed., 1995).

19. *Id.* at 13; *see also* L.C. Green, The Contemporary Law of Armed Conflict 69 (1998).

20. 6 Thomas Aquinas, Summa Theologica 159 (2007) (1265).

21. Jean-Jacques Rousseau, Du Contrat Social 111 (1762).

military forces of the enemy." Although the overall purpose of the St. Petersburg Declaration was the prohibition of weapons causing unnecessary suffering for combatants, this provision confirms the immunity of the civilian population from attack.

Neither the Hague Conventions of 1899 and 1907 nor the Geneva Conventions of 1949 contain specific statements of the principle of distinction, but its force as customary law remained in effect. By 1977, when the Additional Protocols were drafted, the nature of warfare demonstrated the need for a clear restatement of the principle of distinction and reinforcement of its central role in LOAC.

ARTICLE 48 OF ADDITIONAL PROTOCOL I: THE BASIC RULE

In order to ensure respect for and protection of the civilian population and civilian objects, the Parties to the conflict shall at all times distinguish between the civilian population and combatants and between civilian objects and military objectives and accordingly shall direct their operations only against military objectives.[22]

Distinction thus lies at the core of LOAC's seminal goal of protecting innocent civilians and persons who are *hors de combat* (literally "out of the fight"). The purpose of distinction — to protect civilians — is emphasized in Article 51 of Additional Protocol I, which states that "[t]he civilian population as such, as well as individual civilians, shall not be the object of attack." Article 51 continues, stating:

Indiscriminate attacks are prohibited. Indiscriminate attacks are:
(a) those which are not directed at a specific military objective;
(b) those which employ a method or means of combat which cannot be directed at a specific military objective; or
(c) those which employ a method or means of combat the effects of which cannot be limited as required by this Protocol; and consequently, in each such case, are of a nature to strike military objectives and civilians or civilian objects without distinction.

Furthermore, Article 85(3) of Protocol I declares that nearly all violations of distinction constitute grave breaches of the Protocol, including:

(a) making the civilian population or individual civilians the object of attack;

22. Article 48 is considered customary international law.

(b) launching an indiscriminate attack affecting the civilian population or civilian objects in the knowledge that such attack will cause excessive loss of life, injury to civilians or damage to civilian objects, as defined in Article 57, paragraph 2(a)(iii); . . .

(d) making non-defended localities and demilitarized zones the object of attack; [and]

(e) making a person the object of attack in the knowledge that he is *hors de combat* . . . .

QUESTIONS FOR DISCUSSION

1. The treaty provisions excerpted above highlight the two different components of distinction: the prohibition on indiscriminate weapons and the obligation to distinguish between those who are fighting and those who are not. Think about current and recent past conflict situations—which present issues about each aspect of distinction?

2. In current conflicts where fighters meld into the civilian population and use civilian areas to hide weapons, it is increasingly difficult for soldiers to distinguish between combatants and non-combatants and to protect civilians. Can the principle of distinction still be relevant? What are the consequences of relaxing the obligations mandated by distinction? Keep in mind that the principle of distinction also obligates parties to a conflict to distinguish themselves from innocent civilians.

3. In many conflicts, insurgents, terrorist groups, and even some State militaries deliberately design their strategy and tactics around the exploitation of the civilian population. Consider how one senior Islamist militant in Egypt's Sinai Peninsula explains their change in strategy:

> At the start of the fighting we used to hide in mountains but now we are present in the villages among residents, because it is safer there . . . . When we were in the mountains it was easy for the army to strike us with helicopters. But as long as we are with the people it is hard to reach us.[23]

4. In 2008, the U.S. Army's Task Force Rock was building a new combat outpost (COP) in Wanat, a village high in the Hindu Kush of Konar Province in Afghanistan's rugged northeast. Three days after the platoon began construction on the new COP, it was attacked, leaving nine U.S. soldiers dead and thirty-one wounded. The process of acquiring the land for the COP had taken months of negotiation, so everyone knew the exact location of the Americans' next COP. When the attack commenced, the intensity and scale of the attack surprised the undermanned platoon the most:

> It was hard to believe the enemy had so many grenades to shoot. Everyone kept waiting for a lull, but it didn't come. The village had clearly been in on the attack, stealthily stockpiling RPGs for days, if not weeks. There

23. *Special Report: Egyptian Militants Outwit Army in Sinai Battlefield*, REUTERS, March 16, 2014.

had been clues: unoccupied young men just sitting and watching the post under construction over the last few days, as if measuring distances, observing routines, counting men and weapons. The men of the platoon had sensed that they were being sized up, but what could they do? They couldn't shoot people for just standing and watching. There had been a few warnings that the attack was coming, one just the night before, but they believed on the basis of long experience that they had time. Ordinarily the enemy would work up to a big attack, preceding it with a small unit assault on one position, a lobbed grenade, or a few mortars from the distance. This is what experience had taught them to expect. Not a massive attack completely out of the blue.[24]

At a most basic level, the principle of distinction's mandate to distinguish between fighters and civilians and to only attack fighters rests on a presumption that a soldier actually *can* differentiate between them. Could the soldiers have determined who was hostile and who was not in the days and weeks leading up to the attack? Were there any targets for the soldiers to identify in this situation?

LOCATION: BAGHDAD, IRAQ

This was during the "Shock and Awe" phase of the war. This particular event started in Sadr City and concluded in Baghdad.

Our unit just arrived in Baghdad after encountering fierce fighting during our push from Sadr City. We just traversed through what many have described as the world's largest "drive by"—a 2-3-mile strip of road with buildings on both sides the entire way, infested with enemy fighters. Concealed by the cover of night, the enemy unleashed an unbelievable volume of fire consisting of RPGs [rocket-propelled grenades] and heavy machine guns. Through my NVG's [night vision goggles], it truly looked like a scene from *Star Wars* with all the green flashes streaking through the air in every direction.

Casualties were mounting and continued as we fought to gain a foothold in the city. Eventually, we made our way to Saddam's Presidential Palace, which we secured to establish a fighting position and to medevac our casualties. Just moments before arriving, my AAV [amphibious assault vehicle] was hit with 2 RPGs, gravely wounding several Marines.

While the fighting in the streets continued throughout the city, an alarming number of civilians began entering the streets and started looting, taking anything they could get their hands on. As a result, our tactical picture became blurred, making it hard to distinguish

24. MARK BOWDEN, THE THREE BATTLES OF WANAT AND OTHER TRUE STORIES 13 (2016).

combatants from civilians due to the melting pot of fighters we were encountering—most of whom didn't wear uniforms, making it difficult to identify Iraqi civilians from enemy combatants. This was not something that was anticipated nor was there any direction on how to proceed during greater civilian involvement.

In addition to looting, vehicular traffic started to increase around the palace, becoming an additional concern. My unit made a hasty roadblock at the front of the palace using anything we could find to pile into the streets to prevent traffic from funneling in our direction: furniture, tires, scrap wood, metal appliances, etc. There wasn't time or the resources to make signs or use a traditional barrier system which might have been more obvious to traffic; this was very primitive, essentially a pile of garbage in the middle of the street that we hoped would discourage inbound traffic away from the palace. And if that wasn't enough, hopefully the backdrop of heavily armed Marines and fighting vehicles would make them choose more cautiously.

Shortly after the roadblock was established, we were approached by a series of vehicles. The first was a small truck with three men inside that appeared to be unarmed. They pulled up to our hasty roadblock and stopped within sight of us and sat motionless inside of their truck. We yelled and waved our hands for them to turn around, but it failed to produce any type of response. One of our gunners decided to shoot warning shots towards them, after which the driver hit the gas and accelerated towards us at an alarming rate of speed. We held our fire for as long as we reasonably could and then decided to engage the vehicle with our weapons, rendering it inoperable.

As the truck came to a stop, it was obvious all were either dead or critically injured. But before anyone could assess the actual conditions, we were approached by a van. The van, unfortunately, even with the bullet-ridden truck in front of them, would make the same series of decisions, which ended in the same manner. This would also be the case for the third vehicle, which resembled a Greyhound bus with many passengers. In total, more than 30 people were killed, every one of them civilians.

We didn't know if they were suicide car bombers or if they were going to veer off at the last moment down an adjacent street that wasn't known to be frequented by civilians. We tried to deter them by designating one Marine to shoot tracer rounds only, even though the rules of engagement (ROEs) stated otherwise. But unfortunately each time we fired tracer rounds it resulted in the driver accelerating towards us at a high rate of speed, leaving us no other choice but to identify them as hostile and engage them as if they were intending to kill us. It was obvious the tactical picture was changing, but the current ROEs didn't have a chance to catch up.

— U.S. Marine

D.   *PROPORTIONALITY*

The principle of proportionality requires that parties refrain from attacks in which the expected civilian casualties will be excessive in relation to the anticipated military advantage gained. It is important to note that this *jus in bello* principle of proportionality differs substantially from the *jus ad bellum* proportionality discussed briefly in Chapter 1, which is focused on the nature and extent of force allowed in self-defense in response to an attack. In LOAC, this principle balances military necessity and humanity and is based on the confluence of two key ideas. First, the means and methods of attacking the enemy are not unlimited. Rather, the only legitimate object of war is to weaken the military forces of the enemy. Second, the legal proscription on targeting civilians does not extend to a complete prohibition on all civilian deaths. The law has always tolerated "the incidence of some civilian casualties . . . as a consequence of military action,"[25] although "even a legitimate target may not be attacked if the collateral civilian casualties would be disproportionate to the specific military gain from the attack."[26] That is, the law requires that military commanders and decision-makers evaluate the advantage to be gained from an attack and assess it in light of the likely civilian casualties.[27]

Additional Protocol I contains three separate statements of the principle of proportionality. The first appears in Article 51, which sets forth the basic parameters of the obligation to protect civilians and the civilian population and prohibits any "attack which may be expected to cause incidental loss of civilian life, injury to civilians, damage to civilian objects, or a combination thereof, which would be excessive in relation to the concrete and direct military advantage anticipated." This language demonstrates that Additional Protocol I contemplates incidental civilian casualties, and appears again in Articles 57(2)(a)(iii)[28] and 57(2)(b),[29] which refer specifically to precautions in attack.

---

25. Judith Gardham, *Necessity and Proportionality in* Jus ad Bellum *and* Jus in Bello, *in* INTERNATIONAL LAW, THE INTERNATIONAL COURT OF JUSTICE AND NUCLEAR WEAPONS 283-284 (Laurence Boisson de Chazoumes & Philippe Sands eds., 1999).

26. Legality of the Threat or Use of Nuclear Weapons, 1996 I.C.J. 226, ¶ 936 (July 8) (Dissenting Opinion of Judge Higgins).

27. The term "collateral damage" is often used in the media and by the public to refer to the incidental (meaning not deliberate) civilian casualties from an attack on a military target.

28. "With respect to attacks, the following precautions shall be taken: (a) those who plan or decide upon an attack shall: . . . (iii) refrain from deciding to launch any attack which may be expected to cause incidental loss of civilian life, injury to civilians, damage to civilian objects, or a combination thereof, which would be excessive in relation to the concrete and direct military advantage anticipated."

29. "[A]n attack shall be cancelled or suspended if it becomes apparent that the objective is not a military one or is subject to special protection or that the attack may be expected to cause incidental loss of civilian life, injury to civilians, damage to civilian objects, or a combination thereof, which would be excessive in relation to the concrete and direct military advantage anticipated."

The Rome Statute of the International Criminal Court also incorporates the principle of proportionality in criminalizing war crimes. Article 8(2)(b)(iv) forbids

> [i]ntentionally launching an attack in the knowledge that such attack will cause incidental loss of life or injury to civilians or damage to civilian objects or widespread, long-term and severe damage to the natural environment which would be clearly excessive in relation to the concrete and direct overall military advantage anticipated.

Both formulations emphasize that proportionality is not a mathematical concept, but rather a guideline to help ensure that military commanders weigh the consequences of a particular attack and refrain from launching attacks that will cause excessive civilian deaths. The principle of proportionality is well-accepted as an element of customary international law applicable in all armed conflicts.

PROPORTIONALITY?

- During the first Gulf War, the U.S. bombed the Al Firdus bunker, a former air raid shelter then used as a bunker. It was camouflaged, surrounded by barbed wire, guarded day and night, and used as a command and control post. U.S. reconnaissance recorded military vehicles, command and control radio traffic, and other evidence of its use as a military post—but no evidence of any civilians. On February 12, 1991, two U.S. F-117 stealth fighters bombed the bunker, destroying it. When morning came, news footage of over 200 dead civilians being removed from the bunker flashed around the world.
- During the 1982 Falklands War, the Royal Navy sunk the Argentine cruiser *General Belgrano*, killing 368 Argentine sailors and seamen, the largest single loss of life of the entire conflict.
- In Afghanistan, U.S. soldiers and Marines faced attacks from Taliban militants who fired from residential compounds. If the U.S. soldiers and Marines fired back, they would likely endanger or kill civilians living in those compounds.
- During the 2006 war between Israel and Hezbollah in Lebanon, Hezbollah used villages in southern Lebanon as bases, storing weapons in and firing rockets from civilian houses. Attacking Hezbollah fighters and stopping the rocket attacks often meant bombing civilian houses and villages.
- The Battle of Fallujah in 2004 was one of the harshest battles of the second Gulf War. In fighting to root out hardcore Sunni insurgents

who controlled the city (and supported and harbored the killers of four U.S. civilian contractors), the U.S. anticipated heavy civilian casualties.

Which of these scenarios implicates the principle of proportionality? Why or why not?

QUESTIONS FOR DISCUSSION

1. LOAC therefore constitutes a careful balancing between military necessity and humanity, between the needs of the military force to defeat the enemy and the humanitarian considerations of minimizing suffering during wartime. As you read the following excerpt, think about how this balance should be struck. What are the consequences of upending this delicate balance?

> [LOAC] cannot be oblivious to the exigencies of war and to the military necessity impelling each Belligerent Party to take the requisite measures to defeat the enemy. Still, military necessity must be dissociated from wanton acts that have no operational rhyme or reason. The objective need to win the war is not to be confounded with the subjective whim or caprice of an individual soldier (whatever his rank). Lawful violence in war must be leveraged to the attainment of some discernible military advantage as a direct result. . . .
>
> The fact that there is military advantage in pursuing a particular mode of action is not the end of the matter. Had it been the end, if military necessity were the sole beacon to guide the path of armed forces in wartime, no limitation of any significance would have been imposed on the freedom of action of Belligerent Parties. Such a reversion to the outdated adage *à la guerre comme à la guerre* (all's fair in war) would negate the major premise that the choice of means and methods of warfare is not unlimited. . . . But the determination of what action or inaction is permissible in wartime does not rest on the demands of military necessity alone. There are also countervailing humanitarian considerations — shaped by the global Zeitgeist — that affect the general practice of States and goad the drafters of treaties. . . . These considerations are both inspiring and instrumental, yet they too cannot monopolize the course of warfare. If benevolent humanitarianism were the only factor to be weighed in hostilities, war would have entailed no bloodshed, no human suffering and no destruction of property; in short, war would not be war. [LOAC] must be predicated on a subtle equilibrium between the two diametrically opposed stimulants of military necessity and humanitarian considerations. In doing that, [LOAC] takes a middle road, allowing Belligerent Parties much leeway (in keeping with the demands of military necessity) and nevertheless curbing their freedom of action (in the name of humanitarianism). The furnace in which all [LOAC] norms are wrought is stoked — in the words of the Preamble to the St. Petersburg Declaration of 1868 . . . by the desire

to fix "the technical limits at which the necessities of war ought to yield to the requirements of humanity".

The paramount precept of [LOAC]—to reiterate the language of the same St Petersburg Declaration . . . is "alleviating as much as possible the calamities of war". The humanitarian desire to attenuate human anguish in any armed conflict is natural. However, the thrust of the concept is not absolute elimination of the calamities of war (a goal which would manifestly be beyond reach), but relief from the tribulations of war "as much as possible" bearing in mind that war is fought to be won. . . .

[LOAC] amounts to a checks-and-balances system, intended to minimize human suffering without undermining the effectiveness of military operations. Military commanders are often the first to appreciate that their professional duties can, and should, be discharged without causing pointless distress to the troops. It is noteworthy that the St. Petersburg Declaration was crafted by an international conference attended solely by military men. The input of military experts to all subsequent landmark treaties governing the conduct of hostilities has been enormous. As for customary international law, it is forged in the crucible of State practice during hostilities, predominantly through the action of armed forces.

Every single norm of [LOAC] is moulded by a parallelogram of forces: it confronts an inveterate tension between the demands of military necessity and humanitarian considerations, working out a compromise formula. While the outlines of the compromise vary from one [LOAC] norm to another, it can be categorically stated that no part of [LOAC] overlooks military requirements, just as no part of [LOAC] loses sight of humanitarian considerations. All segments of this body of law are animated by a pragmatic (as distinct from a purely idealistic) approach to armed conflict.[30]

2. Think about how many different ways law uses the term proportionality. The term is tossed around in a variety of ways and settings with regard to the use of force by states and individuals, against both individuals and objects. It is a central principle of LOAC, a key normative requirement framing the right to use force in self-defense, and an essential factor limiting the use of force within law enforcement and human rights parameters. Each concept of proportionality plays a central role in its own legal regime; each has important protective purposes. In understanding how to apply LOAC and other related legal paradigms to the acts of states and individuals in armed conflict and situations of violence (see Chapter 4 regarding how to identify armed conflict), it is essential to understand the key differences between what proportionality means in each of these legal regimes. The primary issue in analyzing *jus ad bellum* proportionality is whether the defensive use of force is appropriate in relation to the ends sought, measuring the extent of the use of force against the overall military goals, such as

---

30. Yoram Dinstein, The Conduct of Hostilities Under the Law of International Armed Conflict 4-5 (2010).

fending off an attack or subordinating the enemy. The LOAC principle of proportionality, in contrast, focuses solely on the protection of civilians and minimization of civilian casualties, and requires that parties refrain from attacks in which the expected civilian casualties will be excessive in relation to the anticipated military advantage gained. Finally, proportionality in human rights law refers to the measure of force directed at the intended target of the attack. Law enforcement authorities can use no more force than is absolutely necessary to effectuate an arrest, defend themselves, or defend others from attack. This proportionality does not address the unintended victims of the use of force, thus differing again in a fundamental manner from LOAC proportionality. Consider the consequences for legal protections and accountability when one form of proportionality is substituted for another—or the ramifications of blurring the lines between legal paradigms.

CHAPTER 3

HISTORICAL DEVELOPMENT OF LOAC

Despite examples of atrocities and brutality in any era, LOAC has a long pedigree and "attempts to regulate war are as old as war itself."[1] Throughout history and around the globe, belligerents have created war codes and recognized their value. Although LOAC was not codified in one collection of volumes until the mid-eighteen hundreds, it was nevertheless an essential part of the evolution of humankind and the evolution of warfare on every continent.

A. ANTIQUITY THROUGH THE CODE OF CHIVALRY

Cultures throughout the ancient world developed laws and rules to govern armed conflict. The Old Testament, for example, contains "numerous admonitions for, and records of, the slaughter of men, the transplanting of the women and children, the plunder of beasts and other property, the looting and wanton destruction of cities, etc."[2] The wars between Egypt and the Sumerians in the second millennium B.C.E. were "governed by a complex set of rules obligating belligerents to distinguish combatants from civilians and providing procedures for declaring war, conducting arbitration, and concluding peace treaties."[3] The Code of Hammurabi provided for, among other things, "the protection of the weak against oppression by the strong and ordered that hostages be released on payment of ransom,"[4]

---

1. HOWARD LEVIE, TERRORISM AND WAR: THE LAW OF WAR CRIMES 55 (1992).

2. *Id.* at 9 (citing Numbers 31:7-12; Deuteronomy 3:6-7, 20:14-17; Samuel 15:3).

3. Chris Jochnick & Roger Normand, *The Legitimation of Violence: A Critical History of the Laws of War*, 35 HARV. INT'L L.J. 49, 60 (1994).

4. *See* THE AVALON PROJECT (2008), http://avalon.law.yale.edu/default.asp. Hammurabi was the king of Babylon and he lived from 1728-1686 B.C.E. Articles 133-135 of the Code of Hammurabi specifically address "prisoners of war."

and Cyrus I, King of the Persians in the seventh century B.C.E, ordered that the enemy wounded were to be treated the same as their own wounded soldiers.

Similarly, the Greeks and Romans restricted warfare in a manner familiar to us today. In Alexander the Great's war against the Persians, the Greeks viewed respect for war victims as a central principle, observed truces, and respected the inviolability of the enemy's temples, embassies, priests, and envoys. Mercy was shown to "helpless captives" and prisoners of war were ransomed and exchanged. "It was considered wrong to cut off or poison the enemy's water supply, or to make use of poisoned weapons. Treacherous weapons of every description were condemned as being contrary to civilized warfare. . . ."[5] The Romans also spared the lives of their prisoners of war.[6]

Many of the modern international humanitarian law principles have their roots in India, China, Southwest Asia, and Japan, including the Indian epic, *Mahabharata* (c. 400 B.C.E.), and the *Manava Dharma-Sastra* (or the *Laws of Manu*), which foreshadowed many central provisions of the 1907 Hague Regulations. In Japan, the *Bushi-Do* (the "medieval code of honour of the warrior caste of Japan") exhorted the exercise of humanity in "battle and towards prisoners of war," regardless of whether or not the prisoner of war surrendered peacefully or fought to his "last arrow."[7] Prominent Chinese writers similarly detailed some of the most fundamental tenets of LOAC and prohibited the military from attacking cities, pillaging, enslaving civilians, murdering innocents, or attacking an incapacitated, sick, or wounded enemy. The Koran also requires the victor to extend humanitarian efforts "[t]o feed for the love of Allah, the indigent, the orphan and the captive."[8] Although Islamic warfare was often on par with the brutality of warfare conducted by Christians, in the twelfth century, Sultan Saladin observed the laws of war "in an exemplary manner."[9] To that end, the first Caliph, Abu Bakr, stated in his orders to his commanders,

> O people! I charge you with ten rules; learn them well! Stop, O people, that I may give you ten rules for your guidance in the battlefield. Do not commit treachery or deviate from the right path. You must not mutilate dead bodies. Neither kill a child, nor a woman, nor an aged man. Bring

---

5. L.C. Green, *Cicero and Clausewitz or Quincy Wright: The Interplay of Law and War*, 9 A.F. ACAD. J. LEG. STUD. 59, 69 (1998).

6. *See* Christopher Greenwood, *Historical Development and Legal Basis, in* THE HANDBOOK OF HUMANITARIAN LAW IN ARMED CONFLICT 1, 13 (Dieter Fleck ed., 1995). However, both the Greeks and Romans "distinguished between those peoples whom they regarded as their cultural equals and those whom they considered to be barbarians." *Id.*

7. *Id.* at 15.

8. L.C. Green, *Cicero and Clausewitz or Quincy Wright: The Interplay of Law and War*, 9 A.F. ACAD. J. LEG. STUD. 59, 69 (1998).

9. Christopher Greenwood, *Historical Development and Legal Basis, in* THE HANDBOOK OF HUMANITARIAN LAW IN ARMED CONFLICT 1, 14 (Dieter Fleck ed., 1995).

no harm to the trees, nor burn them with fire, especially those which are fruitful. Slay not any of the enemy's flock, save for your food. You are likely to pass by people who have devoted their lives to monastic services; leave them alone.[10]

In the Middle Ages, which certainly produced its share of brutal engagements, war was regarded as a formal process, a contest between two sovereigns during which formal rules of combat and conduct would apply. Although declarations of war are now rarely, if ever, used and have no legal effect with regard to the application of LOAC, for hundreds of years they formed the formal trigger for the application of relevant codes of conduct.

During this period, an unwritten Code of Chivalry developed among knights. Along with the Christian writings of St. Augustine and St. Thomas Aquinas, these rules of chivalry prohibiting attacks on the sick, the wounded, women, and children thus offered some guidance in this period. However, the rules only applied to knights, not to the ordinary people. Moreover, many of the rules developed not for humanitarian purposes but to preserve existing power structures—namely, the authority of the Church. For example, "the attempt by the Lateran Council in 1137 to ban the crossbow was motivated as much by a desire to get rid of a weapon which allowed a foot soldier to threaten an armoured knight as by humanitarian concern at the injuries which crossbow bolts could cause."[11] Tribunals of knights adjudicated disputes over and violations of the rules of chivalry. These courts judged the accused knight on the manner in which he treated fellow knights, not on his treatment of any number of other "lowly" combatants. Worse, they frequently dispensed victors' justice. For example, in 1268, Charles of Anjou had Conraddin executed after "mock proceedings" for "having illegally waged war as a rebel."[12] Sir William Wallace was put to death without a trial in 1305 for "having spared 'neither age nor sex, monk nor nun.'"[13] Arguably the first "international war crimes" trial was of Peter von Hagenbach in 1474 for his violations of the law of war. Charles the Bold, Duke of Burgundy, made von Hagenbach governor of the city of Briesach, where von Hagenbach proceeded to rape, murder, confiscate private property, and illegally tax its citizens.[14] He was convicted, deprived of his knighthood, and then executed.

As the Middle Ages drew to a close, the chivalric orders declined, the firearm was invented, and sovereigns created armies by hiring mercenaries.

---

10. Youssef H. Aboul-Enein & Sherifa Zuhur, Islamic Rulings on Warfare 22 (2004).

11. Christopher Greenwood, *Historical Development and Legal Basis, in* The Handbook of Humanitarian Law in Armed Conflict 1, 14 (Dieter Fleck ed., 1995).

12. Howard Levie, Terrorism and War: The Law of War Crimes 3, 11 (1992).

13. *Id. See also* Steven R. Ratner, *Categories of War Crimes, in* Crimes of War 374 (Roy Gutman & David Rieff eds., 1999).

14. *See* Howard Levie, Terrorism and War: The Law of War Crimes 11 (1992).

The mercenaries viewed war as a means for private gain and no longer followed the chivalric code, making no distinction between combatants and civilians. The problems of mercenary armies who had no regular pay and inadequate supplies and were thus forced to ravage the countryside by living off the land produced important lessons. It became generally understood that "soldiers who were regularly fed and paid, and who did not have to forage for food and shelter, could be disciplined and trained. . . ."[15] As a result, "soldiering became a profession, and the distinction between soldier and civilian was stabilized. And so were born the customs and rules governing the conduct of occupying troops, requiring respect for the lives and livelihoods of the civilian inhabitants, as long as they remained non-combatants."[16]

Hugo Grotius' definitive work, *De jure belli ac pacis*, published in 1625, was the first comprehensive codification of international law. The father of modern international law, Grotius insisted that the conduct of war had strict legal limits and parameters. Enlightenment thinkers, such as Rousseau, recognized that "[w]ar . . . is not a relation of man to man, but of State to State, in which individuals are enemies only accidentally, and not as men, nor even as citizens, but as soldiers; not as members of their country, but as its defenders."[17] His clarity on this issue opened the way for subsequent leaders, statesmen, and authors to make clear the duties and privileges owed to the soldier. For example, in a letter to Napoleon, Talleyrand praised LOAC for the civility Europe showed when at peace:

> Three centuries of civilization have given Europe a law of nations, for which . . . human nature cannot be sufficiently grateful. According to the maxim that war is not a relation between one man and another, but between state and state, in which private persons are only accidental enemies, not as men, nor even as members or subjects of the state, but simply as its defenders, the law of nations does not permit that the rights of war, and of conquest thence derived, should be applied to peaceable, unarmed citizens, to private properties and dwellings, to the merchandise of commerce, to the magazines which contain it, to the vehicles which transport it, to unarmed ships which carry it on streams and seas, in one word, to the person and the goods of private individuals.

15. TELFORD TAYLOR, THE ANATOMY OF THE NUREMBERG TRIALS: A PERSONAL MEMOIR 11 (1992). "Administrative staffs handled supplies, pay, and other logistical necessities. Military police helped enforce discipline. . . ." *Id.*

16. *Id.* ("Execution was the usual punishment for troops who pillaged or otherwise molested the citizenry. It is reported that General Thomas Gage, commander of British troops in Boston in 1774-1775, had two of his soldiers hanged for breaking into a colonist's store.").

17. David J. Bederman, *Reception of the Classical Tradition in International Law: Grotius' De Jure Belli ac Pacis*, 10 EMORY INT'L L. REV. 1, 5 (1996). Rousseau's *Du Contrat Social* was published in 1762.

> The law of war, born of civilization, has favored its progress. It is to this that Europe must ascribe the maintenance and increase of her prosperity, in the midst of the frequent wars that have divided her.[18]

At the same time, states began to develop customs for the treatment and protection of prisoners of war. The 1785 Treaty of Amity and Commerce between the United States and Prussia was one of the first attempts to memorialize legal obligations in written form, affirming that prisoners of war

> shall not be confined in dungeons, prison-ships, nor prisons, nor be put into irons, nor bound, nor otherwise restrained in the use of their limbs; that the officers shall . . . have comfortable quarters, and the common men be . . . lodged in barracks as roomly and good as are provided by the party in whose power they are for their own troops. . . .[19]

B. *LIEBER CODE AND SOLFERINO*

By the middle of the nineteenth century, the idea that certain practices should be forbidden because they were inhumane, regardless of their military utility, began to take hold in military law. Humanitarian considerations thus increasingly occupied a central place and began to displace notions of expedience.

The introduction of the war correspondent arguably proved to be one of the most important events in this period of the evolution of LOAC. When the first war correspondent filed the first war report (to London from Balaklava via the telegraph) during the Crimean War of 1854-56, the public's view of war changed forever. Prior to that report, the public received a healthy helping of "self-serving accounts of military commanders" with an "emphasis . . . on deeds of bravery, not on the pain and suffering of noncombatants in harm's way or of combatants captured or injured."[20] William Howard Russell's "Dispatch to the Times" on November 14, 1854, brought home the horrors of war directly with a gripping description of the Charge of the Light Brigade and the terrible destruction as the "Russian gunners . . . poured a murderous volley of grape and canister on the mass of struggling men and horses, mingling friend and foe in one common ruin" and killing their own troopers along with the British cavalry.[21]

The next major event in the evolution of LOAC grew directly out of this nascent trend of exposing the general public to the horrors of war. The

---

18. TELFORD TAYLOR, THE ANATOMY OF THE NUREMBERG TRIALS: A PERSONAL MEMOIR 7 (1992).

19. Treaty of Amity and Commerce, Pru.-U.S., July 9, 1785, 8 Stat. 84.

20. ARYEH NEIER, WAR CRIMES: BRUTALITY, GENOCIDE, TERROR, AND THE STRUGGLE FOR JUSTICE 13-14 (1998).

21. William Howard Russell, *Dispatch to the Times*, LONDON TIMES, November 14, 1854.

Battle of Solferino, during the Italian War of Unification in 1859, was a typical mid-nineteenth-century battle — but one which shocked an observer, Swiss businessman Henri Dunant. Horrified by the "lack of any systematic effort by the armies" involved to retrieve and care for their fallen comrades left "on the battlefield, and often robbed and murdered by local inhabitants," Dunant was driven to organize the efforts of volunteers to collect and provide for the wounded despite the fact that medical providers were left "unprotected from attack or capture."[22] Dunant published his reflections in *A Memory of Solferino* and, capitalizing on its great success and popular influence, founded the International Committee of the Red Cross (ICRC) in Geneva in 1863. One year later, the ICRC promulgated its first convention for the purpose of caring for the victims of war: the Convention for the Amelioration of the Condition of the Wounded in Armies in the Field, signed by twelve European states on August 22, 1864. This first Geneva Convention defined the legal status of medical personnel and further stated that "[w]ounded or sick combatants, to whatever nation they may belong, shall be collected and cared for."[23]

Across the Atlantic, the American Civil War raged and extensive coverage in American newspapers of battles and the horrors of war opened the eyes of ordinary citizens to the dangers war posed for both soldiers and civilians caught in the combat zone. Although there is no reported correlation to the public receiving vivid descriptions of the war, President Lincoln ordered that a code be written for the Union Army's conduct in the conflict and commissioned Professor Francis Lieber of Columbia University to draft the code.[24] Implemented on April 24, 1863, by the United States Army as General Orders No. 100, Lieber's *Instructions for the Government of Armies of the United States in the Field* quickly became commonly referred to as the Lieber Code and is recognized as the first modern codification of the law of war.

Czar Alexander II of Russia took the next step in the development of LOAC in 1868 when he convened the first international conference on the laws of war, with the goal of alleviating the calamities of war. The result, the 1868 Declaration of St. Petersburg, was the first international effort to limit the types of weapons used in war, and prohibited weapons that caused unnecessary suffering. The Declaration states that "the employment of such arms would, therefore, be contrary to the laws of humanity."[25] The 1864

22. Christopher Greenwood, *Historical Development and Legal Basis, in* The Handbook of Humanitarian Law in Armed Conflict 1, 18 (Dieter Fleck ed., 1995).

23. Convention for the Amelioration of the Condition of the Wounded in Armies in the Field, arts. 2, 6, Aug. 22, 1864, 129 Consol. T.S. 361.

24. Burrus M. Carnahan, *Lincoln, Lieber and the Laws of War: The Origins and Limits of the Principle of Military Necessity*, 92 Am. J. Int'l L. 213, 214-215 (1998).

25. Declaration Renouncing the Use, in Time of War, of Certain Explosive Projectiles, Nov. 29, 1868, 138 Consol. T.S. 297.

Geneva Convention was already in operation and was soon put to the test during the 1870 Franco-Prussian War. However, one major country had not yet signed the treaty: the United States. Clara Barton, a significant American player in the provision of relief to the wounded and other victims of war, championed the cause of U.S. ratification of the 1864 Geneva Convention and, by 1882, secured U.S. participation.

C.   FROM THE HAGUE TO WORLD WAR II

On August 24, 1898, Czar Nicholas II circulated a letter to diplomats in St. Petersburg proposing an international conference in The Hague to discuss peace and disarmament. Handicapped by suspicions that the Czar viewed the conference as a way to overcome Russia's relative military weakness and by government instructions to reject limitations on arms, the Hague Conference ultimately prohibited the use of only three weapons: asphyxiating gases, dum-dum bullets, and balloon-launched munitions. However, it was more successful in addressing the laws and customs of land warfare, producing the Convention (II) with Respect to the Laws and Customs of War on Land, a formative LOAC document still relied on today. Using the Lieber Code as a major source, the Convention focused primarily on prisoners of war and the relations between occupation troops and the non-combatant civilian inhabitants. It then went further, however, and unequivocally prohibited declaring "no quarter" or attacking enemy soldiers who had surrendered.[26]

The preamble of the 1899 Hague Convention (II) has had an unusually lasting impact on LOAC. Known as the Martens Clause after the Convention's principal draftsman, noted Russian jurist Frederic de Martens, this formative section contained themes repeated in the subsequent Hague and Geneva Conventions. It reads in part:

> Animated by the desire to serve, even in this extreme hypothesis, the interests of humanity and the ever-increasing requirements of civilization;
>
> Thinking it important, with this object, to revise the laws and general customs of war, either with the view of defining them more precisely or of laying down certain limits for the purpose of modifying their severity as far as possible;
>
> Until a more complete code of the laws of war is issued, the High Contracting Parties think it right to declare that in cases not included in the Regulations adopted by them, populations and belligerents remain under the protection and empire of the principles of international law, as

26. *See* Convention (II) with Respect to the Laws and Customs of War on Land and Its Annex: Regulations Concerning the Laws and Customs of War on Land, art. 23(d), July 29, 1899, 32 Stat. 1803.

they result from the usages established between civilized nations, from the
laws of humanity, and the requirements of the public conscience. . . .[27]

Throughout the nineteenth century, therefore, ideas that gained acceptance in the late eighteenth century were given practical effect. Several
major international treaties codified customary rules of warfare and helped
to develop those rules. Many of these treaties remain in force today and
continue to govern conduct during wartime.

The next century began as the last one ended, with wars waged in several parts of the world. Notwithstanding states' efforts to uphold LOAC
or, at the very least, declarations of such intent, the need for continued
development of new treaty law was evident. A first step was the 1906 Geneva
Convention for the Amelioration of the Condition of the Wounded and
Sick in Armies in the Field, building on and replacing the 1864 Geneva
Convention. On the heels of the 1905 Russo-Japanese War, Italy's invasion
of Turkey, and mounting tensions in Europe, Czar Nicholas II called for a
Second Hague Conference in 1907. Like its predecessor, the 1907 Hague
Convention focuses on the laws and customs of land warfare; it retained the
Martens Clause in the preamble and differed only slightly from the 1899
Convention in substance. In addition, by 1914 the United States replaced
General Orders No. 100 with *The Law of Land Warfare*, the Army field man-
ual that, now updated, remains in force.[28]

World War I produced gas warfare, a genocide, and many states pro-
claiming to respect the law of war while at the same time condemning their
adversaries' "illegal" acts. The Ottoman Empire's "Young Turk" government
entered the war in November 1914 as an ally of Germany and began the
deportation and massacre of its Armenian population. But because the
Armenians were citizens of the Ottoman Empire — the entity that carried
out the genocide — the Hague Conventions were wholly inapplicable. A
joint Allied declaration in May 1915 nonetheless denounced the Turkish
actions as "crimes against humanity and civilization."[29]

At the conclusion of the war there was a strong movement among the
victorious Allies both to hold accountable those who violated LOAC and to
advance LOAC's ideals by addressing the devastating technological innovations revealed by the conflict but largely unaddressed by the Hague Conventions. Efforts at accountability produced mixed results. In February 1920,
the Allied Powers presented the new German government with a list of 854

---

27. *Id.* at pmbl. Essentially, the preamble establishes the precedent of a "catch-all"
protection of customary international law to provide protection where it is not yet codified.
Fifty-one nations have ratified the 1899 Hague Convention, including the United States.

28. The current version is DEPARTMENT OF THE ARMY & U.S. MARINE CORPS, FM 6-27/
MCTP 11-10C, COMMANDER'S HANDBOOK ON THE LAW OF LAND WARFARE (2019).

29. TELFORD TAYLOR, THE ANATOMY OF THE NUREMBERG TRIALS: A PERSONAL MEMOIR
12-13 (1992).

individuals for trial, including a number of leading military and political figures. The German government countered with a proposal to try accused persons before the German Supreme Court in Leipzig and the Allied Powers ultimately agreed, presenting the Germans with a list of forty-five individuals for initial prosecutions. Included on the list was Lieutenant Patzig, commander of a U-boat that sank a hospital ship and then destroyed two lifeboats with survivors. Two of Patzig's subordinates (he was unavailable for trial) were convicted of manslaughter but soon "escaped" from jail.[30] The Allies also had great interest in accountability for Turkish atrocities against the Armenians, Assyrians, Pontic, and Anatolian Greeks, as well as for the mistreatment of British prisoners in Turkish hands. With some cooperation from the Sultan, in April 1919, a Turkish military tribunal convicted two officials (one sentenced to death by hanging) for the murder of Armenians. The 1923 Treaty of Lausanne then granted amnesty to other alleged perpetrators, cutting short any post-war efforts to enforce LOAC accountability.

Much of the extraordinary cost of human lives during World War I was attributable to technological innovations that were not governed by the Hague Conventions, such as the submarine, airplane, and poison gas. The slaughter in Europe "sparked a public outcry for new methods of controlling the consequences of war," and, "[s]purred by the public clamor, diplomats and jurists again assembled to devise a means of regulating war."[31] This time period was marked particularly by efforts to ban war altogether (such as the Kellogg-Briand Pact) or to prohibit certain weapons. For example, the 1922 Treaty of Washington was drafted by the five victorious powers in World War I—France, Great Britain, the United States, Italy, and Japan—to be a new commitment against the use of gas. When France failed to ratify it, the treaty never entered into effect and was regarded as a failure. Three years later in Geneva, the provisions of the defunct 1922 Treaty of Washington that addressed asphyxiating gases and biological weapons were revived as the 1925 Geneva Gas Protocol, to which 145 states are parties.[32]

On July 1, 1929, forty-seven states sent representatives to Geneva to discuss two conventions. The Diplomatic Conference met "to redraft the 1906 Geneva Wounded and Sick Convention and, for the first time, to draft a separate Convention Relative to the Treatment of Prisoners of War which would, when ratified, complement Articles 4 to 20 of the 1907 Hague Regulations."[33] During World War I, all parties struggled with how to handle

---

30. *Id.* at 17.

31. Chris Jochnick & Roger Normand, *The Legitimation of Violence: A Critical History of the Laws of War,* 35 Harv. Int'l L.J. 49, 83 (1994).

32. On a number of occasions, States Parties have violated the 1925 Geneva Gas Protocol, including Italy in Ethiopia (1935-1936), Egypt in Yemen (1963-1967), and Iraq in Iran (1980-1988). It is generally considered to still be in force.

33. Howard Levie, Terrorism and War: The Law of War Crimes 37 (1992).

an overwhelming, indeed record, number of prisoners of war. As a result, the 1929 Geneva Convention for the Amelioration of the Condition of the Wounded and Sick in Armies in the Field and the 1929 Geneva Convention relative to the Treatment of Prisoners of War were born. The two treaties did not break any new ground with regard to doctrine, but were significantly more detailed and comprehensive than their predecessor agreements.

D.   THE GENEVA CONVENTIONS, THE ADDITIONAL PROTOCOLS, AND OTHER POST–WORLD WAR II DEVELOPMENTS

On the night of December 25 [1941], Japanese soldiers from the main invasion force of Hong Kong had forced their way into the emergency hospital set up at Stanley College, killed two doctors, and raped British nurses. . . . Dr. Black, the British director of the hospital (which was at the time flying a Red Cross flag), tried to explain to Japanese soldiers that the building was a hospital. He was shot at the entrance. The Japanese soldiers then threw grenades into the hospital, killing injured soldiers. Those patients still alive were bayoneted. The Japanese then forced British and Chinese nurses as well Chinese volunteers into one room and gang-raped them throughout the night.[34]

The Japanese invasion and occupation of Nanking, the capital of China at that time, produced some of the most horrific acts ever undertaken against a civilian population. Torture of civilians included live burials, mutilation, "death by fire," "death by ice," and "death by dogs," to name but a few favored methods.[35] "The Japanese saturated victims in acid, impaled babies with bayonets, hung people by their tongues."[36] The Japanese forces seemed especially fond of rape and "[e]stimates range from as low as twenty thousand to as high as eighty thousand" rapes, and "[t]he rape of women frequently accompanied the slaughter of entire families."[37]

German atrocities in occupied territories across Europe are well known: death squads, death camps, medical experimentation, starvation of civilian populations in ghettos, and more. With regard to international law, Hitler simply ignored provisions of the Geneva Conventions that interfered with his military plans. In particular, he issued the infamous "Commando Order,"[38] mandating that any Allied commandos found in Europe or Africa

34. YUKI TANAKA, HIDDEN HORRORS: JAPANESE WAR CRIMES IN WORLD WAR II 82-83 (1998).
35. *Id.* at 87-88.
36. *Id.*
37. *Id.* at 87-91, 99.
38. Hitler Commando Order, 18th October 1942 (498-PS, USA 501, Part 3, p. 213; Part 4, p. 2).

were to be executed on the spot, even if they were in uniform or attempted to surrender. The order was a clear violation of the Geneva Convention and was to be passed along only orally to commanders and not distributed beyond that.[39]

The United States and her allies were not above the law and committed violations of LOAC as well. For instance, "the U.S. Army in Europe during the period from June 1944 to the conclusion of hostilities in May 1945 court-martialed and executed 95 American soldiers" for law of war violations.[40] In retaliation for the fire-bombings of London and Coventry, and in keeping with accepted warfare strategies of the times, the Allies carpet-bombed Dresden and other German cities, causing untold civilian casualties and the total destruction of the cities. The use of atomic weapons at Hiroshima and Nagasaki effectively ended the war sooner, but also caused extraordinary human suffering and hundreds of thousands of casualties. However, certainly nothing the Allied Powers did could match the unspeakable horrors of the Nazi and Japanese militaries and their respective regimes.

The events of World War II made apparent the gaps in the international laws of war during the era and demonstrated the need for a comprehensive humanitarian standard during armed conflict. At the Diplomatic Conference held at Geneva from April 21 to August 12, 1949, the international community, represented by over fifty countries, amended the existing three conventions and drafted a new one, the Fourth Geneva Convention relative to the Protection of Civilian Persons in Time of War. The revisions to the previous conventions include prohibitions of conduct during armed conflict that read like a laundry list of the very actions committed mainly by the Axis Powers during World War II. The new protections afforded to killed, captured, or injured combatants sought to prevent the brutal abuses visited upon the combatants of World War II. The new Fourth Convention's introduction notes that the events of World War II "were to show the disastrous consequences of the failure to provide . . . an international Convention for the protection of civilians in wartime, particularly of those in occupied territories; this tragic period was one of deportations, mass extermination, taking and killing of hostages, and pillage."[41]

---

39. Robert E. Conot, Justice at Nuremberg 308 (1983).

40. W. Hays Parks, *Crimes in Hostilities*, Marine Corps Gazette, Aug. 1976, at 17. For an example of more recent law of war violations, *see* Gary Solis, Son Thang: An American War Crime 211 (1997). General courts-martial "convicted twenty-seven Marines of the murder or manslaughter of Vietnamese noncombatants. Ninety-five Army soldiers were convicted of the same offenses. Between January 1965 and September 1973 there were eighty-one substantiated cases, excluding My Lai, of war crimes involving U.S. Army personnel, and thirty-one soldiers were convicted." The United States Marine Corps did not keep "war crime" records.

41. International Committee of the Red Cross, The Geneva Conventions of August 12, 1949 18 (2009).

The most terrible act of the war years, the Holocaust, was foremost in the formation of post–World War II international law. The United Nations adopted the Convention on the Prevention and Punishment of the Crime of Genocide through U.N. General Assembly Resolution 260A (III) in December 1948. The memory of millions being murdered proved a catalyst to unanimously usher in what the President of the General Assembly, Mr. H. V. Evatt of Australia, declared "the supremacy of international law."[42] The term genocide did not exist before World War II and was coined in direct response to the mass exterminations of Jews during the Holocaust. In addition to setting forth the primary elements of the crime of genocide, the Genocide Convention establishes an obligation for all State parties to prevent and punish acts of genocide. However, it has remained unclear precisely what an obligation to "undertake to prevent"[43] genocide entails.

Memories of World War II drove the creation of additional pieces of international law as well. In 1954, the Convention for the Protection of Cultural Property in the Event of Armed Conflict was signed at The Hague, the first international treaty to address exclusively the protection of cultural property. Before World War II, there had not necessarily been a significant need for international law to protect cultural property. However, in World War II the Nazis actively targeted cultural property as a method of defeating enemies.[44] In its preamble, the Hague Convention thus states that "damage to cultural property belonging to any people whatsoever means damage to the cultural heritage of all mankind, since each people makes its contribution to the culture of the world."[45]

Heretofore, major historical catalysts spurred the development of the international law of armed conflict, and the same pattern held true with the adoption of the Additional Protocols of 1977: the Protocol Additional to the Geneva Conventions of August 12, 1949, and relating to the Protection of Victims of International Armed Conflicts (Additional Protocol I) and the Protocol Additional to the Geneva Conventions of August 12, 1949, and relating to the Protection of Victims of Non-International Armed Conflicts (Additional Protocol II). By June 1977, "the Vietnam War, the protection of human rights in occupied territories . . . and the armed conflicts during decolonization" had demonstrated that civilians remained in danger of

---

42. Matthew Lippman, *A Road Map to the 1948 Convention on the Prevention and Punishment of the Crime of Genocide*, 4 J. GENOCIDE RES. 177-195 (2002).

43. Convention on the Prevention and Punishment of the Crime of Genocide, art. 1, U.N. GAOR, G.A. Res 260A(III) (1948), 78 U.N.T.S. 277.

44. Naomi Mezey, *The Paradoxes of Cultural Property*, 107 COLUM. L. REV. 2004, 2009 (2007).

45. Convention for the Protection of Cultural Property in the Event of Armed Conflict, pmbl., May 14, 1954, S. TREATY DOC. NO. 106-1 (1999), 249 U.N.T.S. 215.

extreme levels of violence, leading some to suggest that LOAC did not reflect the realities of modern warfare.[46] According to Theodor Meron,

> the principal object of Protocol I was to bring up to date in a single treaty both the 1949 Geneva Conventions for the protection of war victims (Geneva law) and the 1907 Hague Convention (No. IV) on the Laws and Customs of War on Land (Hague law or the law governing means and methods of conducting war).[47]

The influence of the time is clear in Additional Protocol I's provisions and protections: protection of medical aircraft, medical personnel, and relief efforts for the civilian population, and reinforced norms for recovering the missing and the dead and disposing of the remains of the dead, for example. Building on 1949 Geneva Conventions' major step forward for humanitarian protections in non-international armed conflicts in Common Article 3, Additional Protocol II is the first treaty focused on the law applicable in non-international armed conflicts.

Nearly thirty years later, contemporary conflicts manifested the need for another protocol. By 2000, conflicts in Somalia, Chechnya, and Afghanistan indicated a waning respect for the red cross and red crescent emblems. The explanation was "that they have been identified with religious/ethnic groupings and thus lost their neutral and impartial character."[48] In addition, some national societies had some difficulty selecting one or the other of the two emblems. The Protocol Additional to the Geneva Conventions of August 12, 1949, and relating to the Adoption of an Additional Distinctive Emblem (Protocol III) thus created a new symbol, the red crystal, and new rules: states could now use one of the following symbols: the red crescent, the red cross, or the red crystal. Signatories intended for this new Protocol to "provide for new opportunities, such as temporary change of a protective emblem, 'where this may enhance protection.'"[49]

Concurrent with the major twentieth-century developments in the modern history of LOAC was the series of protocols and conventions addressing the use of various weapons. Eleven international conventions over thirty years covered various forms of weaponry, from landmines to lasers. Two final significant developments at the end of the twentieth century were the Convention Against Torture and Other Cruel, Inhuman, or

---

46. *See, e.g.*, Michael Bothe, Carl Bruch, Jordan Diamond & David Jensen, *International Law Protecting the Environment During Armed Conflict: Gaps and Opportunities*, 92 INT'L REV. RED CROSS 569, 571 (2010).

47. Theodor Meron, *The Time Has Come for the United States to Ratify Geneva Protocol I*, 88 AM. J. INT'L L. 679 (1994).

48. Dominic McGoldrick, *The Geneva Conventions and United Nations Personnel (Protocols) Act 2009: A Move Away from the Minimalist Approach*, 59 INT'L & COMP. L.Q. 173 (2010).

49. Baptiste Rolle & Edith Lafontaine, *The Emblem that Cried Wolf: ICRC Study on the Use of the Emblems*, 91 INT'L REV. RED CROSS 778 (2010).

Degrading Treatment or Punishment, which came into force in June 1987, and the Rome Statute of the International Criminal Court, opened for signature in 1998 and entered into force in 2002. Building on the work of the International Criminal Tribunals for the former Yugoslavia and Rwanda and a multi-decade advocacy effort, the International Criminal Court manifests the international community's belief that "the imposition of individual responsibility for massive human rights violations, even for seemingly untouchable leaders, was now a distinct possibility."[50] The Rome Statute also serves as a contemporary and forward-looking compilation of the elements of the major violations of LOAC and the foundation for criminal accountability going forward.

---

50. Payam Akhavan, *The International Criminal Court in Context: Mediating the Global and Local in the Age of Accountability*, 97 Am. J. Int'l L. 712-721 (2003) (book review).

PART II

WHAT AND WHEN

CHAPTER 4

WHAT IS ARMED CONFLICT?

States deploy military forces in a wide range of situations encompassing far more than what might traditionally be termed "war." Disaster relief, peacekeeping, peace enforcement, humanitarian relief, counterterrorism operations—these can all involve significant commitments of personnel, matériel, and technological military resources—and yet such operations will not necessarily engage legal obligations under LOAC. The law of armed conflict applies only during armed conflict, not during peacetime, so understanding what armed conflict is and what situations trigger the applicability of LOAC is an essential first step in any analysis.

A. GENEVA CONVENTIONS FRAMEWORK

Before the 1949 Geneva Conventions, existing treaty and customary law only applied to situations of declared war. For example, Article 2 of the Hague Convention of 1899 stated that the annexed Regulations on the Laws and Customs of War on Land applied "in case of war." The classic definition of war appears in Oppenheim's treatise on international law: "war is a contention between two or more States through their armed forces, for the purpose of overpowering each other and imposing such conditions of peace as the victor pleases."[1] Subsequent conventions, such as the 1907 Hague Convention and the 1929 Geneva Convention relative to the Treatment of Prisoners of War, did not address a threshold of applicability but rather relied on the plain meaning found in their titles. Although the definition of war seemed obvious, this paradigm left open multiple possibilities for states to argue that the laws of war—and their concomitant obligations—were not applicable because there was no declared war. For example, during World War II, the Japanese claimed that their operations in China and Manchuria were "police operations" and, therefore, did not trigger the law of war. As the International Military Tribunal for the Far East explained,

---

1. L. OPPENHEIM, II INTERNATIONAL LAW 202 (H. Lauterpacht ed., 7th ed. 1952).

> from the outbreak of the Mukden Incident till the end of the war[,] the successive Japanese Governments refused to acknowledge that the hostilities in China constituted a war. They persistently called it an "Incident." With this as an excuse[,] the military authorities persistently asserted that the rules of war did not apply in the conduct of the hostilities.[2]

The Tribunal rejected the Japanese argument, applied the law of war and convicted numerous Japanese defendants of war crimes and other atrocities.

The drafters of the 1949 Geneva Conventions sought to address a number of such problems:

> Since 1907 experience has shown that many armed conflicts, displaying all the characteristics of a war, may arise without being preceded by any of the formalities [of declaring war]. Furthermore, there have been many cases where Parties to a conflict have contested the legitimacy of the enemy Government and therefore refused to recognize the existence of a state of war. In the same way, the temporary disappearance of sovereign States as a result of annexation or capitulation has been put forward as a pretext for not observing one or other of the humanitarian Conventions.[3]

Another way in which states tried to evade obligations under the law of war was to claim that the opposing government or people were not deserving of adherence to the law, that they did not have a legitimate right to the reciprocity that for hundreds of years formed the foundation of LOAC's obligations. Hitler's approach to the Eastern Front against the Soviet Union offered a telling example, just years before the 1949 Geneva Conventions. In a speech to the army chiefs of staff in March 1941, Hitler pronounced:

> The war against Russia . . . will be such that it cannot be conducted in a knightly fashion. This struggle is one of ideologies and racial differences and will have to be conducted with unprecedented, unmerciful and unrelenting harshness. . . . The commissars are the bearers of ideologies directly opposed to National Socialism. Therefore the commissars will be liquidated. German soldiers guilty of breaking international law . . . will be excused.[4]

After World War II, it was obvious that all "justifications"—political or otherwise—for denying the application of LOAC had to be put to rest. The

---

2. International Military Tribunal for the Far East, Judgment of 4 November 1948, at 490. The Mukden Incident was a staged event by the Japanese military used as the pretext for the invasion of Manchuria.

3. INT'L COMM. RED CROSS, COMMENTARY ON THE GENEVA CONVENTION (III) RELATIVE TO THE TREATMENT OF PRISONERS OF WAR 19-20 (Jean de Preux ed., 1960).

4. WILLIAM SHIRER, THE RISE AND FALL OF THE THIRD REICH: A HISTORY OF NAZI GERMANY 830 (1990).

drafting of the Geneva Conventions in 1949 marked a sea change in the terminology used to describe armed violence between two states or other entities. Motivated by a common determination to identify more clearly when LOAC governed conduct during wartime, the drafters sought to ensure that legal terminology did not undermine the humanitarian goal of protecting war victims. The 1949 Geneva Conventions thus create a framework of law applicable based on the situation on the ground, not based on the claims or objectives of the parties to the conflict. Common Article 2 sets forth the parameters of international armed conflict.

COMMON ARTICLE 2

. . . the present Convention shall apply to all cases of declared war or of any other armed conflict which may arise between two or more of the High Contracting Parties, even if the state of war is not recognized by one of them.

   The Convention shall also apply to all cases of partial or total occupation of the territory of a High Contracting Party, even if the said occupation meets with no armed resistance. . . .

Any conflict between two states involving their armed forces, no matter how minor or short-lived, thus triggers the application of Common Article 2 and the full body of the law of armed conflict. Because today every state is a party to the Geneva Conventions, the treaties enjoy universal application.

Many conflicts, however, involve fighting between a state and non-state entities within the state, or among multiple non-state groups competing for power and authority in a state or particular region of a state. By the straightforward terms of Common Article 2, such conflicts are not international armed conflicts. States have historically sought to minimize the application of international law—including the law of armed conflict—to events and situations within their boundaries. The law of war did not apply in any comprehensive manner to conflicts inside the boundaries of the state—whether between the state and a rebel group or among rebel groups fighting for control. Over the course of the twentieth century, however, a growing recognition developed that the very protections LOAC guaranteed to those engaged in and caught up in international armed conflicts should not be denied to those enmeshed in internal conflicts. The 1949 Geneva Conventions took the groundbreaking step of codifying, for the first time, legal principles applicable in non-international armed conflicts.

COMMON ARTICLE 3

In the case of armed conflict not of an international character occurring in the territory of one of the High Contracting Parties, each Party to the conflict shall be bound to apply, as a minimum, the following provisions:

(1) Persons taking no active part in the hostilities, including members of armed forces who have laid down their arms and those placed *hors de combat* by sickness, wounds, detention, or any other cause, shall in all circumstances be treated humanely, without any adverse distinction founded on race, colour, religion or faith, sex, birth or wealth, or any other similar criteria.

To this end, the following acts are and shall remain prohibited at any time and in any place whatsoever with respect to the above-mentioned persons:

(a) violence to life and person, in particular murder of all kinds, mutilation, cruel treatment and torture;

(b) taking of hostages;

(c) outrages upon human dignity, in particular, humiliating and degrading treatment;

(d) the passing of sentences and the carrying out of executions without previous judgment pronounced by a regularly constituted court affording all the judicial guarantees which are recognized as indispensable by civilized peoples.

(2) The wounded and sick shall be collected and cared for.

An impartial humanitarian body, such as the International Committee of the Red Cross, may offer its services to the Parties to the conflict.

The Parties to the conflict should further endeavour to bring into force, by means of special agreements, all or part of the other provisions of the present Convention.

The application of the preceding provisions shall not affect the legal status of the Parties to the Conflict.

Often termed a "convention in miniature," Common Article 3 effectively establishes a minimum threshold of treatment and conduct for all situations of armed conflict. As the next section will explore in significant detail, Common Article 3 provides the threshold of applicability for conflicts not falling within the definition in Common Article 2, thus creating and defining the category of non-international armed conflict. However, Common Article 3's impact on LOAC goes far beyond definitional purposes and scope. As the Commentary to the Geneva Conventions explains, Common Article 3

> has the merit of being simple and clear. It at least ensures the application of the rules of humanity which are recognized as essential by civilized nations and provides a legal basis for interventions by the International Committee of the Red Cross or any other impartial humanitarian organization—interventions which in the past were all too often refused on the ground that they represented intolerable interference in the internal

affairs of a State. This text has the additional advantage of being applicable automatically, without any condition in regard to reciprocity. Its observance does not depend upon preliminary discussions on the nature of the conflict or the particular clauses to be respected. It is true that it merely provides for the application of the principles of the Convention, but it defines those principles and in addition lays down certain rules for their application. Finally, it has the advantage of expressing, in each of the four Conventions, the common principle which governs them.[5]

The 1949 Geneva Conventions therefore established a two-pronged approach to armed conflict and the application of LOAC to the parties and events so engaged. Under the Geneva Conventions framework, any armed conflict will be either an international armed conflict falling within Common Article 2 or a non-international armed conflict falling with Common Article 3. Internal disturbances and tensions—such as riots and looting—not rising to the level of armed conflict, in contrast, do not trigger the application of LOAC.

QUESTIONS FOR DISCUSSION

1. Was the switch from the term "war" to the term "armed conflict" a positive development? Do you see any downsides?

2. What would happen if both parties to a conflict denied that there was an armed conflict? What if they signed an agreement establishing the absence of an armed conflict and thus sought to prevent the application of LOAC?

3. How does the very existence of Common Article 3 fulfill the historic purposes of LOAC?

4. What is the importance of the last sentence of Common Article 3, both historically and for the application of the law?

As you consider these questions, think about the basic purposes and principles of LOAC discussed in Chapters 1 and 2.

B. DEFINING ARMED CONFLICT

When events in a particular locale suggest the existence of armed conflict, the first questions must be: Is there an armed conflict and if so, what kind of armed conflict? Although the parties to a conflict, as alluded to above, will often seek to characterize it in the way most advantageous

---

5. INT'L COMM. RED CROSS, COMMENTARY ON THE GENEVA CONVENTION (III) RELATIVE TO THE TREATMENT OF PRISONERS OF WAR 35 (Jean de Preux ed., 1960).

to their political, strategic and legal position—usually by denying the existence of an armed conflict at all—the Geneva Conventions clearly choose not to leave these determinations to the parties. Rather, as the International Criminal Tribunal for Rwanda (ICTR) emphatically stated in *Prosecutor v. Jean-Paul Akayesu*, the first prosecution for genocide:

> It should be stressed that the ascertainment of the intensity of a non-international conflict does not depend on the subjective judgment of the parties to the conflict. It should be recalled that the four Geneva Conventions, as well as the two Protocols, were adopted primarily to protect the victims, as well as potential victims, of armed conflicts. If the application of international humanitarian law depended solely on the discretionary judgment of the parties to the conflict, in most cases there would be a tendency for the conflict to be minimized by the parties thereto. Thus, on the basis of objective criteria, [LOAC] will apply once it has been established there exists an . . . armed conflict which fulfills [the] predetermined criteria.[6]

As noted above, the Geneva Conventions establish two categories of armed conflict but do not codify explicit definitions of either international or non-international armed conflict. States, courts, and organizations such as the ICRC frequently characterized situations as armed conflict and specified whether they constituted international or non-international armed conflict in the years after 1949. However, it was not until the establishment of the *ad hoc* international criminal tribunals to try those accused of atrocities in the former Yugoslavia and Rwanda that a formal definition of armed conflict was set forth. The International Criminal Tribunal for the former Yugoslavia (ICTY) was an *ad hoc* international tribunal established by the U.N. Security Council under Chapter VII of the U.N. Charter in 1993 to try perpetrators of war crimes, crimes against humanity, and genocide during the conflict in the former Yugoslavia. The ICTY's first case, *Prosecutor v. Tadić*, produced the first, and by any measure, seminal, international judicial opinion analyzing the existence of an internal armed conflict.

Determining the existence of an armed conflict was an essential jurisdictional prerequisite for the imposition of criminal responsibility, because charges brought under Article 2 (grave breaches of the Geneva Conventions) and Article 3 (violations of the laws and customs of war) of the Statute of the ICTY applied only to situations of armed conflict. In a decision on interlocutory appeal in the *Tadić* case, the Appeals Chamber of the ICTY set forth the modern definition of armed conflict: "[A]n armed conflict exists whenever there is a resort to armed force between States or

---

6. Prosecutor v. Akayesu, Case No. ICTR-96-4-T, Judgement, ¶ 603 (Int'l Crim. Trib. for Rwanda Sept. 2, 1998).

protracted armed violence between governmental authorities and orga-nized armed groups or between such groups within a State."[7] With regard to the application of Common Article 3, the Appeals Chamber emphasized that the notion of armed conflict has a broad geographical and temporal scope. This broad scope is directly related to the protective purposes of the Geneva Conventions; the ICTY specified in *Tadić* that "the rules contained in Article 3 also apply outside the narrow geographical context of the actual theatre of combat operations" and that "the temporal scope of the applica-ble rules clearly reaches beyond the actual hostilities."[8] This definition of armed conflict has not only been the driving factor in the ICTY's jurispru-dence, but was also adopted by the drafters of the Rome Statute establishing the International Criminal Court (ICC) and by the ICTR. It continues to be the most common and oft-cited contemporary definition of armed conflict.

DEFINITION OF ARMED CONFLICT

An armed conflict exists whenever there is a resort to armed force between States or protracted armed violence between governmen-tal authorities and organized armed groups or between such groups within a State.

---

1. *International Armed Conflict*

Common Article 2 applies to any conflict between two states involving their armed forces, no matter how minor or short-lived, even if one or both states deny the existence of the conflict. As the Commentary to the Geneva Conventions explains:

> By its general character, [the first] paragraph deprives belligerents, in advance, of the pretexts they might in theory put forward for evading their obligations. There is no need for a formal declaration of war, or for the recognition of the existence of a state of war, as preliminaries to the application of the Convention. The occurrence of *de facto* hostilities is sufficient.
>
> It remains to ascertain what is meant by "armed conflict." The substi-tution of this much more general expression for the word "war" was delib-erate. It is possible to argue almost endlessly about the legal definition of "war." A State which uses arms to commit a hostile act against another

---

7. Prosecutor v. Tadić, Case No. IT-94-1-I, Decision of Defence Motion for Interlocutory Appeal on Jurisdiction, ¶ 70 (Int'l Crim. Trib. for the Former Yugoslavia Oct. 2, 1995).

8. *Id.* at ¶ 69.

State can always maintain that it is not making war, but merely engaging in a police action, or acting in legitimate self-defence. The expression "armed conflict" makes such arguments less easy. Any difference arising between two States and leading to the intervention of members of the armed forces is an armed conflict within the meaning of Article 2, even if one of the Parties denies the existence of a state of war. It makes no difference how long the conflict lasts, how much slaughter takes place or how numerous are the participating forces; it suffices for the armed forces of one Power to have captured adversaries falling within the scope of Article 4. Even if there has been no fighting, the fact that persons covered by the Convention are detained is sufficient for its application. The number of persons captured in such circumstances is, of course, immaterial.[9]

Notwithstanding the Geneva Conventions' firm requirement that the existence of an armed conflict is based solely on objective determinations based on the facts on the ground, the application of the law of international armed conflict is not always straightforward. In some situations, a seemingly minor confrontation or situation will meet the threshold for international armed conflict, even though neither country will be beating the drums of war. Thus, for example, the Iranian detention of fifteen British sailors in the Persian Gulf in March 2007[10] triggered the law of international armed conflict and the Third Geneva Convention governed the treatment of the detained sailors. The fact that neither the United Kingdom nor Iran recognized a state of war or the existence of an armed conflict had no bearing on the application of LOAC. The Commentary clarifies that even if both states deny the existence of an armed conflict, the Geneva Conventions still apply based objectively on the *de facto* situation: "[e]ven in that event it would not appear that they could, by tacit agreement, prevent the Conventions from applying. It must not be forgotten that the Conventions have been drawn up first and foremost to protect individuals, and not to serve State interests."[11]

In other situations, a State may simply deny the existence of an armed conflict for any number of reasons, such as domestic political consumption, efforts to seek legitimacy, or other goals. In the case of Operation Just Cause in 1989 in Panama, for example, the United States initially argued that there was no armed conflict triggering the Geneva Conventions because there was no dispute between the two states. With 30,000 U.S. troops in Panama and

9. INT'L COMM. RED CROSS, COMMENTARY ON THE GENEVA CONVENTION (III) RELATIVE TO THE TREATMENT OF PRISONERS OF WAR 22-23 (Jean de Preux ed., 1960).

10. Sarah Lyall, *Iran Detains British Sailors in Waters Off Iraq*, N.Y. TIMES (Mar. 23, 2007).

11. INT'L COMM. RED CROSS, COMMENTARY ON THE GENEVA CONVENTION (III) RELATIVE TO THE TREATMENT OF PRISONERS OF WAR 23 (Jean de Preux ed., 1960).

armed hostilities between the two sides, however, the U.S. argument was difficult to reconcile. Indeed, when General Manuel Noriega raised the issue of prisoner of war status at his sentencing hearing for multiple counts of drug-trafficking in the Southern District of Florida federal court, the court held that "[h]owever the government wishes to label it, what occurred in late 1989-early 1990 was clearly an 'armed conflict' within the meaning of Article 2. Armed troops intervened in a conflict between two parties to the treaty."[12]

Russia's invasion of Crimea offers a useful reminder of the key purpose behind the low threshold for triggering international armed conflict. On February 27-28, 2014, armed men in unmarked uniforms (understood to be and later identified as Russian troops) seized Crimea's parliament building and two airports, and subsequently spread out to secure control over Crimea, a province of Ukraine. Ukraine's government described the Russian intrusion as an invasion, put troops on high alert and appealed to NATO for assistance. Within a few weeks, Russia formally (although illegally) annexed Crimea after a referendum widely viewed as rigged by pro-Russian forces. Russia continues to assert control over Crimea and has incorporated it into Russia. Unlike the situation that developed a few months later in eastern Ukraine, the situation in Crimea involved very little, if any, kinetic violence. Beyond reports of one or two shots being fired, Russian and Ukrainian military forces did not engage directly in hostilities. Nonetheless, LOAC applied to the situation in Crimea from the moment Russian forces entered Ukrainian territory without Ukraine's consent. Consider why—indeed, it may seem counterintuitive in the absence of fighting and in light of reports that Ukrainian soldiers were unarmed in most confrontations.

The immediate application of LOAC upon any dispute between states leading to the engagement of their armed forces is fundamental to LOAC's core purposes and effectiveness. Think back to the arguments by German and Japanese authorities regarding the application of LOAC during WWII, described earlier in this chapter. The threshold for international armed conflict is designed to maximize LOAC's protective purposes. Once Russian forces entered Ukrainian territory, the need for LOAC's protective framework became evident. From what body of law could soldiers detained—by either side—seek protection for treatment, repatriation or other rights? This low threshold helps to ensure that there are no gaps in legal protection, guarding against situations in which "no law governs the conduct of military operations below that level of intensity, including the opening phase of hostilities."[13]

---

12. U.S. v. Noriega, 808 F. Supp. 791, 795 (S.D. Fla. 1992).

13. Dapo Akande, *Classification of Armed Conflicts: Relevant Legal Concepts, in* INTERNATIONAL LAW AND THE CLASSIFICATION OF CONFLICTS 32, 41 (Elizabeth Wilmshurst ed., 2012).

QUESTIONS FOR DISCUSSION

1. As the situation in Crimea demonstrated, waiting until sustained fighting breaks out between the armed forces of two states may well exclude situations in which LOAC's protective purposes are needed. Indeed, LOAC may be the only mechanism for individuals in one state to seek redress or protection from the other state. Think about possible scenarios in which a higher threshold for the application of LOAC in the case of conflict between two states would risk a gap in protection—is anyone left unprotected? Who and in what situations?

2. On November 24, 2015, the Turkish military shot down a Russian Su-24 fighter jet in the Turkish-Syria border area.[14] Russia condemned the attack on its warplane and suspended military contracts, but did not take any further action. Did this incident trigger the application of the law of international armed conflict? What about the U.S. missile strikes against the Shayrat air base in Syria—the airfield from which the chemical attacks on civilians in Syria were launched—on April 6, 2017?[15] Did those strikes constitute an international armed conflict between the United States and Syria?

3. On March 1, 2007, 170 Swiss troops crossed the border from Switzerland into Liechtenstein in the middle of the night. According to reports, the "incident occurred in bad weather and in the middle of the night, when Switzerland is hard to tell apart from its neighbors."[16] Did this incursion into Liechtenstein start an international armed conflict? In May 2020, Polish soldiers mistakenly crossed the border with the Czech Republic and set up a border fence as part of operations guarding the closed border during the pandemic, refusing to allow Czech citizens to access an area within their own country.[17] The mistake was immediately corrected—but did it create an international armed conflict? What about March 2014, when Lebanese media reported that a stray bullet from an Israel Defense Forces training exercise in the north of Israel near the Lebanese border struck the windshield of a car driving in Ramia, on the other side of the border in Lebanon?[18]

2. Non-International Armed Conflict

Common Article 3 is the primary measure of the existence of a non-international armed conflict. Given the universal ratification of the 1949

---

14. Dion Nissenbaum et al., *Turkey Shoots Down Russian Military Jet*, WALL STREET J. (Nov. 24, 2015).

15. Jennifer Griffin, Lucas Tomlinson, *U.S. Missiles Target Syria Airfield in Response to Chemical Weapons Attack*, FoxNews.com (Apr. 7, 2017).

16. Peter Stamm, *Switzerland Invades Liechtenstein*, N.Y. TIMES (Mar. 12, 2007).

17. Rob Picheta, *Poland Invaded the Czech Republic Last Month, But Says It Was Just a Big Misunderstanding*, CNN.COM (June 12, 2020).

18. Yaakov Lapin, *Lebanese Media Reports Stray IDF Bullet Strikes Car in Lebanon, None Hurt*, JERUSALEM POST (Mar. 2, 2014).

Geneva Conventions among all countries around the world, Common Article 3 applies in all situations that could constitute non-international armed conflict under the conditions as explicated in the cases discussed below. For states that are party to Additional Protocol II relating to non-international armed conflicts, however, that text sets forth a slightly different, and more exacting, standard for the application of the law contained therein.

a.   Common Article 3

According to the Commentary to the Geneva Conventions, no specific test for determining the applicability of Common Article 3 exists; rather the goal is to interpret Common Article 3 as broadly as possibly. The Commentary does, however, offer some guidance in the form of indicative — but not dispositive — factors or characteristics of a Common Article 3 conflict, based on the nature and behavior of both state and non-state parties:

> What is meant by "armed conflict not of an international character"? That was the burning question which arose again and again at the Diplomatic Conference. The expression was so general, so vague, that many of the delegations feared that it might be taken to cover any act committed by force of arms — any form of anarchy, rebellion, or even plain banditry. For example, if a handful of individuals were to rise in rebellion against the State and attack a police station, would that suffice to bring into being an armed conflict within the meaning of the Article? In order to reply to questions of this sort, it was suggested that the term "conflict" should be defined or — and this would come to the same thing — that a list should be given of a certain number of conditions on which the application of the Convention would depend. The idea was finally abandoned — wisely, we think. Nevertheless, these different conditions, although in no way obligatory, constitute convenient criteria, and we therefore think it well to give a list drawn from the various amendments discussed. . . . [The Commentary then lists several criteria, including that the rebelling party has an organized military force with a responsible command, the government is obliged to resort to military force, and that the dispute has been submitted to the U.N. Security Council as a threat to or breach of the peace, among other criteria.]
>
> The above criteria are useful as a means of distinguishing a genuine armed conflict from a mere act of banditry or an unorganized and short-lived insurrection.
>
> Does this mean that Article 3 is not applicable in cases where armed strife breaks out in a country, but does not fulfill any of the above conditions (which are not obligatory and are only mentioned as an indication)? We do not subscribe to this view. We think on the contrary, that the scope of application of the article must be as wide as possible.[19]

---

19. INT'L COMM. RED CROSS, COMMENTARY ON THE GENEVA CONVENTION (IV) RELATIVE TO THE PROTECTION OF CIVILIAN PERSONS IN TIME OF WAR 35-36 (Oscar M. Uhler & Henri Coursier eds., 1958).

Whereas Common Article 2 applies to any situation in which the armed forces of two states engage with each other—no matter how short-lived or minimal the use of force or extent of hostilities—Common Article 3 essentially sets a minimum threshold for the existence of armed conflict. It thus distinguishes situations of armed conflict from riots, internal disturbances and tensions, and so-called "acts of banditry." For example, the looting and violence in Los Angeles in response to the 1992 Rodney King verdict were riots: uncoordinated violence triggering a massive police response, with assistance from the U.S. Marines, but not the law of armed conflict. Determining the existence of a non-international armed conflict first requires an assessment of whether the facts on the ground demonstrate that the hostilities in question have risen above this preliminary threshold.

At the same time that the ICTY was elaborating on the definition of armed conflict in *Tadić* and other early ICTY cases, the Inter-American Commission on Human Rights faced much the same question: when is internal violence an armed conflict that triggers the obligations and protections of Common Article 3? Assessing the legal characterization of a 30-hour firefight resulting from an attack on an Argentine military barracks by a group of armed individuals, the Commission focused on the difference between "internal disturbances" and armed conflict:

> In contrast to . . . situations of domestic violence, the concept of armed conflict, in principle, requires the existence of organized armed groups that are capable of and actually do engage in combat and other military actions against each other. In this regard, Common Article 3 simply refers to, but does not actually define "an armed conflict of a non-international character." However, Common Article 3 is generally understood to apply to low intensity and open armed confrontations between relatively organized armed forces or groups that take place within the territory of a particular State. Thus, Common Article 3 does not apply to riots, mere acts of banditry or an unorganized and short-lived rebellion. Article 3 armed conflicts typically involve armed strife between governmental armed forces and organized armed insurgents. It also governs situations where two or more armed factions confront one another without the intervention of governmental forces where, for example, the established government has dissolved or is too weak to intervene. It is important to understand that application of Common Article 3 does not require the existence of large-scale and generalized hostilities or a situation comparable to a civil war in which dissident armed groups exercise control over parts of national territory.
>
> The most difficult problem regarding the application of Common Article 3 is not at the upper end of the spectrum of domestic violence, but rather at the lower end. The line separating an especially violent situation of internal disturbances from the "lowest" level Article 3 armed conflict may sometimes be blurred and, thus, not easily determined. When faced

with making such a determination, what is required in the final analysis is a good faith and objective analysis of the facts in each particular case.[20]

This analysis relied on the interpretive tools provided in the Commentary to Common Article 3, as described above. However, as the jurisprudence of the ICTY demonstrated, further elaboration of the definition of non-international armed conflict proved essential for the effective characterization of conflicts and application of LOAC. As a first step, the ICTY Trial Chamber in *Tadić* elaborated on the broad guidelines in the definition of armed conflict set forth by the Appeals Chamber in the interlocutory appeal:

> The test applied by the Appeals Chamber to the existence of an armed conflict for the purposes of the rules contained in Common Article 3 focuses on two aspects of a conflict; the intensity of the conflict and the organization of the parties to the conflict. In an armed conflict of an internal or mixed character, these closely related criteria are used solely for the purpose, as a minimum, of distinguishing an armed conflict from banditry, unorganized and short-lived insurrections, or terrorist activities, which are not subject to international humanitarian law.[21]

Subsequent cases at the ICTY, as well as other cases at the ICTR, the ICC, and the Special Court for Sierra Leone, relied on the *Tadić* definition of armed conflict as protracted violence between the government and organized armed groups or between two or more armed groups as the paradigm for identifying the existence of an armed conflict. Over time, the factors highlighted in the initial *Tadić* merits decision — intensity and organization — have become the international community's foundational framework for analyzing the existence of non-international armed conflict.

When the ICTY began to hear cases stemming from the violence in Kosovo, it had to address conflict characterization anew. Unlike the fighting in Croatia and Bosnia, the nature of the violence in Kosovo raised questions as to whether the situation met the threshold for an armed conflict. In *Prosecutor v. Limaj*, the ICTY analyzed the situation in Kosovo and developed a comprehensive and detailed framework for applying the definition. First, to analyze intensity, the Tribunal examined multiple factors, including: the number, duration, and intensity of individual confrontations; the types of weapons and other military equipment used; the number of persons and types of forces engaged in the fighting; the geographic and temporal distribution of clashes; the territory that has been captured and held; the number of casualties; the extent of material destruction; the number of civilians fleeing combat zones; and the involvement of the United Nations Security Council.

---

20. Abella v. Argentina, Judgment, Inter-Am. Ct. H.R., No. 55/97, ¶¶ 152-3 (Nov. 18, 1997).

21. Prosecutor v. Tadić, Case No. IT-94-1-T, Judgment, ¶ 562 (Int'l Crim. Trib. for the Former Yugoslavia May 7, 1997).

To assess organization, the Tribunal then explored the nature and operations of the Kosovo Liberation Army, looking at: the existence of a hierarchical structure; territorial control and administration; the ability to recruit and train combatants; the provision of uniforms and salaries; the ability to launch operations using military tactics; the ability to enter peace or cease-fire agreements and to negotiate with other parties; the ability to issue internal regulations and operational orders; and the ability to coordinate multiple units.

The *Tadić* framework thus offers a useful analytical starting point for identifying the existence of a non-international armed conflict and the application of Common Article 3.

REFUGEES OR POWS?

After returning from a court-martial one Thursday afternoon in 1994, I had a note on my desk to report to a staging area for immediate deployment. Upon reporting to duty, I was told that the United States military had been tasked to respond to a mass exodus of Haitian and Cuban migrants. Although our final mission would end up changing no less than seven times, our underlying duty was to respond expeditiously and provide humanitarian relief.

The military operation involved rescuing Haitian and Cuban migrants on the high seas and reviewing their standing to determine whether they should receive refugee status in the United States. The majority of the legal review took place at Guantanamo Naval Base in Cuba (GTMO). At the time, GTMO was a very small naval base and the influx of tens of thousands of migrants was a logistical challenge. Part of the evolution of the operation involved the inclusion of Non-Governmental Organizations (NGO) as observers. One senior member of a well-known NGO made a very public announcement that the United States military was violating the Geneva Conventions by not providing adequate living space for detainees.

Was he right? Did the Geneva Conventions apply to this situation? If not, what law governed how the U.S. treated the migrants?

— *Lieutenant Colonel Kurt Larson,*
USMC (Ret.) judge advocate

---

b.   Additional Protocol II

Additional Protocol II seeks to build on Common Article 3 and ensure better protection for victims of non-international armed conflicts by setting forth more comprehensive standards and norms of LOAC applicable in non-international armed conflicts. Like Common Article 3, it does not apply to internal disturbances and tensions, riots, and other isolated acts of violence, which do not rise to the level of armed conflict. However, Additional Protocol II sets a stricter standard than that found in Common Article 3, which, as discussed above, is commonly understood to be interpreted as broadly as possible. Article 1 of Additional Protocol II states that the Protocol applies to all armed conflicts that

> take place in the territory of a High Contracting Party between its armed forces and dissident armed forces or other organized armed groups which, under responsible command, exercise such control over a part of its territory as to enable them to carry out sustained and concerted military operations and to implement this Protocol.

Although Additional Protocol II was not at issue in the conflict in the former Yugoslavia, it did arise in the context of conflict characterization for the conflict in Rwanda. In the first case before the International Criminal Tribunal for Rwanda, *Prosecutor v. Jean-Paul Akayesu*, the ICTR held that the conflict in Rwanda satisfied the requirements of Additional Protocol II. The Tribunal explained:

> It has been shown that there was a conflict between, on the one hand, the RPF [Rwandan Patriotic Front], under the command of General Kagame, and, on the other, the governmental forces, the FAR [Forces Armées Rwandaises]. The RPF increased its control over the Rwandan territory from that agreed in the Arusha Accords to over half of the country by mid-May 1994, and carried out continuous and sustained military operations until the cease fire on 18 July 1994 which brought the war to an end. The RPF troops were disciplined and possessed a structured leadership which was answerable to authority. The RPF had also stated to the International Committee of the Red Cross that it was bound by the rules of International Humanitarian law. The Chamber finds the said conflict to have been an internal armed conflict within the meaning of Additional Protocol II.[22]

QUESTIONS FOR DISCUSSION

1. The drafters of the Geneva Conventions saw no drawbacks to a broad scope for Common Article 3, because it would not limit the state's right to respond or increase the rebel group's authority to fight. In noting that the rights and obligations set forth in Common Article 3 were already recognized as fundamental and essential components of the law in all civilized nations, the Commentary explains: "What Government would dare to

---

22. Prosecutor v. Akayesu, Case No. ICTR-96-4-T, Judgement, ¶ 627 (Int'l Crim. Trib. for Rwanda Sept. 2, 1998).

claim before the world, in a case of civil disturbances which could justly be described as mere acts of banditry, that, Article 3 not being applicable, it was entitled to leave the wounded uncared for, to torture and mutilate prisoners and take hostages?"[23] In essence, the view at the time was that a government was not adding to its legal obligations in any way by recognizing the application of Common Article 3. And yet states remain—historically and at present—reluctant to countenance international intrusions into what they view as domestic matters and often deny the application of Common Article 3 altogether. Consider what might explain this continued resistance.

2. In 1995, the Constitutional Court of the Russian Federation examined the constitutionality of certain presidential decrees regarding the use of armed force in Chechnya. One of those decrees stated that "disarmament of the unlawful armed militia raised in that republic, which were using tanks, missile launchers, artillery systems and war planes, 'was impossible in principle without the use of regular troops.'" In the course of the decision, the court declared that Additional Protocol II was applicable to the conflict.[24]

3. Since 2006, the government of Mexico has deployed 45,000 soldiers and federal police to northern Mexico to combat the drug cartels that operate there. Despite this unprecedented application of federal power, over 300,000 Mexicans have been killed since 2006, and cartels have controlled territory, levied taxes and imposed order.[25] While many of the deaths have been related to kidnappings, extortion, or other examples of criminal activity, the cartels have also attacked the Mexican state directly—for example, on May 6, 2011, the Zetas attacked a Mexican military convoy with automatic weapons and grenade launchers, killing one civilian and wounding five others caught in the crossfire.[26]

> a. Was the Mexican state engaged in a non-international armed conflict with the Zeta cartel or any other cartels? A Common Article 3 conflict? Could it be an Additional Protocol II conflict, if Mexico were a party to Additional Protocol II? What would the ICTY say? What would the Inter-American Commission say? What other information would you need to reach a determination?

23. Int'l Comm. Red Cross, Commentary on the Geneva Convention (IV) Relative to the Protection of Civilian Persons in Time of War 36 (Oscar M. Uhler & Henri Coursier eds., 1958).

24. Decision of the Constitutional Court of the Russian Federation on the Constitutionality of Presidential Decrees, July 31, 1995, *Rossijskaia Gazeta* of August 11, 1995, pp. 3-7, *reprinted in* 17 Hum Rts. J. 133 (1996).

25. Council on Foreign Relations, *Mexico's Long War: Drugs, Crime, and the Cartels*, Feb. 26, 2021.

26. Martha Mendoza, *Drug Violence Makes U.S. Firms Wary About Expanding in Mexico*, Associated Press (May 16, 2011).

    b. Does it matter that the Zeta cartel also fought with other cartels over illicit drug and human trafficking routes into the United States?

    c. Some argue that the violence in Mexico cannot be a non-international armed conflict because the drug cartels do not have political motivations to overthrow the government.[27] Does LOAC require a political motive for conflict identification?[28]

4. In December 2009, Iranian government forces responded forcefully to large demonstrations outside the grounds of Tehran University and elsewhere in the capital, demonstrations that grew out of the opposition to the disputed June 2009 election of Mahmoud Ahmadinejad. Thousands of members of the Basij, a pro-government paramilitary group that falls under the command of Iran's elite Republican Guard, assaulted a group of several hundred students with steel clubs, electric batons, pepper spray, and tear gas. For a few days, running battles between student demonstrators and the Basij paramilitary forces took place, with injuries on both sides. Regular police units were also out in full force and hundreds of student demonstrators were arrested. The government's chief prosecutor stated that the government would "show no mercy" to the protestors or their families and that "[i]ntelligence and security . . . forces have been ordered not to give any leeway to those who break the law, act against national security and disturb public order."[29]

    a. Was this an armed conflict under Common Article 3? Under Additional Protocol II? How does this situation compare to or differ from the events in the *Abella v. Argentina* case?

    b. If this is not an armed conflict, what law applies?

5. Which of the following situations would trigger the law of armed conflict:

    a. The 1995 bombing of the Alfred P. Murrah Federal Building in Oklahoma City?

    b. U.S. airstrikes on a chemical plant in Sudan in response to the 1998 U.S. Embassy bombings in Kenya and Tanzania?

---

27. Pierre Hauck and Sven Peterke, *Organized Crime and Gang Violence in National and International Law*, 92 INT'L REV. RED CROSS 407, 433 (2010). *See also* EMILY CRAWFORD, IDENTIFYING THE ENEMY: CIVILIAN PARTICIPATION IN ARMED CONFLICT 185-186 (2015).

28. *See* INT'L COMM. RED CROSS, COMMENTARY TO GENEVA CONVENTION I FOR THE AMELIORATION OF THE CONDITION OF THE WOUNDED AND SICK IN THE ARMED FORCES IN THE FIELD ¶¶ 447-451 (2d ed. 2016) ("[i]t should also be considered that introducing political motivation as a prerequisite for non-international armed conflict could open the door to a variety of other motivation-based reasons for denying the existence of such armed conflicts. Furthermore, in practice it can be difficult to identify the motivations of a non-State armed group. What counts as a political objective, for example, might be controversial; non-political and political motives may co-exist; and non-political activities may in fact be instrumental in achieving ultimately political ends.").

29. Thomas Erdbrink, *Iran Steps Up Crackdown, Assaults Protesters at University of Tehran*, WASHINGTONPOST.COM (Dec. 9, 2009).

  c. U.S. unmanned airstrikes against Taliban militants in Pakistan?

  d. An exchange of mortar fire along the Georgia-South Ossetia border?

  e. The 2013 Boston Marathon bombing?

  f. The riots and unrest in Ferguson, Missouri in 2014, in Baltimore, Maryland in 2015, or across the United States after the death of George Floyd in 2020?

6. How should the end of a non-international armed conflict be determined? In December 2014, President Barack Obama stated that "our combat mission in Afghanistan is ending, and the longest war in American history is coming to a responsible conclusion."[30] Mukhtar Yahia Naji al Warafi, a detainee held by the United States at the Guantanamo Bay detention facility, subsequently challenged his detention on the grounds that, because the conflict between the United States and the Taliban was over—as President Obama had stated—the United States no longer had authority to detain him.[31] Was he correct? Is a statement by the President of the United States sufficient to end a conflict for the purposes of the application of LOAC?[32] What other approaches make sense? Some argue that a "reverse-*Tadić*" analysis is the correct approach, essentially looking for evidence to demonstrate that either or both the intensity of the conflict and the organization of the parties have fallen below the threshold for triggering such a conflict. How should such an analysis be undertaken?

UPRISING IN SYRIA: EARLY CHALLENGES OF ARMED CONFLICT RECOGNITION

In the wake of popular uprisings in Egypt, Libya, and Tunisia, Syrian activists called for a national day of rage on March 18, 2011. Syrian troops opened fire on demonstrations in Dera'a, killing five, accelerating the pace of the discontent in Syria that had simmered since

---

30. Statement by the President on the End of the Combat Mission in Afghanistan, The White House, Office of the Press Secretary, December 28, 2014, https://obamawhitehouse.archives.gov/the-press-office/2014/12/28/statement-president-end-combat-mission-afghanistan.

31. Al Warafi v. Obama, No. 09-2368 (RCL), 2015 WL 4600420 (D.D.C. July 30, 2015), at *1.

32. The court rejected the detainee's argument—and the government's argument that other presidential statements demonstrated that the conflict continued—stating that "the President's position, while relevant, is hardly the only evidence that matters to this issue." *Id.* at *5. Rather, the court considered the facts on the ground; that is, evidence demonstrating that "U.S. involvement in the fighting in Afghanistan, against al Qaeda and Taliban forces alike, has not stopped," to conclude that the conflict had not ended. *Id.* at *7.

December 2010. Between March and June 2011, demonstrations spread throughout Syria. The Assad regime used force—including Syrian infantry and mechanized units—to quell the demonstrations. Throughout this period, Syrian refugees, including Syrian army deserters, fled to Turkey.

On July 29, 2011, a group of deserted Syrian officers released a video announcing the formation of the Free Syrian Army (FSA). At the same time, disparate groups of Syrians began resisting the regime with armed violence on a local level. After the formation of the FSA, some of the local groups professed allegiance to the FSA while others did not. These civilians armed themselves with automatic weapons and rocket-propelled grenades, as well as improvised explosive devices.

On August 14, 2011, Syria laid siege to Latakia and Syrian navy gunboats opened fire on its waterfront with automatic weapons. By September, defectors and armed civilians based in Rastan had become a sufficient threat that the Assad regime dispatched 250 armored vehicles to engage in a four-day siege to recapture that city from September 27 to October 1. Throughout the spring and summer of 2012, Syrian rebels increasingly demonstrated an ability to inflict damage on the Syrian regime and stand and fight. By May 2012, the Syrian rebels could boast numbers of at least 40,000. The increased effectiveness of Syrian rebels may have been attributable to weapons, training, and logistical support from Turkey, Qatar, and Saudi Arabia. As local cadres of Syrian rebels became more effective and cohesive fighting units, their cooperation with other groups and relative integration with the Free Syrian Army's command structure increased.

Following a massacre at Houla, and a failed attempt by the international community to broker a ceasefire, the FSA launched a nationwide offensive in June. On June 2, the FSA killed fifty-seven Syrian soldiers in ambushes around the country. On June 7, the FSA killed twenty-four Syrian soldiers. Throughout June and July, similar numbers of Syrian soldiers were killed each day. At the same time, each day, tens of Syrian civilians were killed either as a result of hostilities or the use of state violence against unarmed civilians.

The International Legal Analysis

1. In November 2011, the newly constituted United Nations Independent International Commission of Inquiry on the Syrian Arab Republic found that over 3,500 civilians had been killed and the military was carrying out operations in several cities, including direct targeting of residential areas. With regard to the applicable law, the Commission concluded that it could not verify either

the intensity of the fighting or the organization of the rebel forces and therefore the situation did not rise to the level of an armed conflict.

2. In February 2012, the Commission's second report noted that the situation had become increasingly violent and militarized, the government had intensified its violent repression, and the rebels had launched operations against government forces, checkpoints, and police stations, among other targets. With regard to the applicable law, the Commission concluded that although it "is gravely concerned that the violence in certain areas may have reached the requisite level of intensity, it was unable to verify that the Free Syrian Army (FSA), local groups identifying themselves as such or other anti-Government armed groups had reached the necessary level of organization."[33]

3. In its May 2012 update, the Commission referred to the situation as one in which "gross violations continue unabated in an increasingly militarized context."[34] It also noted the increased organization of the opposition entities.

4. In the summer of 2012, the international community began to speak more about armed conflict and the ICRC noted that there was limited armed conflict in specified areas of Syria. On July 15, 2012, the ICRC declared that it believed an armed conflict exists and international humanitarian law applied throughout Syria.

Questions

1. Did the ICRC's July 15, 2012 declaration announce an armed conflict or was it merely an acknowledgment of what had long been clear in Syria? Who were the parties?

2. If an armed conflict existed in Syria before July 15, 2012, when did it start? Should we answer the question by considering the intensity of the conflict and then the organization of the Free Syrian Army in isolation? Are other factors relevant? What about the nature of the Assad regime's response? Would a totality of the circumstances approach—accounting for intensity and organization as two key factors—be more useful or effective here?

3. Is it relevant to your analysis that the international community was attempting to impose a ceasefire in Syria by April 2012? Does that attempt imply a degree of cohesion for the Syrian rebels not otherwise apparent?

33. Report of the Independent International Commission of Inquiry on the Syrian Arab Republic, A/HRC/19/69, Feb. 22, 2012, ¶ 13.

34. Independent International Commission of Inquiry on the Syrian Arab Republic, Periodic Update, May 24, 2012, ¶ 2.

> 4. Did the provision of arms and support to the Free Syrian Army by Turkey, Qatar, and Saudi Arabia affect the legal character of the situation in Syria?
>
> 5. What are the consequences of not finding an armed conflict in Syria before July 2012?

C.   COUNTERTERRORISM AS ARMED CONFLICT?

The existence of an armed conflict is the trigger for the application of LOAC. The attacks of September 11th and the resulting military operations and conflict between the United States and al Qaeda and other terrorist groups introduced new complications in this area. When looking at the traditional framework of international armed conflict (Common Article 2) and non-international armed conflict (Common Article 3), what is the impact of a conflict between one or more states and a transnational terrorist group that conducts terrorist attacks in a number of different countries and military operations in more than one country? Can it constitute an armed conflict within the definition of armed conflict as understood in LOAC? These questions were at the center of the debates surrounding U.S. policy and decisions for at least the first decade after the 9/11 attacks.

From the start, the United States has asserted that it is engaged in an armed conflict with terrorist groups—namely, al Qaeda and, over time, other groups and offshoots. Thus, the Authorization for Use of Military Force of September 18, 2001—the foundation upon which U.S. targeting and detention policy rests—states:

> the President is authorized to use all necessary and appropriate force against those nations, organizations, or persons he determines planned, authorized, committed, or aided the terrorist attacks that occurred on September 11, 2001, or harbored such organizations or persons, in order to prevent any future acts of international terrorism against the United States by such nations, organizations or persons.

In November 2002, the United States targeted Abu Ali al-Harithi, an al Qaeda operative suspected of planning the October 2000 attack on the U.S.S. *Cole,* using a Predator drone to attack the car in which al-Harithi was traveling in Yemen. Al-Harithi and five other men died in the attack. In response to a request from the U.N. Special Rapporteur on Extrajudicial, Summary or Arbitrary Executions for an explanation of and justification for the attack, the United States relied on an armed conflict framework, arguing that any allegations stemming from military operations fell outside the purview of the Special Rapporteur. Specifically, the United States declared that

Al Qaida and related terrorist networks are at war against the United States. They have trained, equipped, and supported armed forces and have planned and executed attacks around the world against the United States on a scale that far exceeds criminal activity. Al Qaida attacks have deliberately targeted civilians and protected sites and objects [including the 1998 Embassy bombings, the 2002 Bali nightclub bombing, the failed shoe-bomber attack, attacks on the U.S. Consulate in Karachi and others].

Despite coalition successes in Afghanistan and around the world, the war is far from over. . . . The continuing military operations undertaken against the United States and its nationals by the Al Qaida organization both before and after September 11 necessitate a military response by the armed forces of the United States. To conclude otherwise is to permit an armed group to wage war unlawfully against a sovereign state while precluding that state from defending itself.[35]

Since 9/11, the rhetoric of U.S. administrations regarding counter-terrorism has been and continues to be one of war. Israel takes a similar approach, consistently characterizing its conflicts with Hezbollah and Hamas as armed conflict. Other countries have been the victim of terrorist attacks and are engaged in comprehensive military or law enforcement operations in response, but traditionally do not necessarily take an armed conflict approach: the United Kingdom, India, Spain, and Russia, to name a few. The characterization of the conflict, both whether there is an armed conflict and, if so, what type of conflict, has profound implications for determining the applicable legal framework.

QUESTIONS FOR DISCUSSION

1. In contrast to the U.S. view of an armed conflict, many have argued that U.S. operations against al Qaeda and other terrorist groups do not fall within the definition of armed conflict as understood in international law. They argue that the rhetorical concept of a "war on terror" does not necessarily equate with an armed conflict as understood in LOAC. First, a conflict between a state (the United States) and a non-state group (al Qaeda) cannot be an international armed conflict because it is not between two states, as set forth in Common Article 2 of the Geneva Conventions. In addition, according to this argument, the "transnational nature of the operations . . . , coupled with the fact that an international coalition is currently involved in

---

35. Response of the Gov't of the United States of America to the Letter from Special Rapporteur on Extrajudicial, Summary or Arbitrary Executions to the Secretary of State Dated November 15, 2002 and to the Findings of the Special Rapporteur Contained in Her Report to the Commission on Human Rights, E/CN.4/2003/G/80, April 22, 2003.

those operations, directly excludes the possibility of qualifying that 'war' as an internal armed conflict."[36] Who has the better argument?

2. Others critique the notion of an armed conflict against terrorist groups on broader policy grounds as well:

> What are the boundaries of the Bush administration's "war on terrorism?" The recent battles fought against the Afghan and Iraqi governments were classic wars between organized military forces. But President George W. Bush has suggested that his campaign against terrorism goes beyond such conflicts; he said on September 29, 2001, "Our war on terror will be much broader than the battlefields and beachheads of the past. The war will be fought wherever terrorists hide, or run, or plan."
>
> This language stretches the meaning of the word "war." If Washington means "war" metaphorically, as when it speaks about a "war" on drugs, the rhetoric would be uncontroversial, a mere hortatory device intended to rally support for an important cause. Bush, however, seems to think of the war on terrorism quite literally—as a real war—and this concept has worrisome implications. The rules that bind governments are much looser during wartime than in times of peace. The Bush administration has used war rhetoric precisely to give itself the extraordinary powers enjoyed by a wartime government to detain or even kill suspects without trial. In the process, the administration may have made it easier for itself to detain or eliminate suspects. But it has also threatened the most basic due process rights. . . .
>
> By literalizing its "war" on terror, the Bush administration has broken down the distinction between what is permissible in times of peace and what can be condoned during a war. In peacetime, governments are bound by strict rules of law enforcement. Police can use lethal force only if necessary to meet an imminent threat of death or serious bodily injury. Once a suspect is detained, he or she must be charged and tried. These requirements—what one can call "law-enforcement rules"—are codified in international human rights law.
>
> In times of war, law-enforcement rules are supplemented by a more permissive set of rules: namely, international humanitarian law, which governs conduct during armed conflict. Under such "war rules," unlike during peacetime, an enemy combatant can be shot without warning (unless he or she is incapacitated, in custody, or trying to surrender), regardless of any imminent threat. If a combatant is captured, he or she can be held in custody until the end of the conflict, without any trial.
>
> These two sets of rules have been well developed over the years, both by tradition and by detailed international conventions. There is little law, however, to explain exactly when one set of rules should apply instead of the other. For example, the Geneva Conventions—the principal

---

36. Silvia Borelli, *Casting Light on the Legal Black Hole: International Law and Detentions Abroad in the "War on Terror,"* 857 INT'L REV. RED CROSS 39, 45 & n.25 (2005).

codification of war rules—apply to "armed conflict," but the treaties do not define the term. Fortunately, in its commentary on them, the International Committee of the Red Cross (ICRC), the conventions' official custodian, has provided some guidance. One test that the ICRC suggests can help determine whether wartime or peacetime rules apply is to examine the intensity of hostilities in a given situation. The Bush administration, for example, has claimed that al Qaeda is at "war" with the United States because of the magnitude of its attacks on September 11, 2001, its bombings of the U.S. embassies in Kenya and Tanzania, its attack on the U.S.S. *Cole* in Yemen, and the bombing of residential compounds in Saudi Arabia. Each of these attacks was certainly a serious crime warranting prosecution. But technically speaking, was the administration right to claim that they add up to a war?[37]

3. On November 13, 2015, ISIS attackers targeted six locations around Paris, killing 130 people and wounding hundreds more. A few months later, on March 21, 2016, ISIS claimed responsibility for twin bombings at the Brussels airport and a subway station, which killed thirty-two people and wounded 320 more. What law applied to these attacks and the attackers? How does French President François Hollande's pronouncement, speaking before a joint session of the French parliament, that "France is at war"[38] with ISIS impact your analysis? What about the fact that France had already been engaged in air strikes against ISIS, first in Iraq since September 2014 and then in Syria beginning in September 2015?[39]

Consider the implications of treating counterterrorism as armed conflict. What are the ramifications for the planning and implementation of operations? For the treatment of persons? For the law of armed conflict as a legal regime?

D.   CYBER OPERATIONS AS ARMED CONFLICT?

Revolutionary advances in technology now enable both militaries and civilians to engage in cyber activity to achieve objectives—whether related to protest and revolution, crime, terrorism, espionage, or military operations. At one end of the spectrum, both governments and private companies face a nearly constant onslaught of cyber activity seeking to access information, undermine or damage systems, or otherwise gain a financial, political, or strategic advantage of some kind. At the other end of the spectrum, we

37. Kenneth Roth, *The Law of War in the War on Terror: Washington's Abuse of "Enemy Combatants,"* For. Affairs, Jan./Feb. 2004, at 2, 2-3.

38. Krishnadev Calamur, *Is France at War*, TheAtlantic.com (Nov. 16, 2015).

39. David A. Graham, *What is France Doing in Syria*, TheAtlantic.com (Nov. 15, 2015).

see acts that some commentators call cyber war or cyber attacks, including the cyber operations in Georgia during the August 2008 conflict between Russia and Georgia, the Stuxnet virus, or the comprehensive computer network operations launched against the Estonian government in the summer of 2007. Governments and companies alike have established mechanisms for countering these rapidly developing threats and operations in cyberspace, including, for example, U.S. Cyber Command, China's People's Liberation Army (PLA) General Staff Department (GSD) 3rd Department, the Iranian Sun and Cyber Armies, Israel's Unit 8200, and the Russian Federal Security Service's 16th Directorate.

Cyber warfare has been defined broadly to include, among other actions: defending information and computer networks, deterring information attacks, denying an adversary's ability to defend networks and deter attacks; engaging in offensive information operations against an adversary; or dominating information on the battlefield.[40] Used this way, the term is descriptive rather than legal and does not necessarily offer guidance or conclusions regarding the application of LOAC to cyber activity. The growing use of cyber tools and concern over cyber attacks highlight key questions regarding whether and when LOAC applies to cyber operations. Questions relating to the application of LOAC to specific cyber actions within a broader, already-existing armed conflict will be addressed in later chapters; in such cases, the application of LOAC to the conflict is not in question. But what about when some type of conflict scenario develops comprised entirely of cyber interactions? Could solely cyber conduct trigger LOAC?

The answer could be fairly straightforward in the context of two states using cyber force against each other. If two states are involved and engage in acts amounting to armed hostilities using cyber operations or cyber capabilities, an international armed conflict would exist, even if short and limited in scope. Thus, "it is generally accepted that cyber operations having similar effects to classic kinetic operations [i.e., destruction of civilian or military assets or the death or injury of individuals] would amount to an international armed conflict."[41] Two particular challenges make the identification of an armed conflict difficult in a solely cyber context: whether the damage is sufficient to qualify as "armed" force and whether it is possible to attribute the act to a state or to individuals whose conduct is attributable to a state.

---

40. *See* STEVEN A. HILDRETH, CONG. RESEARCH SERV., RL 30735, CYBERWARFARE (2001).

41. INT'L COMM. RED CROSS, COMMENTARY TO GENEVA CONVENTION I FOR THE AMELIORATION OF THE CONDITION OF THE WOUNDED AND SICK IN THE ARMED FORCES IN THE FIELD ¶ 255 (2d ed. 2016). The Tallinn Manual offers the example of "a cyber operation that causes a fire to break out at a small military operation" as sufficient to trigger an international armed conflict. TALLINN MANUAL 2.0 ON THE INTERNATIONAL LAW APPLICABLE TO CYBER OPERATIONS 383 (Michael N. Schmitt ed., 2017).

First, consider the requirement that a conflict be "armed" and that the states involved are using "armed force" against each other. Cyber operations raise the question of whether force that is not kinetic and does not involve traditional "weapons" can still be considered "armed" for the purposes of conflict identification. Even in the absence of kinetic force, however, cyber operations can cause highly destructive effects, including death and injury to persons. "Armed" therefore refers to the nature of the force, not necessarily the nature of the agency or entity that carries out the cyber operation—a cyber operation constituting armed force carried out by an intelligence agency could trigger an international armed conflict while cyber espionage carried out by the armed forces would not.[42] One common approach to determining whether a cyber operation constitutes "armed force" is to equate the operation to "attacks" as defined in Article 49 of Additional Protocol I, which are "acts of violence against the adversary, whether in offence or defence."[43] Cyber operations can cause violent consequences, so "[t]o the extent that they result in injury or death of persons or damage or destruction of property, they are attacks satisfying the armed criterion of armed conflict."[44]

A second challenge for the identification of armed conflict in the cyber context alone is the difficulty of attribution, of identifying where an attack originated and who carried it out. An international armed conflict is between two states — as a result, the use of armed force in the cyber arena must be attributable to a state to trigger an international armed conflict. Acts by the armed forces or any other state agency clearly qualify, but cyber operations are often carried out by private actors or masked in a manner so as to make identification of the actors difficult or impossible. When these issues have arisen in more traditional contexts, "private individuals acting within the framework of, or in connection with, armed forces, or in collusion with State authorities may be regarded as de facto State organs,"[45] meaning that cyber attacks that such individuals launch will be regarded as state acts. As a result, uncertainty regarding the existence of an international armed conflict and the application of LOAC can remain; indeed, at this time, "no international armed conflict has been publicly characterized as having been solely precipitated in cyberspace."[46]

---

42. Tallinn Manual 2.0 on the International Law Applicable to Cyber Operations 384 (Michael N. Schmitt ed., 2017).

43. Protocol Additional to the Geneva Conventions of 12 August 1949, and relating to the Protection of Victims of International Armed Conflicts (Protocol I) art. 49(1), June 8, 1977, 1125 U.N.T.S. 3.

44. Michael N. Schmitt, *Classification of Cyber Conflict*, 17 J. Conflict & Sec. L. 245, 251 (2012).

45. Prosecutor v. Tadić, Case No. IT-94-1-A, Appeal Judgement ¶ 144 (Int'l. Trib. for the Former Yugoslavia, July 15, 1999).

46. Tallinn Manual 2.0 on the International Law Applicable to Cyber Operations 384 (Michael N. Schmitt ed., 2017).

In the non-international armed conflict context, however, classifying cyber activity and operations as armed conflict can be significantly more complicated. Applying the existing analytical structure—protracted armed violence between a government and an organized armed group or between two or more organized armed groups—raises a host of questions. Can a group using only cyber capabilities be considered to be "armed"? How would you define "armed" in such a context? Beyond that, however, consider the two main criteria of intensity and organization. Intensity could likely be characterized in a manner similar to the methodology used now, with appropriate qualifications made to fit within a cyber framework. Given the nature of cyber operations, it is unlikely that cyber operations alone would satisfy the intensity requirement. At present, "network intrusions, the deletion or destruction of data (even on a large scale), computer network exploitation, and data theft do not amount to a non-international armed conflict," nor would the "blocking of certain Internet functions and services" or "defacing governmental or other official websites."[47] In contrast, cyber operations that have the same violent consequences as kinetic attacks could meet the requisite intensity threshold.

The second factor, organization, will often forestall any conclusion that a non-international armed conflict exists. Of course, a non-state armed group that is "sufficiently organized to be a Party to a conventional non-international armed conflict would be sufficiently organized to be a Party to a conflict that includes or is solely based on cyber operations."[48] However, many of the entities engaging in cyber operations are entirely virtual; that is, the members of the ostensible group have never met each other or even spoken to one another, other than through the Internet and cyber media. Can such a collection of people—ranging from hackers to "a distinct online group with a leadership structure that coordinates its activities by, for instance, allocating specified cyber targets amongst themselves, sharing attack tools, conducting cyber vulnerability assessments, and doing cyber damage assessment to determine whether 'reattack' is required"[49]—be considered "organized"? Although the first set of hackers would not be organized, much like rioters who descend upon the same protest without any coordination, the latter would likely satisfy the organization criterion. Significantly more common, however, are informal groupings of individuals that have a shared purpose and may have access to a common website with tools and information about targets but do not act with coordination in any manner. For example, during the conflict between Georgia and Russia in the summer of 2008, numerous

47. *Id.* at 388.

48. Int'l Comm. Red Cross, Commentary to Geneva Convention I for the Amelioration of the Condition of the Wounded and Sick in the Armed Forces in the Field ¶ 437 (2d ed. 2016).

49. Tallinn Manual 2.0 on the International Law Applicable to Cyber Operations 390 (Michael N. Schmitt ed., 2017).

cyber attacks were launched against Georgia. Most of these attacks were initiated using a website that provided cyber tools and lists of Georgian government websites and cyber targets. The attacks were not coordinated with regard to timing, target and effect, or in any other aspect. If such activity were being considered for possible designation as a non-international armed conflict (as opposed to the international armed conflict between Georgia and Russia), where should such collections of individuals fall along a spectrum of organization? Is there something about the cyber realm that should require a higher level of organization? A lower threshold?

QUESTIONS FOR DISCUSSION

1. What indicators of intensity will prove effective in the cyber realm? Think about the indicators set forth by the ICTY in *Tadić*, *Limaj* and other cases — how well do they translate to the cyber context? What indicators might be more useful?

2. In April 2007, the government of Estonia moved a statue of a Soviet Red Army soldier from the center of Tallinn to a military cemetery outside the city. Riots and protests by ethnic Russians led to two days of violence and, beginning on April 27, a massive series of cyber attacks hit nearly every sector of Estonian society. Banks could not operate their online services, cash machines no longer worked, and government and other websites were taken down by distributed denial of service attacks causing previously unseen levels of Internet traffic.[50] The attacks came from Russian IP addresses, but there was no clear evidence that the attacks were carried out by the Russian government, and they were routed through over 100 countries around the world. Did the attacks constitute an international armed conflict? Non-international armed conflict? Why or why not?

3. Consider other recent cyber operations — how would you characterize the following:

    a. On November 24, 2014, a hacker group leaked a release of confidential data from Sony Pictures, including emails, personal information about employees and their families, executive salary data, copies of then-unreleased Sony films, and other confidential information. The hackers demanded that Sony cancel release of *The Interview*, a Sony comedy about a plot to assassinate North Korean leader Kim Jong-Un, and threatened violence against movie theaters showing the film. U.S. officials confirmed a few weeks later that North Korea was responsible for the hack.[51]

---

50. Damien McGuinness, *How A Cyber Attack Transformed Estonia*, BBC.COM (April 27, 2017).

51. Lori Grisham, *Timeline: North Korea and the Sony Pictures Hack*, USATODAY.COM (Dec. 18, 2014).

b. On June 27, 2017, a massive cyberattack crippled Ukraine's national bank, largest airport, state power company, and government offices. The attack also shut down radiation monitoring in the Chernobyl exclusion zone and affected the postal service, transportation systems, and television stations. The attack soon spread internationally, affecting the Danish shipping conglomerate Maersk and appearing in France, Spain, and India.[52]

c. In 2016, Russian entities engaged in massive interference in the U.S. presidential election, including hacking into Democratic candidate Hillary Clinton's emails, spreading false or damaging information, and hacking into electoral systems at the state and local level.

---

52. Lizzie Dearden, *Ukraine Cyber Attack: Chaos as National Bank, State Power Provider and Airport Hit by Hackers*, THE INDEPENDENT (June 27, 2017).

CHAPTER 5

CLASSIFYING CONFLICTS

The application of LOAC depends fundamentally on the existence of an armed conflict. This first determination, as discussed in the previous chapter, marks the legal demarcation between wartime and peacetime. But that is not the end of the matter. The legal inquiry necessarily extends to the identification of and differentiation between international and non-international armed conflicts. Although in 1949, Common Article 3 and its threshold of humane treatment was the full range of law applicable during non-international armed conflicts, over the ensuing decades the gap between the two legal frameworks has narrowed considerably. The law of targeting—for both persons and objects—for example, is nearly identical in international and non-international conflicts. The protections for cultural property and the prohibitions on the use of chemical and biological weapons extend across both types of conflicts as well. The most significant remaining area of differentiation involves the status of persons and the detention regimes applicable in the two types of conflict. In addition, classifying conflicts is essential for understanding who the parties to the conflict are and against whom each party is fighting, which is critical to determining the relevant rights, obligations, and privileges.

A. DISTINGUISHING AND TRANSITIONING BETWEEN INTERNAL AND INTERNATIONAL ARMED CONFLICT

In some situations, the characterization of a conflict as international or non-international is straightforward. Many conflicts, however, are more complicated and display characteristics of both international and internal conflicts. Other conflicts may start as one type of conflict and morph into the other, depending on developments over the course of the conflict. For example, the U.S. invasion of Afghanistan in 2001 triggered an international armed conflict. Most observers recognize that, with the initial defeat of the Taliban and the establishment of the government of Afghan President Hamid Karzai, the conflict then became a non-international armed conflict between the Karzai government and insurgent Taliban forces, with the United States and NATO forces invited to support the Karzai government. Many view U.S. operations to combat al Qaeda in Afghanistan as a separate non-international armed conflict, raising questions about whether there can be more than one conflict occurring in the same geographical area at the same time. Indeed, this notion of two different conflicts—often one international and one non-international—occurring at the same time and in the same location is not new. In its 1986 judgment in *Military and Paramilitary Activities in and against Nicaragua*, for example, the ICJ characterized the conflict in Nicaragua as follows:

> the conflict between the *contras'* forces and those of the Government of Nicaragua is an armed conflict which is "not of an international character." The acts of the *contras* towards the Nicaraguan Government are therefore governed by the law applicable to conflicts of that character; whereas the actions of the United States in and against Nicaragua fall under the legal rules relating to international conflicts.[1]

Interestingly, despite U.S. intervention on behalf of the non-state actor against a state in an ongoing non-international armed conflict, the court did not apply Common Article 2 to the *contras*. Instead, the court treated U.S. intervention—particularly the mining of Nicaraguan ports—as a conflict distinct from the conflict between Nicaragua and the *contras*. Similar characterizations have been suggested for the war in Lebanon in the 1970s—a non-international armed conflict between the Lebanese government and militia groups alongside an international armed conflict between Israel and Lebanon once Israel invaded in 1978—and the conflict in Cambodia during the same decade.[2] More recently, the 2011 conflict in Libya offers a classic example of the transition from peacetime to non-international armed conflict to international armed conflict.

LIBYA 2011

On February 15, 2011, the Libyan government arrested a human rights attorney who represented the families of prisoners killed in a 1996 prison uprising. The next day, a crowd of several hundred gathered in Benghazi, Libya's second largest city, to demand his release. The crowd was organized by the families represented by the imprisoned attorney.

---

1. Military and Paramilitary Activities in and against Nicaragua (Nicar. v. U.S.), 1986 I.C.J. 114, ¶ 219 (June 27).

2. *See* Hans-Peter Gasser, *Internationalized Non-International Armed Conflicts: Case Studies of Afghanistan, Kampuchea, and Lebanon*, 33 Am. U. L. Rev. 145, 153-157 (1983).

Armed with Molotov cocktails and rocks, the crowd clashed with Libyan riot police. That same day, hundreds of protestors marched in protest against the Qaddafi regime in the cities of Al Beyda and Zentan, where they set fire to the local security headquarters.

On February 17, 2011, protests broke out in Tripoli, Benghazi, and Al Beyda. The Libyan government reportedly responded to these protests with police and snipers, killing as many as twenty-four protesters. By February 19, daily clashes between protesters and Libyan security forces had resulted in the deaths of at least 100 protesters. By February 21, protesters had taken control of Benghazi and the Libyan government responded with military helicopters and airstrikes, as well as Libyan special forces, who reportedly fired indiscriminately into crowds, in an effort to quell mounting protests.

At the same time, protests spread, apparently spontaneously, to other cities all over Libya. The cities of Misurata and Zawiyah joined the rebellion, giving rebel forces access to a Libyan army arsenal. The U.N. Security Council took notice of the situation in Libya and referred the matter to the International Criminal Court for investigation. By February 27, whole units of Libyan armed forces were defecting to the rebels. Defecting officers of the Libyan armed forces established a unified command and a rebel political leadership, the National Transitional Council, formed to coordinate anti-Qaddafi actions.

By February 28, the Libyan government was launching attacks against cities controlled by the popular forces. The government's attack on Zawiyah resulted in a sustained, six-hour long engagement between government and popular forces, with the latter ultimately driving the government forces into retreat. The popular forces began to train with captured weapons belonging to the Libyan government and donned captured military garb. During this period, 140,000 Libyan refugees fled to Tunisia.

By March 17, 2011, government forces using infantry, tanks, artillery, and helicopters had driven anti-Qaddafi forces out of Ras Lanuf, Adjadibya, Brega, and were positioned on the outskirts of Benghazi—the heart of the anti-Qaddafi uprising and home to its political front. Also on March 17, the U.N. Security Council authorized the imposition of a "No Fly Zone" over Libya under its Chapter VII authority in the U.N. Charter, and authorized all "necessary measures" to protect civilians. Almost immediately, U.S., French, and British air and sea forces launched attacks targeting the Libyan air defense network, air force, and ground troops.

1. Was there an armed conflict in Libya on February 17, 2011? What about on February 28? Or March 18?
2. If there was an armed conflict in Libya on any of those dates, what was its character?

3. When do "protests" become "rebellion"?
4. Did the U.S., U.K., and French airstrikes enforcing the U.N. Security Council Resolution place any of those countries in an armed conflict with Libya? If so, does that change the nature of the hostilities between the government of Libya and the anti-Qaddafi forces?

In June 2011, the United Nations International Commission of Inquiry on Libya issued a report on violations committed during the conflict. With respect to the characterization of the conflict and the applicable law, the Commission stated the following:

60. The escalation of the situation in Libya has particular consequences in terms of the application of international law. In legal terms, the periods can be demarked as (i) "peace-time," (ii) "non-international armed conflict" and (iii) "co-existing international armed conflict." For the purposes of the application of relevant legal standards, it is necessary to define more closely the relevant time periods involved.

61. **Peace-time Libya:** When the demonstrations began in mid-February, Libya could be classified as being in a normal state of peace.

62. **Non-International Armed Conflict:** The precise date for determining when this change from peace to non-international armed conflict occurred is somewhat difficult in the current circumstances. The Commission notes that other organisations that have been examining this question such as the Prosecutor of the ICC and the International Committee of the Red Cross (ICRC) have not put forward a particular date.

63. The Commission notes the definition of non-international armed conflicts in Additional Protocol II to the Geneva Conventions Relating to the Protection of Victims in Non-International Armed Conflict (to which Libya is a party), namely conflicts "which take place in the territory of a High Contracting Party between its armed forces and dissident armed forces or other organized armed groups which, under responsible command, exercise such control over a part of its territory as to enable them to carry out sustained and concerted military operations and to implement this Protocol." The situation must constitute more than either isolated acts of violence, a mere internal disturbance or riot and involve protracted violence, engaging both the Government forces and an organised armed group. No definition of non-international armed conflict is provided for in the four Geneva Conventions (which include[] the protections of Common Article 3). Jurisprudence has developed, however, defining non-international armed conflict as whenever there is "protracted armed violence between governmental authorities and organized armed groups or between such groups within a State."

64. In determining whether a non-international armed conflict exists, the Commission has thus had to consider the intensity of the conflict, the extent of relevant control of territory and the nature of the armed group in opposition to the Government. Examining the nature of

the armed group involves considering such factors as whether there is a hierarchical command structure, the extent to which it is able to carry out organized operations (e.g., organises into zones of responsibility, means of communication); discipline systems, the nature of logistical arrangements and how the group presents itself (e.g., whether it is capable of involvement in negotiations).

65. Information is more readily available concerning the intensity of the conflict and how the opposition forces have gained territorial control than many aspects of the organisation of the armed opposition forces. On 19 February, Government opponents assumed control over the *Katiba* premises in Benghazi, and also took control of the airport in Benghazi. On the same day in Tobruk, Government opponents took over Omar al-Mukhtar *Katiba* and confiscated weaponry. On 20 February, demonstrators controlled the town of Al-Shahat, east of Libya, and reportedly "arrested" persons fighting with the Qadhafi forces. By 24 February, anti government forces appear to have taken control of Tobruk, and Misrata. By 26 February, Security Council Resolution 1970 welcomed various institutions' condemnation of serious violations of human rights and humanitarian law in Libya[.] Whilst the Commission lacks full information concerning several aspects of the opposition forces organization, it has reached the preliminary view that by or around 24 February, a non-international armed conflict had developed sufficient to trigger the application of AP II and Common Article 3 of the Geneva Conventions.

66. **Co-existing International Armed Conflict:** The airstrikes to enforce the no-fly zone imposed by the Security Council through Resolution 1973 which began on 19 March brought into being an international armed conflict between the States participating in this military action and the Libyan state. The Commission has noted that the objective of this international military action is to enforce Security Council Resolution 1973. It is also satisfied that the actions of NATO and other foreign States involved are not exercising control over the military actions of either of the parties to the non-international armed conflict. As such, it concludes that the international armed conflict is legally separate to the continuing non-international armed conflict, and is thus a "co-existing international armed conflict."[3]

The lines between international armed conflict and non-international armed conflict are not always so clear, however, and the involvement, role and goals of various parties can be murky at best. In the conflict in the former Yugoslavia, conflict characterization was put to the test multiple times over the course of the conflict. In May 1991, Croatia and Slovenia declared independence from the Federal Republic of Yugoslavia. After ten days of fighting, Yugoslav forces withdrew from Slovenia, after which Slovenia

---

3. Human Rights Council, Report of the International Commission of Inquiry to investigate all alleged violations of international human rights law in the Libyan Arab Jamahiriya, U.N. Doc A/HRC/17/44 (June 1, 2011).

remained at peace. Fierce fighting continued in Croatia and spread to Bosnia in May 1992 when Bosnia and Herzegovina declared independence as well. Serbs in Bosnia formed a separate Bosnian Serb entity, called Republika Srpska, and fighting between and among all three ethnic groups exploded. Over the next three years, the world learned of concentration camps, ethnic cleansing, mass killings, and other atrocities throughout Bosnia and the contested portions of Croatia. In 1993, the U.N. Security Council exercised its Chapter VII powers under the U.N. Charter and established the ICTY to prosecute individuals charged with committing violations of LOAC during the then still ongoing conflict. After the tribunal determined that there was indeed an armed conflict in the former Yugoslavia (the subject of the previous chapter), it had to characterize the conflict at different times in order to determine the applicable law.

As an initial step, the Tribunal first concluded, in the *Tadić* interlocutory appeal decision referenced in Chapter 4, that the conflict included both international aspects and non-international aspects at varying times and in varying places. This basic description was sufficient for the initial process of asserting jurisdiction over Mr. Tadić. However, applying LOAC, especially for the purposes of criminal accountability, requires greater delineation and examination of the various factors that can help characterize a conflict. In particular, several recent and ongoing conflicts demonstrate the complex arena of conflict classification. This section highlights three challenging issues: foreign state involvement in an ongoing non-international armed conflict; extraterritorial force against a non-state armed group; and complex conflicts with many parties and shifting allegiances.

1.   *Foreign State Involvement in a Non-International Armed Conflict*

State involvement in some way in a conflict that is taking place within another state is quite common. The question then is whether the foreign state's involvement changes the characterization of the conflict such that it converts a non-international armed conflict into an international armed conflict. Foreign state involvement in a conflict can take several different forms, including financial assistance to one party, transfer of weapons and matériel, assistance through advisors and trainers, introduction of some soldiers and units, or even full-scale intervention of combat units.

Armed intervention by a third-party state into an ongoing non-international armed conflict will complicate that armed conflict both politically and legally. In particular, the characterization of an armed conflict that an intervening state is engaged in — regardless of the legality of the intervention under the *jus ad bellum* — impacts the extent of the applicable LOAC. Intervention in support of a non-state actor against the territorial state internationalizes the conflict and places the intervening state and the territorial state in an international armed conflict, as in the Libya discussion above. In contrast, intervention in support of the government of the territorial state against a non-state actor—assuming the intervening state and the non-state actor engage in hostilities sufficient to establish an armed conflict—puts the intervening state and the non-state actor in a non-international armed conflict. For example, consider the conflict in Afghanistan and how the characterization has changed from before 9/11, when the Northern Alliance and the Taliban were engaged in a struggle for control, to now. Similarly, nearly forty years ago, Soviet intervention in Afghanistan on behalf of the Soviet-installed puppet government of Afghanistan against the *mujahedeen* placed the Soviet Union in a non-international armed conflict with the *mujahedeen*. In a similar vein, the U.S. engagement in Vietnam—supporting the government of the Republic of Vietnam against the National Liberation Front (the Viet Cong)—constituted third state intervention in support of a government against a non-state actor, placing the United States, the intervening state, in a non-international armed conflict with the Viet Cong, the non-state actor. The United States chose to treat the conflict as an international armed conflict as a matter of policy—an approach the ICRC urged and supported—lending credence to the view that once the United States intervened, the whole conflict was internationalized.[4] In a wide variety of conflicts, courts and other national and international entities have addressed conflict characterization both during and after a conflict, in order to assess operational needs and accountability parameters.

The question of third-party involvement and internationalization of armed conflict arose throughout the conflict in the former Yugoslavia. In the *Tadić* case, the Trial Chamber found that Tadić was not guilty of numerous grave breaches of the Geneva Conventions because, according to the Trial Chamber's findings, the armed conflict in the former Yugoslavia was not an international armed conflict at the time of the alleged crimes. Grave breaches are crimes under the law of international armed conflict and therefore, if the conflict was not international, the crimes could not constitute grave breaches. On appeal, the Appeals Chamber rejected the characterization of the post-May 1992 conflict in Bosnia as internal and determined that the involvement of the Federal Republic of Yugoslavia (FRY) rendered the conflict international. The Tribunal found that the Bosnian Serb forces were "acting under the overall control of and on behalf of the FRY" and therefore "even after 19 May 1992 the armed conflict in Bosnia and Herzegovina between the Bosnian Serbs and the central authorities of Bosnia

---

4. Hans-Peter Gasser, *Internationalized Non-International Armed Conflicts: Case Studies of Afghanistan, Kampuchea, and Lebanon*, 33 Am. U. L. Rev. 145, 147 (1983).

and Herzegovina must be classified as an *international* armed conflict."[5] In particular, the Tribunal pointed to several factors in finding such "overall control": the FRY continued to determine military strategies and objectives, to pay the Bosnian Serb forces' salaries, and to provide critical combat support. In addition, the FRY and the Bosnian Serb entity negotiated as a unified delegation at the Dayton Accords and the FRY pledged to ensure that the Bosnian Serb entity complied with any peace agreement.

QUESTIONS FOR DISCUSSION

1. In the spring of 2014, conflict broke out between Ukraine and pro-Russian separatists in the eastern Ukraine regions of Donetsk and Luhansk. By the summer of that year and continuing to the present, numerous reports of Russian involvement have emerged. Which of the following reports would change the characterization of a non-international armed conflict[6] in Ukraine and why:

   a. Photographs released in April 2014 showing that the "little green men" who seized government buildings across Donetsk and Luhansk were actually Russian military and intelligence forces.[7]

   b. Hundreds of Russian troops train and equip Ukrainian separatists in eastern Ukraine.[8]

   c. Russian military personnel fighting alongside separatists in eastern Ukraine claim to be volunteers, heading across the border to fight while on vacation from military service in Russia.[9]

   d. Ukrainian forces capture ten Russian paratroopers in Donetsk.[10]

   e. Russian helicopters fire rockets at Ukrainian border guards.[11]

5. *Prosecutor v. Tadić*, Case No. IT-94-1-A, Judgement, ¶ 162 (Int'l Crim. Trib. for the Former Yugoslavia July 15, 1999).

6. In July 2014, the International Committee of the Red Cross issued a public statement calling on all sides to comply with LOAC and reiterating that the "rules and principles [of LOAC] apply to all parties to the non-international armed conflict in Ukraine." Press Release, Int'l Comm. Red Cross, *Ukraine: ICRC Calls on All Sides to Respect International Humanitarian Law*, July 23, 2014, https://www.icrc.org/eng/resources/documents/news-release/2014/07-23-ukraine-kiev-call-respect-ihl-repatriate-bodies-malaysian-airlines.htm.

7. Andrew Higgins, Michael R. Gordon & Andrew E. Kramer, *Photos Link Masked Men in East Ukraine to Russia*, N.Y. TIMES, April 20, 2014, at A1.

8. Michael R. Gordon & Andrew E. Kramer, *Russia Continues to Train and Equip Ukraine Rebels, NATO Official Says*, N.Y. TIMES, Nov. 4, 2014, at A4.

9. Corey Flintoff, *Russia Reports Troop Deaths in Ukraine, But Calls them "Volunteers,"* NPR.ORG (Sept. 8, 2014).

10. Adam Swain, *Further Claims of Russian Troop Deployments Follow Capture of Soldiers in Donetsk*, THECONVERSATION.COM (August 27, 2014).

11. *Id.*

      f. Russia supplies heavy weaponry (including the BUK anti-aircraft missile used to shoot down the civilian commercial airliner Malaysian Airlines flight 17), advisors, command and control, and funding to Ukrainian separatists.[12]

2. What is the effect on conflict characterization when multiple states intervene in a non-international armed conflict? If multiple states intervene on the side of the state, such as in Afghanistan after the fall of the Taliban? What if multiple states are involved on both sides of the conflict? Consider Syria — Russia, the United States, the United Kingdom, France, and Iran are all involved militarily in the conflict against one or more groups. Does that change the non-international armed conflict between Syria and various opposition groups into an international armed conflict? Why or why not? Some argue that the conflict with ISIS is an international armed conflict because ISIS calls itself a state. Is that correct?[13]

3. When the United Nations or a regional security organization sends peacekeeping forces to help stabilize a conflict, the presence of those multinational or United Nations peacekeeping forces does not change the characterization of the conflict. Why not? In what circumstances would the participation of an international force alter the legal nature of the conflict?

4. The International Court of Justice addressed the role of a state providing assistance to a rebel group a decade before the ICTY in the *Nicaragua* case. Although the question addressed appears similar to the question of conflict characterization in the *Tadić* decision discussed above, the ICJ holding focused on the level of control necessary for attribution of the non-state armed group's activities to a foreign state for purposes of state responsibility (effective control) — not for characterization as an international or non-international armed conflict (overall control).[14]

---

12. Jens David Ohlin, *Control Matters: Ukraine & Russia and the Downing of Flight 17*, OPINIOJURIS.ORG, July 23, 2014, http://opiniojuris.org/2014/07/23/control-matters-ukraine-russia-downing-flight-17/; Tom Parfitt, *Ukraine and MH17: Who are the Separatists*, THE TELEGRAPH (July 18, 2014).

13. *See* INT'L COMM. RED CROSS, COMMENTARY TO GENEVA CONVENTION I FOR THE AMELIORATION OF THE CONDITION OF THE WOUNDED AND SICK IN THE ARMED FORCES IN THE FIELD ¶ 447 (2d ed. 2016) ("Common Article 3 or humanitarian law more generally does not give an answer on whether an entity is a State under international law; it is the rules of general international law that set out the relevant criteria").

14. In the *Application of the Genocide Convention* case, the ICJ ruled that the effective control test remains the standard for state responsibility for the acts of a non-state group, while the overall control test is the appropriate standard for classifying a conflict where a state is exercising some measure of control or authority over a non-state group in a non-international armed conflict. Application of the Convention on the Prevention and Punishment of the Crime of Genocide (Bosn. & Herz. v. Serb. & Montenegro), Judgment, 2007 I.C.J. 43, ¶¶ 404-407 (Feb. 26).

5. Consider the challenges of applying the overall control test in the cyber context. When "viruses, Trojan horses, or computer worms could be routed through various computers and countries, making the originators and their controllers almost impossible to identify with much certainty,"[15] how should overall control be assessed for purposes of determining whether a state is controlling a non-state group so as to internationalize a non-international armed conflict? The *Tallinn Manual* offers the following explanation:

> Applying the [overall control] test, if State A exercises overall control over an organized group of computer hackers that penetrate State B's cyber infrastructure and cause significant physical damage, the armed conflict qualifies as "international" in nature. State A need not have instructed the group to attack particular aspects of the infrastructure, but, instead, only needs to have exerted sufficient control over the group to instruct it to mount a campaign against cyber infrastructure. . . .[16]

6. In some conflicts, an international armed conflict may be "internalized," that is, transformed into a non-international armed conflict. The conflict in Afghanistan, for example, was first a non-international armed conflict between the Taliban regime and the opposition led by the Northern Alliance. After 9/11, the U.S. invasion of Afghanistan created an international armed conflict between the U.S. and Afghanistan—although the Taliban regime was not recognized by the international community (with the exception of three states), the Taliban was the *de facto* government and military forces of Afghanistan. Precisely because recognition, or the lack thereof, of governments was historically a means of avoiding the application of the law of war, "it is *de facto* government and not recognition that matters" in modern LOAC.[17] After the Taliban regime fell and the new Afghan government was established, the conflict became a non-international armed conflict, with the U.S. and other international forces fighting alongside and at the invitation of the new Afghan government against the now-insurgent Taliban forces.

2.   *Extraterritorial Force Against Non-State Armed Groups*

The conflicts in Bosnia and Herzegovina, in Libya, and in Syria, for example, all involve armed violence between a state and one or more armed

---

15. THE 1949 GENEVA CONVENTIONS: A COMMENTARY 23 (Andrew Clapham et al. eds., 2015).

16. TALLINN MANUAL ON THE INTERNATIONAL LAW APPLICABLE TO CYBER WARFARE 80-81 (Michael N. Schmitt ed., 2013) (Rule 22).

17. Marko Milanovic, *The Applicability of the Conventions to "Transnational" and "Mixed" Conflicts, in* THE 1949 GENEVA CONVENTIONS: A COMMENTARY 32 (Andrew Clapham et al. eds., 2015).

groups inside the same territory—or perhaps between two or more armed groups in that territory, such as in Somalia. However, not all conflicts are contained within the boundaries of a state. Recent and current conflicts demonstrate that armed conflict can and does occur in many varieties and many combinations, irrespective of borders, nationality, or geographical distance. Consider the following types of conflicts identified by the ICRC in a report on contemporary challenges in LOAC:

- Spill-over conflicts in which a non-international armed conflict between government forces and one or more organized armed groups within the territory of a state "spill over" into the territory of neighboring states;
- Multi-national non-international armed conflicts, where multi-national armed forces fight alongside the forces of a "host" state, in its territory, against one or more organized armed groups;
- A subset of multi-national non-international armed conflicts where United Nations or regional forces support a "host" government involved in hostilities against one or more organized armed groups in its territory; or
- Cross-border conflicts where the forces of a state are involved in hostilities with a non-state party operating from the territory of a neighboring "host" state without that state's control or support.[18]

The law applicable to these different types of non-international armed conflict is the same: Common Article 3 and all customary law applicable to non-international armed conflict. Although Common Article 3 uses the term "non-international armed conflict," at the time the Geneva Conventions were drafted, a more accurate description might have been "internal armed conflict." The conflicts into which the drafters of the Geneva Conventions sought to inject some humanitarian norms and some regulation were most often understood as conflicts between a government and a domestic uprising.[19] Interestingly, although this may have been the primary or only construct in the minds of the drafters and the state delegates, the actual language of Common Article 3 is not limited to such intra-state conflicts, but rather encompasses any conflict "not of an international character." Figuring out when and where it applies, and to which parties, in such conflicts can be more complicated, however.

Spillover conflicts primarily raise questions about the geographic reach of an existing armed conflict and whether the crossing of a border

18. *See* INT'L COMM. OF THE RED CROSS, DOC. NO. 31IC/11/5.1.2, INTERNATIONAL HUMANITARIAN LAW AND THE CHALLENGES OF CONTEMPORARY ARMED CONFLICTS 9-11 (2011).

19. INT'L COMM. RED CROSS, COMMENTARY ON THE GENEVA CONVENTION (IV) RELATIVE TO THE PROTECTION OF CIVILIAN PERSONS IN TIME OF WAR 26-27 (Oscar M. Uhler & Henri Coursier eds., 1958).

has any consequence for the application of LOAC. The conflict in Afghanistan repeatedly spilled over into the border regions of Pakistan as the Taliban sought breathing room in the tribal areas of Northwest Pakistan and launched attacks on U.S. and Afghan forces from safe havens there. Similarly, in the course of the ongoing non-international armed conflict between the government of Somalia and al-Shabaab, al-Shabaab militants regularly cross the border and launch attacks in Kenya. In response, Kenyan forces have engaged with al-Shabaab operatives both within Kenya and across the border back in Somalia. Article 1 of the Statute of the ICTR acknowledged the spillover of the Rwanda conflict into the Democratic Republic of the Congo (Zaire at the time) and other nearby states in its statement of jurisdiction, declaring the tribunal competent to "prosecute persons responsible for serious violations of international humanitarian law in the territory of Rwanda and Rwandan citizens responsible for such violations committed in the territory of neighbouring States. . . ." The spread of hostilities into an adjacent state raises the question of whether and how LOAC applies to acts and persons in that adjacent state. Although some argue that LOAC will only apply if the hostilities in that adjacent state meet the intensity and organization requirements of the *Tadić* test independently, the ICRC and state practice support an extension of LOAC application at least to the hostilities between the two parties. The ICRC explained as follows in its 2011 report on challenges in contemporary armed conflicts:

> relations between parties whose conflict has spilled over remain at a minimum governed by Common Article 3 and customary [LOAC]. This position is based on the understanding that the spillover of a [non-international armed conflict] into adjacent territory cannot have the effect of absolving the parties of their [LOAC] obligations simply because an international border has been crossed. The ensuing legal vacuum would deprive of protection both civilians possibly affected by the fighting, as well as persons who fall into enemy hands.[20]

A more difficult question is how far the conflict can spill over into the neighboring country with regard to the application of LOAC. Should LOAC apply throughout the entire neighboring country even if the spillover is confined to a small area near the border? Think about the object and purpose of LOAC, as well as broader policy concerns that might affect your answer.

Finally, a "cross-border" non-international armed conflict is one that takes place between a state and a non-state armed group located entirely outside the state's territory. Since 9/11, the idea of an external non-international armed conflict—a conflict between a state and a non-state group occurring outside that state and in the territory of one or more

---

20. INT'L COMM. OF THE RED CROSS, DOC. NO. 31IC/11/5.1.2, INTERNATIONAL HUMANITARIAN LAW AND THE CHALLENGES OF CONTEMPORARY ARMED CONFLICTS 9-10 (2011).

other states—has become significantly more prevalent. The 2006 conflict between Israel and Hezbollah fit this description, as has the U.S. conflict with al Qaeda in the Arabian Peninsula (AQAP) in Yemen. One challenge here is determining the appropriate methodology for conflict recognition, because the development of such conflicts does not necessarily match that of more traditional non-international armed conflicts. According to the "classic" story of non-international armed conflict, a state faces internal disturbances or other domestic unrest, responds with ordinary law enforcement measures to restore and maintain public order and security, the unrest increases, and at some point, the military is called upon to counter the continued threat from the uprising. As clashes between the non-state forces and the military continue and develop in degree and frequency, we reach the threshold of non-international armed conflict. This is how a non-international armed conflict comes into being, as told in the Commentary and through the *Tadić* analysis and its progeny. But does this "story" hold true when a state acts against a non-state group outside its territory?

Although intensity and organization will be the primary tools for assessing the existence of a conflict, the notion that the state will first use law enforcement to respond to the attack and to restore public order and security—inherent in the Common Article 3 analysis—may not be an option at all. Rather, the state likely needs to rely on its military to stop the attack and deter the attackers from continuing their operations as a first step, because there would be no other option. Think about one of the important considerations highlighted in the Commentary to Common Article 3: whether "the legal Government is obliged to have recourse to the regular military forces."[21] Can this consideration still help demarcate a threshold for armed conflict when law enforcement is not an option? More importantly, is it likely that cross-border non-international armed conflicts will eventually rest on a lower threshold of any exchange of hostilities between a state and a non-state armed group outside its borders? If so, what might be the benefits or risks of such a development?

QUESTIONS FOR DISCUSSION

1. In 2008, Colombia launched air strikes and a raid against a jungle camp of the Revolutionary Armed Forces of Colombia (FARC) across the border in Ecuador, killing a top FARC commander. Did Colombia's use of force against the FARC in Ecuador trigger an international armed conflict with Ecuador? If one state uses force in the territory of another state, but against a non-state armed group rather than the state, that conflict

---

21. INT'L COMM. RED CROSS, COMMENTARY ON THE GENEVA CONVENTION (IV) RELATIVE TO THE PROTECTION OF CIVILIAN PERSONS IN TIME OF WAR 35 (Oscar M. Uhler & Henri Coursier eds., 1958).

is between the state and the non-state armed group, because it does not involve two states as the opposing parties. But if the territorial state does not consent to the use of force on its territory against the non-state armed group, is there also a separate international armed conflict between the state using force and the territorial state? Did the United States trigger an international armed conflict with Pakistan when U.S. Navy SEALs undertook the Osama bin Laden raid in 2011? The U.S. did not notify Pakistan in advance that it was entering its airspace and attacking a target in Abbottabad or ask for Pakistan's consent to do so.

2. What if the non-state armed group is part of the government in the territorial state? Consider a potential future conflict between Israel and Hezbollah in southern Lebanon. The 2006 conflict between Israel and Hezbollah was generally considered a non-international armed conflict—an example of a cross-border conflict between a state and a non-state group in the territory of another state.[22] Now that Hezbollah is part of the government of Lebanon after winning ten seats in Parliament and a place in the unity government in 2009, however, what type of conflict would ensue if hostilities break out between Israel and Hezbollah?

3. The question of the application of LOAC to cross-border hostilities and the classification as a non-international armed conflict is different from the question of the state's authority to use force in such a situation. The latter issue is a *jus ad bellum* question and is an equally important part of the analysis, but does not and should not alter the LOAC analysis. What is the legal authority for a state to use force against a non-state armed group attacking it from outside its borders? Does that authority depend on the actions or inaction of the territorial state from where the non-state armed group is operating? Does the existence of an ongoing non-international armed conflict that has spilled over provide sufficient justification for the use of force—even if the non-state armed group has not launched attacks from the spillover state but is merely seeking safe haven there—and obviate the need for a separate *jus ad bellum* analysis?

3. Complex Conflicts

In many conflicts, a multitude of groups—both state and non-state—may be fighting, some against each other, some in concert, some simply in the same area but unrelated to each other in goal or strategy. A study of conflicts worldwide concluded that over thirty percent of the active conflicts in 2002 and 2003 involved more than one rebel group, for

---

22. Note that many argue that there was also a parallel international armed conflict between Israel and Lebanon as a result of Israel's use of force in Lebanon without Lebanon's consent. *See, e.g.*, Marko Milanovic, *The Applicability of the Conventions to "Transnational" and "Mixed" Conflicts, in* THE 1949 GENEVA CONVENTIONS: A COMMENTARY 38 (Andrew Clapham et al. eds., 2015).

example.[23] When foreign states intervene as well, conflict characterization becomes highly complex. The conflict in the Democratic Republic of the Congo (DRC) offers an excellent example and was the subject of the first judgment of the ICC, *Prosecutor v. Thomas Lubanga Dyilo*. In brief, after years of Belgian colonial rule and decades of autocratic rule by the independent country's first leader, Mobutu Sese Soku, the DRC (then known as Zaire) became embroiled in conflict in the aftermath of the 1994 genocide in Rwanda. Extremist Hutu militias responsible for most of the genocidal killings in 1994 fled from Rwanda and sought safe haven in the eastern part of the DRC. Rwanda subsequently sent forces to combat them. Over the next few years, anti-Mobutu rebels fought the government with the support of Rwanda and in 1997 installed a new government under President Laurent Kabila, renaming the country the Democratic Republic of the Congo. Violence continued, with Rwanda and Uganda ultimately supporting Kabila's opponents after a rift between erstwhile allies, and Angola, Namibia, and Zimbabwe assisting the government forces.

Against the backdrop of this ongoing broader conflict, violence erupted between and among militia groups in the Ituri region of eastern DRC in 2002 and 2003.

CIA Fact Book: http://www.globalissues.org/article/87/the-democratic-republic-of-congo.

23. Lotta Harbom, Erik Melander & Peter Wallensteen, *Dyadic Dimensions of Armed Conflict, 1946-2007*, 45 J. OF PEACE RESEARCH 697-710 (2008).

This situation was the subject of the first case before the ICC, the prosecution of Thomas Lubanga Dyilo. Lubanga, a member of the Hema ethnic group, was the president of the Union of Congolese Patriots (Union des Patriotes Congolais, UPC), a brutal armed group fighting in the Ituri region, part of a local armed conflict between the Hema and Lendu ethnic groups. Before and during the course of the fighting, Ugandan forces invaded the border areas, in response to the cross-border attacks by anti-Uganda militias, and occupied the area for several years. Competition for the DRC's extensive natural resources only exacerbated and extended the conflict. The local militias, with the backing of foreign armies in many cases, engaged in a horrific and brutal conflict, resulting in over 60,000 civilian deaths and massive atrocities, including summary executions, torture, rape, pillage, and the abduction and use of children as soldiers. Thousands of children, even as young as seven, were recruited by all sides and used as fighters. The ICC indicted Lubanga for the war crimes of enlisting and conscripting children under age fifteen as soldiers and using them as active participants in hostilities in 2002-2003.

In order to apply the Rome Statute correctly, the ICC had to determine whether the conflict was international or non-international at the times of the alleged crimes. Finding that multiple armed conflicts were occurring at the same time, the Trial Chamber recognized that different legal frameworks can apply to distinct conflicts occurring in the same location or country. Applying the *Tadić* overall control test, the Trial Chamber determined that the conflict between the UPC and other armed groups was not internationalized because there was not sufficient evidence that the UPC had acted under the overall control of any of the states involved (Rwanda, Uganda or the DRC).[24] Thus, the situation involved an international armed conflict between the DRC and Uganda alongside multiple non-international armed conflicts between various armed groups.

CONFLICT CLASSIFICATION IN SYRIA

Beginning in 2014, the conflict in Syria morphed into an extraordinarily complex conflict with multiple states and hundreds of armed groups involved in hostilities in various localities and at various times. A brief summary of the parties involved between 2014 and the present includes:

Government of Syria and Allies

- The Syrian regime engaged in hostilities against both Syrian opposition groups and ISIS and lost and regained control of territory

---

24. Prosecutor v. Thomas Lubanga Dyilo, Case No. ICC-01/04-01/06, Judgment ¶¶ 561-567 (March 14, 2012).

over the course of several years. The Syrian Army is supported by the National Defense Forces, a large pro-government militia.
- Russia, Iran, Hezbollah, and other Shia militias engaged in military operations in support of the Syrian regime.

Opposition Groups in Syria

- Moderate Syrian opposition (Free Syrian Army and many other loosely coordinating secular groups)
- Mainstream Islamic opposition groups, primarily organized as the Islamic Front
- Jihadi groups, primarily the al Qaeda-linked al Nusra Front, which coordinated with some mainstream Islamic opposition groups and clashed with secular opposition groups at times
- Syrian Kurdish militias, principally the People's Protection Units (YPG), working in close coordination with the anti-ISIS coalition

Islamic State of Iraq and Syria (ISIS)

- ISIS grew out of the Iraqi al Qaeda affiliate known as al Qaeda in Iraq and subsequently split with al Qaeda and al Nusra. ISIS drew its rank-and-file fighters from disaffected Sunnis upset with the Shia-led government of Iraq. ISIS took control of large portions of Syrian and Iraqi territory in 2014 and 2015 and launched or took responsibility for attacks against Western coalition partners, including the United States, France, Belgium, and the United Kingdom. By the end of 2017, ISIS had been expelled from all but a small portion of the territory it had once controlled.

The Anti-ISIS Coalition

- The U.S.-led anti-ISIS coalition included, at various times, France, the United Kingdom, Canada, Australia, Bahrain, United Arab Emirates, the Netherlands, Jordan, Saudi Arabia and Turkey.

Questions:

1. What type of conflict took place or is taking place in Syria? Is there one conflict or many parallel conflicts? Who are the parties?
2. The United States and the coalition began airstrikes against ISIS in Syria in September 2014 on the basis of collective self-defense in response to ISIS's advance into Iraq and ISIS attacks on one or more coalition partners. The Syrian government did not consent to the use of force on its territory. Does that affect your analysis of the situation?
3. The United States has provided assistance and training to several moderate opposition groups fighting against the Assad regime. Does that alter your analysis of the conflict? Why or why not?

4. In April 2017, the United States struck the government-controlled Sharyat air base in central Syria in response to a poison gas attack against civilians launched by the Syrian military from that air base.[25] In April 2018, the United States, the United Kingdom, and France struck chemical weapons–related targets near Damascus and Homs in response to a second wave of chemical weapons attacks by the Syrian regime against civilians. Was there an international armed conflict between the U.S. and Syria on either occasion as a result? Between the U.S. and Russia, which had numerous Russian military personnel and aircraft stationed at the Sharyat air base?

QUESTIONS FOR DISCUSSION

1. The situation in the DRC involved many more players, both state and non-state, than even the complex conflict in the Balkans. Interestingly, in its *Decision on the Confirmation of Charges*, the ICC Pre-Trial Chamber had taken a different approach, finding that Uganda's occupation of portions of Ituri turned the conflict into an international armed conflict for that period of time, but that Rwanda's role in supporting the UPC did not constitute overall control as understood in *Tadić*. The Trial Chamber's recharacterization of the conflict did not have any significant effect on the specific charges because use of child soldiers is a war crime in both international and non-international armed conflicts. Does it matter then how the court characterizes the conflict?

2. One complicating factor in the *Lubanga* case was Uganda's occupation of part of the Democratic Republic of the Congo and what effect that occupation had on the characterization of the conflict overall. Occupation is a subset of international armed conflict. If Uganda was occupying part of the DRC's territory, should that mean that any and all armed conflicts taking place in that area of occupation are international armed conflicts, even if such conflict is only between non-state armed groups and does not involve either Uganda or the government of the DRC?

3. In recent years, scholars and policy makers have debated whether the dichotomy between non-international and international armed conflict is as strict as it appears from a first examination of the law. Modern conflicts—like that in the DRC—certainly challenge the easy characterization of conflict into only two different types. Does this pose a problem for the application and implementation of the law? Or can LOAC accommodate

---

25. Luis Martinez, David Caplan & Adam Kelsey, *US Launches Strike on Syria Air Base After Chemical Weapons Attack*, ABCNews.com (Apr. 7, 2017).

multiple variations on a theme, in effect, by looking not just to specific provisions but also to the object and purpose of the law?

4. In a complex conflict such as Syria or the DRC, consider whether there is one "global" conflict with many parties in several different oppositional relationships, or a "mixed" conflict with several parallel conflicts occurring at the same time. The "global" approach considers that "the full body of [LOAC] applicable to [international armed conflicts applies] to all armed groups, state and non-state, in an entire territory that contains multiple conflicts of international and internal origin."[26] The "mixed" approach views each conflict, and the relevant applicable law, separately based on the nature of the parties and the hostilities.[27]

4. *Special Agreements*

Parties to a non-international armed conflict may choose to enter into an agreement to apply provisions of the Geneva Conventions beyond Common Article 3. Common Article 3 even encourages such agreements: "the Parties to the conflict should further endeavour to bring into force, by means of special agreements, all or part of the other provisions of the present Convention." In this way, even though the codified law applicable in non-international armed conflicts is limited, particularly compared to that applicable in international armed conflicts, the Conventions seek ways to expand the applicable law in an *ad hoc* manner as well. Note, however, that parties to a conflict cannot enter into an agreement that would limit the application of the Geneva Conventions in their entirety during international armed conflict. For example, during the conflict in the former Yugoslavia, the factions involved in the conflict in Bosnia negotiated an agreement, with the help of the ICRC, that "committed the parties to abide

---

26. James G. Stewart, *How Would War Crimes Prosecutors Classify the Syrian Conflict(s)?*, Oct. 20, 2016, http://jamesgstewart.com/how-would-war-crimes-prosecutors-classify-the-syrian-conflicts/.

27. *See e.g.*, Prosecutor v. Tadić, Case No. IT-94-1, Decision on Defence Motion for Interlocutory Appeal on Jurisdiction ¶ 72 (Int'l. Crim. Trib. for the Former Yugoslavia Oct. 2, 1995) ("the conflicts in the former Yugoslavia could have been characterized as both internal and international, or alternatively, as an internal conflict alongside an international one, or as an internal conflict that had become internationalized because of external support, or as an international conflict that had subsequently been replaced by one or more internal conflicts, or some combination thereof"); Military and Paramilitary Activities in and Against Nicaragua (Nicar. v. U.S.), Judgment, 1986 I.C.J. 14, ¶ 219 (June 27) ("The conflict between the contras' forces and those of the Government of Nicaragua is an armed conflict which is 'not of an international character.' The acts of the contras towards the Nicaraguan Government are therefore governed by the law applicable to conflicts of that character; whereas the actions of the US in and around Nicaragua fall under the rules relating to international conflict.").

by the substantive rules of internal armed conflict contained in common Article 3 and [the leaders] in addition agreed, on the strength of common Article 3, paragraph 3, to apply certain provisions of the Geneva Conventions concerning international conflicts."[28]

QUESTIONS FOR DISCUSSION

1. Think back to the key role the ICRC plays with regard to humanitarian protection in conflict situations. The ICRC relies on its impartiality and neutrality as essential tools in gaining access to conflict areas, detention facilities, refugee camps, and other locales. For this reason, the ICRC rarely, if ever, comments publicly about warring parties' specific adherence to the law or specific violations. Nonetheless, the ICRC is sometimes accused of "taking sides" or "being political." How do these various concerns affect their work?

2. Is there any other entity (such as a nongovernmental organization, international or regional organization, or other country) that could fill a comparable role in facilitating agreements for the protection of persons and application of LOAC? What would the pros and cons be?

B.   CLASSIFYING GLOBAL CONFLICT WITH TERRORIST GROUPS

In the wake of consistent U.S. statements that it is engaged in an armed conflict with al Qaeda, debates arose early on regarding the nature of that conflict. An international armed conflict under Common Article 2 must be between two High Contracting Parties—i.e., states—which therefore seems to disqualify the conflict with al Qaeda from being an international armed conflict. The next question, therefore, was whether Common Article 3 applied to conflicts with non-state actors occurring across borders or outside the territory of the state party. The argument centered, in many ways, on a textual interpretation of Common Article 3.

Consider the arguments made by different agencies within the U.S. government at the time regarding individuals captured in the course of military action in Afghanistan after the attacks of September 11, 2001. The Department of Justice's Office of Legal Counsel (OLC) argued that the conflict with al Qaeda fell entirely outside the Geneva Convention framework:

> Common article 3 complements common article 2. Article 2 applies to cases of declared war or of any other armed conflict that may arise between two or more of the High Contracting Parties, even if the state of

28. Prosecutor v. Tadić, Decision on Defence Motion for Interlocutory Appeal on Jurisdiction ¶ 73 (Int'l Crim. Trib. for the Former Yugoslavia Oct. 2, 1995).

war is not recognized by one of them. Common article 3, however, covers "armed conflict not of an international character"—a war that does not involve cross-border attacks—that occurs within the territory of one of the High Contracting Parties.

Common article 3's text provides substantial reasons to think that it refers specifically to a condition of civil war, or a large-scale armed conflict between a State and an armed movement within its own territory. First, the text of the provision refers specifically to an armed conflict that a) is not of an international character, and b) occurs in the territory of a state party to the Convention. It does not sweep in all armed conflicts, nor does it address a gap left by common article 2 for international armed conflicts that involve non-state entities (such as an international terrorist organization) as parties to the conflict. Further, common article 3 addresses only non-international conflicts that occur within the territory of a single state party, again, like a civil war. This provision would not reach an armed conflict in which one of the parties operated from multiple bases in several different states. . . .

If the state parties had intended the Conventions to apply to all forms of armed conflict, they could have used broader, clearer language. To interpret common article 3 by expanding its scope well beyond the meaning borne by its text is effectively to amend the Geneva Conventions without the approval of the State parties to the agreements. Further, as we have discussed, article 3 was ratified during a period in which the traditional, State-centered view of international law was still dominant and was only just beginning to give way to a human-rights-based approach. Giving due weight to the state practice and doctrinal understanding of the time, the idea of an armed conflict between a nation-State and a transnational terrorist organization (or between a nation-State and a failed State harboring and supporting a transnational terrorist organization) could not have been within the contemplation of the drafters of common article 3. Conflicts of this kind would have been unforeseen and were not provided for in the Conventions.[29]

In a response memorandum to an earlier draft of the OLC memorandum, the Legal Advisor of the Department of State warned that if the Justice Department and Defense Department position in the memo above were accepted, "[f]or the first time, the United States would deny the applicability of the Geneva Conventions to opposing forces in an armed conflict involving U.S. forces. This would be contrary to consistent U.S. practice aimed at promoting the widest possible application of those conventions." Furthermore, the memorandum explained:

Common Article 3 picks up where Common Article 2 leaves off—that is, with armed conflicts not of an international character. Such conflicts are almost always, and typically so, internal armed conflicts, or civil wars. And

29. Office of Legal Counsel, Department of Justice, Memorandum for Alberto R. Gonzales, Counsel to the President, and William J. Haynes II, General Counsel of the Department of Defense, Re: Application of Treaties and Laws to al Qaeda and Taliban Detainees, January 22, 2002.

indeed, the negotiators of the Geneva Conventions had internal conflicts in mind. Nonetheless, the negotiators did not choose the most available formulations, such as "internal armed conflicts" or "armed conflicts arising solely in the territory of one party." Their formulation indicates a readiness to ensure that all armed conflicts that were not international as between High Contracting Parties would be covered. The combination of Articles 2 and 3 was intended to cover *all armed conflicts.* . . . It would be extremely difficult to defend a U.S. position premised on the notion that the conflict in Afghanistan is not an armed conflict of any sort as contemplated under the Geneva Conventions.[30]

Challenges to the detention regime at Guantanamo began in 2004, thus bringing the question of the nature of the conflict, and the applicable law, to the fore. After ruling that year in *Hamdi v. Rumsfeld* and *Rasul v. Bush* that detainees at Guantanamo do have certain due process rights, the Supreme Court of the United States addressed the nature of the conflict two years later in *Hamdan v. Rumsfeld.* In ruling that the Common Article 3 does apply to the conflict between the U.S. and al Qaeda, the Supreme Court reiterated the Commentary's admonition that the scope of Common Article 3 must be "as wide as possible." To that end, the Court stated:

> The term "conflict not of an international character" is used here in contradistinction to a conflict between nations. So much is demonstrated by the "fundamental logic [of] the Convention's provisions on its application." . . . Common Article 2 provides that "the present Convention shall apply to all cases of declared war or of any other armed conflict which may arise between two or more of the High Contracting Parties." . . . High Contracting Parties (signatories) also must abide by all terms of the Conventions *vis-à-vis* one another even if one party to the conflict is a nonsignatory "Power," and must so abide *vis-à-vis* the nonsignatory if "the latter accepts and applies" those terms. . . . Common Article 3, by contrast, affords some minimal protection, falling short of full protection under the Conventions, to individuals associated with neither a signatory nor even a nonsignatory "Power" who are involved in a conflict "in the territory of" a signatory. The latter kind of conflict is distinguishable from the conflict described in Common Article 2 chiefly because it does not involve a clash between nations (whether signatories or not). In context, then, the phrase "not of an international character" bears its literal meaning. . . .[31]

QUESTIONS FOR DISCUSSION

1. Who has the better argument—the Office of Legal Counsel, the State Department, or the Supreme Court? Does it make sense to fit the conflict within Common Article 3? If so, is there any downside to that approach?

---

30. United States Department of State, Memorandum from William H. Taft IV, State Department Legal Advisor, January 11, 2002.
31. Hamdan v. Rumsfeld, 548 U.S. 557, 630 (2006).

2. Since 1998, it has been the policy of the Department of Defense that the armed forces of the United States "comply with the law of war during all armed conflicts, however such conflicts are characterized, and with the principles and spirit of the law of war during all other operations."[32] Does it matter how the conflict is characterized in a legal sense if policy is to apply the law of international armed conflict in all operations?

3. Another approach is to recognize that the conflict with al Qaeda is an armed conflict, but one that does not fit neatly into the Common Article 2—Common Article 3 framework of the Geneva Conventions.

> Unfortunately, this "either/or" analytical approach fails to acknowledge the possibility [that] an extraterritorial non inter-state combat operation launched by a state using regular armed forces could qualify as an armed conflict triggering law of war regulation. Such an operation would fail to satisfy the requisite "dispute between states" necessary to qualify as an international armed conflict within the meaning of Common Article 2. However, based on the traditional understanding of "non-international" armed conflict—an understanding shared by virtually all scholars and practitioners prior to 9/11—the possibility that an armed conflict falling somewhere between an internal armed conflict and an inter-state . . . armed conflict could theoretically be subject to the regulatory effect of the laws of war was necessarily excluded. Accordingly, these "transnational" armed conflicts fell into a regulatory gap—a gap necessitating application of regulation by way of policy mandate. . . .
>
> . . . The ultimate question, therefore, is whether it is best to continue to try and fit the proverbial square "armed conflict" peg into the round "Common Article 3" hole, or whether the time has come to endorse a new category of armed conflict. . . .
>
> Accordingly, the time has come for states to reject any interpretation of the Common Article 2/3 paradigm that results in denial of applicability of these principles to situations of armed conflict where the regulatory effect of the law is essential to ensure this mitigation of suffering and the disciplined application of combat power. Accordingly, the ongoing evolution in the nature of warfare requires acknowledgment that *any* armed conflict triggers the foundational principles of the laws of war. If this outcome is achieved by characterizing such military operations as "Common Article 3" conflicts that trigger the humane treatment obligation *plus* additional customary law of war principles, the regulatory purpose of the law can be achieved. However, because Common Article 3 conflicts have become generally synonymous with *internal* conflicts, it is more pragmatic to expressly endorse [a] hybrid category of armed conflict: *transnational* armed conflict.[33]

---

32. U.S. Dep't of Defense, Dir. 2311.01E, DoD Law of War Program (2006).

33. Geoffrey S. Corn, Hamdan, *Lebanon, and the Regulation of Hostilities: The Need to Recognize a Hybrid Category of Armed Conflict*, 40 Vand. J. Transnat'l L. 295, 309-310, 329-330 (2007).

4. On September 30, 2011, a U.S. drone killed Anwar al-Awlaki, a radical Muslim cleric in Yemen. Al-Awlaki was a dual Yemeni-American citizen who became a leading proponent and propagandist of violent jihad against the United States. The United States government also stated that he assumed a high-ranking operational role in AQAP and planned or inspired numerous terrorist plots against the United States and U.S. interests, such as the failed "underwear bomber" plot and the failed Times Square bomb attempt. Both before and after al-Awlaki's killing, an extensive debate raged over whether targeting an American citizen overseas—albeit one who is part of a hostile terrorist organization—is lawful. As with other targeted strikes, the United States argued that it has the right to target al-Awlaki as part of an armed conflict or under the international law of self-defense. First, al-Awlaki posed an imminent threat to Americans because of his participation in the plots to blow up Northwest flight 253 to Detroit in December 2009 (the so-called "underwear bomber") and to bomb two cargo planes in 2010. Second, he fought with the enemy in the ongoing armed conflict against al Qaeda. Third, the United States had no feasible way to arrest him in Yemen. Does the U.S. claim that it can target al-Awlaki—or others in Yemen or elsewhere—as part of an armed conflict make sense within LOAC? Who is the enemy—al Qaeda generally or AQAP specifically? Where is the armed conflict—everywhere? Or only in Yemen?

5. In a speech two weeks before the al-Awlaki strike, President Obama's top counterterrorism advisor, John O. Brennan, made the following remarks:

> First, our definition of the conflict. As the President has said many times, we are at war with [al Qaeda]. In an indisputable act of aggression, [al Qaeda] attacked our nation and killed nearly 3,000 innocent people. And as we were reminded just last weekend, [al Qaeda] seeks to attack us again. Our ongoing armed conflict with [al Qaeda] stems from our right—recognized under international law—to self defense.
>
> An area in which there is some disagreement is the geographic scope of the conflict. The United States does not view our authority to use military force against [al Qaeda] as being restricted solely to "hot" battlefields like Afghanistan. Because we are engaged in an armed conflict with [al Qaeda], the United States takes the legal position that—in accordance with international law—we have the authority to take action against [al Qaeda] and its associated forces without doing a separate self-defense analysis each time. And as President Obama has stated on numerous occasions, we reserve the right to take unilateral action if or when other governments are unwilling or unable to take the necessary actions themselves.
>
> That does not mean we can use military force whenever we want, wherever we want. International legal principles, including respect for a state's sovereignty and the laws of war, impose important constraints on our ability to act unilaterally—and on the way in which we can use force—in foreign territories.

Others in the international community—including some of our closest allies and partners—take a different view of the geographic scope of the conflict, limiting it only to the "hot" battlefields. As such, they argue that, outside of these two active theatres, the United States can only act in self-defense against [al Qaeda] when they are planning, engaging in, or threatening an armed attack against U.S. interests if it amounts to an "imminent" threat.

In practice, the U.S. approach to targeting in the conflict with [al Qaeda] is far more aligned with our allies' approach than many assume. This Administration's counterterrorism efforts outside of Afghanistan and Iraq are focused on those individuals who are a threat to the United States, whose removal would cause a significant—even if only temporary—disruption of the plans and capabilities of [al Qaeda] and its associated forces. Practically speaking, then, the question turns principally on how you define "imminence."

We are finding increasing recognition in the international community that a more flexible understanding of "imminence" may be appropriate when dealing with terrorist groups, in part because threats posed by non-state actors do not present themselves in the ways that evidenced imminence in more traditional conflicts. After all, [al Qaeda] does not follow a traditional command structure, wear uniforms, carry its arms openly, or mass its troops at the borders of the nations it attacks. Nonetheless, it possesses the demonstrated capability to strike with little notice and cause significant civilian or military casualties. Over time, an increasing number of our international counterterrorism partners have begun to recognize that the traditional conception of what constitutes an "imminent" attack should be broadened in light of the modern-day capabilities, techniques, and technological innovations of terrorist organizations.[34]

Brennan states that even though the U.S. believes that it is in an armed conflict with al Qaeda, it cannot use military force wherever and whenever it wants. Where do we draw the line? What parameters should frame the question of where a state can use force in a conflict with a transnational terrorist group?[35]

6. During the final years of the Obama Administration, the U.S. issued a Presidential Policy Guidance entitled *Procedures for Approving Direct Action Against Terrorist Targets Located Outside the United States and Areas of Active Hostilities.* In detailing rules and procedures for targeted strikes against terrorist operatives in locations outside areas of recurring combat activity—termed

---

34. Remarks of John O. Brennan, "Strengthening our Security, by Adhering to our Values and Laws," Program on Law and Security, Harvard Law School, Cambridge, Massachusetts, September 16, 2011, http://www.whitehouse.gov/the-press-office/2011/09/16/remarks-john-o-brennan-strengthening-our-security-adhering-our-values-an.

35. *See* Laurie R. Blank, *Defining the Battlefield in Contemporary Conflict and Counterterrorism: Understanding the Parameters of the Zone of Combat,* 39 Georgia J. Int'l L. 1 (2010).

"areas outside active hostilities"—the PPG requires that lethal action in such areas be limited to circumstances in which there is an imminent threat to American lives, where capture is not feasible, and where there is a near certainty of no civilian casualties. Does the imposition of policy-based rules that constrain ordinary LOAC authorities change the nature of the conflict or where it is located? What is the effect of policy on the applicability of the law?

PART III

WHO

CHAPTER 6

COMBATANTS

LOAC's key goals are to regulate the conduct of hostilities and protect persons and objects during conflict. In order to do so, we must know not only whether there is an armed conflict but also who is involved in the conflict. Therefore, once we have analyzed the nature of the conflict and determined that the situation in question does trigger the application of LOAC—such as an international armed conflict, non-international armed conflict, or occupation—the next step is to identify the status of the persons in the zone of combat and their rights, obligations, and privileges. Individual status, whether on the battlefield or off, determines whether a person can lawfully engage in hostilities, is immune from attack, enjoys the privileges of prisoner of war (POW) status upon capture, and a host of other issues. This chapter addresses the legal category of combatants in LOAC, including defining who is a combatant and what rights and privileges combatants have, such as the privileges of combatant immunity and the treatment owed to prisoners of war. The following chapter discusses civilians, the protections they enjoy during armed conflict and the conditions under which they forfeit some of those protections.

A. DEFINITION AND CLASSIFICATION

The Lieber Code explained that "[a]ll enemies in regular war are divided into two general classes—that is to say, into combatants and non-combatants, or unarmed citizens of the hostile government."[1] From a practical standpoint, this classification of persons is essential to the basic spirit and purpose of LOAC: the principle of distinction mandates that persons who are fighting distinguish between those who are fighting and those who are not. Combatant status enables exactly that distinction. In addition, the law of war does not outlaw all killing in war; rather, lawful belligerents do not commit crimes when they engage in lawful killing or destruction of property in the course of hostilities. Understanding who has the right to

---

1. FRANCIS LIEBER, WAR DEPARTMENT, INSTRUCTIONS FOR THE GOVERNMENT OF ARMIES OF THE UNITED STATES IN THE FIELD art. 155 (1863).

bear arms, in essence, requires an understanding of who falls within the category of lawful belligerents—or combatants—and who does not. As the Commentary to the Third Geneva Convention explains, therefore, "[o]nce one is accorded the status of a belligerent, one is bound by the obligations of the laws of war, and entitled to the rights which they confer."[2]

1.   *Combatant Status and the Four-Part Test*

The legal term "combatant" is only applicable in international armed conflict; in non-international armed conflict, LOAC does not include combatant status or prisoners of war. When assessing an individual's status during armed conflict, therefore, the nature of the conflict is the first level of inquiry, as discussed in Chapters 4 and 5. To that end, this discussion of combatant status will focus on the law applicable in international armed conflict and will identify key issues relative to non-international armed conflict as appropriate.

The 1899 Hague Convention established the earliest delineation of the components of combatant status in Article 1 of the attached Regulations Respecting the Laws and Customs of War on Land:

The laws, rights, and duties of war apply not only to armies, but also to militia and volunteer corps fulfilling the following conditions:

- To be commanded by a person responsible for his subordinates;
- To have a fixed distinctive emblem recognizable at a distance;
- To carry arms openly; and
- To conduct their operations in accordance with the laws and customs of war.

As the determining framework for the privileges associated with lawful belligerency—prisoner of war status and combatant immunity, most importantly—these criteria not only reinforce the classic conception and structure of regular armed forces, but also create strong incentives for militia and other volunteer forces to conform to these same structures and conduct in order to qualify for the same privileges.[3]

In the aftermath of World War II, which showed that significant uncertainty remained regarding the status of certain groups, such as resistance fighters, the drafters of the 1949 Geneva Conventions sought to specify clearly the categories of persons entitled to the protections and privileges of combatant status. To that end, Article 4 of the Third Geneva Convention sets forth the categories of persons who qualify for POW status in international armed conflict.

---

2. INT'L COMM. RED CROSS, COMMENTARY ON THE GENEVA CONVENTION (III) RELATIVE TO THE TREATMENT OF PRISONERS OF WAR 46 (Jean de Preux ed., 1960).

3. *See* Sean Watts, *The Notion of Combatancy in Cyber Warfare*, 2012 4TH INTERNATIONAL CONFERENCE ON CYBER CONFLICT 235, 238 (C. Czosseck, R. Ottis & K. Ziolkowski eds., 2012), https://ccdcoe.org/cycon/2012/proceedings/d2r1s10_watts.pdf.

ARTICLE 4 OF THE THIRD GENEVA CONVENTION

A. Prisoners of war, in the sense of the present Convention, are persons belonging to one of the following categories, who have fallen into the power of the enemy:

(1) Members of the armed forces of a Party to the conflict, as well as members of militias or volunteer corps forming part of such armed forces.

(2) Members of other militias and members of other volunteer corps, including those of organized resistance movements, belonging to a Party to the conflict and operating in or outside their own territory, even if this territory is occupied, provided that such militias or volunteer corps, including such organized resistance movements, fulfill the following conditions:

(a) that of being commanded by a person responsible for his subordinates;

(b) that of having a fixed distinctive sign recognizable at a distance;

(c) that of carrying arms openly;

(d) that of conducting their operations in accordance with the laws and customs of war.

(3) Members of regular armed forces who profess allegiance to a government or an authority not recognized by the Detaining Power.

(4) Persons who accompany the armed forces without actually being members thereof, such as civilian members of military aircraft crews, war correspondents, supply contractors, members of labour units or of services responsible for the welfare of the armed forces, provided that they have received authorization, from the armed forces which they accompany, who shall provide them for that purpose with an identity card similar to the annexed model.

(5) Members of crews, including masters, pilots and apprentices, of the merchant marine and the crews of civil aircraft of the Parties to the conflict, who do not benefit by more favourable treatment under any other provisions of international law.

(6) Inhabitants of a non-occupied territory, who on the approach of the enemy spontaneously take up arms to resist the invading forces, without having had time to form themselves into regular armed units, provided they carry arms openly and respect the laws and customs of war.

As the definitional framework for the Geneva Convention focused on protections and treatment due to prisoners of war, Article 4 "is in a sense the key to the Convention."[4] Note that the categories of prisoner of war and combatant are not completely coextensive, however. Two of the categories in Article 4—subparagraphs (4) and (5)—are civilians accompanying and providing services to the armed forces and therefore do not fall into the category of combatants, even though they are entitled to POW status if

---

4. INT'L COMM. RED CROSS, COMMENTARY ON THE GENEVA CONVENTION (III) RELATIVE TO THE TREATMENT OF PRISONERS OF WAR 49 (Jean de Preux ed., 1960).

captured because they are with the armed forces in a formal capacity. Combatants, therefore, are persons falling within subparagraphs (1), (2), (3) and (6) of Article 4.[5]

The first, and most obvious, category of combatants are members of the regular armed forces to a party to the conflict. Any person serving in the military of a High Contracting Party (which today is every country in the world) engaged in a Common Article 2 conflict (i.e., international armed conflict) is therefore a combatant. He or she can lawfully engage in hostilities, is a legitimate target of attack by enemy forces, and is entitled to POW status if captured in an international armed conflict. The other key categories for our analysis are those listed in Article 4(A)(2), (3) and (6) above. The last category in Article 4 is the *levée en masse*, or spontaneous civilian uprising, which dates back to the French Revolution. Although it is rarely applicable in modern conflicts, this provision "affords combatant status to all civilians who spontaneously take up arms to defend their national soil against invaders during the short period of time that a foreign army is advancing onto the territory of their state."[6] Because such persons do not wear a uniform or other distinctive sign, the requirement emphasized in subparagraph (6) that they carry arms openly is of particular importance to ensure that they are recognizable as combatants.[7] Subparagraph (3) refers to members of regular armed forces of a government not recognized by the detaining power and was a direct response to the situation in World War II when some states refused to grant combatant status to units professing allegiance to a government they did not recognize. The classic example was the Free French forces under General Charles de Gaulle, to whom the Germans originally denied POW status under the Franco-German armistice until the intervention of the ICRC.

Militias and other armed groups belonging to a party to the conflict pose the most complicated set of issues. Beyond the preliminary requirements that such militias fight in an international armed conflict and belong

---

5. *See* Additional Protocol I, art. 50(1), explaining that a "civilian is any person who does not belong to one of the categories of persons referred to in Article 4(A)(1), (2), (3) and (6) of the Third Convention and in Article 43 of this Protocol."

6. Robert Kolb & Richard Hyde, An Introduction to the International Law of Armed Conflicts 198 (2008).

7. *See* Trial of Carl Bauer, Ernst Schramek and Herbert Falten, Case No. 45, Judgment (Permanent Mil. Trib. at Dijon Oct. 18, 1945), *reprinted in* U.N. War Crimes Comm'n, III Law Reports of Trials of War Criminals 15, 18-19 (1949) (finding that members of the French resistance—the French Forces of the Interior (FFI)—were entitled to POW status at a minimum, *inter alia*, because they satisfied the requirements of a *levée en masse*: "Inhabitants resorting to arms ['on the approach of the enemy'] would enjoy the rights of belligerents. It is immaterial whether they wear civilian clothes or any other kind of dress. The sole conditions are that they carry arms openly and respect the laws and customs of war when fighting. In our case the German witness Spielberg testified that the three F.F.I. men had committed no violations of the laws of war, and from the fact that they were captured while fighting it follows that they carried arms openly.").

to a party to that conflict, the Third Geneva Convention, like the Hague Convention before it, sets forth four additional criteria such groups must meet before their members are entitled to POW status and thus to be called "combatants." Specifically, such militia must be 1) under responsible command; 2) have a fixed distinctive sign; 3) carry arms openly; and 4) conduct operations in accordance with the laws of war. The second requirement often engenders the most discussion and debate and, as the Commentary explains, could be an armband, "a cap (although this may frequently be taken off and does not seem fully adequate), a coat, a shirt, an emblem or a coloured sign worn on the chest."[8] The key purpose of this criterion is to reinforce the principle of distinction, to ensure that members of such militia groups distinguish themselves from the civilian population.

2. *Classifications in Practice*

Understanding whether individuals are combatants or civilians has ramifications across the targeting, detention and accountability frameworks. First, members of the regular armed forces and other combatants are legitimate targets of attack at all times by dint of their status as soldiers or other combatants. Thus, an American soldier in his barracks is a lawful target, even if he is merely brushing his teeth or engaged in other non-combat activities. This status-based targeting is at the heart of the law of armed conflict framework—the right to use lethal force as a first resort against hostile forces solely on the basis of their status, rather than on the basis of identified hostile conduct. In contrast, as discussed in Chapter 7, civilians are immune from attack and can only be targeted if, and for so long as, they take a direct part in hostilities. Targeting in such situations is therefore conduct-based.

SLEEPING TARGETS?

In 1998, the United States launched Operation Desert Fox—a series of airstrikes aimed at eroding Iraq's weapons of mass destruction capabilities. The United States targeted a number of military and security targets in Iraq that contributed to Iraq's ability to produce, store, maintain and deliver weapons of mass destruction. During the operation, I was approached by a young intelligence officer concerned about the targeting of the barracks of the Special Republican Guard, an elite Iraqi

---

8. INT'L COMM. RED CROSS, COMMENTARY ON THE GENEVA CONVENTION (III) RELATIVE TO THE TREATMENT OF PRISONERS OF WAR 60 (Jean de Preux ed., 1960).

security unit. The officer was troubled by the idea that the Iraqi troops might be asleep and, therefore, present no immediate threat to coalition forces.

Was the officer correct? Did the United States have to wait until the Iraqi troops were "in fighting position" before they struck at the target?
— *Major General Charles Dunlap, Jr., JAGC,*
U.S. Air Force (Ret.), former Deputy Judge Advocate General

Questions of combatant status also arise in the context of detention. Upon capture, an individual will naturally seek to have POW status to enjoy the rights and privileges accorded to such status. The Third Geneva Convention mandates that all persons detained in the course of armed conflict are entitled to an individual determination of their status by a competent tribunal, which can take a variety of forms.

ARTICLE 5 OF THE THIRD GENEVA CONVENTION

The present Convention shall apply to the persons referred to in Article 4 from the time they fall into the power of the enemy and until their final release and repatriation.

Should any doubt arise as to whether persons, having committed a belligerent act and having fallen into the hands of the enemy, belong to any of the categories enumerated in Article 4, such persons shall enjoy the protection of the present Convention until such time as their status has been determined by a competent tribunal.

Members of the regular armed forces enjoy POW status upon capture, a determination that will usually be made with little complication. Notably, Article 5 provides for a presumption of POW status for all persons whose status is uncertain upon capture, until their status is determined. Such persons could be members of irregular militia, civilians claiming to be members of a *levée en masse*, or others accompanying the armed forces, for example. The term "competent tribunal" encompasses a wide range of possible decision-makers, from a military tribunal to a civilian court or more typically one or more military officers at a table set up at the forward detention center or collection point. In Operation Iraqi Freedom, for example, the United States held Article 5 tribunals for thousands of detainees. Typically, the "tribunal" was composed of three military officers, one of whom was a judge advocate — although the presence of a judge advocate is not necessary.[9] Other countries have met this requirement with just one judge advocate acting as the "tribunal." Ultimately, the purpose of the Article 5 tribunal is to ensure that all persons are afforded all appropriate protections under the law and to pass the captured individual up the chain of command to leadership, removing any determination decisions from junior enlisted personnel who theoretically may be more likely to take inappropriate actions.

Well before the 1949 Geneva Conventions, courts were called upon to ascertain the status of persons detained in the course of conflict or terrorist acts. During the U.S. Civil War, for example, questions arose as to the use of military commissions to try individuals captured and suspected of belligerent activity. In *Ex Parte Milligan*, the U.S. Supreme Court overturned the conviction of an Indiana resident convicted by a military commission for "1. 'Conspiracy against the Government of the United States;' 2. 'Affording aid and comfort to rebels against the authority of the United States;' 3. 'Inciting insurrection;' 4. 'Disloyal practices;' and 5. 'Violation of the laws of war.'" Declaring that "[n]o graver question was ever considered by this court, nor one which more nearly concerns the rights of the whole people; for it is the birthright of every American citizen when charged with crime, to be tried and punished according to law,"[10] the Court held that Milligan could not be tried before a military commission because he was a civilian, not a member of the Confederate forces and not involved in hostilities.

Finally, classification as a combatant or a civilian determines whether an individual can be prosecuted for certain acts during wartime and in what type of forum. Combatants enjoy immunity from prosecution under domestic law for lawful belligerent acts committed during conflict—that is, a combatant cannot be prosecuted for the lawful killing of combatants fighting for the other side or for attacks on lawful military objectives. In addition, if a prisoner of war is prosecuted for war crimes, she must be tried in the same forum as the detaining power uses to try members of its own forces. The classification of persons also drives the type of crimes that can be charged in any national or international court. Consider the war crime of unlawful attacks on civilians, for example. One key element of that crime is that the victims were civilians, demonstrating yet another need for effective categorization of individuals in implementing and enforcing the law.

QUESTION FOR DISCUSSION

1. Why are combatants targetable at all times? Consider the basic presumptions underlying LOAC in comparison to the human rights law or law enforcement paradigm. Do the categories of combatants match the

---

9. U.S. Dep't of Army, Reg. 190-8, Enemy Prisoners of War, Retained Personnel, Civilian Internees and Other Detainees paras. 1-6.a, 1-6.c (Oct. 1, 1997).

10. *Ex Parte* Milligan, 71 U.S. 2, 118-119 (1866).

categories of persons you think should be targetable or detainable without charge given the operational realities and fundamental presumptions of armed conflict? Why or why not?

a.   Members of Regular Armed Forces

Milligan involved a civilian unaffiliated with the armed forces. In many cases, however, persons captured are either soldiers or irregular fighters, and the courts or other competent authorities must determine whether they fit within the categories of lawful combatants or, perhaps, have engaged in conduct that causes them to lose otherwise privileged status. As the fundamental covenant set forth in the Hague Convention suggests: in order to enjoy the privileges of LOAC, one must abide by the obligations as well. *Ex Parte Quirin*, a landmark U.S. Supreme Court decision on wartime authorities, addresses this question. In June 1942, eight German soldiers infiltrated the United States to engage in a two-year campaign of sabotage against numerous targets around the United States. Tried by a secret military tribunal, they were convicted of violations of the laws of war and sentenced to death. On appeal to the U.S. Supreme Court, the defendants challenged the jurisdiction of a U.S. military tribunal to try enemy soldiers. In upholding the military commission's jurisdiction and sentence, the Supreme Court declared:

> By universal agreement and practice, the law of war draws a distinction between the armed forces and the peaceful populations of belligerent nations and also between those who are lawful and unlawful combatants. Lawful combatants are subject to capture and detention as prisoners of war by opposing military forces. Unlawful combatants are likewise subject to capture and detention, but in addition they are subject to trial and punishment by military tribunals for acts which render their belligerency unlawful. The spy who secretly and without uniform passes the military lines of a belligerent in time of war, seeking to gather military information and communicate it to the enemy, or an enemy combatant who without uniform comes secretly through the lines for the purpose of waging war by destruction of life or property, are familiar examples of belligerents who are generally deemed not to be entitled to the status of prisoners of war, but to be offenders against the law of war subject to trial and punishment by military tribunals.[11]

QUESTIONS FOR DISCUSSION

1. The Geneva Conventions do not use or include the term unlawful combatant. As used here in *Quirin*, the term refers solely to individuals

---

11. *Ex Parte* Quirin, 317 U.S. 1, 30-31 (1942).

who would qualify as combatants but engage in conduct that causes them to lose the privileges of that status; hence the term "unlawful" before the word "combatant." The term "unlawful combatant" is now commonly used to refer to persons who fight without the right to engage in hostilities; that is, persons who are not part of any regular army or militia and would never qualify as combatants or prisoners of war. What are the consequences of this broadening of the definition or conception of the term?

2. After the Geneva Conventions entered into force, similar questions arose regarding the status of soldiers engaged in spying, sabotage, or hostilities in civilian clothing. In 1966, the courts in Singapore (then part of Malaysia) heard several cases involving attempted sabotage in Malaysia by Indonesian soldiers disguised in civilian clothing. In *Krofan v. Public Prosecutor*, the court analyzed the status of soldiers who "came to Singapore at night in a boat which carried no lights, wearing civilian clothing and carrying explosives with them for the purpose of exploding these explosives in Singapore at a time when there was a state of armed conflict between Indonesia and Malaysia." Applying both customary law and the Geneva Conventions, the court held that "a regular combatant who chooses to divest himself of his most distinctive characteristic, his uniform, for the purpose of spying or of sabotage thereby forfeits his right on capture to be treated as other soldiers would be treated i.e. as a prisoner of war."[12]

3. In late September 2001, U.S. Special Forces entered Afghanistan to link up with the Northern Alliance, the forces fighting against the Taliban regime, in preparation for the launch of Operation Enduring Freedom on October 8, 2001. U.S. soldiers in combat fatigues, buzz cuts, and standard-issue gear certainly would stand out among the local tribesmen and fighters in the mountains of Afghanistan. As a result, these units dressed in the traditional Northern Alliance *pakol* (brown or gray hat) and checkered scarf, grew beards, traveled on horseback, and carried weapons and equipment more similar to their Northern Alliance counterparts. What would have been their status if captured?

4. In June 2014, Ukrainian separatists captured Lieutenant Nadia Savchenko, a Ukrainian Air Force fighter pilot. Lieutenant Savchenko was in uniform and carrying her weapons. Shortly thereafter, the separatists handed her over to Russian agents who transferred her to Russia, where she was arrested and placed in a civilian prison.[13] What was Savchenko's status? Was she a POW?

5. The United States killed General Qassem Soleimani, commander of the Quds force of the Iranian Revolutionary Guard, in a drone strike

---

12. Krofan v. Public Prosecutor, (1966) (Sing.), *reprinted in* 1 MALAYAN L.J. 133 (1967); 52 I.L.R. 497 (1979).

13. Neil Buckley et al., *Russia Releases Ukrainian Pilot Nadia Savchenko*, FIN. TIMES (May 25, 2016); Mark Feygin, *Russia's Illegal Prisoners of War*, WASH. POST (Dec. 24, 2014).

that targeted his convoy as it departed Baghdad International Airport in the early morning hours on January 3, 2020. Iran's top military commander, General Soleimani was also the primary mastermind of Iran's proxy forces throughout the region. The United States asserted that he was planning imminent attacks on U.S. forces and facilities. Was General Soleimani a combatant—and if so, a lawful target of attack—as he traveled from the airport to his next destination? Does the fact that he was in Iraq, not Iran, change your analysis? If the strike initiated an armed conflict between the United States and Iran, is it lawful to target a specific individual or leader (sometimes called a "decapitation strike") as the first act in a conflict?

6. On March 3, 2011, prior to NATO's involvement in the conflict in Libya, news reports surfaced of three Dutch marines captured by Libyan forces during a helicopter evacuation of European civilians trapped in the chaos in Libya. How would you analyze the status of the three marines? What law governs their treatment? Would your answer change if the same event took place after the NATO operation began?

7. On December 17, 1994, U.S. Army Chief Warrant Officer Bobby Hall was shot down over North Korean airspace and captured by North Korean forces. He was held for thirteen days before being released. North Korea stated that it was treating him as a POW. On April 1, 2001, a collision between a U.S. Navy EP-3E ARIES II signals reconnaissance aircraft and a Chinese fighter jet off the coast of China disabled the American plane, forcing it to land without clearance on Hainan Island in China. The crew was taken into custody and detained for ten days. Were they POWs? If not, what would the difference be between them and Chief Warrant Officer Bobby Hall?

8. In 2007, the U.S. military launched the Human Terrain System (HTS), which embedded social scientists with military units on the ground in Afghanistan to help improve commanders' and soldiers' understanding of the local population and culture. According to an early HTS mission statement, this was

> the first time that social science research, analysis, and advising has been done systematically, on a large scale, and at the operational level. We advise brigades on economic development, political systems, tribal structures, etc.; provide training to brigades as requested; and conduct research on topics of interest to the brigade staff.[14]

Were anthropologists and other social scientists embedded with military units through HTS entitled to POW status if captured? Does it matter who captured them or what they were doing or who they were with when captured?

---

14. Beth Schwartzapfel, *Hearts & Minds*, BROWN ALUM. MAG., Sep./Oct. 2010, at 32, 34.

b. Militia and Irregular Fighters

The 1907 Hague Convention accords POW status to militia and other volunteer groups meeting the four requirements of responsible command, distinctive sign, carrying arms openly, and abiding by the laws of war. The treatment of resistance movements and partisans became a challenging issue during World War II, as debates arose over whether they fit within the category of militia. As states were occupied or absorbed into other states,

> national groups continued to take an effective part in hostilities although not recognized as belligerents by their enemies, and members of such groups, fighting in more or less disciplined formations in occupied territory or outside their own country, were denied the status of combatant, regarded as 'francs-tireurs' and subjected to repressive measures.[15]

At Nuremberg, the U.S. Military Tribunal upheld reprisals and other harsh measures against partisans, in keeping with the state of the law pre-Geneva Conventions. In the *Hostages Trial*, high-ranking German officers were charged with reprisal killings in Greece, Yugoslavia, Albania, and Norway. The defendants claimed that the persons killed were guerrillas and partisans and thus not entitled to treatment as POWs. The Tribunal held that civilians and members of partisan bands who do not meet the requirements of international law for lawful belligerent status are not entitled to be treated as prisoners of war, and therefore "no crime can properly be charged against the defendants for the killing of such captured members of the resistance forces. . . ."[16] Nonetheless, the Nuremberg Tribunal also reaffirmed the growing recognition that partisans and resistance fighters could qualify for combatant status in certain circumstances in the *Einsatzgruppen* case, tried the same year. The Tribunal explained:

> Many of the defendants seem to assume that by merely characterizing a person a partisan, he may be shot out of hand. But it is not so simple as that. If the partisans are organized and are engaged in what international law regards as legitimate warfare for the defense of their own country, they are entitled to be protected as combatants. The record shows that in many of the areas where the Einsatzgruppen operated, the so-called partisans had wrested considerable territory from the German occupant, and that military combat action of some dimensions was required to reoccupy those areas. . . . In reconquering enemy territory which the occupant has lost to the enemy, he is not carrying out a police performance but a

---

15. Int'l Comm. Red Cross, Commentary on the Geneva Convention (III) Relative to the Treatment of Prisoners of War 52 (Jean de Preux ed., 1960).

16. United States v. Wilhelm List and Others (The Hostages Trial), Case No. 47, Judgment (U.S. Mil. Trib., Nuremberg, Feb. 19, 1948), *in* VIII Law Reports on the Trials of War Criminals 48, 57 (1949).

regular act of war. The enemy combatants in this case are, of course, also carrying out a war performance. They must, on their part, obey the laws and customs of warfare, and if they do, and then are captured, they are entitled to the status and rights of prisoners of war.[17]

These two cases demonstrate the highly fact-intensive nature of the inquiry into combatant status for irregular troops and others fighting against regular armed forces. In both cases, however, there is the beginning of a recognition that partisans may well fit within the category of irregular militia or other groups potentially entitled to combatant status upon meeting the requisite conditions.

The drafters of the 1949 Geneva Conventions focused significant attention on the question of the status and appropriate treatment of members of resistance movements and how they fit within the category of militia and volunteer groups. Traditionally, partisans were only recognized during a period of invasion and once their country was occupied, the population was obligated to respect the occupier's measures to restore public order and security. Article 4 of the Third Geneva Convention thus represents a major leap forward in the protection of such persons in 1) emphasizing that militia and volunteer corps include organized resistance movements, and 2) according treatment to resistance movements operating inside or outside their own territory, even if the territory is occupied. At the same time, however, the requirements of Article 4(A)(2) remain in effect for such groups, of course, a key step in upholding distinction and other central principles of LOAC.

In *Military Prosecutor v. Kassem*, the Israeli military court in 1969 applied Article 4 of the Third Geneva Convention to determine the appropriate status for members of the Organization for the Popular Front for the Liberation of Palestine captured in the occupied territories and prosecuted for numerous acts of terrorism. The court's ruling highlights Article 4's methodology and key components. First, as the court explained, the question of whether members of a militia can qualify for prisoner of war status only arises in the context of an international armed conflict — a conflict between two states — and when the militia "belong[s] to a Party to the conflict." Second, the court affirmed that "to be entitled to treatment as a prisoner of war, a member of an underground organization on capture by enemy forces must clearly fulfill all the four . . . conditions and that the absence of any of them is sufficient to attach to him the character of a combatant not entitled to be regarded as a prisoner of war." The members of the PFLP did not abide by the four conditions, in particular the last condition in Article 4(A)(2): the obligation to abide by the law of war:

17.   United States v. Otto Ohlendorf et al (Einsatzgruppen case), United States Military Tribunal II, Nuremberg Case No. 9, Judgment (April 9, 1948), *in* IV TRIALS OF WAR CRIMINALS BEFORE THE NUERNBERG MILITARY TRIBUNALS UNDER CONTROL COUNCIL LAW NO. 10 411, 492-493 (1946-1949).

If an armed band operates against the forces of an occupant in disregard of the accepted laws of war . . . then common sense and logic should counsel the retention of its illegal status. . . . The attack upon civilian objectives and the murder of civilians . . . were all wanton acts of terrorism aimed at men, women and children who were certainly not lawful military objectives. . . . Immunity of non-combatants from direct attack is one of the basic rules of the international law of war. The presence of civilian clothes among the effects of the defendants is, in the absence of any reasonable explanation, indicative of their intent to switch from the role of unprotected combatants to that of common criminals.[18]

QUESTIONS FOR DISCUSSION

1. In the early years after 9/11, the first debates centered on whether the Third Geneva Convention applied to the conflict with al Qaeda and, if so, whether al Qaeda operatives were entitled to POW status. The U.S. government concluded that al Qaeda militants did not merit POW status, even if the Third Geneva Convention did apply:

Even if Article 4, however, were considered somehow to [apply], captured members of al Qaeda still would not receive the protections accorded to POWs. Article (4)(2), for example, further requires that the militia or volunteers fulfill the conditions first established by the Hague Convention IV of 1907 for those who would receive the protection of the laws of war. Hague Convention IV declares that the "laws, rights and duties of war" only apply to armies, militia, and volunteer corps when they fulfill four conditions: command by responsible individuals, wearing insignia, carrying arms openly, and obeying the laws of war. . . . Al Qaeda members have clearly demonstrated that they will not follow these basic requirements of lawful warfare. They have attacked purely civilian targets of no military value; they refused to wear uniform or insignia or carry arms openly, but instead hijacked civilian airliners, took hostages, and killed them; they have deliberately targeted and killed thousands of civilians; and they themselves do not obey the laws of war concerning the protection of the lives of civilians or the means of legitimate combat.[19]

This explanation focuses primarily on the final requirement in Article (4)(2), the obligation to comply with the laws of war. Consider as well how al Qaeda members fail to fulfill the first three requirements.

18. Military Prosecutor v. Omar Mahmud Kassem and Others, 42 I.L.R. 470 (Isr. Mil. Ct. 1969).

19. Memorandum for William J. Haynes II, General Counsel, Department of Defense, Application of Treaties and Laws to al Qaeda and Taliban Detainees (Jan. 22, 2002), *reprinted in* THE TORTURE PAPERS: THE ROAD TO ABU GHRAIB 38, 50 (Karen J. Greenberg & Joshua L. Dratel eds., 2005).

2. At first blush, LOAC seems to require that any person who is not a combatant—one who does not qualify for POW status—must be a civilian. Indeed, the very definition of civilian, both in Additional Protocol I and in U.S. doctrine, is any person who is not a combatant. How does the concept of enemy combatant, which drove U.S. detention policy in the so-called "war on terror" for several years after the fall of 2001, fit within this framework? Are enemy combatants civilians?

3. In 2003, the United States trained exiled Iraqis—generally members of the exile opposition group then known as the Iraqi National Congress—and formed them into units called the Free Iraqi Forces. These units wore uniforms similar to those worn by U.S. troops (often a different color camouflage) with a patch noting "FIF" for Free Iraqi Forces:

The FIF troops were deployed in Iraq with some U.S. units in the initial phases of the conflict in 2003. How would you characterize these units? What would be their status if captured by the Iraqi military?

4. In anticipation of possible conflict with Russia, the Estonian Defense League holds training and competitions on "skills useful for partisans," including weapons use, survival skills, IED assembly, and other tactics to use against a potential occupying army. The Estonian government encourages its citizens to be ready to engage in partisan warfare given the fear of Russian incursion and the inability to match Russia in conventional

warfare.[20] If a conflict breaks out, would any Estonians fighting against the Russians in this manner qualify for combatant status? Why or why not?

c. Article 44 of Additional Protocol I

Although numerous conflicts post-9/11, such as those in Afghanistan, Iraq, Lebanon, and Gaza, have triggered extensive discussions about these challenges, it is important to note that it is not a new issue. Any treatment of the Vietnam War, for example, whether news article, book, or movie, highlights the complex nature of the fight against the Viet Cong as they blended into the civilian population and used civilian villages for cover. The rise of guerrilla movements and the wars of decolonization in the decades after World War II served as a catalyst for efforts to expand the notion of lawful combatancy. The nature of conflict changed as the armed struggles for self-determination across Africa and other regions took the form of guerrilla warfare. Under Article 4(A)(2) of the Third Geneva Convention, members of militia or volunteer corps must fulfill the four conditions to be entitled to combatant status, including wearing a fixed insignia and carrying arms openly. These two requirements are the functional embodiment of distinction—both enable fighters on the other side to determine whether one is a fighter or an innocent civilian meriting protection. Yet conflicts around the world involve persons fighting who do not adhere to these obligations. When the international community convened in the mid-1970s to draft the two Additional Protocols, the question of the appropriate parameters for combatant status thus garnered extensive attention. Additional Protocol I sought to address these problems in international armed conflict by relaxing the standards for POW status for persons traditionally understood to be unprivileged belligerents, i.e., persons who engage in hostilities without being entitled to lawful combatant status.

First, Article 43 of Additional Protocol I expands the notion of combatant to include all resistance movements fighting on behalf of a party to the conflict. It is important to note that this formulation is significantly broader than past frameworks—because Additional Protocol I includes wars of national liberation within the regime of international armed conflict, guerrilla movements and insurgents operating on behalf of a party (even though it is not a state) will fall within the notion of combatants. Article 44 then introduces a revised conception of distinction.

---

20. Andrew E. Kramer, *Spooked by Russia, Tiny Estonia Trains a Nation of Insurgents*, N.Y. TIMES.COM (Oct. 31, 2016).

ARTICLE 44 OF ADDITIONAL PROTOCOL I

3. In order to promote the protection of the civilian population from the effects of hostilities, combatants are obliged to distinguish themselves from the civilian population while they are engaged in an attack or in a military operation preparatory to an attack. Recognizing, however, that there are situations in armed conflicts where, owing to the nature of the hostilities an armed combatant cannot so distinguish himself, he shall retain his status as a combatant, provided that, in such situations, he carries his arms openly:

(a) during each military engagement, and

(b) during such time as he is visible to the adversary while he is engaged in a military deployment preceding the launching of an attack in which he is to participate.

Acts which comply with the requirements of this paragraph shall not be considered as perfidious within the meaning of Article 37, paragraph 1(c).

4. A combatant who falls into the power of an adverse Party while failing to meet the requirements set forth in the second sentence of paragraph 3 shall forfeit his right to be a prisoner of war, but he shall, nevertheless, be given protections equivalent in all respects to those accorded to prisoners of war by the Third Convention and by this Protocol.

The goal of these provisions is to encourage greater compliance with the law of war by insurgents by offering them combatant and prisoner of war status. In effect, Article 44(3) removes the obligation to wear a fixed distinctive sign as long as individuals carry their arms openly when visible to the enemy and preparing to launch an attack. The Commentary to Additional Protocol I notes that

[g]uerrilla fighters will not simply disappear by putting them outside the law applicable in armed conflict, on the basis that they are incapable of complying with the traditional rules of such law. Neither would this encourage them to at least comply with those rules which they are in a position to comply with, as this would not benefit them in any way. . . . The text of Article 44 is a compromise, probably the best compromise that could have been achieved at the time. It is aimed at increasing the legal protection of guerrilla fighters as far as possible, and thereby encouraging them to comply with the applicable rules of armed conflict, without at the same time reducing the protection of the civilian population in an unacceptable manner.[21]

Critics of this provision — including, in particular, the United States and other states that have declined to ratify Additional Protocol I — argue

21.   CLAUDE PILLOUD, YVES SANDOZ, CHRISTOPHE SWINARSKI & BRUNO ZIMMERMAN, COMMENTARY ON THE ADDITIONAL PROTOCOLS OF 8 JUNE 1977 TO THE GENEVA CONVENTIONS OF 12 AUGUST 1949 521-522 (1987).

that it undoes one of the fundamental "*quid pro quos* of humanitarian law: in exchange for making yourself more easily distinguishable from the civilian population (and as a result facilitating the ability of an enemy to lawfully attack you), the law granted you the benefit of POW status with its accordant combatant immunity."[22] Numerous countries submitted reservations or formal statements to Additional Protocol I on the basis of this provision, and the U.S. declined to ratify it altogether. In sending Additional Protocol II regarding non-international armed conflict to the Senate for ratification, President Ronald Reagan stated that he could not submit Additional Protocol I as well, partly on the basis of Article 44. In his letter of transmittal to the Senate, President Reagan offered the following reason, among others, why he would not seek ratification of Additional Protocol I:

> Another provision would grant combatant status to irregular forces even if they do not satisfy the traditional requirements to distinguish themselves from the civilian population and otherwise comply with the laws of war. This would endanger civilians among whom terrorists and other irregulars attempt to conceal themselves. These problems are so fundamental in character that they cannot be remedied through reservations, and I therefore have decided not to submit the Protocol to the Senate in any form. . . . In fact, we must not, and need not, give recognition and protection to terrorist groups as a price for progress in humanitarian law.[23]

In essence, Article 44(3) raises significant concerns that it encourages perfidious behavior, allowing combatants to hide within the civilian population for protection. The United Kingdom issued a formal statement upon ratification of Additional Protocol I, noting that the exception in Article 44(3) could only apply in extremely limited situations (notably, occupied territory or wars of national liberation triggering Article 1(4) of AP I). Otherwise, "[w]ide application of this special rule would reduce the protection of civilians to vanishing point. Members of the opposing armed forces would come to regard every civilian as likely to be a combatant in disguise and, for their own protection, would see them as proper targets for attack."[24]

Those who view Article 44(3) as an advance argue that the recognition of the nature of guerrilla warfare makes it more possible for nonstate actors to abide by some aspects of LOAC. In a response to President

---

22. Geoffrey S. Corn, *Thinking the Unthinkable: Has the Time Come to Offer Combatant Immunity to Non-State Actors?*, 22 STAN. L. & POL'Y REV. 253, 274 (2011).

23. *See* Message from the President of the United States transmitting the Protocol II Additional to the Geneva Conventions of August 12, 1949, and Relating to the Protection of Victims of Noninternational Armed Conflicts, Concluded at Geneva on June 10, 1977 (Jan. 29, 1987).

24. UNITED KINGDOM MINISTRY OF DEFENCE, JSP 383: THE JOINT SERVICE MANUAL OF THE LAW OF ARMED CONFLICT 4.5.1 (2004).

Reagan's letter above, a legal advisor from the ICRC penned the following response in an effort to explain how the provision developed and how its key purposes were understood at the time:

> The Diplomatic Conference had to negotiate a solution to an age-old challenge to the law of war: guerrilla warfare. The issue, in short, is the following: there are times in armed conflicts when one side, the weaker side, comes to the conclusion that unless it accepts defeat, it cannot abide by the classic requirements that combatants must fulfill under current law, in particular the requirement to wear a uniform. It was contended that such situations arise mainly during occupations by foreign armed forces or in wars of national liberation. History provides many examples in which guerrilla warfare was the only way for a people to survive and to save its honor. On the other hand, the ability to distinguish between combatants and noncombatants is crucial to the proper functioning of the law of war. The principle of distinction requires that those who may be attacked (because they themselves are exercising the right to attack) must distinguish themselves from those who may not be attacked. Only thus does it become possible, in practical terms, to spare the civilian population from the effects of hostilities.
>
> In other words, the new law recognizes that there are exceptional situations in which combatants may dispense with the necessity of identifying themselves: under certain conditions they may "go underground" or hide in the civilian population, as guerrilleros have done since time immemorial. But they may not fight in civilian disguise! Indeed, in these exceptional circumstances combatants must carry their arms openly and thus distinguish themselves from the civilian population at the very least during the actual military engagement and in the preceding phase of deployment. . . .
>
> There are two crucial notions in Article 44(3) that require some comment. First, what is to be understood by "situations in armed conflicts where, owing to the nature of the hostilities, an armed combatant cannot so distinguish himself"? The legislative history leaves no doubt about the intentions of the lawmakers, and its interpretation does not seem to be controversial: such exceptional circumstances, which allow combatants to invoke the new rule, can arise only in occupied territory and in a war of national liberation. The meaning of the second crucial notion, "military deployment preceding the launching of an attack," is less evident. The United States and the United Kingdom, on signing Protocol I, declared that the phrase means "any movement towards a place from which an attack is to be launched." . . . Nobody can reasonably claim that such an interpretation may further terrorism. The President's letter of transmittal and the State Department's report give the odd impression that the American Government has relinquished this sensible interpretation of the rule and instead now understands it to mean that a combatant must distinguish himself only in the last moment before the shot is fired. It is not helpful for the future of humanitarian law for the United States Government to be on record as adhering to such an interpretation of an

extremely important and delicate rule of Protocol I. A treaty should be understood "in good faith in accordance with the ordinary meaning to be given to the terms of the treaty in their context and in the light of its object and purpose." The purpose of the rules on combatant status is to make the distinction between combatants and civilians possible "[i]n order to promote the protection of the civilian population." The "worst case" approach is not an appropriate way to understand an international agreement as delicate as a humanitarian law treaty.[25]

QUESTIONS FOR DISCUSSION

1. What is the impact of Article 44(3) for the principle of distinction and the implementation of combatant status? Can the principle of distinction survive the application of this provision in practice?

2. Is the ICRC Commentary or the U.S argument more convincing? What does each emphasize in its interpretation of the value or challenges of the provision? Do they highlight different LOAC principles or goals? Does the potential for more groups complying with some of LOAC outweigh the danger of diluting the key protections of distinction? Is that really the trade-off here?

3. Now consider that many current conflicts include large numbers of contractors, mercenaries, and other persons fighting or providing support to those who are fighting, but who are not part of an army or organized armed group. How does the relaxed standard found in Additional Protocol I affect how we think about, establish, and enforce their obligations under LOAC?

4. From the perspective of the soldier who must have clarity and predictability—as much as possible—regarding his or her obligations on the battlefield regarding the mission at hand and the protection of civilians, consider whether Article 44(3) makes those two central tasks (mission fulfillment and protection of civilians) harder to accomplish.

d. Medical and Religious Personnel

Protection for medical personnel dates back to the very first Geneva Convention in 1864, which states that "[h]ospital and ambulance personnel, including the quarter-master's staff, the medical, administrative and transport services . . . shall have the benefit of the same neutrality [as military hospitals and ambulances] when on duty, and while there remain any wounded to be brought in or assisted." These protections appear in

---

25. Hans-Peter Gasser, *The U.S. Decision Not to Ratify Protocol I to the Geneva Conventions on the Protection of War Victims: An Appeal for Ratification by the United States*, 81 AM. J. INT'L L. 912, 918-921 (1987).

subsequent Geneva Conventions and include members of volunteer aid societies and civilian medical personnel. The four 1949 Geneva Conventions build on this long-standing practice and incorporate extensive protections for medical personnel and medical facilities, both in the First Geneva Convention (relating to the wounded and sick) and in the Fourth Geneva Convention (relating to the protection of civilians). These same protections extended to religious personnel, defined in the Geneva Conventions as "chaplains attached to the armed forces."

Beyond these protections, medical and religious personnel have a specific and unique status upon capture. Although they are members of the regular armed forces, they are not prisoners of war. Rather, medical personnel who are exclusively engaged in the medical service of their armed forces and chaplains who fall into the hands of the enemy are both "retained personnel." They nonetheless benefit from all the protections granted to POWs under the Third Geneva Convention. Under the Geneva Conventions, the detaining power must allow these medical and religious personnel to continue to perform their medical or religious duties, preferably for POWs of their own country. When their services are no longer needed for these duties, the detaining power is obligated to return them to their own forces.

WHO IS A MEDIC?

During late 2010 and early 2011, I was assigned to Joint Task Force 435 located at the Detention Facility in Parwan (DFIP), Bagram Air Field, Afghanistan. I was a legal advisor to the Detainee Review Boards held at the DFIP. These Boards consisted of a recorder (analogous to a prosecuting attorney), three field-grade military officers serving as voting Board members, and a personal representative (somewhat analogous to a defense attorney, although a non-JAG officer). All detainees were entitled to a Board every six months to review their detention status.

It was not uncommon that detainees would challenge their detention status based on the general principles of the law of armed conflict, or at least their own idiosyncratic understanding of those principles. As the legal advisor, it was my duty to the Board to provide them guidance on these LOAC concepts, and in particular, whether a detainee's alleged activities qualified him for noncombatant status under international law. For instance, a large number of individuals seemed to believe that being an itinerant preacher of the Koran entitled them to protection under the laws of armed conflict, and there were a surprisingly large number of wrongly detained village principals of girls' schools. There were claims of mistaken identity, undercover activities, double-crosses, tribal disputes and run-of-the-mill local feuds.

One of the most interesting legal issues under the laws of armed conflict that arose from my time as a legal advisor in the Boards concerned the status of medical personnel. In these cases, we would work closely with the International Committee of the Red Cross representative located at the detention facility. It is an inviolable principle of the laws of war that medical personnel have protected status. However, there are reciprocal requirements to abide by certain rules as codified in the Geneva Conventions. One major obvious requirement is the need for a distinctive emblem that would designate the individual as a member of a medical unit, such as a Red Cross or in this setting, a Red Crescent.

In many situations, this is a fairly simple, straightforward factual analysis. In the U.S. and most developed or developing countries, we have specialized medical personnel, wearing distinctive emblems, and organized into separate medical units. They work in hospitals, which have distinctive markings visible from the air, and are geographically separated from combatant units. When these medical personnel travel, it is in ambulances, which are themselves given distinctive markings.

These systems do not necessarily hold true in modern-day Afghanistan. The Taliban have no distinctive military identification for themselves, let alone their medical personnel. There are no hospitals, no ambulances, and no separate medical units. Even Taliban personnel who have some cross-training as medical personnel are not separated from combatants; it is unclear from what I have seen if they know that there is a requirement for nonparticipation in active hostilities.

On these Boards, we did our best to piece together the facts and attempt to determine if captured detainees who claimed this protected status were, in fact, legitimate medical personnel. The International Committee of the Red Cross has attempted to address this problem with the distribution of a type of identity card for Taliban medical personnel; of course, these cards could be subject to abuse or perfidy by the Taliban, but at least it is a start.

— *Captain Benjamin May, JAGC, U.S. Air Force*

QUESTIONS FOR DISCUSSION

1. As stated above, in most militaries, medical personnel wear distinctive emblems and are organized into separate medical units. But what happens when a medic does not wear an emblem of any kind?

2. In the U.S. military, U.S. Navy Corpsmen are assigned to support the U.S. Marines. A Fleet Marine Force (FMF) Corpsman, also known as a "combat medic," typically serves with a Marine unit, in contrast to non-FMF Corpsmen,

who work in hospitals. Corpsmen have a long tradition of serving side-by-side with the Marines and have been decorated for valor more than any other Navy rating (specialty). However, the Corpsman role has evolved over time. In the early days, Corpsmen went into combat with only a medical kit and were not armed; if they did have a weapon, it was only to protect their patients. Today's Corpsman is essentially a Marine infantryman with a medic bag—he or she does not wear any distinctive emblem, and can and will operate any weapon to put rounds down range. The medics in *Saving Private Ryan* and *Band of Brothers* have given way to the next generation of warfare, as seen in *Generation Kill* with Hospitalman Second Class (HM2) Robert "Doc" Bryan. In a Humvee with four men riding inside and a gunner standing up with the top half of his body exposed, each team member must be covering the area in front of him. If one of these team members is a medic, is that a LOAC violation?

B.   COMBATANT PRIVILEGES AND PROTECTIONS

1.   Combatant Immunity

War consists largely of acts that would be criminal if performed in time of peace—killing, wounding, kidnapping, destroying or carrying off other people's property. Such conduct is not regarded as criminal if it takes place in the course of war, because the state of war lays a blanket of immunity over the warriors.

— General Telford Taylor at Nuremberg

One definition of a combatant is a person who has a right to participate in hostilities. This privilege is based on the doctrine of combatant immunity, which mandates that lawful combatants cannot be held criminally responsible for lawful belligerent acts during wartime. Thus, a soldier who kills the enemy in accordance with the law of war (i.e., the person killed was a legitimate target, the attack complied with basic LOAC principles, etc.) is not engaging in what would, under domestic law, be murder. As the Lieber Code stated, "so soon as a man is armed by a sovereign government and takes the soldier's oath of fidelity, he is a belligerent; his killing, wounding, or other warlike acts are not individual crimes or offenses."[26] Indeed, the principle of combatant immunity dates back centuries: the medieval authority Gratian stated, "The soldier who kills a man in obedience to authority is not guilty of murder."[27] The Third Geneva Convention

---

26. FRANCIS LIEBER, WAR DEPARTMENT, INSTRUCTIONS FOR THE GOVERNMENT OF ARMIES OF THE UNITED STATES IN THE FIELD art. 57 (1863).

27. C.23 q.5 c.8; *see also* TELFORD TAYLOR, NUREMBERG AND VIETNAM: AN AMERICAN TRAGEDY 19 (1970).

includes two articles that form the parameters of combatant immunity. Article 87 prohibits sentencing combatants to any penalties other than those provided for members of the armed forces of the detaining power. Article 99 then states that POWs cannot be tried or sentenced for any act that was not forbidden by international law or the law of the detaining power at the time the act was committed. In this way, the law effectively legalizes some acts that would be criminal during peacetime, reflecting the fact that soldiers act as agents of the sovereign state. Persons who do not qualify for combatant status, in contrast, can be prosecuted for acts on the battlefield under domestic law, because they do not enjoy the privilege of combatant immunity.

Combatant immunity will thus be raised as a defense to prosecution in some cases. In order to determine whether the defendant indeed merits combatant immunity, the court must determine whether he or she is a lawful combatant under the definition in Article 4 of the Third Geneva Convention, much like the analysis for POW status. This question arose soon after the 9/11 attacks, when the United States captured an American citizen fighting with the Taliban in Afghanistan. John Walker Lindh, charged with conspiracy to murder U.S. nationals, among other crimes, argued that he was entitled to combatant immunity as a Taliban soldier. Applying Article 4 of the Third Geneva Convention, the court held that Lindh was not entitled to combatant immunity because the Taliban did not satisfy the four conditions for members of a militia to qualify for combatant status: 1) the Taliban did not have the "command structure necessary to fulfill the first criterion, as it is manifest that the Taliban had no internal system of military command or discipline"; 2) "the Taliban typically wore no distinctive sign that could be recognized by opposing combatants"; and 3) "although it appears that Lindh and his cohorts carried arms openly in satisfaction of the third criterion for lawful combatant status, it is equally apparent that members of the Taliban failed to observe the laws and customs of war[,] regularly target[ing] civilian populations in clear contravention of the laws and customs of war."[28]

QUESTIONS FOR DISCUSSION

1. The Court does not focus on whether the Taliban qualify for combatant status as the regular armed forces of Afghanistan. In a memo in response to the January 7, 2002, Office of Legal Counsel memo analyzing the application of the Geneva Conventions to the conflict in Afghanistan, the State Department Legal Advisor stated the following:

---

28. U.S. v. John Walker Lindh, 212 F. Supp. 2d 541, 558 (E.D. Va. 2002).

> The Geneva Conventions are applicable by their terms to the Taliban forces. The GPW is intended to apply in the broadest set of circumstances, with "recognition" of the adversary not a prerequisite to its application. Article 4(A)(3) of GPW specifically applies to "members of the regular armed forces who profess allegiance to a government or an authority not recognized by the Detaining Power." The Taliban qualify as a "government or authority" and, as a category, Taliban forces could meet factual tests of "regular armed forces." In cases of doubt as to specific individuals associated with the Taliban, Article 5 of the Prisoners of War Convention requires that protection be provided until their status has been determined by a competent tribunal. . . .[29]

Which approach is better? Does one approach align more closely with the Geneva Conventions? With the object and purpose of LOAC?

2. What about Taliban fighters captured in 2009? Irek Hamidullin, a former Russian army officer fighting with the Taliban and the al Haqqani network, was captured by Afghan Border Police and U.S. forces after an attack on a border post in Afghanistan. When transferred to U.S. federal court in Virginia and charged with multiple crimes, including attempting to destroy an aircraft of the United States and attempting to kill an officer or employee of the United States, Hamidullin argued he was entitled to combatant immunity and therefore could not be prosecuted for such crimes. Would he qualify for combatant status? Why or why not?[30]

3. Recall Lieutenant Nadia Savchenko, the Ukrainian fighter pilot captured by Ukrainian separatists and transferred to Russian custody. The Russian authorities charged her with murder for acting as an artillery spotter for an attack on a rebel checkpoint inside Ukraine where two Russian journalists were killed; she was convicted and sentenced to twenty-two years in prison before being released in a prisoner exchange.[31] Was the trial in a Russian domestic court lawful?

4. Combatant immunity depends not only on the lawful combatant status of the person in question, but also on the existence of an armed conflict and the commission of the relevant acts during that conflict. Thus, a member of the Revolutionary Armed Forces of Colombia (FARC) was not entitled to combatant immunity as a defense to charges of hostage-taking, material support for terrorists and other crimes arising out of the attack on a small plane, the murder of one American and one Colombian, and the detention of three more Americans in the jungles of Colombia for more than five years. Beyond the fact that the defendant did not qualify

---

29. United States Department of State, Memorandum from William H. Taft IV, State Department Legal Advisor, January 11, 2002.

30. United States v. Hamidullin, No. 15-4788, 2018 WL 1833604 (4th Cir. Apr. 18, 2018).

31. Andrew E. Kramer, *Ukrainian Pilot, Nadiya Savchenko, Is Exchanged for 2 Russian Prisoners*, NYTIMES.COM (May 25, 2016).

for combatant status as a member of the FARC—which fails the fourth criteria of adhering to the law of war—the District Court for the District of Columbia also highlighted the absence of an armed conflict between the United States and the FARC as an immediate bar to any claim of combatant immunity.[32]

2. *Protection for Wounded and* Hors de Combat

Henri Dunant's horror at the carnage and suffering of the wounded during the Battle of Solferino launched the corpus of LOAC dedicated to the protection of wounded, sick, and shipwrecked combatants. LOAC mandates three categories of obligations: respect, protection, and care. Respect requires that injured personnel not be targeted or made the object of any assault whatsoever. Thus, "belligerents must not engage in hostile acts against such persons, which includes a requirement to abstain from threats, intimidation and harassment directed against those placed *hors de combat*."[33] Second, persons who are *hors de combat* must be protected from the dangers of war—such as the obligation to keep prisoners of war away from the combat zone, as discussed below. Finally, the obligation to care for the wounded means that belligerent parties must search for and collect wounded and sick personnel regardless of nationality or other criteria. These obligations are set forth in the First and Second Geneva Conventions.

After the Falklands War, for example, a British military surgeon was not only awarded the Order of the British Empire for his work saving lives under enemy fire—but was also awarded the equivalent honor in Argentina, "for saving the lives of their soldiers too."[34] As Surgeon-Captain Rick Jolly explained afterwards, "[o]ur attitude was simple . . . to treat the injured Argentinians in a way we would like to be treated," telling the story of an Argentine fighter pilot the British navy rescued from the South Atlantic's freezing waters. "He was coming in to attack one of our ships when he got a missile right up his tail pipe. He ejected at the last minute, badly broke his knee and was fished out of the water. When he came to us I said to him, 'Welcome, you're a pilot, I'm an aviation doctor and we admire you. You've got this broken knee and we are going to try to mend it.'"[35]

---

32. U.S. v. Pineda, 2006 U.S. Dist. LEXIS 17509, at *11 (D.D.C. Mar. 28, 2006).

33. ROBERT KOLB & RICHARD HYDE, AN INTRODUCTION TO THE INTERNATIONAL LAW OF ARMED CONFLICTS 189 (2008).

34. Will Payne & Andrew Dagnell, *Incredible Story of the Falklands War Hospital that Treated Victims from Both Sides of Conflict*, MIRROR ONLINE (Mar. 12, 2012).

35. *Id.*

News reports from the 2003 war in Iraq highlighted the same emphasis on the provision of medical treatment based only on need, regardless of which side the injured person fought on. For example, at one base in Iraq, doctors treating a wounded Iraqi insurgent—shot while planting a roadside bomb (IED)—administered unit after unit of blood. When they sent out a call for volunteer blood donors, dozens of soldiers lined up, even though the recipient of the blood donation was, a few minutes before, attacking them. As one soldier said, "A human life is a human life."[36]

QUESTIONS FOR DISCUSSION

1. In July 1950, during the Battle of Taejon, North Korean troops set up a roadblock, cutting off the American 34th Infantry Division's supply line and preventing them from evacuating their wounded from a mountaintop. As the division retreated, twenty or thirty wounded soldiers too hurt to walk were left behind with a U.S. medic and U.S. Military Chaplain Herman G. Felhoelter, who was identified by a white cross on his uniform. Although the medic was able to escape, soldiers from the NK 3d Division shot Felhoelter in the back while he prayed over the wounded and then killed all the remaining wounded. The incident, known as the "Medic-Chaplain Massacre," was one of several incidents that prompted a U.S. investigation into North Korean war crimes.

2. "Double-tapping" describes the practice of shooting wounded or apparently dead enemy fighters to ensure that they are dead and not feigning death. Although not new, double-tapping received news coverage in Iraq after reports of U.S. soldiers and Marines allegedly shooting wounded insurgents. One account from a battle in 2007 in Iraq sets the scene for such situations:

> Stark saw a wounded insurgent on the ground with a hand behind his back. "Turn on your stomach!" Gilbertson, the gunner, yelled, intending to detain the man. But the insurgent hurled a grenade at the truck. The pin failed, and Gilbertson shot him with his machine gun. The Humvee lurched forward, and Stark saw an insurgent curled in the fetal position but still moving. Wary after the grenade incident, Gilbertson recalled, he pulled out his 9mm pistol and shot the man, who then detonated his suicide vest. Flesh and ball bearings splattered the right side of Stark's Humvee, which was lifted off its wheels and thrown down, causing its third flat tire. After that, the soldiers said, they decided to kill any wounded insurgents able to move.[37]

In other cases, the knowledge that a day or two before, wounded insurgents pretending to be dead had shot and killed a fellow soldier or Marine will

36. Robert Bazell, *A Human Life Is a Human Life*, NBC NEWS (Mar. 2, 2007).
37. Ann Scott Tyson, *A Deadly Clash at Donkey Island*, WASH. POST (Aug. 19, 2007).

lead others to "double tap" in order to prevent the same thing from happening again.[38] LOAC is clear that the wounded and others who are *hors de combat* are protected from attack and that the wounded must be cared for, regardless of whether they are the enemy. Is a wounded fighter who can still attack considered to be *hors de combat*?

3. Article 41(2) of Additional Protocol I states that a "person is *hors de combat* if: . . . (c) he has been rendered unconscious or is otherwise incapacitated by wounds or sickness, and therefore is incapable of defending himself; provided that in any of these cases he abstains from any hostile act and does not attempt to escape." A person who is wounded and still actively fighting is not *hors de combat* under this definition. Note that the protection for those who are *hors de combat* is framed as such in Article 41(1): "[A] person who is recognized or who, in the circumstances, should be recognized to be *hors de combat* shall not be made the object of attack." The determination, like many others in LOAC, is not entirely subjective but depends on what is reasonable in the circumstances. Thus, delivering an extra bullet to the head of every wounded person because one might be feigning death or serious wounds in order to attack again is unlawful.

4. By the same token, the individual right of self-defense protects the right to defend against an enemy who is feigning death or serious wounds for hostile purposes (which also constitutes the war crime of perfidy, discussed below in Chapter 10). In a critical battle to save the U.S. forces conducting a fighting retreat from the Chosin Reservoir in the Korean War, the Marines of Fox Company faced this exact scenario:

> Out of the corner of his eye Bonelli saw a Chinese soldier who was playing dead at the top of the hill rise up from a pile of frozen corpses and point an automatic weapon. Before Bonelli could react another Marine cut him in half with a BAR. For Captain Barber, this presented a moral dilemma. He was aware that Chinese battlefield strategy included playing dead in order to lure a Marine into proximity and then kill him, and he considered this premeditated murder. But did this tactic give him the right, in order to protect his men, to summarily execute wounded enemy soldiers? His company was taking a severe beating on this hill, and he could not afford to lose even one more Marine in this way. If the enemy surrendered that was one thing — although how many men he could spare to guard prisoners was another complicating factor he'd have to figure out later. For now, however, he issued orders to put all "dead" and wounded Chinese out of their misery. Such were the exigencies of war and the burden of command in combat.[39]

---

38. *TV Report Says Marine Shot Prisoner*, Assoc. Press (Nov. 16, 2004).

39. Bob Drury & Tom Clavin, The Last Stand of Fox Company: A True Story of U.S. Marines in Combat 114 (2009).

When is double-tapping, also sometimes called a "dead check," a LOAC violation and when is it reasonable conduct on the battlefield? Can it ever be lawful? What if a unit has a policy of double-tapping?

WHO TO PROTECT?

I was commanding an armored cavalry troop conducting search and destroy operations just south of the DMZ in Quang Tri Province during the Vietnam War. We were engaged in a firefight with small North Vietnamese Army (NVA) elements for about half a day. After the battle, we determined that there was at least one if not more North Vietnamese soldiers still hiding in a large patch of tall elephant grass. I told our Kit Carson Scout attached to our troop (former North Vietnamese soldier who had deserted and rallied to the South) to call out saying that anyone hiding in the grass should come out with hands raised and without weapons.

After yelling this several times, we received one response from an NVA soldier (we could not see him) who said that he was wounded and could not come out. His voice sounded strong. Through the interpreter, I instructed him to crawl out. I did not want to send any dismounted soldiers into the tall grass because of the possibility that the hiding soldier would shoot. This had happened to us before when a wounded NVA soldier had shot and killed one of our men as we were attempting to capture him.

After a pause, with no further response from the NVA soldier, through the interpreter I told him that if there was no attempt by him in the next five minutes to come out I would send our armored vehicles into the tall grass (these were Armored Cavalry Assault Vehicles, modified/tracked M113s), and there was a good possibility that he would be run over. When he did not come out, I sent two vehicles into the grass (our men were protected inside the vehicles, but because their hatches would be closed, they had limited visibility). One vehicle did in fact run over the NVA soldier. That surely killed him. Not sure whether he would have died from his gunshot wounds.

— U.S. Army officer

1. Was this a LOAC violation? What if the NVA soldier was faking being wounded in order to attack soldiers who came to help him? How could the commander make that decision?
2. Should the nature of combat in a particular conflict—such as the particular known tactics of the enemy—affect the application of LOAC principles and obligations on the ground? What are the consequences of allowing such flexibility? Of not allowing it?

3. *Respect for the Dead*

Honorable treatment does not end with the death of an enemy fighter. LOAC allows for searching of the dead for intelligence purposes but not for personal gain. It also contains several prescriptions designed to ensure dignified treatment and appropriate burial or disposal of the dead. The First and Second Geneva Conventions obligate parties to an international armed conflict to "search for the dead and prevent their being despoiled."[40] This duty applies in non-international armed conflict as well, as enshrined in Article 8 of Additional Protocol II. The requirement to treat the dead with respect fits directly within LOAC's core principle of humanity and the overarching concept of human dignity that accompanies the principle of humanity. Furthermore, the prohibition on mistreatment of the dead is one of the most ancient prescriptions in LOAC's long pedigree. For example, in depicting the Trojan War, Homer's *Iliad* offers some of the bloodiest battle scenes a reader may find, a veritable catalogue of the horrors of war. Yet Homer hints strongly at customs mandating respect for the bodies of the dead, particularly after the great battle between Hector and Achilles. Achilles kills Hector, ties his body to his chariot, and drags it around. The gods, however, protect Hector's body from desecration, and Homer's condemnation is stern: "nothing is gained thereby for his good, or his honour."[41] The reader is left with little doubt that Achilles' conduct is dishonorable and violates existing codes of conduct.

Unfortunately, modern wars have brought new renditions of these violations, such as scenes of American servicemen being dragged through the streets of Mogadishu in 1993.

> They were dragging the body on the street when an outnumbered and outgunned squad of Saudi Arabian soldiers drove up on vehicles. Even though they were with the UN, the Saudis were not considered enemies of the Somalis, and even on this day their vehicles were not attacked. What the Saudis saw made them angry. "What are you doing?" one of the soldiers asked. "We have Animal Howe," answered an armed young Somali man, one of the ringleaders. "This is an American soldier," said another. "If he is dead, why are you doing this? Aren't you a human being?" the Saudi soldier asked the ringleader, insulting him. One of the Somalis pointed his gun at the Saudi soldier. "We will kill you, too," the gunman said. People in the back of the crowd shouted at the Saudis, "Leave it. Leave it alone! These people are angry. They might kill you."
>
> "But why do you do this?" the Saudi persisted. "You can fight, but this man is dead. Why do you drag him?" More guns were pointed at the Saudis. The disgusted [Saudi] soldiers drove off.[42]

---

40. First Geneva Convention, art. 15; Second Geneva Convention, art. 18.
41. HOMER, THE ILIAD, 24:52.
42. MARK BOWDEN, BLACK HAWK DOWN 292 (1999).

It is easy to see how the failure to uphold these obligations not only undermines core values, but also can endanger the broader mission. In January 2012, a video of four U.S. Marines urinating on the corpses of three dead Taliban fighters circulated around the world. Provoking anger and drawing condemnation in Afghanistan and elsewhere, the video sparked fears of rising anti-American sentiment, especially at a time of tense relations between the United States and Afghanistan. Notwithstanding immediate and firm U.S. condemnation of the desecration of the bodies, the "Taliban and Mr. Karzai each pointed to the images as evidence of American brutality, a message with broad appeal in Afghanistan."[43] In this case, the violation not only served to renew the motivation of the enemy forces (the Taliban) to fight, but also weakened relations with the United States' partners in the war in Afghanistan (the Karzai government).

QUESTIONS FOR DISCUSSION

1. On May 2, 2011, the United States killed Osama bin Laden in a raid on his hideout in Abbottabad, Pakistan. Bin Laden's body was photographed for identification purposes (blood and saliva samples were collected as well), immediately flown out of Pakistan, transferred to a U.S. military vessel, prepared according to Islamic tradition, and then buried at sea. Was this the correct treatment under LOAC? The United States sought to end the matter as quickly as possible and with no possibility of a martyr's grave or other future rallying point. Was this an acceptable reason for burial at sea? What else could or should the United States have done with the body? In comparison, when U.S. forces killed Saddam Hussein's sons during the war in Iraq, they turned the bodies over to the family members for burial. Should the United States have sought out a member of bin Laden's family to take the body?

2. Burying the dead can often pose logistical challenges and tactical dangers. For example, one U.S. veteran of the Vietnam War remembers:

> As I mentioned, this was a day-long action at platoon level where two of my three platoons kept making contact with and engaging small size North Vietnamese forces. I don't recall the exact number, but by about 4 pm in the first platoon area we had 6 or so NVA KIA [Killed in Action]. The few we captured (some wounded) had been flown out by helicopter.
>
> We usually buried any killed NVA in shallow graves. Because it was getting late in the day I decided that it was too late to take time to bury them. We always went into a night defensive position in troop strength. I had to get all three platoons together into a circular perimeter and find

43. Graham Bowley & Matthew Rosenberg, *Video Inflames a Delicate Moment for U.S. in Afghanistan*, N.Y. Times (Jan. 12, 2012).

a relatively large flat area that had no dead space out in front. (We did have three D-9 bulldozers with us that could help flatten an area pretty quickly.) It would take us about two hours to prepare the defensive position which included putting out concertina wire, registering artillery fires, selecting night observation positions outside of the wire for dismounted OPs, putting out trip flares, emplacing claymore mines, digging fighting positions and mounting M-60 machine guns in them, digging a mortar pit and dismounting one of our 4.2-inch mortars and getting illumination rounds ready. Whenever we took fire at night the first thing done was for the mortar crews to put up illumination. We also had to eat. All of this had to be completed before dark.

I have since wondered whether not properly burying the NVA dead that afternoon (it would not have taken long using a bulldozer) was some sort of violation. The next day we went back to the area where we left the unburied dead and found that they had been buried during the night in a shallow grave covered by a black tarp and a little dirt. The only thing I can think happened is that NVA left in the area buried them during the night and then moved out of the area as we made no more contact.

Was the failure to bury the dead a violation of LOAC? Or was the obligation simply to respect and protect from despoliation? How should this commander have weighed the obligations towards the dead NVA and the force protection needs of his unit? What if they started burying the dead bodies and came under fire? Could they leave them there?

3. The Marines of Fox Company in Korea were undermanned and in constant danger of being overrun. The men needed more protection from the constant onslaught of advancing Chinese soldiers:

> Men hopped from their foxholes and began dragging Chinese bodies to use as sandbags. Although there were fewer enemy dead on the west slope of the hill, Bob Kirchner managed to find half a dozen corpses to pile in front of his hole, including the two men he had bayoneted and the bugler Sergeant Komorowski's grenade had beheaded. To his everlasting sorrow, he also dragged Roger Gonzales's body out of his hole and added it to the stack. He was sure the dead Marine would have understood; Kirchner certainly would have if the tables were turned.[44]

Can dead combatants ever be used for tactical advantage? Does it matter if it is defensive or offensive?

4. In October 2011, Libyan leader Muammar Qaddafi was found in a drainpipe after an attack on his convoy as it fled from Sirte, his hometown. He was then either killed in the course of a gunfight or killed once in the hands of his captors. The treatment of Qaddafi's body in the immediate

---

44. BOB DRURY & TOM CLAVIN, THE LAST STAND OF FOX COMPANY: A TRUE STORY OF U.S. MARINES IN COMBAT 129-130 (2009).

aftermath of his death in October 2011 was in some ways eerily reminiscent of the scene described above from *The Iliad*: by most accounts, he was stripped to the waist, tied to some sort of vehicle, and dragged through the streets. Desecrating his body and dragging it around constituted a violation of Common Article 3 (and the Fourth Geneva Convention, if it had been an international armed conflict) and a war crime as defined by customary international law and the Rome Statute of the International Criminal Court.

C.   *DETENTION IN INTERNATIONAL ARMED CONFLICT: PRISONERS OF WAR*

Under the POW detention regime in the Third Geneva Convention and earlier customary and conventional law, preventing a return to hostilities is the underlying purpose of detention. "The object of capture is to prevent the captured individual from serving the enemy. He is disarmed and from then on he must be removed as completely as practicable from the front, treated humanely and in time exchanged, repatriated or otherwise released."[45] In particular, POWs are not liable to prosecution for their lawful wartime acts, which reinforces the fact that they are not held as a form of punishment for engaging in combat. Thus, the detention of a combatant has only "one purpose: to preclude the further participation of the prisoner of war in the ongoing hostilities. The detention is not due to misgivings about previous reprehensible conduct on the part of the prisoner of war, and he cannot be prosecuted and punished 'simply for having taken part in hostilities.'"[46] In effect, "it should always be remembered that prisoners of war are not convicted criminals in need of corrective training or punishment,"[47] but are simply held so as to remove them from the battlefield.

The essentially non-punitive nature of POW detention and the fundamental purpose of removing combatants from the battlefield forms the foundation for the comprehensive protective framework that the Third Geneva Convention establishes for POW treatment. Thus, the regulations set forth—and any restrictions on POWs—serve this protective purpose and seek to balance the respective interests of the POW, the detaining state, and the POW's state. As the International Military Tribunal for the Far East

---

45. *In re Territo*, 156 F.2d 142, 145 (9th Cir. 1946).

46. YORAM DINSTEIN, THE CONDUCT OF HOSTILITIES UNDER THE LAW OF INTERNATIONAL ARMED CONFLICT 35 (2010) (citing A. ROSAS, THE LEGAL STATUS OF PRISONERS OF WAR: A STUDY IN INTERNATIONAL HUMANITARIAN LAW APPLICABLE IN ARMED CONFLICTS 82 (1976)). *See also* Third Geneva Convention, arts. 87, 99.

47. UNITED KINGDOM MINISTRY OF DEFENCE, JSP 383: THE JOINT SERVICE MANUAL OF THE LAW OF ARMED CONFLICT 8.1.1 (2004).

(Tokyo War Crimes Trial) explained, the "responsibility for the care of prisoners of war and of civilian internees . . . is not limited to the duty of mere maintenance but extends to the prevention of mistreatment."[48]

1.   Treatment and Protection of POWs

Customary principles and values regarding the treatment of POWs find direct reflection in the Third Geneva Convention's detailed framework for the protection of prisoners of war in the modern law of war. The starting point is the basic rule in Article 13 mandating humane treatment at all times:

> Prisoners of war must at all times be humanely treated. Any unlawful act or omission by the Detaining Power causing death or seriously endangering the health of a prisoner of war in its custody is prohibited and will be regarded as a serious breach of the present Convention. In particular, no prisoner of war may be subjected to physical mutilation or to medical or scientific experiments of any kind which are not justified by the medical, dental or hospital treatment of the prisoner concerned and carried out in his interest.
>
> Likewise, prisoners of war must at all times be protected, particularly against acts of violence or intimidation and against insults and public curiosity.

More specifically, the Third Geneva Convention requires that detaining powers take proactive steps to protect POWs from the hazards of combat. Articles 19 and 23 mandate that POWs be held "far enough from the combat zone for them to be out of danger" and cannot be "detained in . . . areas where [they] may be exposed to the fire of the combat zone." Reprisals against POWs are also prohibited because, as the Commentary states, among other reasons, "the feelings which lie behind such practices are absolutely contrary to the spirit of the Geneva Conventions."[49] Furthermore, detaining powers retain a measure of responsibility for the treatment of POWs even after they are transferred to another power, demonstrating the strong protective underpinnings of POW custody. The Commentary thus explains that "it was never the intention of the authors of the Convention thereby to relieve the transferring Power of all responsibility with regard to the prisoners who are transferred."[50]

48. The Tokyo War Crimes Trial, Judgment (Int'l Mil. Trib. for the Far East November 1948), *reprinted in* THE LAW OF WAR: A DOCUMENTARY HISTORY 1037, 1040 (L. Friedman ed., 1972).

49. INT'L COMM. RED CROSS, COMMENTARY ON THE GENEVA CONVENTION (III) RELATIVE TO THE TREATMENT OF PRISONERS OF WAR 142 (Jean de Preux ed., 1960).

50. *Id.* at 137.

This notion of an extensive framework relying not just on the specific provisions of the Third Geneva Convention but also on the spirit and purpose of the Conventions as a whole can be seen in the comprehensive applicability of POW protections under customary international law as well. Customary international law does not only apply to the broad strokes of POW treatment and detention, therefore, but also to most of the obligations and privileges set forth in the Third Geneva Convention, as shown in the work of the Eritrea-Ethiopia Claims Commission (EECC). The EECC was established pursuant to the December 2000 Agreement ending hostilities between Eritrea and Ethiopia and was tasked with deciding all claims relating to the conflict and/or arising out of international humanitarian law, including the Geneva Conventions. In deciding Eritrea's claim for loss, damage and injury suffered as a result of Ethiopia's treatment of Eritrean prisoners of war, the EECC relied primarily on customary international law, because Eritrea had not ratified the Geneva Conventions until August 2000, just before the end of the war. Addressing a wide range of complaints regarding Ethiopia's treatment of Eritrean POWs, the EECC concluded that:

- "[F]requent physical abuse of Eritrean POWs by their captors" violated international law and "at a minimum, Ethiopia failed to take effective measures, as required by international law, to prevent such abuse."
- Ethiopia was "liable for inhumane treatment during evacuations from the battlefield as a result of its forcing Eritrean POWs to go without footwear during evacuation marches," because "although the harshness of the terrain and weather on the marches to the camps may have been out of Ethiopia's control, to force the POWs to walk barefoot in such conditions unnecessarily compounded their misery."
- Programs of "enforced indoctrination" and the segregation of various groups of POWs from each other constituted mental and emotional abuse in violation of the Geneva Conventions.
- Sub-standard health conditions and severely restricted diets leading to malnutrition violated customary international law.[51]

QUESTIONS FOR DISCUSSION

1. The Third Geneva Convention does allow the detaining power to employ POWs in various forms of labor, both within POW camps and outside in ordinary industries. Why does the law allow for detaining powers to use the labor of POWs? Does that comport with the basic premises and

---

51. Eri.-Eth. Cl. Comm'n, Prisoners of War–Eritrea's Claim 17 (2005).

purposes of the Third Geneva Convention? Why might labor be a positive aspect of detention for POWs? Any such labor may not have any direct connection to the war effort or military operations, however. For example, numerous German military officers were convicted, both at Nuremberg and in national courts, for the use of POWs as slave labor connected to the war effort, including working in the metallurgical industry, building ammunition depots, coal mines, and the armament industry.[52] Similarly, the Hague Regulations and the Third Geneva Convention forbid compelling POWs to serve in the armed forces of a hostile party.

2. LOAC — both in the Geneva Conventions and in customary law — seeks to protect and ensure the dignity of POWs. POWs are also protected from "public curiosity," meaning that photographing POWs, parading them in the streets or broadcasting of videos is prohibited. For example, a U.S. Military Commission convicted a German general for war crimes for exposing POWs to insults and violence:

> Some time in January, 1944, Field Marshal Kesselring, commander-in-chief of the German forces in Italy, ordered the accused who was commander of Rome garrison to hold a parade of several hundreds of British and American prisoners of war in the streets of the Italian capital. This parade, emulating the tradition of the triumphal marches of ancient Rome, was . . . to bolster the morale of the Italian population in view of the recent allied landings, not very far from the capital. The accused ordered the parade which took place on 2nd February, 1944. 200 American prisoners of war were marched from the Coliseum, through the main streets of Rome under armed German escort. The streets were lined by forces under the control of the accused. The accused and his staff officers attended the parade. According to the Prosecution witnesses (some of whom were American ex-prisoners of war who had taken part in the march), the population threw stones and sticks at the prisoners, but, according to the defence witnesses, they threw cigarettes and flowers. . . . A film was made of the parade and a great number of photographs taken which appeared in the Italian press under the caption "Anglo-Americans enter Rome after all . . . flanked by German bayonettes." The accused . . . stated that the march was to quell rumours of the German defeat and to quieten the population of Rome, not to scorn or ridicule the prisoners. . . .
>
> The march through Rome was a violation of Article 2, sub-paragraph 2 of the [1929] Geneva Convention which says "They" (prisoners of war)

---

52. France, General Tribunal at Rastadt of the Military Government for the French Zone of Occupation in Germany, *Roechling case*, Judgment, 30 June 1948; Netherlands, Temporary Court-Martial of Makassar, *Koshiro case*, Judgment, 5 February 1947; The I.G. Farben Trial, United States Military Tribunal, Nuremberg, X Law Reports of Trials of War Criminals, United Nations War Crimes Commission 1 (1949); Trial of Alfred Krupp et al., United States Military Tribunal, Nuremberg, X Law Reports of Trials of War Criminals, United Nations War Crimes Commission 69 (1949).

"shall at all times be humanely treated and protected particularly against acts of violence, from insults and from public curiosity." The charge was obviously framed in accordance with this regulation. There can be no doubt that the prisoners of war were exposed to public curiosity. . . . The court found that the accused in whose care the prisoners were at the time, and who had ordered and attended the march, was guilty of a war crime.[53]

What purpose do these protections serve? How do these protections and prohibitions carry out and fulfill the central purposes of LOAC? American aviators were marched through the streets of Hanoi and endured similar abuse. However, what about the three U.S. soldiers who were captured by Serb forces in Macedonia along the Yugoslav border in 1999 and then broadcast on state television — is this the same as marching them through the streets? Is it in violation of LOAC? Or was being put on TV "good news" for those service members and their families because the international community now knew they were alive, making it much more difficult for the Serbs holding them to kill them or make them disappear?

3. Would release of photographs for purposes of revealing prisoner abuse and deterring future abuse of prisoners fall within the protection against "public curiosity"? Consider the object and purpose of the public curiosity provision as well as the broader mandate to ensure humane treatment.[54]

4. Can POWs be held as hostages? Or is it only civilians who become hostages when held for bargaining or similar purposes? Hostage-taking violates the Geneva Conventions and the Rome Statute of the International Criminal Court. As the ICRC explains, hostage-taking occurs when "[a] person has been captured and detained illegally [and a] third party is being pressured, explicitly or implicitly, to do or refrain from doing something as

53. United States v. Maelzer, Case No. 63 (U.S. Military Comm. Sept. 9, 1946), XI Law Reports of Trials of War Criminals, United Nations War Crimes Commission 53, 54-55 (1949).

54. *See* ACLU v. Dep't of Defense, 543 F.3d 59, 90 (2d Cir. 2008) (release of photos of detainee abuse at Abu Ghraib, with identifying features obscured, "is consistent with the purpose of furthering humane treatment of captives, which animates Article 13 of the Third Geneva Convention and Article 27 of the Fourth Geneva Convention. . . . Release of the photographs is likely to further the purposes of the Geneva Conventions by deterring future abuse of prisoners. To the extent the public may be 'curious' about the Army photos, it is not in a way that the text of the Conventions prohibits; curiosity about 'enemy prisoners being subjected to mistreatment through the streets,' . . . is different in kind from the type of concern the plaintiffs seek to inspire. . . . Heightened public awareness of events depicted in the Army photos—some of which appear to violate the Geneva Conventions—would serve to vindicate the purposes of the Geneva Conventions without endangering the lives or honor of detainees whose identities are protected.").

a condition for releasing the hostage or for not taking his life or otherwise harming him physically."[55] The ICTY held that detaining POWs in this manner does constitute hostage-taking, in an opinion that directly affirmed the protective purposes of the POW regime in the Third Geneva Convention:

> [T]he protection of POWs is covered by an extensive net of provisions within the Third Geneva Convention which, read together, lead to the conclusion that any conduct of hostage-taking involving POWs could not but be in violation of the Third Geneva Convention. . . . The lawfulness of detention does not depend on the circumstances in which any individual comes into the hands of the enemy but rather depends upon the whole circumstances relating to the manner in which, and reasons why, they are held. Thus, the unlawfulness of detention relates to the idea that civilians or those taking no active part in hostilities are taken or held hostage not to ensure their safety or to protect them, but rather to gain an advantage or obtain a confession.[56]

DETENTION IN THE FIELD

During the Iraq war of 2003, a patrol is operating in the forward areas and captures an enemy prisoner who is carrying important documents. His status is unclear as he was not in any recognizable uniform and refuses to reveal his identity. The patrol commander considers that he may have further intelligence to reveal and needs to be removed from the area of hostilities to the rear areas where he can be subject to further interrogation. The patrol is being resupplied by a helicopter, which carries sensitive equipment.

   The prisoner has been transferred to a rear holding area where he is to be interrogated. In addition to restraining the prisoner, the senior interrogator asks that the prisoner remain subject to sight deprivation

55. *ICRC Position on Hostage-taking*, 846 INT'L REV. RED CROSS 467 (2002); *see also* United Nations Preparatory Commission for the International Criminal Court, Report of the Preparatory Commission for the International Criminal Court, Addendum, Part II, Finalized Draft Text of the Elements of Crimes Art. 8(2)(a)(viii) War Crime of Excessive Incidental Death, Injury, or Damage (2 Nov. 2000); KNUT DÖRMANN, ELEMENTS OF WAR CRIMES UNDER THE ROME STATUTE OF THE INTERNATIONAL CRIMINAL COURT: SOURCES AND COMMENTARY 124-27 (2005). The elements of the crime of hostage taking draw heavily from the International Convention Against the Taking of Hostages, Nov. 17, 1979, 1316 U.N.T.S. 205. *See* Prosecutor v. Sesay, Kallon and Gbao (RUF case), Case No. SCSL-04-15-A, Appeals Judgment, ¶ 579 (Oct. 26, 2009).

56. Prosecutor v. Radovan Karadžić, Case No. IT-95-5/18-AR72.5, Decision on Appeal of Trial Chamber's Decision on Preliminary Motion to Dismiss Count 11 of the Indictment, ¶¶ 21, 65 (Int'l Crim. Trib. for the Former Yugoslavia July 9, 2009).

in order to "soften him up" for interrogation. The interpreter recognizes the prisoner as someone from his own village and also worries that he might identify the interpreter. The interpreter fears for the safety of his family who are still in the village, under enemy control.

The only means available to achieve sight deprivation is hessian sacks because blacked out goggles have not been issued. The only way to get the goggles is to wait for the next supply helicopter a day later, increasing the risk to the prisoner by requiring him to remain in the area of hostilities and delaying the opportunity to subject him to in-depth interrogation.

Do the unit's procedures comply with LOAC? What are the commander's obligations if he does not know whether the prisoner qualifies for POW status? Is sight deprivation acceptable in this situation? How should the commander balance the prisoner's rights with regard to treatment and protection? How should he or she factor in the need to protect the unit? The village and its inhabitants?

— *Colonel Charles Garraway, U.K. Army Legal Services (Ret.)*

2. *Denial of Quarter*

Two names from World War II stand out in any discussion of murder of POWs: Malmedy and Biscari.

[On December 18, 1944,] the following terse message was received from the U.S. First Army by Twelfth Army Group and Supreme Headquarters, Allied Expeditionary Force (SHAEF):

SS Troops vicinity L8199 captured U.S. soldier, traffic M.P. with about two hundred other U.S. soldiers. American prisoners searched. When finished, Germans lined up Americans and shot them with machine pistols and machine guns. Wounded informant who escaped and more details follow later.

Thirty Americans would eventually be identified as having escaped from a field southwest of the Baugnez crossroads from which the bodies of 72 GIs would later be recovered.

`. . .

[S. Sgt. Henry Roy Zach of the U.S. Thirty-second Armored Regiment testified at trial that he and his small unit were captured by German Waffen-SS on December 17, 1944. They accompanied the German column until it joined up with a larger force at the Baugnez crossroads.] As the column halted, Zach and his companions were hustled off the tanks on which they had been riding and directed to join a large group of American prisoners . . . already standing in a field along the road. . . . All the prisoners seemed to have their hands raised, but there was considerable "shifting and jostling" so that Zach, to his good fortune as events would prove, found himself in the rear of the group. . . . He was never-theless able to see a tracked vehicle mounting a heavy gun maneuvering on the road and seemingly attempting to depress its weapon in order to cover the prisoners. . . . Shortly thereafter, heavy automatic weapons fire was opened on the prisoners, although Zach was unable to see where the firing had originated. He immediately fell to the ground as bullets thud-ded into earth and flesh. . . . After what seemed to Zach a quarter-hour but which was almost certainly a shorter period, the firing stopped and the German vehicles could be heard moving off a few minutes later. Zach dramatically described the subsequent movements on two occasions of small numbers of Germans through the field finishing off survivors.[57]

In the end, a "total of 81 Americans were killed in the single worst atrocity against U.S. troops during World War II in Europe."[58] After the war, the perpetrators were tried in the U.S. Military Tribunals at Dachau and were convicted, with many receiving the death penalty and the rest life imprison-ment or lengthy prison terms.

Over a year earlier, U.S. servicemen engaged in comparable atrocities at the Battle of Biscari, after "the early morning of July 14 witnessed the start of a sharp struggle for control of the airfield north of Biscari":[59]

[O]n 14 July 1943, troopers serving in the 180th Infantry Regiment overcame enemy resistance and . . . had gathered together a group [of] forty-eight prisoners. Forty-five were Italian and three were German. Major Roger Denman, the Executive Officer in the 1st Battalion, 180th Infantry, ordered a noncommissioned officer (NCO), thirty-three-year-old SGT Horace T. West, to take the POWs "to the rear, off the road, where they would not be conspicuous, and hold them for questioning."

After SGT West, several other U.S. Soldiers assisting him, and the forty-eight POWs had marched a mile, West halted the group. He then directed that "eight or nine" POWs be separated from the larger group and that these men be taken to the regimental intelligence officer (S-2) for interrogation. . . .

West then took the remaining POWs "off the road, lined them up, and borrowed a Thompson Sub-Machine Gun" from the company first sergeant (1SG). When that NCO asked West what he intended to do, "SGT West replied that he was going to kill the 'sons of bitches.'" After telling the Soldiers guarding the POWs to "turn around if you don't want to see it," SGT West then singlehandedly murdered the disarmed men by shooting them.

---

57. JAMES J. WEINGARTNER, CROSSROADS OF DEATH: THE STORY OF THE MALMÉDY MASSACRE AND TRIAL 65, 69-70 (1979).

58. *The Malmedy Massacre*, HISTORY PLACE (1997), http://www.historyplace.com/worldwar2/timeline/malmedy.htm.

59. James J. Weingartner, *Massacre at Biscari: Patton and an American War Crime*, 52 THE HISTORIAN 24, 27, 29 (1989).

[In a second incident,] twenty-five year old CPT John T. Compton, then in command of Company A, 180th Infantry, was with his unit in the vicinity of the same Biscari airfield. After the Americans encountered "sniping . . . from fox holes and dugouts occupied by the enemy," a Soldier managed to capture thirty-six enemy soldiers. When CPT Compton learned of the surrender, he "immediately had a detail selected" from his company to execute the POWs. . . .

The following day, after knowledge of Compton's execution of the enemy travelled up the chain of command, LTG Bradley personally questioned the junior officer about his actions. As CPT Compton told Bradley, he "had been raised fair and square as anybody else and I don't believe in shooting down a man who has put up a fair fight." But, said Compton, these enemy soldiers "had used pretty low sniping tactics against my men and I didn't consider them as prisoners."[60]

In two separate court-martial proceedings, Sergeant West was convicted and sentenced to life imprisonment; Captain Compton was acquitted.

The responsibility to care for POWs dates back to well before the 1949 Geneva Conventions or even the 1929 Geneva Convention relative to the Treatment of Prisoners of War. During the U.S. Civil War, both sides treated captured enemy personnel as prisoners of war. One infamous prisoner of war facility was the Andersonville prison, where the Confederate Army held tens of thousands of captured Union soldiers in a facility only suitable for holding a few thousand prisoners. The commandant of the Andersonville prison, Major Henry Wirz, was charged and prosecuted for mistreatment, torture, and murder of prisoners.

QUESTIONS FOR DISCUSSION

1. The prohibition on killing prisoners dates back to long before the Geneva Conventions and the modern law of war. Why does LOAC prohibit killing of prisoners?

2. The Malmedy massacre helped stiffen the resolve of the U.S. forces during the Battle of the Bulge. Word had spread quickly among the troops that surrender equaled death. The killings helped the men endure subfreezing temperatures and constant shelling. This is a perfect example of the effects of violating LOAC. If a nation treats enemy prisoners in accordance with LOAC, the enemy is more likely to surrender, as they did in the 1991 Gulf War by the thousands—sometimes to unmanned aerial vehicles (now commonly called drones) and television camera crews. The end result is fewer casualties, both among friendly forces and possibly civilians, and a quicker path to an end of the conflict.

---

60. Fred L. Borch, *War Crimes in Sicily: Sergeant West, Captain Compton, and the Murder of Prisoners of War in 1943*, Army Law. 1-2 (March 2013). *See also* Rick Atkinson, The Day of Battle: The War in Sicily and Italy, 1943-1944 118-121 (2008).

> ## SCREEN SHOT!
>
> In *The Great Escape*, a movie based upon actual events during World War II, Allied POWs dig tunnels and seventy-six prisoners escape from *Stalag Luft III*, a German POW camp one hundred miles southeast of Berlin. All but three of the POWs are captured in an attempt to reach Switzerland, Sweden, and Spain. Although the Germans return some of the POWs to the camp, they execute fifty of them.
>
> 1. Is it a violation of LOAC to shoot escaping POWs?
> 2. Once the POWs were recaptured, what were the German authorities' obligations to the prisoners? Could they execute them after re-capture?

3. Protecting Powers and Monitoring Mechanisms

The law of international armed conflict establishes a framework for external monitoring and implementation of the obligations of states. The concept of a "protecting power," which first appeared in a treaty in the 1929 Geneva Convention relative to the Treatment of Prisoners of War, relies on neutral third states to protect the rights and duties of parties to international armed conflicts. A Protecting Power is a state asked by another state to safeguard its interests and the interests and rights of its nationals within a third state. This concept has a lengthy history, dating back to the sixteenth century. Large states, which had embassies in other countries, would often protect the interests of smaller states, generally for reasons of prestige and power. According to the Commentary, over time, many small and medium-sized states "asked the great Powers to undertake the protection of their interests in countries where they themselves were not represented."[61] Protecting Powers played an important role in World War I, gaining access, along with the ICRC, to prisoner of war camps and sometimes even civilian detention facilities. However, they had no access to camps or individuals in occupied territory. By World War II, critical deficiencies in the existing Protecting Power system were evident, namely the lack of obligatory supervision and participation in the Protecting Power system.

The drafters of the 1949 Geneva Conventions sought to remedy these problems by ensuring that the Protecting Power system would be obligatory, with no reliance on requests for cooperation and no debates regarding the

---

61. INT'L COMM. RED CROSS, COMMENTARY ON THE GENEVA CONVENTION (IV) RELATIVE TO THE PROTECTION OF CIVILIAN PERSONS IN TIME OF WAR 81 (Oscar M. Uhler & Henri Coursier eds., 1958).

nature of collaboration. In accordance with articles 8 and 9 of the Third and Fourth Geneva Conventions, respectively, the parties are obligated to appoint a Protected Power at the beginning of a conflict and, if the appointment is accepted, permit the state to perform its role. In articles 126 and 143, respectively, the Third and Fourth Geneva Conventions state specifically what is required to facilitate the role of the Protecting Power: "[r]epresentatives or delegates of the Protecting Powers shall have permission to go to all places where protected persons are, particularly to places of internment, detention and work." The territorial state cannot prohibit or interfere with such visits except for reasons of imperative military necessity and as a temporary, exceptional measure. In perhaps the only example of the Protecting Power system being used in the past half-century, during the Falklands conflict, Switzerland acted for the United Kingdom and Brazil acted for Argentina.

The ICRC has the same rights and access under the Third and Fourth Geneva Conventions during international armed conflict and plays an essential role in monitoring implementation of LOAC during armed conflict, particularly with regard to prisoners of war and other detainees. In particular, given that the Protecting Power system has barely, if ever, been used in the years since World War II, "[t]he role of the ICRC has taken on an increasing importance in the light of the failure of states to appoint protecting powers."[62] The law of non-international armed conflict provides almost no obligatory framework for outside monitoring, providing only in Common Article 3 that "[a]n impartial humanitarian body, such as the International Committee of the Red Cross, may offer its services to the Parties to the conflict." These conflicts are, naturally, the ones in which the ICRC's role of ensuring humanitarian protection for victims of war, humane treatment for detainees, and compliance with the law is most essential. Through careful impartiality, the ICRC helps to protect its access and influence, the keys to its ability to fulfill its mission.

4.   Trial and Punishment of POWs

The Third Geneva Convention establishes comprehensive procedures and protections for POWs in the event that the detaining state seeks to prosecute them for crimes committed during the conflict or during captivity. Most importantly, under the principle of combatant immunity explained above, LOAC proscribes the trial of a lawful combatant for lawful acts of war committed within the context of an armed conflict—thus, for instance, a

---

62.   UNITED KINGDOM MINISTRY OF DEFENCE, JSP 383: THE JOINT SERVICE MANUAL OF THE LAW OF ARMED CONFLICT 16.13.1 (2004).

combatant may not be prosecuted for murder for the otherwise lawful act of killing an enemy combatant. As the Lieber Code provides, "[s]o soon as a man is armed by a sovereign government and takes the soldier's oath of fidelity, he is a belligerent; his killing, wounding, or other warlike acts are not individual crimes or offenses."[63] Similarly, Article 43(2) of Additional Protocol I affirms that combatants "have the right to participate directly in hostilities." Consider how the following protections set forth in the Third Geneva Convention preserve and reinforce the principle of combatant immunity:

> **Article 87:** Prisoners of war may not be sentenced by the military authorities and courts of the Detaining Power to any penalties except those provided for in respect of members of the armed forces of said Power who have committed the same acts.
>
> **Article 99:** No prisoner of war may be tried or sentenced for an act which is not forbidden by the law of the Detaining Power or by international law, in force at the time the said act was committed.

Combatants are, however, subject to trial for war crimes, other pre-capture criminal acts unrelated to the conflict, or crimes committed during captivity. For example, in 1945, fourteen German POWs were executed by hanging for murdering other POWs during captivity in U.S. POW camps. Five soldiers of the celebrated Afrika Korps were convicted at court-martial of killing another POW at a camp in Oklahoma. Seven U-boat submariners and sailors were similarly convicted for the murder of a fellow POW at the Papago Park, Arizona camp, and two more German soldiers were convicted of killing a POW in a South Carolina camp. In all three cases, the murdered POWs were suspected by their fellow POWs of disclosing military secrets to the Americans and attacked for being traitors. All fourteen defendants were hanged at Ft. Leavenworth and are buried there.[64] This episode remains one of few examples of POWs tried for crimes committed during captivity; note that the accused were tried in a U.S. court-martial, just as American soldiers would be.

---

63. Francis Lieber, War Department, Instructions for the Government of Armies of the United States in the Field art. 57 (1863). In rejecting a superior orders defense with respect to unlawful acts, the Nuremberg Military Tribunal affirmed this rule, stating that it "cannot be questioned that acts done in time of war under the military authority of the enemy cannot involve criminal liability on the part of officers or soldiers if the acts are not prohibited by the conventional or customary rules of war." United States v. Wilhelm List and Others (The Hostages Trial), Case No. 47, Judgment (U.S. Mil. Trib., Nuremberg, Feb. 19, 1948), in VIII Law Reports on the Trials of War Criminals 50 (1949).

64. *See Questions Surround Executions of WWII POWs*, Spartanburg-Herald J. (Oct. 18, 1992).

If POWs are to be prosecuted for war crimes, they must be tried in the same forum (e.g., a court-martial) and only for the same offenses for which soldiers of the detaining state would likewise be tried.[65] These protections are essential to guard against show trials or arbitrary treatment and sentencing. One of the most important protections appears in Article 85 of the Third Geneva Convention, which mandates that "Prisoners of war prosecuted under the laws of the Detaining Power for acts committed·prior to capture shall retain, even if convicted, the benefits of the present Convention." In essence, this provision prohibits the detaining state from disregarding its obligations with respect to POWs simply by categorizing any or all members of the enemy forces as war criminals. During the Vietnam War, the North Vietnamese pronounced that captured American pilots were not prisoners of war; rather, that "the bombing attacks constitute crimes for which these prisoners will have to answer before the courts and that the Third Geneva Convention (prisoners of war) is consequently not applicable to them."[66] The United States firmly rejected this assertion, based on the key advances of the Third Geneva Convention (to which North Vietnam was a party).[67] Although post–World War II tribunals did not provide the benefits of POW status and protections to soldiers prosecuted for war crimes and such protection was not enshrined in the 1929 Geneva Convention on POWs,[68] the drafters of the Third Geneva Convention deliberately included the rule in Article 85 in order to fill this evident gap in protection for POWs. As the Commentary to the Third Geneva Convention explains:

> The International Committee of the Red Cross followed with some concern the course of justice in the various countries where proceedings were instituted against prisoners of war in respect of offences committed prior to their capture. In its opinion, it was dangerous not to afford to the accused the guarantees provided by an international convention which . . . do not exceed those accruing from the procedural laws of most States. The International Committee's concern was increased by the fact that, in most countries, proceedings against war criminals were based on special *ad hoc* legislation and not on the regular penal legislation of the countries concerned. Furthermore, it seemed illogical and unjust to prejudge the guilt of the accused,

65. Third Geneva Convention, arts. 84, 87.

66. Int'l Comm. Red Cross, *The International Committee and the Vietnam Conflict,* 6 INT'L REV. RED CROSS 399, 403 (1966).

67. In a communication to the ICRC, the U.S. Assistant Legal Advisor for Far Eastern Affairs at the State Department declared that "[n]o nation has reserved the right to nullify its obligations under the Convention by a simple declaration that it regards members of the armed forces of an opposing party in an international conflict as war criminals." George Aldrich, *Entitlement of American Military Personnel Held by North Viet-Nam to Treatment as Prisoners of War Under the Geneva Convention of 1949 Relative to the Treatment of Prisoners of War,* July 13, 1966, X WHITEMAN'S DIGEST 231, 232-33 (§ 7).

68. *See e.g.,* Matter of Yamashita, 327 U.S. 1, 21, 22, 24 (1946).

since they were deprived of the protection of the Convention before actually having been found guilty of war crimes. [Any denial of protection] can only be applicable after a court has given its finding. For under modern law, the accused is presumed innocent until his guilt is proved.[69]

In noting that Article 85 guarantees POWs prosecuted and convicted for pre-capture acts all the protections in the Third Geneva Convention — assistance of counsel, right to call witnesses, receive and send correspondence, and receive relief parcels, visits from the ICRC, and so forth — the Commentary notes that "[t]his is where the present Article makes the most important innovation as compared with the corresponding provisions of the 1929 Convention."[70]

QUESTIONS FOR DISCUSSION

1. What would be the consequence of allowing states to prosecute POWs for participation in hostilities alone? How would that affect the relationship between the law of war and the *jus ad bellum*?

2. In 1916, U.S. President Woodrow Wilson sent forces commanded by General John J. Pershing into Mexico to capture Pancho Villa after he led a raid on the town of Columbus, New Mexico, killing sixteen Americans. In the aftermath of hostilities between American forces and local forces in Mexico, including the government's armed forces, Texas prosecuted four captured Mexican soldiers for the murder of William Oberlies, a corporal in the U.S. Army. If you were the attorney for the four defendants what would you argue?

Noting that the situation between the U.S. and Mexico amounted to "a state of warfare," the court reversed the convictions on the grounds that, as soldiers, the defendants were operating under military command and not acting of their own volition and therefore were not subject to the jurisdiction of the courts of Texas simply for fighting in the conflict.[71]

---

69. INT'L COMM. RED CROSS, COMMENTARY ON THE GENEVA CONVENTION (III) RELATIVE TO THE TREATMENT OF PRISONERS OF WAR 414–15 (Jean de Preux ed., 1960).

70. *Id.* at 423.

71. Arce v. State, 202 S.W. 951 (Tex. Crim. App. 1918). Regarding the existence of the conflict and the application of the law of war, the court noted that the Judge Advocate of the U.S. Army explained in an official opinion:

> It is thus apparent that under the law there need be no formal declaration of war, but that under the definition of Vattel a state of war exists, so far as concerns the operations of the United States troops in Mexico, by reason of the fact that the United States is prosecuting its rights by force of arms and in a manner in which warfare is usually conducted. The statutes which are operative only during a period of war have been interpreted as relating to a condition and not a theory. . . . I am, therefore, of the opinion that the actual conditions under which the field operations in Mexico are being conducted are those of actual war. That within the field of operations of the expeditionary force in Mexico it is a time of war within the meaning of the fifty-eighth article of war. *Id.*

3. The Judicial Committee of the Privy Council, the highest court of appeal for United Kingdom overseas territories and Crown dependencies, provided a succinct explanation for combatant immunity in overturning the convictions of members of the Indonesian armed forces for possession of arms and explosives and other domestic crimes during the conflict between Indonesia and Malaya:

> The Act is an Internal Security measure, part of the domestic law, and not directed at the military forces of a hostile power attacking Malaysia. It would be an illegitimate extension of established practice to read section 58 as referring to members of regular forces fighting in enemy country. Members of such forces are not subject to domestic criminal law. If they were so subject they would be committing crimes from murder downwards in fighting against their enemy in the ordinary course of carrying out their recognised military duties.[72]

5.   *Repatriation*

A fundamental feature of the POW regime is that POWs must be repatriated as soon as possible after the end of active hostilities. Once the fighting is over, the justification for holding enemy personnel—removing them from the battlefield—no longer exists. The Third Geneva Convention then sets forth detailed procedures for such repatriation, including the restoration to POWs of any articles of value and provisions for POWs to take their personal effects with them upon repatriation or have them forwarded. Before the 1949 Geneva Conventions, the framework for repatriation left too much discretion in the hands of the detaining state. Article 75 of the 1929 Geneva Convention stated, "[w]hen belligerents conclude an armistice convention, they shall normally cause to be included therein provisions concerning the repatriation of prisoners of war." States were able to take advantage of the vague language in this provision and keep POWs for longer than anticipated in the spirit of the law. For this reason, the Third Geneva Convention of 1949 specifically talks of repatriating POWs "without delay." In many cases, the parties to a conflict will negotiate specific agreements regarding the repatriation of prisoners at the end of the hostilities. For example, at the end of the conflict between India and Pakistan in the early 1970s, which resulted in the creation of Bangladesh as an independent state, the three countries signed an agreement (the Delhi Agreement) providing for three-way repatriation of prisoners. Over 300,000 prisoners

---

72. Public Prosecutor v. Oie Hee Koi and connected appeals, Judicial Committee of the Privy Council (U.K.), 4 Dec. 1967 [1968], A.C. 829.

were repatriated in 1973 and 1974 under the terms of the agreement.[73] Similarly, at the end of the conflict in the former Yugoslavia, the Dayton Agreement included an agreement between the parties on prisoner exchanges, including provisions on cooperation with the ICRC, lists of prisoners for exchange, prohibitions on reprisals, and obligations to cooperate with the ICTY.[74] Although the POW protections and repatriation obligations apply solely in international armed conflict, these types of special agreements can play a significant protective role in non-international armed conflict by providing a framework for the safe return of detainees from both sides.

QUESTIONS FOR DISCUSSION

1. For the release and repatriation of POWs, how soon after the end of hostilities is "without delay"? Consider the logistics involved in arranging for repatriation, including transport for sick or wounded POWs, safe and orderly movement of POWs, and arrangements for reception upon repatriation. Recognizing that the repatriation obligation is not instantaneous, "repatriation [nonetheless] should occur at an early time and without unreasonable or unjustifiable restrictions or delays."[75]

2. The agreement that brought an end to the fighting in the Korean War required that all POWs be repatriated regardless of the hundreds of war crimes investigations underway. Should war crimes allegations supersede the requirement to repatriate?

3. During the same conflict, tens of thousands of Chinese and North Koreans in U.N. POW camps refused repatriation. Is there a requirement that POWs return to their country of origin?

4. Iran and Iraq fought a brutal war from 1980 to 1988. Both sides delayed and obstructed efforts to repatriate POWs at the end of the conflict, and it was not until 2003 that most POWs had been either repatriated or registered as refusing to go back to their country of origin. Early in the repatriation process, efforts began with swaps of injured and sick POWs, but often faltered on accusations by one side that the other was not fulfilling its obligations under the relevant bilateral arrangements.[76] Can repatriation obligations rest on reciprocity in this way under LOAC or does the law—either the letter or the spirit of the law—require parties to repatriate POWs regardless of the other party's actions?

---

73. Agreement on the Repatriation of Prisoners of War and Civilian Internees, Bangl.-India-Pak., 74 I.L.M. 501 (1974).

74. General Framework Agreement for Peace in Bosnia and Herzegovina, Annex 1A: Agreement on the Military Aspects of the Peace Settlement, art. IX, Dec. 14, 1995, 35 ILM 75 (1996).

75. Eri.-Eth. Cl. Comm'n, Prisoners of War–Eritrea's Claim 17, 65 (2005).

76. *Iran Suspends POW Exchange; Iraq Retaliates*, Los Angeles Times (Nov. 28, 1988).

CHAPTER 7
CIVILIANS

The fundamental distinction between combatant and civilian goes far back into history. In the most basic sense, the principle that some persons are not involved in fighting and thus merit some protection from the effects of war traces its roots back to ancient civilization. Although those protections now may seem minimal, they do demonstrate a long-standing recognition that not all persons constitute an enemy to be killed.[1] In medieval times, this concept was an underpinning of the code of chivalry, which set forth rules for those who were fighting and restricted war only to those authorized to fight on behalf of the sovereign.[2] Nonetheless, until 1949, law of war treaties and conventions focused primarily—if not exclusively—on the conduct of war and the treatment of prisoners of war, the wounded, and other members of the armed forces. The Lieber Code and the Hague Conventions had mandated the differentiation between combatants and civilians, but had not provided any comprehensive protections directly for civilians.

One of the great advances of twentieth-century treaty law is the Fourth Geneva Convention, a multilateral treaty creating a legal regime to protect civilians in times of war. Under the Fourth Geneva Convention, LOAC mandates protection of all civilians and also provides comprehensive protection in particular for two classes of civilians in the hands of an adverse party to the conflict: the inhabitants of occupied territory and the nationals of a belligerent state who are in the territory of the adversary. The events of World War II

---

1. Examples from ancient texts show some differentiation between the effects of war on combatants and on innocent civilian parties. For example, the *Mahabharata* text tracing the history of the Kurukshetra War stated, "he is no son of the Vishni race who slayeth a woman, a boy or an old man." PERCY BORDWELL, THE LAW OF WAR BETWEEN BELLIGERENTS 8 (1908). Similarly, the prophet Elisha warned the king against the killing of civilians: "When thou comest nigh unto a city to fight against . . . thou shalt smite every male therof with the edge of the sword. But the women and the little ones, and the cattle, and all that is in the city . . . thou shalt take unto thyself. . . ." L.C. GREEN, THE CONTEMPORARY LAW OF ARMED CONFLICT 26 (1998). And the Code of Hammurabi ordered "protection of the weak against oppression by the strong and ordered that hostages be released on payment of a ransom." Christopher Greenwood, *Historical Development and Legal Basis, in* THE HANDBOOK OF INTERNATIONAL HUMANITARIAN LAW 12 (Dieter Fleck ed., 1995).

2. *See, e.g.,* PERCY BORDWELL, THE LAW OF WAR BETWEEN BELLIGERENTS 411 (1908) (noting that "priests, monks, lay brothers, pilgrims, merchants, laborers and beasts of burden were not to suffer violence. Those who broke the truce were to be excommunicated.").

had demonstrated that the rules in force at the time inadequately protected these classes of individuals. Citizens of occupied territory throughout Europe and Asia enjoyed little protection from international law (notwithstanding existing protections for civilians and prohibitions on abuses) and endured atrocities, summary executions, inhumane treatment, and other deprivations.

After World War II, this approach was no longer sustainable. As the Commentary to the Fourth Geneva Convention explains, the drafters of the Geneva Conventions sought specifically to address these problems: "the new Geneva Convention could not confine itself, as the earlier Conventions had done, to protecting people who had already become the victims of war — the wounded, prisoners or internees; it had to prevent such people from becoming victims."[3]

As Chapters 1 and 2 discuss, one of the fundamental purposes of LOAC is the protection of civilians from the ravages of war, and one of the cardinal principles of the law is the principle of distinction between those who are fighting and those who are not. These concepts form the foundation of the civilian protections found in the Fourth Geneva Convention, Common Article 3, the Additional Protocols and customary international humanitarian law. The key components of the civilian protection regime include measures to protect civilians during the conduct of hostilities, such as those found in Part II of the Fourth Geneva Convention and in Additional Protocol I, and measures to ensure the protection of civilians in the power of the enemy forces, whether in occupied territory or belligerent territory, such as those found in Part III of the Fourth Geneva Convention. This chapter focuses primarily on who fits within the category of civilian — as well as the subcategories within that broad classification — and the rights and protections such persons are guaranteed in the Fourth Geneva Convention and Additional Protocol I. Chapters 8 and 9 address the protection of civilians within the conduct of hostilities in greater detail. In combination with the specific rights of individuals in occupied territory, these components form a comprehensive framework for the protection of civilians in times of conflict and occupation.

A.   TREATY BASICS: DEFINITIONS AND FRAMEWORK FOR PROTECTION

Consider the environment and the range of dangers civilians encounter in armed conflict. Civilians in all areas of hostilities, particularly contested areas, face the obvious dangers from attacks, firefights, maneuvers, and all types of kinetic activities. Civilians in territory controlled by their own side in

---

3. Int'l Comm. Red Cross, Commentary on the Geneva Convention (IV) Relative to the Protection of Civilian Persons in Time of War 5 (Oscar M. Uhler & Henri Coursier eds., 1958).

the conflict may seem to be in the least danger, but nonetheless encounter deprivations and possibly severe encroachment on basic rights and mistreatment. Civilians in enemy-controlled territory are, as the events of World War II and many other recent conflicts unfortunately demonstrate, in the most precarious position. LOAC seeks to address each of these challenges with a multilayered framework for civilian protection during armed conflict.

The most fundamental protection all civilians enjoy is immunity from attack. Article 51(2) of Additional Protocol I states: "The civilian population as such, as well as individual civilians, shall not be the object of attack." Direct targeting of civilians is therefore strictly prohibited. But the protection for civilians from hostilities is significantly broader than protection from direct attack. Article 51 sets the foundation for a framework of protections to ensure that "the civilian population and individual civilians shall enjoy general protection against dangers arising from military operations." The rest of the article then prohibits indiscriminate attacks, disproportionate attacks, reprisals, and using the presence or movements of the civilian population to shield military objectives or operations. Civilian objects are also protected from attack, with special protection for hospitals, houses of worship, and cultural property.

The second comprehensive protection for all civilians is the humane treatment obligation. The protections in Common Article 3 form a minimum threshold of humane treatment for all persons not participating in hostilities, prohibiting cruel, inhuman, and degrading treatment, including murder, torture, hostage-taking, outrages on personal dignity, extrajudicial executions, and humiliating and degrading treatment, for example. In addition, in international armed conflict, all persons enjoy the protections in Article 75 of Additional Protocol I, considered customary law by most nations,[4] for humane treatment and fair trial protections. Article 75, entitled "Fundamental Guarantees," begins with guarantees of basic protections for all persons not benefitting from more favorable protections, stating that all persons

> shall be treated humanely in all circumstances and shall enjoy, as a minimum, the protection provided by this Article without any adverse distinction based upon race, colour, sex, language, religion or belief, political or

---

4. On March 7, 2011, the White House issued a statement regarding its view of Article 75 of Additional Protocol I: "The U.S. Government will therefore choose out of a sense of legal obligation to treat the principles set forth in Article 75 as applicable to any individual it detains in an international armed conflict, and expects all other nations to adhere to these principles as well." Press Release, The White House, Fact Sheet: New Actions on Guantanamo and Detainee Policy (Mar. 7, 2011). *But see* John Bellinger, *Obama's Announcements on International Law*, LAWFARE (Mar. 8, 2011), http://www.lawfareblog.com/2011/03/obamas-announcements-on-international-law (arguing that it is unclear whether the White House statement will change detention policies because if the White House agrees with the Supreme Court's conclusion in *Hamdan* that war with al Qaeda is a non-international armed conflict, then it might choose not to apply Article 75 to Taliban or al Qaeda detainees).

other opinion, national or social origin, wealth, birth or other status, or on any other similar criteria.

In particular, violence, torture, murder, outrages upon personal dignity and humiliating treatment, hostage-taking, and collective punishment are prohibited in all circumstances. Article 75's fair trial guarantees are a particularly notable addition to the corpus of law protecting civilians during conflict—many of these rights, enshrined in human rights treaties, are subject to derogation under human rights law.[5] Now codified in Article 75(4), these guarantees are no longer rights from which a state can derogate during times of conflict out of reasons of national security or national emergency.

ARTICLE 75(4) OF ADDITIONAL PROTOCOL I

4. No sentence may be passed and no penalty may be executed on a person found guilty of a penal offence related to the armed conflict except pursuant to a conviction pronounced by an impartial and regularly constituted court respecting the generally recognized principles of regular judicial procedure, which include the following:

(a) the procedure shall provide for an accused to be informed without delay of the particulars of the offence alleged against him and shall afford the accused before and during his trial all necessary rights and means of defence;

(b) no one shall be convicted of an offence except on the basis of individual penal responsibility;

(c) no one shall be accused or convicted of a criminal offence on account of any act or omission which did not constitute a criminal offence under the national or international law to which he was subject at the time when it was committed; nor shall a heavier penalty be imposed than that which was applicable at the time when the criminal offence was committed; if, after the commission of the offence, provision is made by law for the imposition of a lighter penalty, the offender shall benefit thereby;

(d) anyone charged with an offence is presumed innocent until proved guilty according to law;

(e) anyone charged with an offence shall have the right to be tried in his presence;

---

5. *See, e.g.*, International Covenant on Civil and Political Rights art. 4, Dec. 16, 1966, 999 U.N.T.S. 171; Convention for the Protection of Human Rights and Fundamental Freedoms art. 15, Nov. 4, 1950, 213 U.N.T.S. 222; American Convention on Human Rights art. 27, Nov. 22, 1963, 1144 U.N.T.S. 123.

(f) no one shall be compelled to testify against himself or to confess guilt;

(g) anyone charged with an offence shall have the right to examine, or have examined, the witnesses against him and to obtain the attendance and examination of witnesses on his behalf under the same conditions as witnesses against him;

(h) no one shall be prosecuted or punished by the same Party for an offence in respect of which a final judgement acquitting or convicting that person has been previously pronounced under the same law and judicial procedure;

(i) anyone prosecuted for an offence shall have the right to have the judgement pronounced publicly; and

(j) a convicted person shall be advised on conviction of his judicial and other remedies and of the time-limit within which they may be exercised.

Article 75 thus delineates in full detail the "judicial guarantees" referred to in Common Article 3 as a necessary component of any criminal procedure and "which are recognized as indispensable by civilized peoples."

Finally, the Fourth Geneva Convention mandates general protections for all civilians in international armed conflict, including the establishment of hospital zones and neutral zones, protections for the wounded and sick, and access to relief consignments of food, clothing, and medical supplies. Especially vulnerable civilians—namely children under fifteen, expectant mothers, mothers of young children, and the elderly, wounded, and sick—are entitled to special protections and benefits, including, for example, special care to ensure education, maintenance, and exercise of religion for children orphaned or separated from their families.

Many civilians face an increasingly complex range of challenges during wartime, beyond the direct effects of hostilities. Internment, occupation, security measures, abusive treatment—the effects of a hostile force in their territory can put civilians at risk in a variety of ways. In particular,

> Geneva Convention IV ordinarily applies to "enemy civilians" because they are thought to be in need of protection on account of their adverse allegiance, and due to the fact that they cannot be protected by the normal mechanism of diplomatic representation as these ties are severed on account of the situation of armed conflict between the belligerents.[6]

The law thus provides a heightened set of protections for a particular category of civilians defined as "protected persons." These civilians, who lack

---

6. Robert Kolb & Richard Hyde, An Introduction to the International Law of Armed Conflicts 222 (2008).

the protections of normal diplomatic mechanisms because they are in occupied or enemy territory, thus benefit from a set of rights and protections that look quite similar to basic human rights protections. Consider why as you read further about the specific protections and the definition of protected persons below.

The Fourth Geneva Convention requires that all protected persons enjoy respect for family, honor, personal integrity, and religious practices and customs. Women are protected from attacks on their honor and all protected persons are protected from any physical or moral coercion. Protected persons are guaranteed access to the International Committee of the Red Cross and protected from any collective punishment. More specifically, protected persons in occupied territory enjoy the following rights:

- Any non-nationals of the occupied territory must be allowed to leave
- Reprisals are prohibited
- Individual or mass forcible transfers or deportations are prohibited
- Protected persons cannot be forced to serve in the armed forces of the occupying power or for essential labor
- Civilian property cannot be destroyed except for imperative military necessity
- Deprivation of liberty is permitted only on the basis of an individual threat to security and is heavily regulated to ensure appropriate procedures and reviews

Protected persons in enemy territory enjoy the following set of rights and protections:

- Protected persons are entitled to leave the territory and have the right to appeal any refusal of such right
- Right to access relief supplies
- Access to medical care in the same manner and on the same basis as nationals
- Equal opportunity to find employment
- Protected persons can only be compelled to work to the same extent as nationals

The first key step in determining an individual's rights and protections—as with combatants—is to determine whether she is a civilian and, if so, whether she also meets the definition of a protected person.

1. *Definition of Civilian*

A specific definition of "civilian" or "civilian population" does not appear in the Geneva or Hague Conventions, even though the Fourth Geneva Convention is devoted to the protection of civilian persons in times of war. Rather, the Fourth Geneva Convention talks of persons in the hands of the enemy and of "the whole of the populations of the countries in conflict" in Article 13. The drafters of the Additional Protocols saw the need for a more precise definition, especially given the fundamental obligation to differentiate between combatants and civilians and the changing categories of persons covered in previous definitions. The definition, which is a negative definition categorizing civilians as all persons who are not combatants, thus appears in Article 50 of Additional Protocol I.

ARTICLE 50 OF ADDITIONAL PROTOCOL I

1. A civilian is any person who does not belong to one of the categories of persons referred to in article 4A(1), (2), (3) and (6) of the Third Convention and in Article 43 of this Protocol. In case of doubt whether a person is a civilian, that person shall be considered to be a civilian.

2. The civilian population comprises all persons who are civilians.

3. The presence within the civilian population of individuals who do not come within the definition of civilians does not deprive the population of its civilian character.

This definition has three critical parts. First, *civilian* is defined in opposition to *combatant*, so that no person is left without a status, and the concomitant protections, under LOAC. Consider the consequences of having a definition of civilian that listed or described certain types or categories of persons qualifying as civilians. The likelihood that someone — or an entire group of people — will fall into a gap between the two definitions of combatant and civilian is, unfortunately, all too evident. LOAC emphatically rejects any such possibility that any individuals could be left without protections — as a result, all persons are either combatants or civilians, and the nature and structure of the definitions ensures this essential framework.

Second, any uncertainty or doubt in a person's status is to be resolved in favor of civilian status, with the goal of ensuring as much protection as possible. In essence, LOAC mandates a default starting point of civilian status for any person whose status is not clear. This presumption in favor of the most protected status takes the same approach as the similar presumption of POW status in Article 5 of the Third Geneva Convention, which requires that in case of doubt, a person suspected of a belligerent act shall benefit from the protections of POW status until his status is determined by a competent tribunal.[7]

Third, the civilian population, which merits its own protection beyond that of individual civilians, does not lose its civilian character merely because some combatants are present, stationed, hiding or otherwise intermingled therein. The ICTY explained:

> Read together, Article 50 of Additional Protocol I and Article 4A of the Third Geneva Convention establish that members of the armed forces, and members of militias or volunteer corps forming part of such armed forces, cannot claim civilian status. Neither can members of organized resistance groups, provided that they are commanded by a person responsible for his subordinates, that they have a fixed distinctive sign recognizable at a distance, that they carry arms openly, and that they conduct their operations in accordance with the laws and customs of war. However, the Appeals Chamber considers that the presence within a population of members of resistance groups, or former combatants, who have laid down their arms, does not alter its civilian characteristic.[8]

Given the nature of hostilities and the unfortunate practice of many fighters exploiting the presence of civilians during military operations, it is essential to prevent any erosion of civilian protections solely due to the presence of fighters in and around civilians, civilian objects and civilian areas.

Overall, the definitions of civilian and combatant are status categories—an individual is a combatant if she falls into one of the categories in Article 4(1), (2), (3) or (6) of the Third Geneva Convention; or a civilian if she does not. Status is based on membership, on belonging to a group, not on one's conduct at a particular moment. A combatant who is unarmed or not engaging in combat does not acquire civilian status as a result of not actually fighting—nor does a civilian become a combatant simply by picking up a weapon and jumping into the fray. The only way to change one's status is to join the armed forces or armed group, or to end one's membership in such a group.

An individual's status as either combatant or civilian determines his or her protections and rights. For example, combatants have the right to participate in hostilities and are entitled to POW status and combatant immunity, but are liable to attack at any time. Civilians are protected from attack and cannot be detained except based on individualized determinations that they pose an imperative threat to security, but do not enjoy the right to

7. Third Geneva Convention, art. 5 ("Should any doubt arise as to whether persons, having committed a belligerent act and having fallen into the hands of the enemy, belong to any of the categories enumerated in Article 4, such persons shall enjoy the protection of the present Convention until such time as their status has been determined by a competent tribunal.").

8. Prosecutor v. Blaškić, Case No. IT-95-14-A, Appeals Judgement ¶ 113 (Int'l Crim. Trib. for the Former Yugoslavia July 29, 2004).

participate in hostilities or combatant immunity. However, an individual's conduct at a particular moment can alter the protections or rights that normally accompany his status. Combatants who are *hors de combat* because they are wounded, sick, or detained are protected from attack as well, but do not become civilians; rather, they receive that protection through the First, Second, or Third Geneva Conventions. As discussed below, a civilian who participates in hostilities will lose his or her immunity from attack, but will still remain categorized as a civilian. A civilian accompanying the armed forces will be a POW if captured because she is entitled to that protection in those circumstances, but will remain a civilian. In the same manner, as cases in the previous chapter demonstrate, a combatant who fights in civilian clothing will lose the privileges of combatant immunity and POW status, but will remain a combatant. Understanding an individual's rights and protections is therefore a two-step process: what is the individual's status—combatant or civilian—and what protections or rights has he gained or lost as a result of his conduct?

2. Protected Persons

The provision of heightened protections for persons in the hands of an enemy force is one of the great innovations of the Fourth Geneva Convention. As noted above, the provisions of Part II of the Fourth Geneva Convention apply to the whole of the population of countries in conflict and provide basic protections for everyone in the conflict area. Part III addresses the status and treatment of protected persons, a category defined in Article 4.

ARTICLE 4 OF THE FOURTH GENEVA CONVENTION: PROTECTED PERSONS

Persons protected by the Convention are those who, at a given moment and in any manner whatsoever, find themselves, in case of a conflict or occupation, in the hands of a Party to the conflict or Occupying Power of which they are not nationals.

Nationals of a State which is not bound by the Convention are not protected by it. Nationals of a neutral State who find themselves in the territory of a belligerent State, and nationals of a co-belligerent State, shall not be regarded as protected persons while the State of which they are nationals has normal diplomatic representation in the State in whose hands they are.

. . .

> Persons protected by the Geneva Convention for the Amelioration of the Condition of the Wounded and Sick in Armed Forces in the Field of August 12, 1949, or by the Geneva Convention for the Amelioration of the Condition of Wounded, Sick and Shipwrecked Members of Armed Forces at Sea of August 12, 1949, or by the Geneva Convention relative to the Treatment of Prisoners of War of August 12, 1949, shall not be considered as protected persons within the meaning of present Convention.

A protected person is therefore:

1. In the hands of a party or occupying power of which he/she is not a national;
2. Not a national of a neutral State or a co-belligerent State;
3. Not protected by the First, Second, or Third Geneva Conventions.

The drafters of the Geneva Convention excluded from the definition of protected persons individuals who are nationals of a neutral or co-belligerent state because it is assumed that such persons will be protected through their state's normal diplomatic relations with the relevant party to the conflict or occupying power. Persons already protected by one of the first three Geneva Conventions are also excluded because they already have the full protection of international law. In this way, Article 4 offers a micro-look at one central underlying theme of LOAC—no one is left without a status under international law; no person will be unprotected by the law. The first requirement—in the hands of a party of which the individual is not a national—raises two primary questions: what is "in the hands of" and what are the parameters of nationality, especially in modern, complex conflicts?

a. "In the Hands Of"

In prosecuting crimes committed during the conflict in the former Yugoslavia, the ICTY frequently faced the challenge of determining protected person status as the parties moved into contested areas, took control of territory, and subjected civilians to abuse, violence, and other atrocities. The question arose whether the requirement of "in the hands of" includes civilians in an area controlled by an adverse party, or whether that component of the definition of protected persons applies only to those in the physical custody of such adverse party. Relying on the Commentary to the Fourth Geneva Convention, the ICTY held, with regard to Bosnian civilians in Croatian-controlled territory, that although the residents "were not directly or physically 'in the hands of' Croatia, they [could] be treated as being constructively 'in the hands of' Croatia, a country of which they were not nationals."[9]

b. Nationality

Article 4 of the Fourth Geneva Convention speaks of "nationals," suggesting that states and nationality are the key determinants of protected person status. However, as many conflicts demonstrate, nationality is often not an appropriate measure of an individual's opportunities for protection, given the complexities of shifting allegiances in complicated ethnic and tribal conflicts. As a result, the international tribunals have focused on allegiance rather than nationality in assessing protected person status. Thus, for example, although the Bosnian Serbs and Bosnian Muslims were the same nationality—all nationals of Bosnia and Herzegovina—they did not share allegiances and in fact were opposing parties in a conflict internationalized by the participation and overall control of the Federal Republic of Yugoslavia. Bosnian Muslims in the hands of Bosnian Serbs were therefore protected persons, as were Bosnian Serbs in the hands of Bosnian Muslims. The Tribunal thus eschewed nationality alone as the marker for protection, affirming that Article 4's "primary purpose is to ensure the safeguards afforded by the Convention to those civilians who do not enjoy the diplomatic protection, and correlatively are not subject to the allegiance and control, of the State in whose hands they may find themselves."[10] The key analysis rests on the "substance of relations" rather than the legal characterization of nationality.

QUESTIONS FOR DISCUSSION

1. The concept of protected persons is only relevant in an international armed conflict, when the Fourth Geneva Convention is applicable, thus presuming that more than one state is involved. But what if the party holding the potential protected persons is not a state or linked to a state, but is still fighting in an international armed conflict? Would that eliminate protected person status? What would be the consequences of such a determination?

2. More broadly, in today's world of conflicts between or involving non-state entities and ranging across state borders, how should we think about protected person status and similar protections for civilians that were originally linked to diplomatic protection and a state's responsibility for its citizens?

---

9. Prosecutor v. Rajić, Case No. IT-95-12-S, Review of the Indictment Pursuant to Rule 61 of the Rules of Procedure and Evidence ¶ 37 (Int'l Crim. Trib. for the Former Yugoslavia Sept. 13, 1996).

10. Prosecutor v. Tadić, Case No. IT-94-1-A, Judgement ¶ 168 (Int'l Crim. Trib. for the Former Yugoslavia July 15, 1999).

3. In the early stages of the conflict in Afghanistan, the United States determined that persons captured and detained in Afghanistan did not qualify for protected person status under the Fourth Geneva Convention. Although the convention applied during the first phase of the conflict, when it was an international armed conflict between the United States and Afghanistan, the Department of Justice concluded that the category of protected persons only included "persons finding themselves in the hands of a party to the conflict only in territory belonging to that party (e.g., the United States) and not in territory belonging to the opposing party (or parties) to the conflict (e.g., Afghanistan)."[11] How does this interpretation compare to that of the ICTY? Does it accord with LOAC's goal of ensuring that no person is left unprotected?

B.   ARE THEY CIVILIANS?

Zones of conflict are not populated solely by soldiers and innocent civilians, of course. In Afghanistan, for example, there have been multinational soldiers, ordinary Afghan civilians, contractors, militants, al Qaeda operatives, and so forth. Other conflicts also include regional or United Nations peacekeepers in the mix. So how do we categorize all of these different people?

1.   Peacekeepers

A peacekeeper is a member of a military force assigned to preserve the peace in a conflict or post-conflict region. Peacekeepers, therefore, are armed (usually lightly but armed nonetheless), are part of a military unit, and function under military command. However, they do not belong to a party to the conflict at hand. In cases involving alleged war crimes perpetrated against peacekeepers, international tribunals and other courts must first find that the peacekeepers enjoy the status of civilians under LOAC, because the offense of attacks against peacekeeping personnel is "a particularisation of the general and fundamental prohibition in international humanitarian law against attacks on civilians and civilian objects."[12] The Special Court for Sierra Leone explained that the essential component of

---

11. U.S. Dep't of Justice, Memorandum, Whether Persons Captured and Detained in Afghanistan are "Protected Persons" under the Fourth Geneva Convention, August 5, 2005, https://www.justice.gov/sites/default/files/olc/legacy/2009/12/30/aclu-ii-080505.pdf.

12. Prosecutor v. Sesay, Kallon and Gbao (RUF Case), Case No. SCSL-04-15-T, Judgement 215 (Special Court for Sierra Leone Mar. 2, 2009).

this analysis is the nature of the peacekeepers' authority to use force: as long as peacekeeping units use force solely in self-defense, they retain civilian status. When peacekeepers take direct part in hostilities or have more robust authority to use force, they can be legitimate targets and therefore lose their protection from attack.

QUESTIONS FOR DISCUSSION

1. One year after the Special Court for Sierra Leone decision cited above, the ICC addressed the status of peacekeepers in the case of Bahar Idriss Abu Garda, a commander of the Justice and Equality Movement, one of the main rebel groups fighting in the conflict in Darfur. Garda was charged with attacking United Nations peacekeepers and peacekeeping matériel and vehicles, killing twelve peacekeepers. In its decision on the Confirmation of Charges, the Pre-Trial Chamber noted that "three basic principles are accepted as determining whether a given mission constitutes a peacekeeping mission, namely (i) consent of the parties; (ii) impartiality; and (iii) the non-use of force except in self-defence."[13] Like the Special Court for Sierra Leone, the ICC determined that peacekeepers are entitled to the protection from attack enjoyed by civilians, except when they directly participate in hostilities or combat-related activities. The use of force in self-defense does not lead to a loss in civilian protections. The court then examined the mission's rules of engagement to determine if the mission was indeed governed by self-defense rules on the use of force. As one member of the mission explained, according to their training, "while they were not allowed to fire at or kill a rebel or any member of any factions, they were allowed to do so when the lives of AMIS personnel were 'totally in danger.'"[14]

2. In the *Garda* decision on the Confirmation of Charges, the ICC also highlighted the difference between peacekeeping missions and peace enforcement missions established under Chapter VII of the United Nations Charter, "which have a mandate or are authorized to use force beyond self-defence in order to achieve their objective."[15] The Convention on the Safety of United Nations and Associated Personnel specifically excludes peace enforcement missions from its scope: "This Convention shall not apply to a United Nations operation authorized by the Security Council as an enforcement action under Chapter VII of the Charter of the United Nations in which any of the personnel are engaged as combatants against organized armed forces and to which the law of international armed conflict

13. Prosecutor v. Abu Garda, Case No. ICC-02/05-02/09, Confirmation of Charges ¶ 71 (Feb. 8, 2010).
14. *Id.* ¶ 117.
15. *Id.* ¶ 74.

applies."[16] Are there other factors that should be considered in assessing the civilian status of peacekeepers? Could their status change during the course of their mission or as a result of events on the ground, beyond the direct participation considerations noted above?

3. How would you analyze the status of peacekeepers if a situation arose in which they were regularly attacked and had to resort to extensive combat operations to repel and deter such attacks? Would that fit within the notion of self-defense? Should it?

2. *Contractors*

In today's conflicts, contractors can often outnumber military personnel. In Iraq alone, hundreds of thousands of contractors have served as engineers, technicians, construction workers, truck drivers, food service providers, and much more—in March 2011, for example, there were 64,253 U.S. Department of Defense contractors in Iraq. However, unlike conflicts in the past when contractors were employed, this was the first time that large numbers of contractors were also acting as very well-armed security. In fact, contractors were the second largest contingent of armed individuals in Iraq, second only to the U.S. military. Similar numbers of contractors have been employed in Afghanistan since the end of 2001, including some 90,339 contractors in March 2011.

In 2008, the ICRC and the government of Switzerland completed an international process to define the international law applicable to private military and security companies in armed conflict. The Montreux Document is a compilation of relevant international law obligations and best practices and reinforces that the personnel of private military and security companies are protected under and obligated by LOAC. Specifically, such personnel are protected as civilians under LOAC except if they are incorporated into the regular armed forces of a state, are members of an organized armed group, or otherwise lose protection. To the extent contractors fall within the category of "persons accompanying the armed forces" in Article 4(A)(4) of the Third Geneva Convention, they will be entitled to prisoner of war status.

In some conflicts, private military contractors engage in active combat. For example, Executive Outcomes, a private military company founded in South Africa, played a significant role in helping the Angolan government defeat the National Union for the Total Independence of Angola (UNITA) rebel movement and the Sierra Leone government defeat the Revolutionary United Front (RUF). More commonly, private companies may contract

---

16. Convention on the Safety of United Nations and Associated Personnel art. 2(2), Dec. 9, 1994, 2051 U.N.T.S. 363.

to perform security monitoring, training, intelligence gathering, and any number of logistics operations. For example, "contractors are or have been training security forces in Iraq, flying gunships in Colombia, training civilian police in Bosnia and Kosovo and protecting Afghanistan President Hamid Karzai."[17] Others specialize in clearing mines or private air reconnaissance. United Nations Secretary General Kofi Annan had even considered engaging a private security company when there was an urgent "need of skilled soldiers to separate fighters from refugees in the Rwandan refugee camps in Goma."[18] The fact that private contractors are often heavily armed, work closely with the military, engage in tasks that assist or even substitute for regular military, and possibly even engage in combat operations presents complex questions regarding the rules applicable to contractors, their status during armed conflict, and their rights, protections, and obligations.

PROTECTORS OR TOO QUICK ON THE TRIGGER?

In the summer of 2008, as the Assistant Director of the Law and Order Task Force, my duties included overseeing the opening of the Judicial Palace in the Al Rusafa District of Bagdad. Located on the edge of Sadr City, and completely under the control of the Iraqi government, the enormous facility housed eleven courts and was visited by as many as 2,000 people per day. With broken metal detectors, unused X-ray machines, and a handful of under-trained, under-armed Iraqi guards, it surprised no one when the U.S. Marshals Service described the courthouse as being "in the most dangerous neighborhood in the most dangerous city in the world."

During one of my initial visits to the Judicial Palace, as I observed the chaos of moving furniture, the press of humanity, and unmistakable undercurrent of tension, I couldn't help but notice the discomfort of my personal security detail. Sensing the concern of these veteran contractors caused me to take a second look at my surroundings, and that's when I noticed that for every Iraqi security guard there were at least seven armed civilians milling about. Eventually, the leader of my security detail came to me and said we need to conclude our business and return to our forward operating base. He then told me that if any shooting began in the building, he fully intended on having his team shoot every person standing between us and the nearest door. That door was over twenty meters and dozens of people away.

---

17. Michael Meyer, *The Dogs of Peace*, NEWSWEEK (Aug. 24, 2003).

18. United Nations Press Release, *Secretary-General Reflects on "Intervention" in Thirty-Fifth Annual Ditchley Foundation Lecture*, SG/SM/6613, June 26, 1998.

> As we left the building, my initial comfort at being well protected was quickly intruded upon by my analysis as a judge advocate. The situation involved a United States military officer, private security contractors, and civilians not wearing uniforms but openly carrying weapons — all the ingredients needed for a Law of Armed Conflict disaster.
>
> — *U.S. Navy judge advocate*

QUESTIONS FOR DISCUSSION

1. As you read the section at the end of this chapter on direct participation in hostilities, consider the implications for a contractor's status if he or she: provides security to dignitaries; stands guard duty at a military post; services airplanes or weapons systems; trains local police or army units; advises local prosecutors or judges; or provides security at detention facilities. What other types of contractor duties could have implications?

2. Military personnel operate unmanned aerial vehicles (UAVs) and make the final decisions regarding targeting. Civilian contractors regularly perform launch and recovery tasks, analyze intelligence, and even assist in determining targets. What is their status?

3. Who is likely to be endangered when a contractor's status is not clear? What are the potential consequences of uncertainty?

4. A mercenary is generally defined, at least colloquially, as a professional soldier hired to serve in a foreign military. The Convention for the Elimination of Mercenarism in Africa and the International Convention Against the Recruitment, Use, Financing and Training of Mercenaries both seek to repress and punish the use of mercenaries. Article 47 of Additional Protocol I provides that a "mercenary shall not have the right to be a combatant or a prisoner of war," thus making such persons liable to criminal prosecution. It further defines a mercenary as any person who:

    (a) is specially recruited locally or abroad in order to fight in an armed conflict;

    (b) does, in fact, take a direct part in the hostilities;

    (c) is motivated to take part in the hostilities essentially by the desire for private gain and, in fact, is promised, by or on behalf of a Party to the conflict, material compensation substantially in excess of that promised or paid to combatants of similar ranks and functions in the armed forces of that Party;

    (d) is neither a national of a Party to the conflict nor a resident of territory controlled by a Party to the conflict;

    (e) is not a member of the armed forces of a Party to the conflict; and

    (f) has not been sent by a State which is not a Party to the conflict on official duty as a member of its armed forces.

Most private military contractors are not hired to serve *in* the military nor are they hired or authorized to engage in offensive military operations. Nonetheless, where is the line between contractor and mercenary and how should it be drawn?

    5. There was a great deal of concern within the military leadership, especially from judge advocates, that the contractors hired by the U.S. government in Iraq and Afghanistan were not properly trained, particularly in the use of force and its appropriate parameters and limits. Contractors did not receive the same level of training as uniformed personnel either prior to deployment or in theatre. What is the obligation of the country that hires contractors to make sure they are properly trained in LOAC?

    6. During much of the conflicts in both Iraq and Afghanistan, contractor misbehavior prompted little accountability beyond firing the individual and sending him home, followed by potential barring from any future contracts. The absence of criminal jurisdiction and lack of prosecution led to a perception of impunity for contractors, with many believing that

> the employees of these companies seem to lack a strong sense of even what the applicable laws and norms are, let alone have any great commitment to them. For example, in congressional testimony, Blackwater CEO Erik Prince appeared to have at best a murky understanding of the precise legal rules and regulations that governed his employees' use of force and available accountability mechanisms for the misuse of that force.[19]

Many judge advocates in theatre believed that contractors were more likely to use force and were "quicker to shoot" than uniformed personnel, in particular, at checkpoints. Should contractors be held to the same use of force standards as the nation's forces they are hired to support?

    7. In 2007, Blackwater military contractors fired indiscriminately into car and foot traffic at Nisour Square in Baghdad while on security detail for the Department of State. Fourteen Iraqi civilians were killed, and more than a dozen others were wounded. After considerable delay, the Department of Justice prosecuted the contractors in U.S. federal court using the Military Extraterritorial Jurisdiction Act (MEJA), which provided federal courts jurisdiction over felonies committed by persons "employed by or accompanying the armed forces"[20] overseas. Congress had amended MEJA in 2004 to include contractors working for other agencies, "to the extent such employment relates to supporting the mission of the Department of

---

    19. Laura A. Dickinson, *Military Lawyers, Private Contractors, and the Problem of International Law Compliance*, 42 N.Y.U. J. Int'l L. & Pol. 355, 380-381 (2010).

    20. Military Extraterritorial Jurisdiction Act of 2000, § 3261(a)(1), Pub. L. No. 106-523, 114 Stat. 2488 (2000).

Defense,"[21] specifically to address the gaps in jurisdiction noted above. The court rejected the defendants' argument that MEJA did not apply because they were Department of State contractors and not accompanying or supporting Department of Defense personnel, and convicted one defendant of murder and the other three of manslaughter in 2014. Three years later, an appeals court threw out the sentences for all four and ordered a new trial for the fourth accused of murder, based on procedural considerations regarding the joint trial and the reliance on an added gun charge.[22]

The 2007 National Defense Authorization Act extended the jurisdiction of the Uniform Code of Military Justice (UCMJ) to apply to "persons serving with or accompanying an armed force in the field" during a "time of declared war or a contingency operation."[23] With the addition of the words "contingency operation," Congress intended to close the "only in a declared war" loophole. As a result, the U.S. military can now investigate and potentially prosecute a contractor who is supporting the Department of Defense at a court-martial for violating the UCMJ.

8. Private contractor firms' use of foreign labor complicates the jurisdictional piece even further—a significant number of contractors in Iraq and Afghanistan were hired from more than thirty countries, and many of these individuals had no ties to the United States. Some of those contractors had committed numerous human rights violations in their home countries. What are the jurisdictional challenges regarding foreign labor to hold them accountable for misbehavior? What is the obligation of the hiring nation to screen potential contractors for prior human rights violations?

3.   Police

On December 28, 2008, Israel launched Operation Cast Lead in the Gaza Strip, a military operation aimed at destroying the ability of Hamas and other Palestinian armed groups to fire rockets at southern Israel. Among the first targets on the first day of the operation were the graduates at the police academy graduation ceremony and several other police stations. Ninety-nine police officers were killed. As a general matter, police are considered civilians except when they are incorporated into the armed forces. Were the police targeted that first day civilians protected from attack or were they combatants or otherwise legitimate targets (civilians directly participating in hostilities, for example)?

---

21. 18 U.S.C. § 3267(1)(A)(ii)(II).

22. Spencer S. Hsu, *Federal Judge Sets June Retrial for Blackwater Guard Accused in 2007 Iraq Massacre*, WASH. POST (Dec. 22, 2017).

23. 10 U.S.C. § 802(a)(10).

After the conflict ended, the United Nations Human Rights Council established an international commission, known as the Goldstone Commission after the lead member, Judge Richard Goldstone. Before the Goldstone Commission issued its report, the State of Israel examined the conduct of the Israel Defense Forces and produced a report detailing the legal framework applicable to the conflict and addressing a range of legal issues arising during the conflict, including the targeting of the police on the first day. The report explained that the police in Gaza were actually part of the Executive Force, a militia formed in 2006 and characterized as "resistance fighters" by its leaders. The Israeli report also documented that many policemen were members of the al-Qassam Brigades, one of the main Hamas armed groups, and that "more than nine out of every ten alleged 'civilian police' were found to be armed terrorist activists and combatants directly engaged in hostilities against Israel." Focusing on the integration of the security apparatus in Gaza, the report concluded: "The reality is that the internal security services have been and continue to be a cadre of terrorist operatives armed with a variety of heavy weapons including anti-tank missile launchers, with standing orders to fight Israeli forces. Under the Law of Armed Conflict, Israel is permitted to target such forces and their bases of operation."[24]

The Goldstone Report took a different approach. In response to Israel's arguments, Hamas argued that the police in Gaza were solely civilian and were engaged only in law enforcement activities and separate from any armed groups or military forces. The Goldstone Commission examined the role of the police in Gaza and in the Hamas infrastructure and concluded that, although most of the police were recruited from the Executive Force and had "clear orders from the leadership to face . . . the enemy, if the Gaza Strip were to be invaded," there was not sufficient evidence to conclude that the police had been incorporated into the armed forces, that sufficient numbers of policemen were members of one or more armed groups, or that the police were directly participating in hostilities. As a result, the Goldstone Report concluded that the attacks on police on the first day were attacks on civilians in violation of LOAC.[25]

QUESTIONS FOR DISCUSSION

1. Israel does not address direct participation in hostilities in its report. Is this an omission? Why would direct participation not be an issue for the Israeli analysis?

24. THE STATE OF ISRAEL, THE OPERATION IN GAZA 27 DECEMBER 2008—18 JANUARY 2009 247-8 (2009), *available at* http://mfa.gov.il/MFA/ForeignPolicy/Terrorism/Palestinian/Pages/Operation_in_Gaza-Factual_and_Legal_Aspects.aspx.

25. U.N. Human Rights Council, Human Rights in Palestine and Other Occupied Arab Territories: Report of the U.N. Fact-Finding Mission on the Gaza Conflict, A/HRC/12/48 (Sept. 15, 2009).

2. Consider Israel's argument that the police are combatants in light of LOAC's categorization of all persons as either combatants or civilians. Do the police at issue in Gaza fit within the categories of combatants in Article 4 of the Third Geneva Convention? How else could the term "combatant" be interpreted here?

3. What are the consequences of the finding in the Goldstone Report that the police are civilians? How does that impact the conduct of the armed conflict? The ability of each side to conduct hostilities in accordance with LOAC's general principles and obligations?

4. In the report of the International Commission of Inquiry on Darfur, the Commission stated:

> in the particular case of the internal conflict in Darfur, the distinction between the police and the armed forces is often blurred. There are strong elements indicating occurrences of the police fighting alongside Government forces during attacks or abstaining from preventing or investigating attacks on the civilian population committed by the Janjaweed. There are also widespread and confirmed allegations that some members of the Janjaweed have been incorporated into the police. President El-Bashir confirmed in an interview with international media that in order to rein in the Janjaweed, they were incorporated in "other areas", such as the armed forces and the police. Therefore, the Commission is of the opinion that the "civilian" status of the police in the context of the conflict in Darfur is questionable.[26]

How does this analysis comport with LOAC's basic framework for understanding status of persons? How does it compare to the analysis used with regard to the police in Gaza?

C.   CIVILIANS AND THE CONDUCT OF HOSTILITIES

1.   Prohibition Against Attacks on Civilians

At the heart of the legal regime protecting civilians in times of war is the prohibition of attacks on civilians. Article 51 of Additional Protocol I prohibits direct attacks on civilians, indiscriminate attacks, and attacks that violate the principle of proportionality, discussed in greater detail in Chapter 9 below. In this way, the complete framework of Article 51 carries

---

26. International Commission of Inquiry on Darfur, *Report of the International Commission of Inquiry on Darfur to the United Nations Secretary-General* 422 (Jan. 25, 2005).

out the object and purpose of the article's first paragraph, which mandates that civilians enjoy general protections from the effects of military operations.

ARTICLE 51 OF ADDITIONAL PROTOCOL I

1. The civilian population and individual civilians shall enjoy general protection against dangers arising from military operations. To give effect to this protection, the following rules, which are additional to other applicable rules of international law, shall be observed in all circumstances.

2. The civilian population as such, as well as individual civilians, shall not be the object of attack. Acts or threats of violence the primary purpose of which is to spread terror among the civilian population are prohibited.

3. Civilians shall enjoy the protection afforded by this Section, unless and for such time as they take a direct part in hostilities.

4. Indiscriminate attacks are prohibited. Indiscriminate attacks are:

   (a) those which are not directed at a specific military objective;

   (b) those which employ a method or means of combat which cannot be directed at a specific military objective; or

   (c) those which employ a method or means of combat the effects of which cannot be limited as required by this Protocol; and consequently, in each such case, are of a nature to strike military objectives and civilians or civilian objects without distinction.

5. Among others, the following types of attacks are to be considered as indiscriminate:

   (a) an attack by bombardment by any methods or means which treats as a single military objective a number of clearly separated and distinct military objectives located in a city, town, village or other area containing a similar concentration of civilians or civilian objects; and

   (b) an attack which may be expected to cause incidental loss of civilian life, injury to civilians, damage to civilian objects, or a combination thereof, which would be excessive in relation to the concrete and direct military advantage anticipated.

6. Attacks against the civilian population or civilians by way of reprisals are prohibited.

7. The presence or movements of the civilian population or individual civilians shall not be used to render certain points or areas immune from military operations, in particular in attempts to shield military objectives from attacks or to shield, favour or impede military operations. The Parties to the conflict shall not direct the movement of the civilian population or individual civilians in order to attempt to shield military objectives from attacks or to shield military operations.

The full spectrum of protections and prohibitions in Article 51 goes well beyond a ban on deliberate attacks, beyond preventing simple disregard for civilian safety, and mandates that parties to a conflict conduct their operations in such a way as to maximize protection for civilians. All too unfortunately, however, the prohibition on direct and deliberate attacks remains essential. Both past and present conflicts demonstrate that the prohibition is both historically rooted and still relevant. Indeed, as a U.S. military judge stated unequivocally in the prosecution of William Calley after the May Lai massacre during the Vietnam War, "an order to kill infants and unarmed civilians who were so demonstrably incapable of resistance to the armed might of a military force . . . is . . . palpably illegal."[27] In the *Calley* case, the accused shot and killed unarmed civilians within his control in a situation in which there were few questions about the nature of the victims and the unlawfulness of the actions. In many situations, however, attacks on civilians occur in the course of hostilities and require an examination of the status of the victims—i.e., whether they are civilians—and the nature of the attacks.

The ICTY addressed countless allegations of unlawful attacks on civilians throughout its twenty-plus year tenure. In *Prosecutor v. Galić*, which addressed crimes committed during the siege of Sarajevo, the longest siege in modern history, the ICTY set forth detailed elements of the crime of unlawful attacks on civilians: 1) the attack causes death or serious bodily injury; 2) to a civilian, as defined in Article 50 of Additional Protocol I; and 3) the presence of individual combatants within the population does not change its civilian character—an essential issue for examining the mortar attacks on the soccer stadium in Sarajevo where some Bosnian soldiers were present along with hundreds or thousands of civilians.

One defense frequently offered for the killing of civilians is the now-rejected justification of reprisals.

> Reprisals are extreme measures to enforce compliance with the law of armed conflict by the adverse party. They can involve acts which would normally be illegal, resorted to after the adverse party has itself carried out illegal acts and refused to desist when called upon to do so. They are not retaliatory acts or simple acts of vengeance. Reprisals are, however, an extreme measure of coercion, because in most cases they inflict suffering upon innocent individuals.[28]

Historically, including through World War II, reprisals were considered an acceptable—if extreme—method of compelling the enemy to cease its own legal violations. Although belligerent reprisals could remain lawful against enemy belligerents under extremely limited circumstances, LOAC

---

27. United States v. William L. Calley, Jr., 22 C.M.A. 534, 544 (1973).

28. UNITED KINGDOM MINISTRY OF DEFENCE, JSP 383: THE JOINT SERVICE MANUAL OF THE LAW OF ARMED CONFLICT 16.16 (2004).

categorically prohibits any reprisals against civilians, civilian objects, protected persons, and other persons and objects enjoying special protection under the law. For example, in the *Kupreškić* case, the ICTY firmly condemned reprisals as an acceptable reason for attacks on civilians. Bosnian Croat soldiers accused of orchestrating a massacre of Bosnian Muslims argued that the attacks were justifiable because Bosnian Muslims were allegedly perpetrating similar attacks against Croats. The Tribunal stressed "the irrelevance of reciprocity, particularly in relation to obligations found within international humanitarian law which have an absolute and non-derogable character. . . . The defining characteristic of modern international humanitarian law is instead the obligation to uphold key tenets of this body of law regardless of the conduct of enemy combatants."[29] Consider the implications if reprisals were to remain a viable option for belligerent parties.

QUESTIONS FOR DISCUSSION

1. Reprisals were fairly common during World War II and were still considered to be a legitimate form of warfare, as "[r]etaliation for illegitimate acts of warfare for the purpose of making the enemy comply in future with the recognised laws of war."[30] Nonetheless, not all acts in reprisal were considered to be lawful. In 1944, members of the Italian resistance detonated a bomb among a company of German police marching in Rome, killing thirty-two. The German High Command ordered that ten Italians be executed for every German killed in the bombing. Although the stated intention was to use prisoners already sentenced to death in the reprisals, the Germans gathered up 335 Italians, including not only existing prisoners but also some teenagers, some elderly, and fifty-seven Jews who had no involvement in partisan activities and were not necessarily even Italians. In what became known as the Ardeatine massacre, the Germans lined them up and shot them in the Ardeatine cave and then buried the cave entrance in an explosion so there would be no survivors and no evidence. After the war, the British Military Court in Rome found the two German commanders in Rome guilty of war crimes and sentenced them to death, which was ultimately commuted to life imprisonment. If reprisals were lawful at the time (before the 1949 Geneva Conventions), why did the Court find that the German actions were unlawful? How did the German actions go beyond the customary parameters of reprisals?

---

29. Prosecutor v. Kupreškić, Case No. IT-95-16-T, Judgement ¶ 511 (Int'l Crim. Trib. for the Former Yugoslavia Jan. 14, 2000).

30. Trial of General Von Mackensen and General Maelzer, Case No. 43 (British Mil. Ct., Rome Nov. 30, 1945), *reprinted in* VIII U.N. War Crimes Comm'n, Law Reports of Trials of War Criminals 1, 5 (1949) (citing War Office, Great Britain, Manual of Military Law (1907)).

2. One of the ICTY's arguments in the *Kupreškić* case is that reprisals are now prohibited because a superior option for compelling adherence to the law exists: international criminal justice. Would a warring party be justified in resorting to reprisals if it could show that there was no hope for any international or domestic criminal process to hold perpetrators on the other side accountable? Could reprisals be justified before the possibility of a criminal justice mechanism is apparent and then prohibited afterwards? What is the value of a blanket prohibition on reprisals?

2. *Obligations to Protect Civilians*

LOAC's protections for civilians do not stop at the prohibition of attacks on civilians, whether direct, indiscriminate, or disproportionate. The very first sentence of Article 51 of Additional Protocol I states: "The civilian population and individual civilians shall enjoy general protection against dangers arising from military operations." There is no doubt that the "dangers arising from military operations" are significantly broader than the dangers arising directly from attacks on civilians or on targets where civilians are likely to be hurt or killed. Given that most contemporary conflicts take place within heavily populated areas and involve frequent, if not constant, contact with civilians, it is important to explore the permissible range of treatment of civilians in the course of military operations. The law definitively prohibits using civilians or civilian objects to shield military objects from attack. In fact, if one party uses human shields or civilian objects it is then responsible for any resulting deaths or damage. But what about using civilians for information or other seemingly innocuous purposes during operations?

The Israeli Supreme Court faced this question in the aftermath of Operation Defensive Wall in the West Bank in 2002, after human rights organizations petitioned the court to enjoin the military's use of the Early Warning Procedure, under which Israeli soldiers seeking to arrest a suspected terrorist could ask a Palestinian civilian to warn the suspect or others in the building in the hopes of minimizing the risk of injury to the suspect or danger to others. The court balanced two conflicting considerations: 1) "the value of human life" and "the general duty of the occupying army to ensure the dignity and security of the civilian population"; and 2) "the occupying army's duty to safeguard the life and dignity of the local civilian sent to relay the warning."[31] The court held that the obligation to protect the local resident prevails, based on the prohibition against using civilians for military purposes or as part of the war effort or occupying army.

31. Adalah—The Legal Center for Arab Minority Rights in Israel v. GOC Central Command, Israel Defense Force PD 11, HCJ3799/02 [2005].

QUESTIONS FOR DISCUSSION

1. In a concurring opinion, one of the justices raised the hypothetical of a father arriving home to find that his house, in which a dangerous terrorist is hiding, is surrounded by military forces with his wife and children inside—and the court's ruling would forbid the army from allowing the father to call his family to evacuate the house. In effect, he argued, the military would face "the following choice: being aided by the father, who will warn his family, or storming the house, involving mortal danger to the residents of the house and to the soldiers."[32] Does the Court's ruling provide a satisfactory answer in light of the issues raised in this hypothetical situation?

2. The Court relies on the law of occupation, but would the Court's conclusions be different if there were no occupation? Would the state's obligations to the civilians be different?

3. Could the military prevent a civilian from providing unsolicited assistance? Would the obligation to protect civilians from the dangers of military operations require that a military unit take action to prevent such assistance?

INFORMANTS, IEDs AND LOAC

You are part of the coalition forces conducting counterinsurgency operations in Iraq. Over the past few weeks, the number of improvised explosive devices (IED) that have been used in your area of operations has dramatically increased. Intelligence sources report that an IED manufacturer has moved into your area and opened up a cell of IED makers and distributors that has then led to an increase in IED use. Recently, you detained an individual who appears to be linked to the IED maker. When questioned, he volunteered to identify the building where the IEDs are made. He cannot seem to identify the building from imagery but is certain that he can take coalition forces there.

1. Do you send the informant to do the identification? If so, do you have a duty to safeguard him?
2. If you do have a duty, how do you propose to satisfy that duty? Do you send him with a dismounted patrol? A mounted patrol? In the back of an armored personnel carrier?

—*Lieutenant Colonel Eric Jensen, JAGC, U.S. Army (Ret.)*

---

32. *Id.* at 14.

4. Consider other ways in which LOAC's general obligations to spare civilians from the "ravages of war" play out in practice, beyond the actual conduct of combat operations. Early in the 2003 war in Iraq, an American unit happened upon an abandoned bottling factory, where they found crate after crate of sodas. It was—as common in Iraq—extremely hot and dry and the commander wondered out loud if it wouldn't be so bad if the soldiers enjoyed the sodas, since they were just sitting there going to waste anyway. Was the commander right that "it wouldn't really matter"?

The Goat Herders

What happens when LOAC is put to the test at the small unit level? The following three events happened when elite forces were discovered by innocent civilians—children, shepherds, and goat herders—deep behind enemy lines. Each unit faced a legal and ethical dilemma in which their lives hung in the balance based on the consequences of their respective decisions. Should they silence those who discovered them by happenstance or let them pass but potentially jeopardize their mission and their lives? In all three cases, the Special Forces units let the goat herders go, and the herders in turn alerted local enemy forces. Some men lost their lives, while others were captured and tortured.

IRAQ: U.S. SPECIAL FORCES

On February 24th, 1991, an eight-man U.S. Special Forces reconnaissance team led by Chief Warrant Officer Two Richard Balwanz is dug into its hiding hole (covered with camouflage netting) for the day after being inserted into Iraq south of Baghdad the night before. In the early morning, three children between five and seven years of age are playing nearby and discover the team. The startled children run away screaming. The team, with silenced automatic pistols, look to CWO2 Balwanz for guidance. His response is immediate, "No, we are not going to shoot children. Or unarmed civilians. I'm sorry, but that is not going to happen."[33] His team moves from the hole to a nearby ditch to continue the mission, but they are discovered for a second time by more children and an adult a few hours later. Again, they do not engage the civilians and the adult makes his way quickly back to the nearby village. Shortly thereafter, a company of Iraqi soldiers and armed Bedouins begin the attack as the team radios for an exfiltration. A fierce six-hour firefight, with close air support, ensues and the team

33. AL SANTOLI, LEADING THE WAY: HOW VIETNAM VETERANS REBUILT THE U.S. MILITARY: AN ORAL HISTORY 316 (1993).

is pinned down in the canal as more and more Iraqi troops come onto the scene. Ultimately all eight men are pulled out safely and survive.

IRAQ: U.K. SPECIAL FORCES

The second incident also happened during the 1991 Gulf War, one month earlier. Eight British Special Air Service (SAS) troops were deep behind enemy lines in Iraq in January 1991 on a reconnaissance and Scud hunting mission. During the day, SAS personnel would hide in carefully camouflaged "lying up positions" in wadis, gullies, or other spots where detection by Iraqi troops would be difficult. The desert, ostensibly empty, was in fact populated with Bedouin goat herders and their families, who were scattered throughout the "Scud alley" operational area. The risk of compromise by the tribesmen was a major concern for the SAS before and during their missions. Although some troopers favored killing any Bedouins they encountered, a "hearts and minds" approach prevailed.[34]

The trouble for the mission started when a young shepherd, and subsequently a man driving a bulldozer, stumbled upon the team. In both situations, the team decided to withdraw and not harm the civilians. Unfortunately, the team could not contact anyone for an exfiltration due to radio issues. Three died (one was killed in action and two died of hypothermia), and Iraqi forces captured (and later abused and tortured) four more. One soldier escaped capture by walking over 100 miles to Syria.

AFGHANISTAN

In June 2005, a four-man SEAL Team from SEAL Team Ten was on a kill/capture mission in Afghanistan.[35] Three shepherds (including a teenage boy) inadvertently discovered the four-man team. According to then-Navy SEAL Petty Officer Second Class Marcus Luttrell, he and his three teammates voted on whether to kill or release the

---

34. When they encountered Bedouins, the SAS teams attempted to co-opt them. "Patrols neither abducted nor killed [them]. They were respectful to them, offered them food and drink, and if necessary bluffed them." KEN CONNOR, GHOST FORCE: THE SECRET HISTORY OF THE SAS 313 (1998).

35. *See* MARCUS LUTTRELL & PATRICK ROBINSON, LONE SURVIVOR: THE EYEWITNESS ACCOUNT OF OPERATION REDWING AND THE LOST HEROES OF SEAL TEAM 10 (2007).

civilians, recognizing that they would probably notify local Taliban fighters if released. Luttrell claims that one team member voted to kill the shepherds, one abstained, and the team leader Navy SEAL Lieutenant Michael Murphy voted to release them but said he would agree with whatever Luttrell voted.[36] Luttrell voted to let them go and within the hour the team faced over 140 Taliban fighters. A two-hour firefight ensued: Luttrell's three SEAL teammates perished, as did sixteen would-be rescuers—eight additional SEALs and eight Army special operations soldiers (160th Special Operations Aviation Regiment "Night Stalkers"), whose MH-47 Chinook helicopter was shot down by a Taliban rocket-propelled grenade.[37]

QUESTIONS FOR DISCUSSION

1. Would restraining or tying up the shepherds have been a reasonable middle ground? But what if tying someone up in the desert or mountains essentially equaled a slow but sure death?

2. If the Special Operations Forces had a reasonable belief that, in fact, these shepherds were acting as lookouts or sentries, then deadly force could have been authorized. Alternatively, once the civilians were restrained in some way—if that option were taken as suggested in the question above—what obligations would they have owed the civilians?

3. Should LOAC allow civilian casualties in circumstances like these? Are there other circumstances where civilian casualties would be allowed? Could these "unlucky" civilians be categorized as "collateral damage" much like the innocent janitor working the night shift at a building that is a legitimate target?

4. In an interview, Luttrell seems conflicted when he states,

I was a soldier following the rules of engagement. We made the judgment call to turn them loose because they weren't armed combatants. And because of that, 19 of my comrades are dead. If you put me back in the same situation, I'd probably do the same thing again, if I didn't know the

36. Lieutenant Murphy's parents dispute this account, maintaining that their son was a decisive person who understood his leadership role and never would have held such a vote. Lieutenant Murphy posthumously earned the Medal of Honor for exposing himself to enemy fire while seeking higher or open ground in order to radio for support. The other team members, including Luttrell, received the Navy Cross (the United States' second highest medal).

37. Luttrell survived by hiding and then receiving shelter from local Pashtun tribesmen who risked their lives to protect him. Sean D. Mayer, *Surviving SEAL Tells Story of Deadly Mission*, ARMY TIMES (Jun. 18, 2007, 6:25 PM), http://www.armytimes.com/news/2007/06/navy_sealbook_070618w.

outcome. Knowing what I know now, knowing what we went through and what I go through every day, hell yeah, I would have killed them.[38]

What do you think about these comments? Do you agree with him or not? What, if anything, is he right or wrong about?

5. Some, including Luttrell, argue that the rules of engagement handicap U.S. soldiers by forcing them to fight with "one hand tied behind their backs" and because the enemy knows exactly what U.S. legal and policy limits are regarding the conduct of hostilities. Do such statements provide a justification for taking more forceful measures against civilians than the law might otherwise allow in different situations?

3. Direct Participation in Hostilities

Although civilian immunity from attack remains a central and defining principle of LOAC, the practical and functional needs of the law lead to one important exception: direct participation in hostilities. Article 51(3) of Additional Protocol I sets forth this exception.

ARTICLE 51(3) OF ADDITIONAL PROTOCOL I

Civilians shall enjoy the protection afforded by this section, unless and for such time as they take a direct part in hostilities.

In certain limited circumstances, therefore, civilians may be directly and intentionally targeted during hostilities: "The principle of distinction acknowledges the military necessity prong of [the law's] balancing act by suspending the protection to which civilians are entitled when they become intricately involved in a conflict."[39] From a practical standpoint, the law's foundational notions of equality of application and equality of arms would no longer make sense if civilians could engage in hostilities but maintain their immunity from attack. Direct participation thus also comports with the basic right of individual self-defense by recognizing that a soldier engaged in conflict has the right to respond with force to someone posing a threat, whether that person is a combatant or a civilian. Defining the parameters of direct participation, however, is challenging and often highly case specific. The Commentary to Additional Protocol I explains that direct participation lies in a middle ground of sorts:

---

38. *See* Sean Naylor, *A Command Decision: SEAL Author Speaks of Regret, Rescue, and the Choice that Cost 19 Lives*, ARMY TIMES (Jun. 18, 2007, 12:41 PM), http://www.armytimes.com /entertainment/books/military_luttrell_qanda_070618w.

39. Michael N. Schmitt, *The Interpretive Guidance on the Notion of Direct Participation in Hostilities: A Critical Analysis*, 1 HARV. NAT'L SEC. J. 5, 12 (2010).

to restrict this concept to combat and to active military operations would be too narrow, while extending it to the entire war effort would be too broad, as in modern warfare the whole population participates in the war effort to some extent, albeit indirectly. The population cannot on this ground be considered to be combatants. . . .[40]

A few key points are essential to the discussion of direct participation in hostilities. First, the rule applies only to civilians. Combatants can be attacked at all times and enjoy no immunity from attack, unless *hors de combat*. Complexities arise in the case of organized armed groups and other non-state entities in which individuals are fighting as a regular course—in essence, as their job—but do not qualify as combatants. In both international and non-international armed conflicts, there is now a general recognition that members of organized armed groups are targetable on the basis of their status as the enemy, or hostile force, meaning that such persons would not qualify as civilians enjoying immunity from attack, i.e., as relevant for a direct participation analysis. However, the question of who constitutes a civilian for the purposes of this discussion continues to be a challenging one in many situations. Second, the question of "for such time"—the temporal aspect of direct participation—is only relevant if there is indeed an underlying act of direct participation.

In a seminal case on direct participation in hostilities, the Israeli Supreme Court thoroughly analyzed the components of the concept of direct participation and highlighted several key issues. The case stemmed from the Israeli practice of preventative strikes against individual Palestinian terrorists in the early 2000s, in response to a wave of Palestinian terrorist attacks against civilians and civilian infrastructure in Israel. Assessing the legality of such strikes, the court first had to determine if the targets of the strikes were legitimate targets of attack by dint of their direct participation in hostilities. As the court explained, direct participation includes three component parts:

1. Hostilities, which "are acts which by nature and objective are intended to cause damage to the army";[41]
2. Taking a direct part, which distinguishes between those taking an active part in hostilities and those who merely generally support the hostilities;
3. For such time, which determines when the civilian's protection from attack resumes. The court reaffirmed that the civilian taking direct part one time or sporadically is entitled to protection from attack once

---

40. CLAUDE PILLOUD, YVES SANDOZ, CHRISTOPHE SWINARSKI, BRUNO ZIMMERMAN, COMMENTARY ON THE ADDITIONAL PROTOCOLS OF 8 JUNE 1977 TO THE GENEVA CONVENTIONS OF 12 AUGUST 1949 516 (1987).

41. Public Committee Against Torture in Israel v. Gov't of Israel 33, HCJ 769/02 [2005].

he disengages from the activity, but emphasized the challenge of the "revolving door," where a civilian regularly engages in hostilities and effectively uses the time between such acts to prepare while enjoying immunity from attack.

The court included in the definition of direct participation the following acts: "a person who collects intelligence on the army"; "a person who transports unlawful combatants to or from the place where the hostilities are taking place; a person who operates weapons which unlawful combatants use; a person who provides service to them, be the distance from the battlefield as it may." In contrast, other types of support would not constitute taking a direct part: "a person who sells food or medicine to an unlawful combatant"; "a person who aids the unlawful combatants by general strategic analysis, and grants them logistical, general support, including monetary aid"; and "a person who distributes propaganda supporting those unlawful combatants."[42]

Civilians have always been present on the battlefield and engaged in hostilities, but the past few decades have seen a dramatic increase in civilian presence, particularly due to the use of civilian contractors, as discussed above, and to the steady increase in conflicts fought in urban areas and among the civilian population. In response to the need for a more thorough understanding of the parameters of direct participation in hostilities, the ICRC initiated a multiyear expert consultation process to analyze and formulate further guidance regarding direct participation in hostilities. The result, released in 2009, was the *Interpretive Guidance on the Notion of Direct Participation in Hostilities under International Humanitarian Law.*

The ICRC's Interpretive Guidance sets forth the constitutive elements of direct participation:

> In order to qualify as direct participation in hostilities, a specific act must meet the following cumulative criteria:
>
> 1. the act must be likely to adversely affect the military operations or military capacity of a party to an armed conflict or, alternatively, to inflict death, injury, or destruction on persons or objects protected against direct attack (threshold of harm), and
> 2. there must be a direct causal link between the act and the harm likely to result either from that act, or from a coordinated military operation of which that act constitutes an integral part (direct causation), and
> 3. the act must be specifically designed to directly cause the required threshold of harm in support of a party to the conflict and to the detriment of another (belligerent nexus).[43]

42. *Id.* at 34-35.

43. Int'l Comm. Red Cross, Interpretive Guidance on the Notion of Direct Participation in Hostilities Under International Humanitarian Law 22 (2009).

Although the immediate consideration in assessing direct participation in hostilities is whether the individual in question can be targeted, civilian participation in hostilities raises additional questions as well. First, civilians who directly participate in hostilities do not become combatants, but remain civilians. As discussed at the start of this chapter, civilian and combatant are status categories based on membership, not conduct. Therefore, a civilian who directly participates in hostilities is still a civilian, but loses her protection from attack for that time. Second, such civilians will be liable to detention as threats to security and can be taken into custody and questioned—in accordance with all humane treatment obligations, of course. Finally, direct participation in hostilities triggers accountability considerations as well. LOAC does not criminalize civilian participation in hostilities *per se*. Rather, under international law, the consequence of direct participation is the loss of civilian immunity from attack. In addition, because they are not combatants, civilians who directly participate will not have any immunity from prosecution if arrested and charged with criminal conduct under domestic law as a result of their participation in hostilities.

QUESTIONS FOR DISCUSSION

1. Does the ICRC *Interpretive Guidance* provide clarification regarding the concept of direct participation in hostilities? Consider the examples in the notes below in light of the definitions in the *Interpretive Guidance*.

2. The *Interpretive Guidance* has fostered extensive discussion and criticisms. One primary criticism is that the guidance skews LOAC's inherent balance between military necessity and humanity too far in the direction of humanity, which will cause states—the primary implementers of LOAC—to view the guidance skeptically. For example, the guidance does not include civilian acts that strengthen their own side's military capacity, focusing instead only on civilian acts that harm the adversary. And yet commanders are going to be equally concerned with acts that strengthen the enemy's capacity as with acts that weaken or harm their own forces' capacity.

One of the major disagreements lies in the treatment of voluntary human shields: the *Interpretive Guidance* treats voluntary human shields as protected civilians not participating in hostilities. Many LOAC experts disagree, arguing that

> From an attacker's perspective (the military necessity prong), it does not matter why an attack cannot be mounted. Whether the obstacle is physical or legal, any military advantage that might have accrued from the attack is forfeited. Indeed, the legal obstacle is often the more effective one. A physical obstacle can be removed or otherwise countered in many situations; a legal prohibition is absolute. . . . Finally, one has to query why [LOAC] would distinguish between those who physically protect a

military objective from those who intentionally misuse the law's protective provisions to prevent an otherwise lawful attack. It would seem that the latter poses the greater risk to humanitarian ends by undermining respect for [LOAC].[44]

A second concern arises in the *Interpretive Guidance*'s treatment of the "revolving door" problem, that is, the civilian who repeatedly participates in hostilities. How does the ICRC's approach compare to the approach in the Israeli Supreme Court's *Targeted Killing* case? What are the consequences of treating such persons as protected civilians in between each engagement in hostilities? Alternatively, what are the consequences of treating such persons as continuously participating in hostilities? Which approach seems more consistent with the fundamental principles of LOAC? Which approach seems more likely to foster effective application of the law and its basic goals and principles?

3. The United States Navy's Commander's Handbook on the Law of Naval Operations explains:

> Direct participation in hostilities must be judged on a case-by-case basis. Some examples include taking up arms or otherwise trying to kill, injure or capture enemy personnel or destroy enemy property. Also, civilians serving as lookouts or guards, or intelligence agents for military forces may be considered to be directly participating in hostilities.[45]

4. The United Kingdom's *Manual of the Law of Armed Conflict* offers the following examples:

> Civilians manning an anti-aircraft gun or engaging in sabotage of military installations are [taking a direct part in hostilities]. Civilians working in military vehicle maintenance depots or munitions factories or driving military transport vehicles are not, but they are at risk from attacks on those objectives since military objectives may be attacked whether or not civilians are present.[46]

5. In *Prosecutor v. Strugar*, the ICTY Appeals Chamber confirmed that a civilian driver for the Dubrovnik Municipal Crisis Staff and the President of the Executive Council of Dubrovnik was not directly participating in hostilities. The Chamber discussed the following examples of direct participation:

> bearing, using or taking up arms, taking part in military or hostile acts, activities, conduct or operations, armed fighting or combat, participating in attacks against enemy personnel, property or equipment, transmitting military

---

44. Michael N. Schmitt, *The Interpretive Guidance on the Notion of Direct Participation in Hostilities: A Critical Analysis*, 1 HARV. NAT'L SEC. J. 5, 32 (2010).

45. DEP'T OF THE NAVY, THE COMMANDER'S HANDBOOK ON THE LAW OF NAVAL OPERATIONS, NWP 1-14M 8.2.2 (2007).

46. UNITED KINGDOM MINISTRY OF DEFENCE, JSP 383: THE JOINT SERVICE MANUAL OF THE LAW OF ARMED CONFLICT 8.1.1 (2004). The manual notes that attacks on military objectives are, of course, subject to the principle of proportionality.

information for the immediate use of a belligerent, transporting weapons in proximity to combat operations, and serving as guards, intelligence agents, lookouts, or observers on behalf of military forces. Examples of indirect participation in hostilities include: participating in activities in support of the war or military effort of one of the parties to the conflict, selling goods to one of the parties to the conflict, expressing sympathy for the cause of one of the parties to the conflict, failing to act to prevent an incursion by one of the parties to the conflict, accompanying and supplying food to one of the parties to the conflict, gathering and transmitting military information, transporting arms and munitions, and providing supplies, and providing specialist advice regarding the selection of military personnel, their training or the correct maintenance of the weapons.[47]

6. In *U.S. v. Salim Ahmed Hamdan*, the prosecution of Osama bin Laden's driver before the Military Commission at Guantanamo Bay, the question arose whether Hamdan was directly participating in hostilities by driving a car with surface to air missiles:

> The Commission also finds that the accused directly participated in those hostilities by driving a vehicle containing two surface-to-air missiles in both temporal and spatial proximity to both ongoing combat operations. The fact that U.S. and coalition forces had the only air assets against which the missiles might have been used supports a finding that the accused actively participated in hostilities *against the United States and its coalition partners*. Although Kandahar was a short distance away, the accused's past history of delivering munitions to Taliban and al-Qaeda fighters, his possession of a vehicle containing surface to air missiles, and his capture while driving in the direction of a battle already underway, satisfies the requirement of "direct participation."[48]

Do these various examples — of both direct and indirect participation — fit within the framework in the Interpretive Guidance?

7. Consider the launching of an attack from an unmanned aerial vehicle (UAV) or "drone." When the drone is operated entirely by the military, the question of direct participation in hostilities does not arise, because once there is an armed conflict, all members of the regular armed forces are combatants and legitimate targets of attack at all times. When contractors or civilian personnel, such as intelligence personnel, operate drones during armed conflict, questions arise as to the status of such persons and the nature of their liability to or immunity from attack. In the context of direct participation, think about who is involved in such an attack (keeping in mind that they are all operating remotely): the drone pilot, the navigator and weapons systems operator, and the mission coordinator.[49] There

---

47. Prosecutor v. Strugar, Case No. IT-01-42-A, Appeals Judgement 176 (Int'l Crim. Trib. for the Former Yugoslavia July 17, 2008).

48. United States v. Hamdan, 1 Mil. Comm'n Rep. 22 (Mil. Comm'n 2007).

49. *Factsheets: MQ-1B Predator*, U.S. Air Force (July 20, 2010), http://www.af.mil /information/factsheets/factsheet.asp?id=122.

is a general consensus that each of these individuals is directly participating in hostilities during the preparation for the attack, during the attack, and on the return. What about the launch and recovery teams? What about the intelligence personnel analyzing the reconnaissance information for the purpose of targeting decisions? Do non-military personnel who operate combat drones during armed conflict violate the law simply by launching attacks?[50]

8.   Another interesting scenario arises in the context of cyber attacks and cyberwarfare. Recent examples include the Stuxnet virus (discovered in 2010 but first released in 2009) that damaged Iran's nuclear capabilities, the 2007 cyber attack on Estonia (most likely emanating from Russia), and assorted cyber attacks during the 2008 war between Georgia and Russia. In the last example, the Russian government denied any role in the attacks, but it is widely believed that the Russian government sponsored or promoted civilian hackers to launch the attacks—and even to coordinate the attacks with the military.[51] China has apparently also encouraged the growth of "hactivists" to attack political targets. Other potential "cyber warriors" could include lone actors or private firms that employ cyber warfare specialists. Analyzing when such persons fall within the concept of direct participation in hostilities, if and when such acts take place during an armed conflict, raises a host of questions. For example, when will a cyber attack be more analogous to firing a gun or launching a missile? When will it be more analogous to merely assembling parts for guns or missiles at a factory far removed from any war? Does the nature of the target matter? Do conventional military operations need to be ongoing or perhaps even coordinating with the cyber attacks for the latter to qualify as participation in hostilities? Is simply writing the code for a virus that will attack a critical infrastructure sufficient to constitute direct participation?[52]

9.   Cyber operations also present questions regarding the "for such time" aspect of direct participation in hostilities. Consider the challenge of identifying *when* an individual might be directly participating:

50.   In 2010, the United States recalled its CIA station chief in Islamabad, Pakistan, after he was named in a legal action for deaths due to drone strikes in Pakistan's tribal areas. Declan Walsh, *CIA Chief in Pakistan Leaves After Drone Trial Blows His Cover*, THE GUARDIAN (Dec. 17, 2010). Although he left primarily because his cover was blown, imagine if the case were a criminal prosecution. Would he be susceptible to prosecution under Pakistani law?

51.   Brian Krebs, *Report: Russian Hacker Forums Fueled Georgia Cyber Attacks*, WASHINGTON-POST.COM (Oct. 15, 2008, 3:15 PM); John Markoff, *Before the Gunfire, Cyberattacks*, N.Y. TIMES, Aug. 13, 2008, at A1, *available at* http://www.nytimes.com/2008/08/13/technology/13cyber.html.

52.   For extensive discussion and commentary regarding the application of international law to cyber operations, see TALLINN MANUAL 2.0 ON THE INTERNATIONAL LAW APPLICABLE TO CYBER OPERATIONS (Michael N. Schmitt ed., 2017).

First, there may be no "deployment" at all since only a computer, and not proximity to the target, is required to mount the operations. The restrictive interpretation of the for such time criterion would suggest that the direct participant can only be attacked while actually launching the operation. This is problematic in that many cyber operations last mere minutes, perhaps only seconds. Such a requirement would effectively extinguish the right to strike at direct participants. Moreover, the effect of a cyber operation may be long-delayed, as in the case of a surreptitiously emplaced logic bomb. Would the target of such an operation only be entitled to attack the direct participant while the logic bomb is being emplaced? The problem is that the very point of these operations is to avoid detection. Therefore, from a practical perspective, there would appear to be no window of opportunity for the victim of an attack to respond. In the cyber conflict environment, therefore, the only reasonable interpretation of "for such time" is that it encompasses the entire period during which the direct cyber participant is engaging in repeated cyber operations.[53]

Does this focus on the actor, rather than the act, make sense as a tool for analysis in cyber? What would be the effect if this analytical approach were to spread to the kinetic environment? Could it make sense in some situations? What risks might it produce?

10. Suicide bomb attacks involve a basic infrastructure of four people: the bomber, the driver or logistical person, the planner or commander (the quarterback, in essence), and the financier. Think about what each of these individuals does and when and how that affects a direct participation analysis. The bomber is chosen both for his (or her) willingness to die and for his (or her) dispensability. He or she straps on the bomb, is taken to the target area, and detonates at the designated time (and—obviously—there will not be a return from deployment in such situations). The driver takes the bomber to the designated area and deposits him or her before driving away. The planner or commander is involved from start to finish—identifying targets; procuring the explosives and other necessary materials; identifying, selecting, and recruiting the bomber; coordinating all the team members; and receiving and dispensing money as needed. The financier is the most attenuated from the process—he may simply wire money or receive money at his bank and transfer it—and yet is also indispensable to the process. Which of these individuals is directly participating in hostilities? Which are participating only "for such time"? Are some of them directly participating in hostilities at all times?

11. Those who are participating in hostilities at all times are thus legitimate targets of attack at all times. What conduct—or perhaps what role in an organization—would shift a person from periodic participation in hostilities to regular, constant, or permanent participation in hostilities? Another

53. Michael N. Schmitt, *Cyber Issues and the* Jus in Bello: *Key Issues*, 87 Int'l L. Stud. 89, 102 (2011).

factor to consider is how such individuals "withdraw" from participation in hostilities, particularly those who are targets all the time. What about those whose involvement is more like a "revolving door," i.e., militants, terrorists, and others who engage in regular attacks but benefit from civilian immunity in between, posing significant challenges for their adversary's efforts to neutralize the threat they pose? One approach is that such persons need to make an affirmative step to withdraw from hostilities in order to regain their civilian immunity. How else could we view the parameters of targeting and direct participation here?

12. Consider the importance of clarity and certainty on the battlefield in analyzing these approaches: how best can the obligations of distinction and protection of the civilian population be upheld in these situations? In order to carry out the obligation of distinguishing between combatants and civilians, between persons who are fighting and those who are not, we need to be able to determine who fits within each category. What happens when those lines are blurred? When persons who are fighting blend into the civilian population in order to avoid being identified as a legitimate target of attack? For example, during Operation Iraqi Freedom, Iraqi insurgents commonly wore civilian clothing when approaching American and British forces in order to get closer without seeming to present a threat. Perhaps most nefariously, insurgent groups that employ suicide bombing as a tactic turned to the use of women and children, for they have proven more likely to evade measures designed to identify suicide bombers. This great fluidity between hostile persons and innocent civilians and the conscious blending of hostile persons into the civilian population can make a soldier's task extraordinarily difficult. For example, a soldier manning a checkpoint sees a jeep speeding toward him. It could be civilians seeking aid or fleeing from danger, or it could be insurgents bent on driving the vehicle into the checkpoint as a suicide bomb. The soldier who reacts too soon and fires on the jeep risks killing innocent civilians; the soldier who waits too long to make a positive identification risks dying in a fiery explosion.

13. Another example from Iraq involves the use of civilians as spotters, or forward observers. Consider the following excerpt from *Generation Kill*:

> Patterson's Alpha Company snipers on the riverfront are dealing with the ambiguities of guerilla war, not covered in the Marine Rules of Engagement [ROE]. The ROE [are] based on the assumption that legitimate targets are people armed with weapons. The problem is Iraqis dressed in civilian clothes who are armed not with guns but with cell phones, walkietalkies and binoculars. These men, it is believed by the Marines, are serving as forward observers for the mortars being dropped into their positions.
>
> Mortars are a weapon of choice for the Iraqis. A mortar is a rocket-propelled bomb that is launched from a tube that's about a meter long. . . . Even the smaller mortars used by the Iraqis will, when they hit, scoop out

about a meter-wide hole in the ground and spray shrapnel for twenty-five meters in all directions. A direct hit from a mortar can disable the biggest American tank, or [destroy] a Humvee.

Since mortars are small and light, they can be moved around easily and fired from rooftops, trenches, alleys, even from the backs of pickup trucks. Even better from the enemy's standpoint, you can't tell which direction they're being fired from. They might be five kilometers away in a trench behind a house or an apartment block.

But since mortar crews are so far away and usually out of sight, they rely on forward observers. These characters tend to hang out near Marine positions with binoculars, cell phones or radios. They watch where the mortars are landing and call back to the guys shooting them to tell them how to adjust their fire. Those who appear to be observers in Nasiriyah are unarmed, dressed in civilian clothes and blend in with the population.

During the first hour . . . , Marine snipers had to request permission up the chain of command to get "cleared hot" to shoot suspected forward observers. Killing unarmed civilians is a dicey issue, but eventually the Marine snipers are given permission to take out Iraqis with binoculars or cell phones on the other side of the river.[54]

Are such spotters or forward observers directly participating in hostilities? How can soldiers or Marines tell the difference between a forward observer and an uninvolved civilian with a cell phone? How does LOAC try to strike the appropriate balance?

THE SUICIDE BOMBER?

You are the Battalion Judge Advocate with the 3d Light Armored Reconnaissance Battalion (3d LAR Bn) deployed in spring 2009 to Nineveh Province, Iraq. Nineveh is the most ethnically diverse province in Iraq, with Sunni Arabs, Kurds, Turkmen, and Yazidi peoples. It also contains the disputed—and important—southern border of Kurdistan.

The current intelligence situation is that you have a Be On the Look Out (BOLO) report for an orange Mercedes dump truck packed with explosives that is looking for elements of 3d LAR Bn throughout the Area of Operations (AO) as a target of opportunity. You've been in Iraq for approximately two months, and your unit has been hit only once by a weak Improvised Explosive Device (IED), although several IEDs have been found prior to detonation. Insurgent attacks have mainly been targeting the Iraqi Army.

---

54. Evan Wright, Generation Kill 102-103 (2004). Similar challenges were portrayed in the movie *Hurt Locker* (Voltage Pictures 2009).

On this particular day, you are travelling in a platoon-size element comprised of six light armored vehicles carrying you (the Battalion Judge Advocate), the Battalion Commanding Officer, and your security detachment to meet with a Kurdish General in the primarily Kurdish city of Sunnuni. This meeting is to discuss rising tensions between the Iraqi Army and Kurdish militia (the Peshmerga). When you arrive at the Kurdish compound, you move with your Battalion Commander and your security detachment from your vehicles via foot patrol approximately 50 meters past a row of homes to the Peshmerga compound. You direct your security detachment to establish an outer cordon of security around the Peshmerga entry control point (ECP) in order for you to establish contact with the Peshmerga and entry into their compound. The ECP is approximately 100 meters long, walled on both sides by two-meter-high walls, and contains four road barrier serpentines to slow incoming vehicle traffic.

The Peshmerga General is not present, so a Marine Officer must enter the compound with a small security detachment to speak with the Peshmerga second in command. Part of your outer security cordon, which is extended out to the end of the ECP, must therefore be pulled off their posts to enter the compound. You immediately identify the security gap and move to the end of the ECP where you have a view down the perpendicularly adjoining road. When you arrive, you see some local males dressed in traditional Iraqi man-dresses. You wave with your right hand to test the atmospherics of the locals and receive no return wave, and only cold stares. You look to your right and see an orange Mercedes dump truck with a single male driver, sitting at the nearest intersection, oriented in your direction. After a moment of sitting at the intersection, the dump truck begins to move slowly in your direction. You begin to move quickly back into the ECP. The truck never passes the front of the ECP, and you don't know where it went or if it stopped.

At that point, an Iraqi male begins walking into the ECP from the direction of the unfriendly locals carrying a black plastic bag and dressed very nicely (which is out of place for this part of Iraq). You look through your Rifle Combat Optic (RCO) to get a better look at the individual's face with its magnified capability. The individual is clearly developmentally disabled as evidenced by defects in his facial structure and the way he is walking. You put your left hand up in a stopping motion, keeping your right on the pistol grip of your M4 Carbine, and say, "quiff, quiff, quiff" ["stop, stop, stop"] loudly in Arabic. The individual keeps walking toward you. You take a few steps aggressively forward and repeat your action with no response. You again look through your RCO to see the individual smile oddly and raise his hands partially in the air, while continuing to walk towards you. Your Battalion

Commander is ten meters behind you, about to exit the compound. You don't know what is in the plastic bag, but you can tell that it does not look very heavy. You are more concerned about an explosive vest or other device on his body. With each step, the danger he poses—to both your unit and the Peshmerga compound and soldiers—*if* he is wearing an explosive device increases exponentially.

What do you do? Is this person a legitimate target? Is he directly participating in hostilities? Is he a civilian immune from attack?

At the last second, as you are assessing whether to shoot this individual, a gust of wind blows from your rear against the individual as he is walking toward you, pushing his pants and shirt tightly against his body. You can see that he has no large explosive vest or anything strapped to his legs.

> *This situation happened to me. I responded by yelling to the Peshmerga ECP guard to address the situation rather than shooting the individual. The Peshmerga guard indicated that he knew the individual and that the situation was safe, although he hurried the individual through the ECP as we were all agitated. Immediately after the situation ended, the Battalion Commander yelled to me, "Hey Judge, the last guy I saw who looked just like that turned into pink mist right in front of me!"*
>
> — *Captain Chad Brooks, U.S. Marine Corps judge advocate*

1. If you shot the individual, would you be violating LOAC? Before the wind gust? Would your answer change after?

2. Apart from the question of whether you could shoot, how do you assess whether you should shoot?

3. Is there a right answer in this situation?

D.   DETENTION OF CIVILIANS

Unlike the detention of combatants during international armed conflict, which is "a fundamental incident of waging war,"[55] the detention of civilians is an extraordinary measure. Under the Fourth Geneva Convention, internment of civilians is the most severe measure that may be taken to address security threats civilians may pose.[56] Most important, detention or internment of civilians is solely conduct-based, in contrast to the status-based detention of POWs. This framework is a direct response to the abuses committed against

---

55. Hamdi v. Rumsfeld, 542 U.S. 507, 519 (2004).

56. Under Article 41 of the Fourth Geneva Convention, "Should the Power in whose hands protected persons may be consider the measures of control mentioned in the present Convention to be inadequate, it may not have recourse to any other measure of control more severe than that of assigned residence or internment, in accordance with the provisions of Articles 42 and 43."

civilians during World War II, when "all too often the mere fact of being an enemy subject was regarded as justifying internment"[57] and internment was the first step to more horrific abuses. Whereas combatants can be detained on the basis of their membership in the enemy's armed forces, LOAC flatly prohibits detention of civilians based on membership or other collective criteria. As the Commentary to the Fourth Geneva Convention explains, "the mere fact that a person is a subject of an enemy Power cannot be considered as threatening the security of the country where he is living; it is not therefore a valid reason for interning him or placing him in assigned residence."[58]

Detention of civilians — more commonly referred to as internment in the language of the Fourth Geneva Convention — may take place in the detaining state's own territory or in occupied territory.

ARTICLE 42 OF THE FOURTH GENEVA CONVENTION

The internment or placing in assigned residence of protected persons may be ordered only if the security of the Detaining Power makes it absolutely necessary.

If any person, acting through the representatives of the Protecting Power, voluntarily demands internment, and if his situation renders this step necessary, he shall be interned by the Power in whose hands he may be.

ARTICLE 78 OF THE FOURTH GENEVA CONVENTION

If the Occupying Power considers it necessary, for imperative reasons of security, to take safety measures concerning protected persons, it may, at the most, subject them to assigned residence or internment. . . .

Detention in both scenarios rests on the necessity demanded by the threat an individual civilian poses to security, but the specific language of the two treaty provisions suggests that internment in situations of occupation "should be even more exceptional than it is inside the territory of the Parties to the conflict,"[59] in order to protect against internment based solely on nationality or allegiance.

---

57. INT'L COMM. RED CROSS, COMMENTARY ON THE GENEVA CONVENTION (IV) RELATIVE TO THE PROTECTION OF CIVILIAN PERSONS IN TIME OF WAR 258 (Oscar M. Uhler & Henri Coursier eds., 1958).

58. *Id.*

59. *Id.* at 367.

Although LOAC does not provide specific guidelines for understanding the security concerns that justify civilian internment, the notions of "imperative reasons of security" or "absolutely necessary" for the security of the detaining power include any civilian who is directly participating in hostilities or has directly participated in hostilities. Given that many activities not meeting the direct participation threshold can pose a security threat to the state, detention authority also extends to civilians who engage in more indirect forms of support or assistance to the war effort. For example, "subversive activity carried on inside the territory of a Party to the conflict or actions which are of direct assistance to an enemy Power," sabotage, espionage, or participation in organizations "whose object is to cause disturbances . . . or . . . seriously prejudice its security by other means"[60] are all sufficient to constitute threats to security justifying detention.

The Fourth Geneva Convention also mandates essential procedural safeguards for civilians. Perhaps most important, and in direct contrast to the detention framework for combatants, civilians can only be detained for such time as the individualized reason for their detention persists. Thus, Article 132(1) of the Fourth Geneva Convention requires that any civilian internee "shall be released by the Detaining Power as soon as the reasons which necessitated his internment no longer exist." This rule reinforces that civilians may only be detained if absolutely necessary for the security of the detaining state — unlike combatants, who may be detained based solely on who they are (e.g., their status), civilians may only be detained based on what they are doing (e.g., their conduct),[61] and therefore must be released as soon as the threat posed by that conduct has abated. In addition, the Fourth Geneva Convention establishes detailed procedures for the review of any civilian internment.

ARTICLE 43 OF THE FOURTH GENEVA CONVENTION

Any protected person who has been interned or placed in assigned residence shall be entitled to have such action reconsidered as soon as possible by an appropriate court or administrative board designated by the Detaining Power for that purpose. If the internment or placing in administrative residence is maintained, the court or administrative board shall periodically, and at least twice yearly, give consideration to his or her case, with a view to the favourable amendment of the initial decision, if circumstances permit.

---

60. *Id.* at 258.

61. Chris Jenks, *Detention Under the Law of Armed Conflict, in* ROUTLEDGE HANDBOOK OF THE LAW OF ARMED CONFLICT 301, 301 (Rain Liivoja & Tim McCormack eds., 2016).

ARTICLE 78 OF THE FOURTH GENEVA CONVENTION

. . . Decisions regarding such assigned residence or internment shall be made according to a regular procedure to be prescribed by the Occupying Power in accordance with the provisions of the present Convention. This procedure shall include the right of appeal for the parties concerned. Appeals shall be decided with the least possible delay. In the event of a decision being upheld, it shall be subject to periodical review, if possible every six months, by a competent body set up by the said Power.

This review process is essential to ensuring that any detention of civilians is justified based on the requisite standard of "absolutely necessary" or "imperative threat to security" and, equally important, to examining whether the continuation of that detention over time is justified. For example, the European Court of Human Rights assessed the detention by British forces of an Iraqi man suspected of involvement in the insurgency in Iraq early in the conflict. The Court first determined that the initial detention was proper because he "was found . . . armed and on the roof of his brother's house, where other weapons and documents of a military intelligence value were retrieved," providing "reason to believe that he might be either a person who could be detained as a prisoner of war or whose internment was necessary for imperative reasons of security, both of which provided a legitimate ground for capture and detention."[62] After an appropriate screening process, however, he was "cleared for release since it was established that he was a civilian who did not pose a threat to security."[63] Based on both the initial justification for the detention and the appropriate process provided, the Court found that the capture and detention "was consistent with the powers available to the United Kingdom under the Third and Fourth Geneva Conventions, and was not arbitrary."[64] In contrast, detention without reasonable grounds to believe it is absolutely necessary for security or without the requisite process to protect the rights of those detained individuals is unlawful and can constitute the grave breach of unlawful confinement of a civilian.[65]

QUESTIONS FOR DISCUSSION

1. The Third Geneva Convention does not prescribe any review process for the detention of POWs. Why does LOAC mandate a regular review

62. Case of Hassan v. United Kingdom, Eur. Ct. Hum. Rts, App. No. 29750/09, ¶ 109 (2014).

63. *Id.*

64. *Id.* ¶ 110.

65. Prosecutor v. Delalić, Case No. IT-96-21-A, Appeals Judgment ¶ 320 (Int'l Crim. Trib. for the Former Yugoslavia Feb 20, 2001).

process for civilians interned in international armed conflict but not for combatants, who can be held without charge until the end of hostilities?

2. The Eritrea-Ethiopia Claims Commission found Ethiopia in violation of international law for detaining civilians as POWs, often for many years. In particular, the Claims Commission noted that, "[w]hile international law allows the internment of civilian nationals of an enemy State under specified conditions and appropriate safeguards,"[66] such requirements were not met and therefore the detention violated international law.

3. Civilian internees must be held separately from POWs or other detainees, including persons detained based on criminal wrongdoing. Why?

4. As you review the various categories of persons who can be detained and the requirements for procedural safeguards and treatment, consider the planning that must take place before any military operations. What are the consequences of a failure to prepare accordingly?

E. HUMANITARIAN ASSISTANCE

In addition to the dangers from hostilities, civilians in situations of armed conflict may face severe shortages of food, medical supplies and other essentials. For example, years of armed conflict in Yemen has produced one of the world's most extreme humanitarian crises. As a leading humanitarian relief agency reported in early 2018:

> 22.2 million people are now in need of humanitarian assistance among which 11.3 million are in acute need of immediate assistance to save or sustain life, mostly women and children.
>
> The conflict has resulted in over 10,000 deaths and two million people displaced, looking for shelter from disease and violence. Yemenis are struggling to survive as fuel, food and medical supplies are critically low due to the closure of land, sea and air routes. Just 14% of national fuel requirements have arrived in country since the end of March putting 10 million people at risk of losing access to water. Over 12 million people are going hungry as wheat and other staples are in increasingly short supply. More than 15 million are without access to health care as most hospitals have shut down due to lack of medical supplies and power cuts.
>
> In addition to constant threat from violence and conflict, an aggressive strain of cholera has broken out, with 1,035,676 suspected cases with . . . 2,224 associated deaths registered since April 2017. Children are particularly vulnerable, as their small systems and malnourished bodies cannot fight the disease.
>
> The United Nations and other NGOs in Yemen have demanded the airport in Sana'a be reopened, as other foreign militaries have restricted

66. Eri.-Eth. Cl. Comm'n, Eritrea's Claim 15, 16, 23 and 27-32, ¶ 121 (2004).

food and medicine from being delivered, literally starving out innocent Yemenis.[67]

LOAC starts from the premise that each party to a conflict bears the primary obligation to fulfill the basic humanitarian needs of the population under its control. The Fourth Geneva Convention and Additional Protocol I both require states to allow free, rapid, and unimpeded passage of essential humanitarian supplies.[68] In occupation, the occupying power has a direct obligation to provide for the public welfare by maintaining food and medical supplies for the population of the occupied territory, and to ensure and maintain medical services, public health, and hygiene.[69] To the extent that portions of occupied territory do not have sufficient supplies, the occupying power must either bring in additional supplies or allow relief operations by other states, the ICRC, or other impartial humanitarian organizations.

Humanitarian relief operations rest on the consent of the parties concerned and must be humanitarian, impartial, and non-discriminatory in nature. First, Article 70(1) of Additional Protocol I provides that relief actions can be undertaken "subject to the agreement of the Parties concerned," specifically the state on whose territory the humanitarian relief operations will take place. Where consent is required, in accordance with fundamental obligations of sovereignty, it may not be arbitrarily withheld. Although international law does not contain a single definition of arbitrariness, there is a general consensus that consent to humanitarian relief operations is arbitrarily withheld if "(i) it is withheld in circumstances that result in the violation by a state of its obligations under international law with respect to the civilian population in question; or (ii) the withholding of consent violates the principles of necessity and proportionality; or (iii) consent is withheld in a manner that is unreasonable, unjust, lacking in predictability or that is otherwise inappropriate."[70] For example, withholding

---

67. *Humanitarian Crisis in Yemen*, CARE, http://www.care.org/emergencies/yemen-humanitarian-crisis.

68. Article 23 of the Fourth Geneva Convention: "Each High Contracting Party shall allow the free passage of all consignments of medical and hospital stores and objects necessary for religious worship intended only for civilians of another High Contracting Party, even if the latter is its adversary. It shall likewise permit the free passage of all consignments of essential foodstuffs, clothing and tonics intended for children under fifteen, expectant mothers and maternity cases." Article 70(2) of Additional Protocol I: "The Parties to the Conflict and each High Contracting Party shall allow and facilitate rapid and unimpeded passage of all relief consignments, equipment and personnel provided in accordance with this Section, even if such assistance is destined for the civilian population of the adverse Party."

69. Fourth Geneva Convention, arts. 55 & 56.

70. Dapo Akande & Emanuela-Chiara Gillard, *Oxford Guidance on the Law Relating to Humanitarian Relief Operations in Situations of Armed Conflict* 22 (U.N. Office for the Coordination of Humanitarian Affairs 2016).

consent so as to cause or contribute to the starvation of the civilian population would violate the prohibition against starvation as a method of warfare, or withholding consent to medical relief operations because such operations would treat wounded enemy personnel would violate the rule mandating treatment of wounded and sick without distinction and with the least possible delay.[71] In both scenarios, the withholding of consent would be arbitrary as a result. In contrast, imperative considerations of military necessity are accepted as valid reasons to withhold consent to relief operations, such as ongoing combat operations or suspicions that the relief personnel are not neutral and are seeking to aid the opposing party in the conflict.

QUESTIONS FOR DISCUSSION

1. Notwithstanding the general rule on consent for relief operations, consent is not required in situations of occupation or if the United Nations Security Council adopts a binding resolution mandating that the parties concerned allow access for humanitarian relief operations. United Nations Security Council Resolution 2139, passed in February 2014 regarding the conflict in Syria, was the first time the Security Council demanded that parties to a conflict allow rapid, safe, and unimpeded access to humanitarian relief operations. In it, the Security Council:

> 5. Calls upon all parties to immediately lift the sieges of populated areas, including in the Old City of Homs (Homs), Nubl and Zahra (Aleppo), Madamiyet Elsham (Rural Damascus), Yarmouk (Damascus), Eastern Ghouta (Rural Damascus), Darayya (Rural Damascus) and other locations, and demands that all parties allow the delivery of humanitarian assistance, including medical assistance, cease depriving civilians of food and medicine indispensable to their survival, and enable the rapid, safe and unhindered evacuation of all civilians who wish to leave, and underscores the need for the parties to agree on humanitarian pauses, days of tranquillity [sic], localized ceasefires and truces to allow humanitarian agencies safe and unhindered access to all affected areas in Syria, recalling that starvation of civilians as a method of combat is prohibited by international humanitarian law;
>
> 6. Demands that all parties, in particular the Syrian authorities, promptly allow rapid, safe and unhindered humanitarian access for United Nations humanitarian agencies and their implementing partners, including across conflict lines and across borders, in order to ensure that humanitarian assistance reaches people in need through the most direct routes; . . .[72]

2. What happens when an opposition party controls portions of a state's territory? Whose consent is required? Can the state refuse consent for relief operations into that portion of its territory? For example, Syria

---

71. *Id.*
72. S.C. Res. 2139, ¶¶ 5-6 (Feb. 22, 2014).

has routinely refused consent for relief operations to cross from Turkey or other neighboring states directly into opposition-controlled areas. Similarly, the government of Sudan has regularly refused access for relief operations into rebel-held areas of Southern Kordofan and Blue Nile, leaving hundreds of thousands without sufficient food or medical supplies.[73]

RELIEF AND REBELS

In 2015, numerous United Nations humanitarian agencies and international non-governmental organizations were carrying out relief operations in parts of the eastern regions of Ukraine no longer under the control of the government. In the summer of 2015, they were informed by the representatives of the Donetsk People's Republic (DPR) — one of two separatist regions in eastern Ukraine — that in order to continue operating in those areas, they would have to register with and be accredited by the "authorities" of the DPR.

- Are the representatives of the DPR entitled to require organizations carrying out humanitarian operations to register with them?
- If they did register, would such registration give legitimacy to the DPR?
- Would such registration be incompatible with United Nations Security Council resolution 2202 (2015) reaffirming its full respect for the sovereignty, independence, and territorial integrity of Ukraine?

> — *Emanuela-Chiara Gillard, former Chief of the Protection of Civilians Section, United Nations Office for the Coordination of Humanitarian Affairs*

---

3. Consider the myriad of ways in which governments might seek to curtail or inhibit relief operations, including onerous entry or visa requirements, extensive delays at border crossings, and harassment, detention, or even targeting of personnel. What tools do relief agencies need to address these obstacles and maximize safe and timely access to the civilian population in need?

---

73. Irina Mosel & Ashley Jackson, *Talking to the Other Side: Humanitarian Negotiations in Southern Kordofan and Blue Nile, Sudan* 4-5 (Humanitarian Policy Group, HPG Working Paper (2013), https://www.odi.org/sites/odi.org.uk/files/odi-assets/publications-opinion-files/8591.pdf.

PART IV

How

CHAPTER 8

IDENTIFYING TARGETS: LEGITIMATE TARGETS AND PROTECTED OBJECTS

The Bombing of Dresden, 1945: In all, over three waves of attacks, 3,300 tons of bombs were dropped on the city. Many of the bombs that were dropped were incendiary bombs. These created so much fire that a firestorm developed. The more the city burned, the more oxygen was sucked in—and the greater the firestorm became. It is thought that the temperature peaked at 1,800 degrees Fahrenheit. The surface of roads melted and fleeing people found that their feet were burned as they ran. Some jumped into reservoirs built in the city centre to assist firefighters. However, these were ten feet deep, smooth-sided and had no ladders—many drowned. Very few of those in the city centre survived—those that did provided a vivid picture of what it was like to be in a firestorm.

"There were no warning sirens. We were completely surprised and rushed back down to the cellars of the hospital. But these quickly became hopelessly overcrowded with people who could no longer find shelter in their own burning buildings. The crush was unbearable, we were so tight you could not fall over."

"Apart from the fire risk, it was becoming increasingly impossible to breath[e] in the cellar because the air was being pulled out by the increasing strength of the blaze."

"We could not stand up, we were on all fours, crawling. The wind was full of sparks and carrying bits of blazing furniture, debris and burning bits of bodies."

"There were charred bodies everywhere."

"The experience of the bombing was far worse than being on the Russian front, where I was a front-line machine gunner."

After the raid had finished, SS guards brought in from a nearby camp . . . burnt the bodies in the city's Old Square (the Altmarkt). There were so many bodies that this took two weeks to complete.

A vast amount of the city was destroyed and when the Red Army took it over, the city had all but ceased to exist.[1]

---

1. *The Bombing of Dresden*, HISTORY LEARNING SITE (2000), https://www.historylearningsite.co.uk/world-war-two/the-bombing-campaign-of-world-war-two/the-bombing-of-dresden/.

The age-old principle that the means and methods of warfare are not unlimited and the mandate that hostilities only be conducted between opposing armed forces and against military targets and objects lie at the core of LOAC. Total war is rejected as a governing principle; rather, the only legitimate military action is that aimed at weakening the military potential of the enemy and bringing about the complete submission of the enemy forces. Thus, as an ancient Greek historian explained, "[i]t is not the object of war to annihilate those who have given provocation for it, but to cause them to mend their ways."[2]

The use of combat power to achieve objectives in war is called targeting. U.S. military doctrine defines targeting as "the process of selecting and prioritizing targets and matching the appropriate response to them, considering operational requirements and capabilities."[3] The targeting process involves "identifying individuals and objects for potential attack, selecting which of those objects will be attacked, executing the attack, and assessing the effects of the attack."[4] LOAC is an essential component of this entire process. Possible targets of attack are identified based on enemy vulnerabilities and capabilities and the possible means and methods of attack are based on the capabilities available and the desired effects on the enemy. All of these decisions take place within the overarching paradigm of LOAC, however, including the identification of targets (discussed in this chapter), the steps required to minimize harm to civilians (Chapter 9), and the means and methods of attack used (Chapter 10).

The rules on the conduct of hostilities thus focus on how parties to an armed conflict can and must conduct their military operations—who and what can be attacked and in what manner, who or what must be protected from attack, and how attacks must be carried out so as to implement LOAC's core purpose of protecting civilians from the hazards of war. At the center of this framework is the principle of distinction, a cornerstone of the "entire system established in The Hague in 1899 and 1907 and in Geneva from 1864 to 1977,"[5] and explicitly codified in Additional Protocol I.

2. Polybius, Histories Bk. V, 11.3 (2nd Century B.C.).
3. Chairman of the Joint Chiefs of Staff, JP 3-60, Joint Targeting I-1 (April 13, 2007).
4. Geoffrey S. Corn and Gary P. Corn, *The Law of Operational Targeting: Viewing the LOAC Through an Operational Lens*, 47 Texas Int'l L.J. 338, 342 (2012).
5. Claude Pilloud, Yves Sandoz, Christophe Swinarski & Bruno Zimmerman, Commentary on the Additional Protocols of 8 June 1977 to the Geneva Conventions of 12 August 1949 598 (1987).

THE BASIC RULE: ARTICLE 48 OF ADDITIONAL PROTOCOL I

In order to ensure respect for and protection of the civilian population and civilian objects, the Parties to the conflict shall at all times distinguish between the civilian population and combatants and between civilian objects and military objectives and accordingly shall direct their operations only against military objectives.

The principle of distinction thus mandates not only differentiation between civilians and combatants, but between civilian objects and military objects as well, a critical component of the protection of the civilian population during armed conflict. Just as civilians may not be made the object of attack, so Article 52 of Additional Protocol I declares that "[c]ivilian objects shall not be the object of attack or of reprisals" and mandates that "[a]ttacks shall be limited strictly to military objectives." In addition, beyond the differentiation between civilian objects and military objects, LOAC grants additional special protection to certain objects of religious, cultural, educational, and environmental significance, as a further means of protecting both the civilian population and its ability to survive during and after conflict.

A key foundational question in the application of LOAC to the conduct of hostilities therefore is the definition of attack. LOAC prohibits attacks against civilians and civilian objects and requires that parties comply with the obligations of proportionality and precautions in launching any attacks, as discussed in Chapter 9. Article 49 of Additional Protocol I defines attacks as "acts of violence against the adversary, whether in offence or in defence." As the Commentary explains, the definition includes both offensive and defensive acts and is not related to who strikes the first blow or the notion of armed attack or aggression in the *jus ad bellum*. Rather, "the term 'attack' means 'combat action' [and] refers simply to the use of armed force to carry out a military operation at the beginning or during the course of armed conflict."[6] Firing a rifle, launching a missile or rocket, dropping a bomb—these are all obvious examples of attacks. Although the definition of "attack" refers to acts of violence against "the adversary," it is now well-accepted that the notion of "attack" also includes acts of violence against civilians or the civilian population.

6. *Id.* at 603.

In general, it is the violence of the act itself or the consequences of the act that qualify it as an attack. The "concept of 'attacks' [therefore] does not include dissemination of propaganda, embargoes, or other non-physical means of psychological or economic warfare."[7] What about cyber operations, which do not involve physical force, but rather the manipulations of ones and zeros and the introduction of worms, viruses and other nefarious computer tools? Consider the following acts from the conflict between Russia and Georgia in August 2008—were they attacks triggering the obligations of distinction, proportionality and precautions as set forth in Articles 48, 49, 51, 52, and 57 of Additional Protocol I?

- On 20 July, President Saakashvili's website was shut down for 24 hours;
- On 7 August, several Georgian servers and the Internet traffic were seized and placed under external control;
- On 8 August, large-scale cyber attacks against sites in Georgia began. The source of the cyber attacks was uncertain. Some reports attributed them to an organization called the "Russian Business Network."
- At this time, it was reported that all Georgian Government websites were unobtainable from US, UK and European cyberspace. The Turkish AS9121 TTNet server, one of the routing points for traffic into the Caucasus, was blocked, reportedly via COMSTAR;
- On 9 August, the Georgian Ministry of Foreign Affairs website was defaced by hackers, who replaced it with offensive photographs. Other Georgian websites which also suffered cyber or hacker attacks included those of the Ministry of Internal Affairs, the Ministry of Defence and the website of [Dmitry] Sanakoyev's pro-Georgian Interim Administration of South Ossetia. In addition, reportedly the National Bank of Georgia was defaced and Georgian news portals were affected by DDoS (distributed denial of service) attacks.
- By 12 August, President Saakashvili's website and a popular Georgian TV website (www.rustavi2.com) were transferred to Tulip Systems. Tulip was then also attacked;
- On 12-13 August, the Ministry of Defence website experienced extensive cyber attacks and two periods of downtime.[8]

These "cyber attacks" took place during an international armed conflict between Georgia and Russia and therefore LOAC applied at the time. However, the simple fact that there was an armed conflict and LOAC applied

---

7. Michael Bothe et al., New Rules for the Victims of Armed Conflicts 289 (1982).

8. 2 Independent International Fact-Finding Mission on the Conflict in Georgia, Report 218 (2009).

does not mean that every act undertaken qualified as an "attack" within the meaning of that term in LOAC and the specific obligations it triggers. Cyber operations can, in fact, qualify as attacks, but it is important to separate the rhetorical use of "cyber attack" from the legal definition of "attack" in LOAC. In assessing whether a cyber action constitutes an attack,

> it is not the violence of the act that constitutes the condition precedent to limiting the occurrence of an attack, but the violence of the ensuing result. . . . Referring back to the requirement of violence, and its development in Additional Protocol I, cyber operations can therefore qualify as "attacks," even though they are not themselves "violent," because they have "violent consequences." A cyber operation, like any other operation, is an attack when resulting in death or injury of individuals, whether civilians or combatants, or damage to or destruction of objects, whether military objectives or civilian objects. By this interpretation, the operations against Georgia were not attacks and therefore not unlawful under international humanitarian law. They involved disruption and defacement, but no physical harm to objects or injury to persons.[9]

The definition of attack is thus an essential preliminary question before analyzing whether an object is a military objective, a civilian object, or an object enjoying special protection under LOAC.

A.   MILITARY OBJECTIVES

The earliest mention of the term "military objective" appears in the 1923 Hague Rules of Air Warfare, a set of rules drafted by a Commission of Jurists established by the Washington Conference of 1922 on the Limitation of Armaments. Article 24(1) of the 1923 Hague Rules states, "[a]erial bombardment is legitimate only when directed at a military objective, that is to say, an object of which the destruction or injury would constitute a distinct military advantage to the belligerent."[10] The second paragraph of that article offers examples of military objectives: "military forces; military works; military establishments or depots; factories constituting important and well-known centres engaged in the manufacture of arms, ammunition, or distinctively military supplies; lines of communication or transportation used for military purposes."[11] Although the 1923 Hague Rules were

9. Michael N. Schmitt, *Cyber Operations and the* Jus in Bello: *Key Issues*, 87 INT'L LAW STUD. 89, 93-95 (2011).

10. Rules concerning the Control of Wireless Telegraphy in Time of War and Air Warfare. Drafted by a Commission of Jurists at The Hague, December 1922 - February 1923, art. 24(1).

11. *Id.*, art. 24(2).

never adopted as a binding legal instrument, they remain important "as an authoritative attempt to clarify and formulate rules of law governing the use of aircraft in war."[12]

Other early categorizations of military objectives included steel works, motor and engineering works, docks and dockside warehouses, waterworks, gasworks, refining and oil storage depots, and oil wells, for example.[13] Finally, one comprehensive survey looking back at the understanding of the notion of military objective at the end of World War II presents the following list of items considered to be military targets:

> Military equipment, units, and bases; economic targets; power sources (coal, oil, electric, hydroelectric); industry (war supporting manufacturing, export and/or import); transportation (equipment, lines of communication, and petroleum, oil, and other lubricants necessary for transportation); command and control; geographic; personnel; military; and civilians taking part in the hostilities, including civilians working in industries directly related to the war effort.[14]

Although the 1949 Geneva Conventions reference the term "military objective," the drafters of the conventions did not include any definition in the treaties. At the time of the drafting of the Additional Protocols in 1977, the drafters recognized the need for a comprehensive definition "if the essential distinction between combatants and civilians and between civilian objects and military objectives was to be maintained."[15]

Like the definition of civilian, the definition of civilian object is a negative one, dependent on the definition of military objective. Article 52 of Additional Protocol I contains the definition of military objective, which is considered to be customary international law.

ARTICLE 52(2) OF ADDITIONAL PROTOCOL I: MILITARY OBJECTIVES

In so far as objects are concerned, military objectives are limited to those objects which by their nature, location, purpose or use make an effective contribution to military action and whose total or partial destruction, capture or neutralization, in the circumstances ruling at the time, offers a definite military advantage.

---

12. 2 OPPENHEIM INTERNATIONAL LAW 519 (7th ed., H. Lauterpacht ed., 1948).

13. A.P.V. ROGERS, LAW ON THE BATTLEFIELD 30 (1996), citing J. STONE, LEGAL CONTROLS OF INTERNATIONAL CONFLICT 624 (1954).

14. W. Hays Parks, *Air War and the Law of War*, 32 A.F. L. REV. 1, 55 (1992).

15. CLAUDE PILLOUD, YVES SANDOZ, CHRISTOPHE SWINARSKI & BRUNO ZIMMERMAN, COMMENTARY ON THE ADDITIONAL PROTOCOLS OF 8 JUNE 1977 TO THE GENEVA CONVENTIONS OF 12 AUGUST 1949 631 (1987).

This definition includes two elements: the object must make an effective contribution to military action and the attack on or destruction of the object must offer a definite military advantage. With regard to the first element, the definition looks to nature, location, use or purpose as the primary criteria. Nature refers to "all objects directly used by the armed forces: weapons, equipment, transports, fortifications, depots, buildings occupied by armed forces, staff headquarters, communications centres etc."[16]

In 1956, the ICRC drew up the following proposed list of categories of military objectives as an annex to the Draft Rules for the Limitation of Dangers incurred by the Civilian Population in Time of War:

I. The objectives belonging to the following categories are those considered to be of generally recognized military importance:

(1) Armed forces, including auxiliary or complementary organisations, and persons who, though not belonging to the above-mentioned formations, nevertheless take part in the fighting.

(2) Positions, installations or constructions occupied by the forces indicated in sub-paragraph 1 above, as well as combat objectives (that is to say, those objectives which are directly contested in battle between land or sea forces including airborne forces).

(3) Installations, constructions and other works of a military nature, such as barracks, fortifications, War Ministries (e.g. Ministries of Army, Navy, Air Force, National Defence, Supply) and other organs for the direction and administration of military operations.

(4) Stores of army or military supplies, such as munition dumps, stores of equipment or fuel, vehicles parks.

(5) Airfields, rocket launching ramps and naval base installations.

(6) Those of the lines and means of communications (railway lines, roads, bridges, tunnels and canals) which are of fundamental military importance.

(7) The installations of broadcasting and television stations; telephone and telegraph exchanges of fundamental military importance.

(8) Industries of fundamental importance for the conduct of the war:

(a) industries for the manufacture of armaments such as weapons, munitions, rockets, armoured vehicles, military aircraft, fighting ships, including the manufacture of accessories and all other war material;

(b) industries for the manufacture of supplies and material of a military character, such as transport and communications material, equipment of the armed forces;

(c) factories or plant constituting other production and manufacturing centres of fundamental importance for the conduct of war, such as the metallurgical, engineering and chemical industries, whose nature or purpose is essentially military;

(d) storage and transport installations whose basic function it is to serve the industries referred to in (a)-(c);

16. *Id.* at 636.

(e) installations providing energy mainly for national defence, e.g. coal, other fuels, or atomic energy, and plants producing gas or electricity mainly for military consumption.

(9) Installations constituting experimental, research centres for experiments on and the development of weapons and war material.

II. The following however, are excepted from the foregoing list:

(1) Persons, constructions, installations or transports which are protected under the Geneva Conventions I, II, III, of August 12, 1949;

(2) Non-combatants in the armed forces who obviously take no active or direct part in hostilities.[17]

A second list was drawn up by Major General A.P.V. Rogers, a former Director of British Army Legal Services, using the Additional Protocol I definition and his own review of state practice:

> military personnel and persons who take part in the fighting without being members of the armed forces, military facilities, military equipment, including military vehicles, weapons, munitions and stores of fuel, military works, including defensive works and fortifications, military depots and establishments, including War and Supply Ministries, works producing or developing military supplies and other supplies of military value, including metallurgical, engineering and chemical industries supporting the war effort; areas of land of military significance such as hills, defiles and bridgeheads; railways, ports, airfields, bridges, main roads as well as tunnels and canals; oil and other power installations; communications installations, including broadcasting and television stations and telephone and telegraph stations used for military communications.[18]

The lists excerpted above include a fairly comprehensive collection of objects that fall within the category of "nature"—that is, they have an intrinsically military character. For most of these objects, their use at a given moment is not necessarily relevant—barring use for a distinct civilian purpose, such as using empty military barracks to house civilian refugees.

Location is an important factor because certain objects, such as bridges, make a direct contribution to military action regardless of whether they have a military function. Another example could be a particular site that is critical for military operations because it must be seized, or because it is important to prevent the enemy from seizing it, or to force the enemy to retreat from it. Similarly, mountain passes, hills, or "known or suspected enemy avenues of approach or withdrawal"[19] all qualify as military objectives by location. The categories of "use" and "purpose" refer respectively to an object's present or intended function and will often involve objects that do not appear to be military upon first impression, thus requiring further

17. *Id.* at 632 n.3.
18. A.P.V. Rogers, Law on the Battlefield 37 (1996).
19. U.S. Department of Defense, Law of War Manual § 5.6.8.4 (2015 rev'd 2016).

examination in given situations. The Commentary to the Additional Protocols explains that many civilian objects are or become useful to the armed forces. "Thus, for example, a school or a hotel is a civilian object, but if . . . used to accommodate troops or headquarters staff, [it will] become [a] military objective[]."[20] Furthermore, the two categories are, while related, distinct from each other: "the criterion of *purpose* is concerned with the intended future use of an object, while that of *use* is concerned with its present function."[21] Examples of civilian objects that make an effective contribution to military action could include "civilian buses or trucks which are being transported to the front to move soldiers from point A to point B, [or] a factory which is producing ball bearings for the military."[22] Nonetheless, Additional Protocol I emphasizes that all doubts as to the civilian or military nature of an object should be resolved in favor of civilian status. Consider, for example, the following two situations:

- *Prosecutor v. Strugar:* "The Chamber has already found that on 6 December 1991 there was an attack launched by the JNA forces against the Old Town of Dubrovnik. It is also the finding of the Chamber, as recorded earlier, that there were no military objectives within the Old Town and the attack was not launched or maintained in the belief that there were. It is possible that there may have been individuals in the Old Town on 6 December 1991 who were connected with the Croatian defending forces, however, any such persons did not fire on JNA forces or undertake any overt military activity. Their presence could not change the character of the population. It was properly characterised as a civilian population, and the objects located there were civilian objects. As regards the Defence submission concerning alleged military activities of the Crisis Staff, the headquarters of which was located in the Old Town, the Chamber notes that no persuasive evidence has been supplied to the effect that the Crisis Staff was conducting military operations from the Old Town. . . . There is nothing in the evidence to suggest that the building of the Crisis Staff made 'an effective contribution to military action' or that its destruction would offer 'a definite military advantage'. Accordingly, the Chamber finds on the evidence in this case that the presence of the Crisis Staff in a building located in the Old Town did not render the building a legitimate military

---

20. Claude Pilloud, Yves Sandoz, Christophe Swinarski & Bruno Zimmerman, Commentary on the Additional Protocols of 8 June 1977 to the Geneva Conventions of 12 August 1949 636 (1987).

21. *Id.*

22. The U.S. Army Judge Advocate General's School, Operational Law Handbook 24 (2010).

objective. The Chamber would also note that the building in question was not proved to have been damaged during the shelling so that this Defence submission apparently lacks factual foundation."[23]

- *Independent International Fact-finding Mission on the Conflict in Georgia:* "Under IHL, schools are by nature civilian objects that are immune from attack. Several cases of damage caused to schools in the course of the hostilities call for specific attention. Referring to the shelling of Tskhinvali by Georgian forces, Human Rights Watch noted that 'the shells hit and often caused significant damage to multiple civilian objects, including the university, several schools and nursery schools. . . . [S]ome of these buildings were used as defence positions or other posts by South Ossetian forces (including volunteer militias), which rendered them legitimate military targets.' For example, witnesses told Human Rights Watch that militias had taken up positions in School No. 12 in the southern part of Tskhinvali, which was seriously damaged by Georgian fire.

  The attack on School No. 7 in Gori on 9 August also exemplifies the need to pay particular attention to the circumstances of an attack. According to Human Rights Watch, relying on one eyewitness: 'Russian aircraft made several strikes on and near School No. 7 in Gori city . . . . [A]bout one hundred Georgian military reservists were in the yard of the school when it was attacked. . . . None of the reservists was injured. The reservists as combatants were a legitimate target, and it is possible that the school was deemed as being used for military purposes. In such circumstances it would lose its status as a protected civilian object. . . .'"[24]

In both of these situations, information about the circumstances at the time of the attack was essential to analyzing whether the civilian object in question (a residential building or a school) had lost its protection from attack by dint of use for military purposes.

Second, the destruction, capture or neutralization[25] of the object must offer a definite military advantage, not one that is hypothetical or speculative. The concept of definite military advantage can often be hard to quantify: at one level, the destruction or neutralization of any object that makes an effective contribution to military action would seem to offer a definite military advantage. However, any assessment of military advantage must be

23. Prosecutor v. Strugar, Case No. IT-01-42-A, Appeals Judgement ¶ 284 (Int'l Crim. Trib. for the Former Yugoslavia July 17, 2008).

24. 2 INDEPENDENT INTERNATIONAL FACT-FINDING MISSION ON THE CONFLICT IN GEORGIA, REPORT 328-329 (2009).

25. Neutralization here means to deny the enemy's ability to use the object without destroying it.

made in light of the circumstances governing at the time, such that a civilian object would not offer a definite military advantage at one moment but then could indeed qualify as such if being used as a command post, to store weapons or to launch attacks. Military advantage also is not limited solely to the tactical gains from the particular attack or parts of an attack, but extends to the attack as a whole and to the security of the attacking force. As an example, the attacking party may see a definite military advantage in an attack that causes the defending party to focus its strategic and tactical energies on one sector, leaving another sector unprotected.

QUESTIONS FOR DISCUSSION

1. The United States maintains that "war-sustaining activities" constitute military objectives. The U.S. Commander's Handbook on the Law of Naval Operations thus defines military objectives as objects that, "by their nature, location, purpose, or use, effectively contribute to the enemy's war-fighting or war-sustaining capability."[26] War-sustaining activities could be, for example, "economic targets of the enemy that indirectly but effectively support and sustain the enemy's war-fighting capability."[27] An example could be oil production or other commodities (like cotton during the Civil War) whose sale provides funds for the purchase of arms or other aspects of the war effort. This category, as framed by the United States, differs from "war-supporting" activities, which are those that indirectly support combat operations—munitions factories, shipyards, etc.[28] Does the notion of "war-sustaining activities" unnecessarily broaden the definition of military objective? Critics argue that the connection is simply too remote between crops or commodities for export and war fighting, and that attacks cannot be justified "solely due to the fact that the destruction of certain objects would deal a heavy economic blow to the enemy."[29]

2. Note that the definition of military objective refers to "the circumstances ruling at the time." Circumstances change constantly during war and must be taken into account in assessing whether a particular object is a military objective. A civilian building may, by dint of being used by one party as a headquarters, become a military objective at a given time. If the party then vacates the building, it returns to its status as a civilian object—it no longer fits within the notion of "use" or "purpose."

---

26. DEP'T OF THE NAVY, THE COMMANDER'S HANDBOOK ON THE LAW OF NAVAL OPERATIONS, NWP 1-14M 8.2 (2017).

27. *Id.* at 8.2.5.

28. Michael N. Schmitt, *Deconstructing Direct Participation in Hostilities*, 42 N.Y.U. J. INT'L L. POL. 697, 718 n.57 (2010).

29. YORAM DINSTEIN, THE CONDUCT OF HOSTILITIES UNDER THE LAW OF INTERNATIONAL ARMED CONFLICT 96 (2d ed. 2010).

3. Consider the problem of "dual-use" targets, which are objects that simultaneously have a civilian and military use. The term is most often applied to infrastructure, such as bridges, electricity generating plants, or oil refineries, that serve both functions at the same time. Does the definition of military objective in Article 52(2) simply render all such objects military objectives because they have some military use? Is the term "dual-use" purely descriptive or does it offer any legal value? How much should the long-term effects on civilian life be taken into account in assessing the lawfulness of targeting such objects?

4. In July 2011, NATO forces implementing the U.N. Security Council Resolution authorizing the use of force to protect civilians in Libya bombed the state television satellite transmitters in Tripoli, to degrade Qaddafi's ability to use television to intimidate the Libyan people and incite violence against them. NATO announced:

> Our intervention was necessary as TV was being used as an integral component of the regime apparatus designed to systematically oppress and threaten civilians and to incite attacks against them. Qadhafi's increasing practice of inflammatory broadcasts illustrates his regime's policy to instill hatred amongst Libyans, to mobilize its supporters against civilians and to trigger bloodshed.
>
> In light of our mandate to protect civilian lives, we had to act. After due consideration and careful planning to minimize the risks of casualties or long-term damage to television transmission capabilities, NATO performed the strike and we are now in the process of assessing its effect. Striking specifically these critical satellite dishes will reduce the regime's ability to oppress civilians while at the same time preserve television broadcast infrastructure that will be needed after the conflict.[30]

Do the satellite transmitters fit within the definition of military objective as set forth above? How does this targeting decision compare with the attack on the Serbian RTS state-owned television station—which was part of the C3 [command, control and communication] network and used for propaganda—during the 1999 NATO bombing campaign? What about targeting the RTLM radio station in Rwanda that was encouraging the killers during the genocide in the spring of 1994?

5. What about factories and other industrial plants, such as steel works, textile factories, automotive plants and so forth? What are the consequences of highly integrated civilian and military infrastructure for civilian protection? For example, in its report on the conduct of the 1991 Persian Gulf War, the U.S. Department of Defense explained that

---

30. Press Release, North Atlantic Treaty Organization, NATO Strikes Libyan State TV Satellite Facility (July 30, 2011), *available at* http://www.nato.int/cps/en/SID-82983FF0-6E3BF21C/natolive/news_76776.htm.

[e]xperience in its 1980-1988 war with Iran caused the Government of Iraq to develop a substantial and comprehensive degree of redundancy in its normal, civilian utilities as back-up for its national defense. Much of this redundancy, by necessity, was in urban areas. . . . Attack of all segments of the Iraqi communications system was essential to destruction of Iraqi military C^2 [Command and Control]. C^2 was crucial to Iraq's integrated air defense system; it was of equal importance for Iraqi ground forces. . . . Baghdad bridges crossing the Euphrates River contained the multiple fiber-optic links that provided Saddam Hussein with secure communications to his southern group of forces. Attack of these bridges severed those secure communications links, while restricting movement of Iraqi military forces and deployment of CW and BW warfare capabilities. Civilians using those bridges or near other targets at the time of their attack were at risk of injury incidental to the legitimate attack of those targets.[31]

6. During the Battle of Fallujah in 2004, U.S. and coalition units employed a variety of methods to stop rocket and mortar attacks on their positions. One tactic for which units frequently requested approval was terrain denial fire, targeting areas insurgents had used to launch attacks or hide weapons. Insurgents may or may not have been in the area when the rounds landed, but it was designed to discourage them from returning to the area to launch attacks. Insurgents often launched attacks from populated areas of the city of Fallujah — meaning that terrain denial fire was aimed at sections of populated areas rather than specific military targets. Were the areas targeted military objectives by location? Was this an acceptable tactic? What if it was used in civilian areas where most or all of the civilians had evacuated?

7. Fuel used to power military vehicles or to make explosives is a military objective by nature. The U.S. targeted ISIS's mobile oil refineries that provided fuel to run ISIS military operations, for example. Similarly, the German Federal Prosecutor General at Germany's Federal Court of Justice ruled that the fuel tankers captured by the Taliban and destroyed by German forces outside Kunduz, Afghanistan, in a controversial incident in September 2009 were lawful military objectives, such that their destruction was not a violation of LOAC.

The fuel tankers and the fuel were originally civilian objects. They became military objectives with the abduction by the Taliban because they were suited to effectively contribute to military action from this moment on. The fuel could be used to refuel vehicles used for attacks and used in combination with explosives as improvised explosive devices. It thus constitutes a military objective in any case as its destruction would offer a considerable military advantage. The fuel tankers also constituted a military

---

31. CONDUCT OF THE PERSIAN GULF WAR: FINAL REPORT TO CONGRESS: APPENDIX ON THE ROLE OF THE LAW OF WAR 612-614 (1992).

objective . . . . The reason is that they could be used for attacks with vehicle-based explosive devices as already happened in Afghanistan five times in 2009 until 4 September 2009. It is irrelevant that the fuel tankers were immobilized on a sandbank. Colonel (*Oberst*) Klein wanted to prevent any future movement of the tankers. There was the risk that the insurgents would successfully free the tankers and use them for military purposes. Therefore they did not constitute civilian objects at the time when Colonel (*Oberst*) Klein ordered the dropping of the bombs. The same holds true for both vehicles present in the immediate surroundings of the fuel tankers. Because of their concrete use they were meant to make an effective contribution to the Taliban's military action.[32]

8. What if oil tankers are being used to transport oil for sale? Can economic and financial targets be military objectives? In 2015 and 2016, the United States targeted over 1,200 ISIS oil tanker trucks, determining that "the tanker trucks formed the core of the oil distribution network[,] without which [ISIS's] oil trade could not flourish."[33] As the U.S. Special Envoy for the Global Coalition to Counter ISIS explained, "We're destroying ISIL's economic base. . . . They cannot pay their fighters."[34] Were these tanker trucks, carrying oil for distribution through sale or smuggling, legitimate military objectives? What about the oil being carried in the trucks? Would you categorize the trucks or the oil as military objectives within the definition in Additional Protocol I or would you consider them to be war-sustaining objects?

9. Vehicle-borne IEDs were one of the deadliest tactics insurgents used in Iraq. Insurgents soon adopted a related tactic—the house-borne IED, or booby-trapped house. U.S. and British patrols often searched houses looking for insurgents and intelligence about insurgents; upon entry into one of these booby-trapped structures, the building would explode, killing the whole patrol. Escalation of force procedures were the common practice with regard to vehicle-borne IEDs: barricades, calls for the vehicle to stop, and warning shots all were part of the procedure designed to stop vehicles before they could get close enough to do damage or be mistakenly taken for a suicide bomber and result in innocent casualties. What about for a booby-trapped house? Could the patrol simply demolish any house suspected of being booby-trapped? What type and amount of information would be needed to make such a determination? Could such an option ever be exercised or would suspect buildings simply need to be avoided?

---

32. Federal Court of Justice, Federal Prosecutor General, Decision ¶ 3(bb) (Apr. 16, 2010), https://www.icrc.org/customary-ihl/eng/docs/v2_cou_de_rule8_sectionf.

33. Jeffrey Miller & Ian Corey, *Follow the Money: Targeting Enemy War-Sustaining Activities*, 87 Joint Forces Q. 31, 33 (2017).

34. White House, press briefing, December 13, 2016, available at www.whitehouse.gov/the-press-office/2016/12/13/press-briefing-press-secretary-josh-earnest-and-special-envoy-global.

10. Can computers or computer networks be military objectives? What about data? A computer is clearly an object, such that one can then assess whether it meets the definition of a military objective. Whether data is an object at all, however, remains the subject of extensive debate. Some argue that data is intangible and therefore cannot be considered an object, noting that the Commentary to Additional Protocol I describes an object as something that is "visible and tangible."[35] Others, however, assert that the drafters of Additional Protocol I would have considered the destruction of data to be the same as physical damage, given the technology at the time. Now, in contrast, "it is perfectly possible to destroy vast quantities of vital data without physically destroying the computers on which they are stored. To place this in context, it raises the question whether a kinetic attack that results in the setting on fire of five hundred mailbags is any more harmful than a cyber operation that permanently deletes five million e-mails."[36] What are the consequences of each argument for the application of LOAC and pursuit of its core objectives? Which approach makes more sense?

CAR BOMBS AND BOOBY TRAPS

April 2005 — Mosul, Iraq

My platoon was conducting a cordon and knock near MSR [Main Supply Route] Tampa. My team was searching homes when we came upon a house that had two cars that had been gutted outside. When we entered the courtyard of the home, we found two more cars that were being gutted. We started talking to the family and their story wasn't adding up. They told us they were brothers and were reconfiguring the vehicles to left-side drive and that was why they had been gutted. The men did not have the "Family" name that should've been common with them. One of my guys was familiar with vehicles and told me they were lying about changing the drive over. Often, vehicles were gutted by insurgents prior to being used as IEDs. We immediately detained the males in the home and contacted our Lieutenant and platoon sergeant to let them know what we had come across.

---

35. CLAUDE PILLOUD, YVES SANDOZ, CHRISTOPHE SWINARSKI & BRUNO ZIMMERMAN, COMMENTARY ON THE ADDITIONAL PROTOCOLS OF 8 JUNE 1977 TO THE GENEVA CONVENTIONS OF 12 AUGUST 1949 634 (1987). *See* TALLINN MANUAL 2.0 ON THE INTERNATIONAL LAW APPLICABLE TO CYBER OPERATIONS 437 (Michael N. Schmitt ed., 2017).

36. Noam Lubell, *Lawful Targets in Cyber Operations: Does the Principle of Distinction Apply?*, 89 INT'L LAW STUD. 252, 267 (2013).

Another team was searching the other side of the road and entered an adjacent home that was abandoned. They immediately ran out of the home. They had discovered 3-105mm artillery shells that were being rigged into improvised devices (IEDs). We contacted the explosive ordinance division (EOD) and requested they come to our location to "demo" the IEDs we had found. While we waited for EOD to arrive we began a thorough search of the "car shop" house. We found excessive amounts of contraband on a hidden ledge in the house, including: 10 AK-47 magazines, two AK bandoleers, multiple cell phones that had been tampered with to be used as detonators, various insurgent propaganda, and maps with locations of coalition positions.

After an hour, EOD showed up and used their remote-controlled bomb robot to disable the IEDs in the house. Once the IEDs were rendered inoperable, my team searched the upper floor of the house and found over twenty 80mm mortar shells and a large container of an unknown powdered substance. EOD placed charges on the IEDs and mortar shells because they were too unstable to move from the location. We convinced EOD to place a small charge on the powder container just in case it was C-4 or a similar substance. My team then took up an overwatch position and waited for detonation.

Each IED was detonated individually to ensure safety for civilians. The first three blasts took out the IEDs; the fourth detonated the mortar shells. The last blast detonated the powder container, which was in fact powdered explosive. The blast was so massive, the second floor of the building collapsed.

Once we returned to the Forward Operating Base, we dropped off the detainees and prepared for our next mission. Interrogators later told us the men were their own terror cell and were trying to impress al Qaeda. They also provided intelligence on other cells operating in our city. At least we caught them before they could do serious harm.

— *U.S. Army soldier*

11. The Afghan version of the house-borne IED challenge proved to be valleys and other areas where multinational troops repeatedly encountered roadside IEDs. Rather than painstakingly—and very dangerously—navigating such routes looking for the IEDs, could units engage in "recon by fire" by lobbing artillery shells or mortars into the valleys to detonate any IEDs buried there? What would be the key considerations in making such a determination?

12. In Gaza, Hamas dug an extensive network of tunnels to use for cross-border attacks into Israel, command centers for Hamas leaders, weapons storage, smuggling, and maneuver without detection from above. During

the 2014 Gaza conflict, Hamas used the tunnels to launch attacks inside Israel, including at least two attacks on Israeli soldiers and attempted attacks on civilian communities.[37] Tunnels used to launch attacks, to store weapons, or as command bunkers easily meet the definition of military objective, but what about tunnels used for smuggling or transit underground? Does the fact that tunnels are underground change the analysis in any way?[38]

13. On January 11, 2016, U.S. forces destroyed an ISIS "cash and finance distribution center" in Mosul, Iraq, in the middle of the night. Shredded pieces of U.S. currency, mostly $100 bills, filled the air. Is money a lawful military objective? Is a building storing cash a lawful military objective? Does it depend on what ISIS was using the money for—paying fighters? Buying weapons or other equipment? Providing social services? Paying civil servants working in its quasi-state?

B.   PROTECTED OBJECTS AND EMBLEMS

The prohibition against attacks on civilian objects, which are all objects not meeting the criteria of military objectives, is a necessary and inherent complement to the prohibition on attacks on civilians and the civilian population. However, LOAC provides additional special protection for several categories of objects in order to ensure either that civilians can continue to benefit from their services and role in society or that civilians will have protection against the added danger such objects could cause if damaged or compromised. Thus, hospitals, religious and cultural property, the environment, objects indispensable for the civilian population, and works and installations containing dangerous forces, such as chemical factories, dams or nuclear power generating stations, all enjoy special protections under LOAC. Beyond the general protection these buildings and sites have as civilian objects, they benefit from additional protections as set forth in Articles 53-56 of Additional Protocol I—in particular, LOAC prohibits the use of such objects for military purposes. In situations where they are used for military purposes (in violation of the law) and meet the test for military objectives, the attacking party is obligated to follow further precautions and only attack in restricted circumstances. Several of these categories have recognized protective emblems that mark objects as deserving of special protection under the law. For medical and religious objects and personnel, the recognized emblems are the Red Cross, the Red Crescent, and the newly

---

37. Harriet Sherwood, *Inside the Tunnels Hamas Built: Israel's Struggle Against a New Tactic in Gaza War*, THE GUARDIAN (Aug. 2, 2014).

38. *See* DAPHNÉ RICHEMOND-BARAK, UNDERGROUND WARFARE (2017).

added Red Crystal.[39] Cultural property is marked by a shield, as denoted in the 1954 Hague Cultural Property Convention, and works and installations containing dangerous forces—such as dams or nuclear power plants—are marked with three bright orange circles.[40]

1.   Hospitals, Medical Units, and Medical Transport

Throughout the final months of 2016, dozens of attacks on hospitals and clinics in opposition-controlled parts of Aleppo were reported. Doctors and nurses, whose chief task during the siege was to care for the victims of bombings and shellings, all too often fell victim to bombs themselves.

As many as 172 verified attacks on medical facilities and personnel were reported across Syria between June and December 2016. According to figures from the Syrian American Medical Society (SAMS), seventy-three of those (42 percent) occurred in the city of Aleppo. The attacks were so frequent, and some key hospitals were struck so many times, that the incidents appear to constitute a systematic attempt to destroy the city's medical support.

These attacks against medical facilities reflected a pattern seen across the country, and documented by groups such as the World Health Organization, Amnesty International, and Médecins Sans Frontières (MSF). Physicians for Human Rights documented 400 attacks on 276 medical facilities, with the deaths of 768 medical personnel, between the beginning of the conflict and the end of July 2016; by their count, 362 of the attacks and 713 of the deaths can be attributed to the Syrian government and allied forces.[41]

Hospitals are—obviously—essential to the protection of both civilians and combatants during armed conflict and receive special protection in both the Geneva Conventions and the Additional Protocols. Article 19 of the First Geneva Convention states that "[f]ixed establishments and mobile medical units of the Medical Service may in no circumstances be attacked, but shall at all times be respected and protected by the Parties to the conflict." Article 18 of the Fourth Geneva Convention protects civilian hospitals with the same prohibition: "[c]ivilian hospitals organized to give care to the wounded and sick, the infirm and maternity cases, may in no circumstances be the object of attack, but shall at all times be respected and protected by the Parties to the conflict." Both provisions mandate that all hospitals be marked with distinctive emblems visible to enemy land, air and naval forces and recommend that all hospitals be located as far as possible from military objectives.

---

39. *See* Protocol Additional to the Geneva Conventions of 12 August 1949, and Relating to the Adoption of an Additional Distinctive Emblem (Protocol III), Dec. 8, 2005, 2404 U.N.T.S. 1. Israel uses the Red Star of David, which is protected as a matter of practice.

40. Convention for the Protection of Cultural Property in the Event of Armed Conflict, arts. 16-17, May 14, 1954, 249 U.N.T.S. 215; Annex I to Protocol Additional to the Geneva Convention of 12 August 1949 and relating to the Protection of Victims of International Armed Conflict (Protocol I), art. 16, June 8, 1977, 1125 U.N.T.S. 3.

41. Atlantic Council, *Hospital Attacks—Breaking Aleppo*, http://www.publications .atlanticcouncil.org/breakingaleppo/hospital-attacks/.

CONSIDER THE MARKINGS ON THIS HOSPITAL IN SYRIA IN THE SUMMER OF 2012[42]

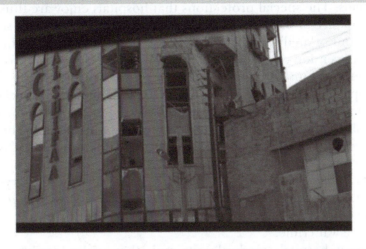

Article 12(1) of Additional Protocol I reinforces this protection of medical units in international armed conflict and Article 11(1) of Additional Protocol II mandates the same protections in the context of non-international armed conflict as well, stating that "[m]edical units and transports shall be respected and protected at all times and shall not be the object of attack." The protection of hospitals in non-international armed conflict can be traced as well to the obligation in Common Article 3 that the "wounded and sick shall be collected and cared for." If hospitals did not enjoy protection from attack, the wounded and sick could not receive the necessary treatment and the protection they are ensured under LOAC, such that "the only logical conclusion is that hospitals are protected in [non-international armed conflicts] as in [international armed conflicts], despite the lack of express provision to this effect in Common Article 3."[43]

The notion of "respect and protect" lies at the heart of the Geneva Convention framework for the protection of the wounded and the establishments necessary to ensure their treatment and safety during armed conflict. Respect means "'to spare, not to attack'" and protect means "'to come to someone's defence, to lend help and support.'"[44] Extended beyond the

42. Human Rights Watch, *Syria Fighter Planes Strike Aleppo Hospital*, August 15, 2012, http://www.hrw.org/news/2012/08/15/syria-fighter-planes-strike-aleppo-hospital.

43. THE 1949 GENEVA CONVENTIONS: A COMMENTARY 223 (Andrew Clapham, Paola Gaeta & Marco Sassòli eds., 2015).

44. INT'L COMM. RED CROSS, COMMENTARY ON THE GENEVA CONVENTION (I) FOR THE AMELIORATION OF THE CONDITION OF THE WOUNDED AND SICK IN THE ARMED FORCES IN THE FIELD 134-135 (Jean Pictet ed., 1952).

individual wounded soldier, the notion of respect and protect then ensures that medical facilities and units are equally safe to perform their essential tasks of treating and protecting the wounded and sick, both combatants and civilians. The special protections that hospitals enjoy are thus "a logical consequence of the principle of inviolability of the wounded, sick, shipwrecked, and of medical personnel."[45] As the Commentary to the Fourth Geneva Convention emphasizes, the obligation to respect and protect puts "belligerents . . . under a general obligation to do everything possible to spare hospitals" and goes beyond a prohibition on deliberate attacks.[46] This protection extends beyond fixed hospitals to medical units in the field, hospital ships, and medical transport, such as ambulances. In the case of deliberate attacks, the Rome Statute criminalizes intentional attacks against buildings, transport, and personnel marked with the distinctive emblems of the Geneva Conventions (i.e., Red Cross, Red Crescent, or Red Crystal) as a war crime. For example, the *International Fact-Finding Mission on the Conflict in Georgia* noted that Russian helicopter attacks on the Gori hospital could amount to a war crime.

However, hospitals, medical units, and other medical facilities can lose their immunity from attack if used for military purposes. Article 19 of the Fourth Geneva Convention states that "the protection to which civilian hospitals are entitled shall not cease unless they are used to commit, outside their humanitarian duties, acts harmful to the enemy." The definition of "harmful to the enemy" is quite broad, and refers not only to direct harm by launching attacks, but also to "any attempts at deliberately hindering his military operations in any way whatsoever."[47] Examples include launching rockets from or storing munitions in a hospital, or using a hospital building as a command post. During Operation Iraqi Freedom, human rights organizations condemned the Iraqi practice of using hospitals and mosques for military uses, noting that, by using hospitals as military headquarters, Iraqi forces turned them into military objectives. Similarly, Hamas used the Shifa hospital, one of Gaza's main hospitals, as a headquarters and fired rockets from inside or on the grounds of hospitals during the 2014 conflict.[48] In the case of hospitals

---

45. THE 1949 GENEVA CONVENTIONS: A COMMENTARY 207 (Andrew Clapham, Paola Gaeta & Marco Sassòli eds., 2015).

46. INT'L COMM. RED CROSS, COMMENTARY ON THE GENEVA CONVENTION (IV) RELATIVE TO THE PROTECTION OF CIVILIAN PERSONS IN TIME OF WAR 147 (Oscar M. Uhler & Henri Coursier eds., 1958).

47. CLAUDE PILLOUD, YVES SANDOZ, CHRISTOPHE SWINARSKI & BRUNO ZIMMERMAN, COMMENTARY ON THE ADDITIONAL PROTOCOLS OF 8 JUNE 1977 TO THE GENEVA CONVENTIONS OF 12 AUGUST 1949 175 (1987).

48. Yoav Zitun, *Video: Terrorists Fire Rockets from Gaza Hospital,* YNETNEWS.COM (July 23, 2014); William Booth, *While Israel Held Its Fire, The Militant Group Hamas Did Not,* WASHINGTON POST (July 15, 2014).

or other medical units that lose their protection from attack due to use for military purposes, LOAC requires that the attacking party may only launch attacks after giving due warning to cease such military activities and providing a reasonable time, where appropriate, for ending the hostile activity or evacuating wounded and sick to a place of safety.[49] Ambulances can create difficult legal and operational issues, particularly in complex urban conflicts. Without a doubt, the ability of ambulances to pass into and through conflict zones is essential to the protection of both civilians and combatants in need of medical care. In many conflicts, however, militants use ambulances to transport fighters and suicide bombers, taking advantage of their special protection. For example, in January 2018, Taliban forces drove an ambulance packed with explosives through a checkpoint and detonated it near a hospital, diplomatic buildings, and other government facilities, killing 95 people and injuring nearly 200 others.[50] Hamas has regularly used ambulances to transport fighters and munitions as well.[51] Consider the consequences of these tactics for the provision of medical care in these conflicts.

LOAC also adds a further layer of protection: in addition to the loss of protection from attack, the use of hospitals or other medical facilities for military purposes, including to shield military objectives, can itself be a violation of LOAC. Article 12(4) of Additional Protocol I declares that "under no circumstances shall medical units be used in an attempt to shield military objectives from attack." As the Commentary to Additional Protocol I explains, placing medical units or facilities "on the periphery of military objectives" in an attempt to immunize those objectives from attack "would completely distort the spirit of humanitarian law and devalue both the victims being cared for and the medical personnel who would be knowingly exposed to very grave danger."[52] Using medical units in this manner goes against the very purposes of the Geneva Conventions, dating back to the first Geneva Convention of 1864. Unfortunately, it is all too common for medical facilities to be used to shield military objectives well beyond this idea of peripheral shielding. Consider the examples in the previous paragraph — placing rocket launchers in a hospital courtyard or on the roof of a hospital, storing weapons or other military equipment in hospitals,

49. First Geneva Convention, Art. 21; Fourth Geneva Convention, Art. 19; Additional Protocol I, art. 13.

50. Ehsan Popalzai and Laura Smith-Spark, *Taliban Attacker Driving Ambulance Packed with Explosives Kills 95 in Kabul*, CNN.COM (Jan. 28, 2018).

51. Yaakov Lapin, *Fighting Terrorists Who Move Around in Ambulances*, JERUSALEM POST (July 20, 2014).

52. CLAUDE PILLOUD, YVES SANDOZ, CHRISTOPHE SWINARSKI & BRUNO ZIMMERMAN, COMMENTARY ON THE ADDITIONAL PROTOCOLS OF 8 JUNE 1977 TO THE GENEVA CONVENTIONS OF 12 AUGUST 1949 170 (1987).

or using medical facilities to shelter combatants or for command and control—each of these acts not only results in the loss of protection from attack, but is a violation of LOAC in and of itself.

Yet another protection is the prohibition on the improper use of the emblems of the Geneva Conventions, such as the Red Cross or Red Crescent used to mark hospitals, as in the photo above. "Improper use" generally means any use that is not authorized by the Conventions or another relevant treaty instrument. As the Commentary explains, the distinctive emblem of the Geneva Conventions

> Allows its bearers to venture on to the battlefield to carry out their humanitarian task. It bears witness to the totally inoffensive character of the persons and objects that it designates, as well as to the impartial, useful and orderly nature of their humanitarian task, and in return, it grants them immunity. Thus it should be displayed in good faith and in accordance with the prescribed conditions, deployed widely wherever possible and permanently under a strict control of the conditions of its use.[53]

The types of acts that constitute improper use coincide with the types of activity that causes civilian objects to become military objectives based on their use and thus lose protection from attack—such as "firing from a building or tent displaying the emblem of the Red Cross; using a hospital train or airplane to facilitate the escape of combatants; . . . and in general using [the emblem] for cloaking acts of hostility."[54] Unfortunately, such practices are not new: after World War II, a U.S. Military Tribunal convicted a German soldier of "wrongfully [using] the Red Cross emblem in a combat zone by firing a weapon at American soldiers from an enemy ambulance displaying such emblem."[55] Noting that misuse of the Red Cross emblem is a violation of the Hague and (pre-WWII) Geneva Conventions, the tribunal declared that "[i]t is hard to conceive of a more flagrant misuse than the firing of a weapon from an ambulance by personnel who were themselves protected by such emblems and by the Conventions, in the absence of an attack upon them."[56] Today, improper or unauthorized use of the distinctive emblems of the Geneva Conventions resulting in death or serious injury is a war crime under the Rome Statute of the International Criminal Court. In effect, LOAC does not rely solely on the loss of immunity from attack as a motivation for parties to a conflict to refrain from misuse of medical facilities, but instead makes that misuse itself a violation of the law to reinforce the prohibition against use of such specially protected objects for military purposes.

53. *Id.* at 450.

54. U.S. DEPARTMENT OF THE ARMY, FM 27-10, THE LAW OF LAND WARFARE ¶ 55 (1956).

55. Trial of Heinz Hagendorf, Case No. 80 (U.S. Intermediate Mil. Gov. Ct., Dachau Aug. 9, 1946), *reprinted in* U.N. WAR CRIMES COMM'N, XIII LAW REPORTS OF TRIALS OF WAR CRIMINALS 146 (1949).

56. *Id.* at 148.

> ## U.S. Air Force as Humanitarian Relief
>
> In Operation Provide Relief, U.S. military transports supported the multinational U.N. relief effort in Somalia in 1992, airlifting aid to remote areas in Somalia to reduce reliance on truck convoys. During the operation, various nongovernmental organizations, including the ICRC, insisted that U.S. Air Force planes display their logos on the outside of the aircraft.
>
> • How would you have responded to these requests? What would be the consequences, for both the U.S. military and the humanitarian relief organizations, if you agreed to the request?
>
> • If you agreed, could the flights also transport U.S. or coalition troops? Or would they be limited to nonmilitary humanitarian relief supplies only?
>
> • Did LOAC apply during the operation? Would your answer change depending on whether LOAC applied?
>
> — *Major General Charles Dunlap, Jr., JAGC,*
> *U.S. Air Force (Ret.), former Deputy Judge Advocate General*

QUESTIONS FOR DISCUSSION

1. What if a hospital is being used to treat wounded combatants or fighters for the enemy forces? Can it be attacked? What if a forward surgical unit is being guarded by armed sentries?

2. How should the appropriate balance be struck between the need to ensure the safety of medical transports and personnel and the provision of medical care on the one hand, and the need to protect against attacks on the other? Imagine being a soldier at a checkpoint who has received intelligence that the enemy is using an ambulance to transport a suicide bomber disguised as a pregnant woman. When an ambulance arrives at your checkpoint, what steps do you take, keeping in mind both your obligation to protect your own forces and civilians and your equally paramount obligation to ensure not just access to medical care and the protection of all civilians (whether on your side or the enemy side), but also the respect for human dignity, decency, and humane treatment. What if you receive intelligence reports that armed groups are using ambulances and other emergency vehicles to move large amounts of weapons and munitions? Can you institute a policy mandating that all emergency vehicles be stopped and searched for contraband? What if the emergency vehicles have their sirens running and appear to be responding to an emergency?

3. In 2002, human rights groups brought a petition to the Israeli Supreme Court in response to incidents where the Israeli Defense Forces allegedly shot at Palestinian ambulances in the course of Israeli combat operations in the West Bank. The Court held: 1) LOAC protects ambulances

and medical services and personnel from attack by combat forces; 2) this protection applies only when the medical teams are exclusively engaged in search, transport and treatment of wounded; and 3) if medical facilities or transportation are used to commit acts harmful to the enemy, they lose their protection on condition that due warning has been given and gone unheeded. In addressing the balance between the essential need to protect medical personnel and facilities and the need for armed forces to protect their forces from attack, the Court stated:

> [W]e see fit to emphasize that our combat forces are required to abide by the rules of humanitarian law regarding the care of the wounded, the ill, and bodies of the deceased. The fact that medical personnel have abused their position in hospitals and in ambulances has made it necessary for the IDF to act in order to prevent such activities but does not, in and of itself, justify sweeping breaches of humanitarian rules. Indeed, this is also the position of the State. . . .
>
> The IDF shall once again instruct the combat forces, down to the level of the lone soldier in the field, of this commitment by our forces based on law and morality—and, according to the State, even on utilitarian considerations—through concrete instructions which will prevent, to the extent possible, and even in severe situations, incidents which are inconsistent with the rules of humanitarian law. . . .
>
> These guidelines should be subject to the circumstances, and should be carried out by the IDF in a way that balances the threat of Palestinian fighters camouflaged as medical teams against the legal and moral obligation to uphold humanitarian rules regarding the treatment of the sick and wounded. Such a balance should take into consideration, among other things, the imminence and severity of any threat.[57]

In June 1987, *Newsweek* magazine ran this photograph from the conflict in Nicaragua:

The caption read, "In Red Cross disguise, a Contra chopper ferries military supplies."[58] How does this misuse of the Red Cross emblem affect both fighters and civilians in the area?

---

57. Physicians for Human Rights v. The Commander of the IDF Forces in the West Bank 4-5, HCJ 2117/02 [2002].

58. Rod Nordland, *The New Contras? Back in Battle, but Losing the War for the People's Hearts and Minds*, NEWSWEEK (June 1, 1987).

4. What about the use of a military helicopter marked with the Red Cross as a low-flying show of force to disperse demonstrators during peacetime?[59] Or the use of the Red Cross emblem by other humanitarian organizations "to avoid a possible attack by insurgents or . . . soldiers who might mistake them for attackers"?[60]

5. Early in the 2003 conflict in Iraq, Kuwait refused to allow any Iraqis (whether wounded or prisoners of war) to be brought into their territory, so U.S. forces brought injured Iraqi soldiers onboard a U.S. Navy hospital ship for treatment. Recognizing that the soldiers could have valuable intelligence about Iraqi operations, capabilities and vulnerabilities, U.S. Army intelligence officers asked for access to question them. If you were the commander of the Navy hospital ship, how would you respond? What would be the consequence of allowing interrogations on a hospital ship? Article 30 of the Second Geneva Convention mandates that the "High Contracting Parties undertake not to use [hospital ships] for any military purpose." What would happen if intelligence derived from an interrogation led to an attack by U.S. forces?

2. *Religious and Cultural Property*

Protection of cultural property and places of worship during armed conflict dates back to the 1899 Hague Convention—and arguably centuries before that. Religious and cultural property is an essential component of the social fabric and an important marker of a community's presence and history, as well as a bulwark against its destruction. Article 27 of the 1907 Hague Regulations thus mandates that "all necessary steps must be taken to spare, as far as possible, buildings dedicated to religion, art, science, or charitable purposes, [and] historic monuments, provided they are not being used for military purposes." Article 56 then states that "[a]ll seizure of, destruction or wilful damage done to [institutions dedicated to religion, charity and education, the arts and sciences], historic monuments, works of art and science, is forbidden." These protections seek to ensure that these central facets of civilian life continue to function during and after armed conflict. As one senior official at UNESCO explained, a "community's cultural heritage reflects its life, history and identity. Its preservation helps to rebuild broken communities, re-establish their identities, and link their past with their present and future."[61] Unfortunately, however, attacks on

---

59. Alex Horton, *Use of Medical Helicopter to Target Protestors is Under Investigation, National Guard Says*, Washington Post (June 2, 2020).

60. Red Cross Warns Against False Use of its Emblem in Cameroon, Aljazeera.com (July 22, 2015).

61. UNESCO, *Re-building Cultural Heritage in Mali*, July 1, 2014, http://whc.unesco.org/en/news/1178/.

such objects also have a long history, including extensive destruction of cultural property belonging to all sides in the conflict in the former Yugoslavia; the looting of the Iraq National Museum in 2003 after the U.S. invasion; the Nazi policy of burning and looting of synagogues across Europe in World War II; and the destruction of Intramuros, the old Spanish colonial district in the center of Manilla, during the Japanese occupation and the U.S. invasion to retake the islands, among many other examples. More recently, ISIS embarked on a campaign to destroy, plunder, and profit from Syria's vast and irreplaceable cultural artifacts during its reign of terror across parts of Syria and Iraq.

ISIS: DESTRUCTION OF CULTURAL HERITAGE IN IRAQ AND SYRIA

Syria

- All six of Syria's certified cultural heritage sites have been officially endangered since 2013 and all had been reported damaged as of March 2016. This includes ancient archaeological sites like the Ancient Roman capital Bosra, Assyrian Tell Sheikh Hamad, Ebla and Mari from the Bronze Age, Dura-Europos, home to the world's best-preserved ancient synagogue, and the Crac des Chevaliers medieval castle complex.
- 30 percent of the historic Old City of Aleppo, one of the oldest continually inhabited cities in the world, has been destroyed.
- ISIS militants destroyed three historic shrines at the Ammar bin Yasir Mosque in Raqqa, a Shiite pilgrimage site.
- In Palmyra, ISIS militants destroyed the Al Lat Lion, a 2,000 year-year-old statute that once guarded an ancient temple. ISIS defaced and looted any remaining artifacts in the Palmyra Museum, selling hundreds on the black market. ISIS bombed the Temples of Bel and Baalshamin and executed Khaled al-Asaad, the head of antiquities at the Palmyra Museum, when he refused to reveal the hiding places of invaluable artifacts. ISIS also destroyed the city's Monumental Arch, the Al Sultaniya Mosque, and the remains of the ancient Roman Tetraplion.

Iraq

- ISIS bulldozed the ancient city of Hatra, a walled city built in the third century BC, and broadcast the destruction in propaganda videos.

- In Mosul, ISIS burned down the historic library, destroyed a tomb believed to be that of the biblical prophet Jonah, destroyed ancient artifacts at the Mosul Museum, and dug tunnels throughout the city to facilitate its looting efforts.
- In Nimrud, ISIS destroyed the palace of Ashurnasirpal II with sledge-hammers, drills and explosives, and then bulldozed the 2900-year-old royal ziggurat, an ancient pyramid mound built as a temple.
- The Adad Gate and parts of the fortification wall of Nineveh, which dated back over 2,500 years, were destroyed, along with 70 percent of the walled city of Nineveh.[62]

The 1954 Hague Convention for the Protection of Cultural Property in the Event of Armed Conflict defines cultural property broadly and sets forth the basic protections during armed conflict.[63] It applies in all armed conflicts, whether international or non-international. Recognizing that the protection of cultural property must begin during peacetime, Article 3 of the Convention requires that states "undertake to prepare in time of peace for the safeguarding of cultural property situated within their own territory against the foreseeable effects of an armed conflict, by taking such measures as they consider appropriate." During armed conflict, Article 4(1) requires all countries to respect cultural property in their own territory and in the territory of the enemy party, to refrain from using the property in any way that would expose it to destruction, and to refrain from any acts of hostility against such property. It is the next paragraph—Article 4(2)—however, that seems to undermine these very protections by providing that the obligations to respect cultural property "may be waived only in cases where military necessity imperatively requires such a waiver." What does military necessity mean here? Can cultural property receive the protection it requires if military necessity is always a justification for an attack?

In the section of Additional Protocol I on "General Protection Against Effects of Hostilities," Article 53 reinforces the special protection for religious and cultural property and objects:

---

62. *See* Alyssa Buffenstein, *A Monumental Loss: Here are the Most Significant Cultural Heritage Sites that ISIS Has Destroyed to Date,* ARTNETNEWS.COM (May 30, 2017).

63. Cultural property includes "movable or immovable property of great importance to the cultural heritage of every people, such as monuments of architecture, art or history, whether religious or secular; archaeological sites; groups of buildings which, as a whole, are of historical or artistic interest; works of art; manuscripts, books and other objects of artistic, historical or archaeological interest; as well as scientific collections and important collections of books or archives . . ."; and buildings or centers containing such property. Convention for the Protection of Cultural Property in the Event of Armed Conflict, art. 1(a), May 14, 1954, 249 U.N.T.S. 215.

Without prejudice to the provisions of the Hague Convention for the Protection of Cultural Property in the Event of Armed Conflict of 14 May 1954, and of other relevant international instruments, it is prohibited:

> (a) to commit any acts of hostility directed against the historic monuments, works of art or places of worship which constitute the cultural or spiritual heritage of peoples;
>
> (b) to use such objects in support of the military effort;
>
> (c) to make such objects the object of reprisals.

Although Article 53 of Additional Protocol I does not define religious and cultural property, it is understood to apply to three categories in particular, to the extent they constitute the cultural or spiritual heritage of peoples: historic monuments, works of art, and places of worship. In addition, it does not provide for any waiver of its obligations: "[a]s long as the object concerned is not made into a military objective by those in control—and that is not allowed—no attack is permitted."[64]

The 1954 Hague Convention applies in all armed conflicts, whether international or non-international. In addition, customary law applicable in non-international armed conflicts also protects against attacks on cultural property, as the ICTY noted in the *Tadić* case. Unfortunately, the conflict in the former Yugoslavia featured numerous attacks on religious and cultural property amidst efforts to destroy the cultural heritage of one or more parties to the conflict. In December 1991, for example, the Yugoslav Peoples' Army repeatedly shelled the Old Town of Dubrovnik, Croatia, a World Heritage site "endowed with an exceptional architectural heritage" with fortifications "widely regarded as some of the finest examples of city fortifications in Europe."[65] Finding that no military objectives were located in the vicinity of the Old Town and that no structures were being used for military purposes, the ICTY found that all elements of the crimes of devastation not justified by military necessity and destruction or willful damage of cultural property were established based on the perpetrators' deliberate attack on the Old Town and awareness of the area's civilian character. More recently, in the first prosecution solely for the war crime of destruction of cultural property, the ICC sentenced Ahmad Al Mahdi to nine years in prison for intentionally directing attacks against ten mausoleums in Timbuktu, Mali. In particular, after noting that the designation of nine of the buildings as UNESCO World Heritage sites "reflects their special importance to international cultural heritage," the court emphasized the war crime of attacks

---

64. Claude Pilloud, Yves Sandoz, Christophe Swinarski & Bruno Zimmerman, Commentary on the Additional Protocols of 8 June 1977 to the Geneva Conventions of 12 August 1949 647 (1987).

65. Prosecutor v. Pavle Strugar, Case No. IT-01-42-T, Judgement ¶ 21 (Int'l Crim. Trib. for the Former Yugoslavia Jan. 31, 2005).

on cultural property is not limited to actions during the conduct of hostilities but also includes acts of violence against protected objects "after [such] object[s] had fallen under the control of an armed group."[66]

PRESERVING CULTURAL HERITAGE IN LIBYA: OPERATION ODYSSEY DAWN

Libya contains a number of archeological sites that reflect the heritage of all mankind. For example, there are five World Heritage sites in Libya, including Cyrene, Leptis Magna, and Sabratha, from the Phoenician, Greek, and Roman periods, the prehistoric rock-art sites of Tadrart Acacus, and the ancient desert town of Ghadames. Along with these prominent sites, there are hundreds of archeological sites scattered throughout the country, many of which were located in the areas fought over during the recent civil war and NATO bombing campaign in support of the Libyan rebels.

What were the law of armed conflict implications? What were the constraints on the NATO forces and the obligations of both sides during the civil war?

The obligation of states parties to an international armed conflict are described in the Hague Rules of 1907, the Geneva Convention for the Protection of Civilians of 1949, the 1954 Hague Cultural Property Convention, and the 1977 Additional Protocol I. All of these references require states to respect and protect cultural property, although there is a fairly significant difference between the legal standards that apply to cultural property as civilian objects and the protections afforded to property that is provided "enhanced protections" under Protocol II to the 1954 Hague Convention. For example, according to Article 27 of the Hague Rules, "In sieges and bombardments all necessary steps must be taken to spare, as far as possible, buildings dedicated to religion, art, science, or charitable purposes, historic monuments . . . provided they are not being used at the time for military purposes." Article 10 of Protocol II to Hague 1954 provides for "enhanced protection" for sites that have been designated by a Committee of States Parties,

---

66 Prosecutor v. Ahmad Al Mahdi, Case No. ICC-01/12/15, Judgment and Sentence ¶¶ 15, 46 (Sept. 27, 2016). The meaning of "attack" and whether it includes acts on persons and objects under the control of the perpetrator, rather than during an active firefight, was a significant point of debate in the *Ntaganda* case before the ICC, with the Appeals Chamber judges failing to reach agreement on the scope of "attack" in Article 8(2)(e)(iv). Prosecutor v. Bosco Ntaganda, Case No. ICC-01/O4-02/06 A A2, Judgment (Mar. 30, 2021).

through a process of nomination similar to the UNESCO World Heritage List designation. Engagement of those sites, even if occupied by military forces, requires warning and the highest operational level of military command to approve for engagement. So it is imperative that military forces identify cultural property before the conflict begins, to highlight the different procedural and tactical approaches to these sites, should they become military objectives by virtue of their occupation by enemy forces. States are obligated to refrain from occupying cultural property sites, unless "imperative military necessity demands it," according to the most liberal Hague Rules approach; but the conversion of a site protected by the Second Hague Protocol requires an analysis of feasible alternatives and approval at a battalion level or higher and sites with enhanced protection cannot be converted to a military objective (without committing a serious violation of the Second Protocol).

Immediately prior to the Libyan operation, several international organizations contacted NATO forces to identify archeological sites. Within the United States, the U.S. Committee of the Blue Shield, which has the charter of supporting U.S. efforts to protect cultural property during armed conflict, provided information to the U.S. armed forces to identify numerous archeological sites and museums. Similar organizations provided notice to NATO and the Libyan forces.

Serious violations of the cultural property protections provided by the law of armed conflict have not been identified in the Libyan conflict, potentially due to the precautions identified above. After the conflict, a team of civil-military experts from the Association of National Committees of the Blue Shield and the International Military Cultural Resources Working Group inspected various critical sites to determine if there was any damage and to recommend means of safeguarding the sites and mitigation of any damage. In addition, UNESCO convened a meeting of experts from inside and outside Libya at its Paris Headquarters to discuss future efforts to protect this critical heritage.

— *Colonel Richard Jackson, JAGC, U.S. Army (Ret.), former Special Assistant to the U.S. Army Judge Advocate General for Law of War Matters*

QUESTIONS FOR DISCUSSION

1. In March 2001, the Taliban destroyed the 1700-year-old sandstone statues of Buddha carved into a cliff in the Bamiyan Valley in the Hindu Kush mountains in central Afghanistan. After first failing to destroy them with anti-aircraft and tank fire, the Taliban used dynamite charges placed into holes drilled in the statues. The Buddhas were destroyed as part of the destruction of all icons and idols in Afghanistan, because they were considered "un-Islamic" by the Taliban. Was this a LOAC violation? Does there have to be a nexus to an ongoing armed conflict?

2. In 2005, U.S. Army snipers took positions at the top of this 1,200-year-old minaret in Iraq:

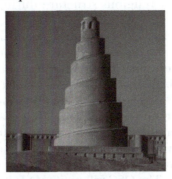

After U.S. soldiers in the town of Samarra faced incessant attacks at the intersection below the minaret, commanders decided to place snipers with powerful scopes and heavy rifles in the minaret, with a bird's eye view of any insurgent activity or threat to U.S. positions or patrols. Upset at the U.S. position atop the minaret, which has been an attraction for Muslim pilgrims for centuries, insurgents began shooting at the minaret with rocket-propelled grenades and small arms fire.[67]

What are the law of war considerations here? Is the U.S. use of the minaret as a vantage point in violation of LOAC? Could there be a valid justification? Is military necessity generally a sufficient justification, or would there need to be no other feasible alternative to achieving the objective of stopping the attacks?[68] Once the U.S. snipers are stationed at the top, how do you assess the legality of the insurgent attacks on the tower?

3. Beyond the legal protections for cultural and religious objects, strategic and operational considerations may loom large in certain conflicts. For example, in Afghanistan, U.S. forces did not enter mosques even if they were in direct pursuit of insurgents seeking shelter therein, but rather relied on Afghan National Army forces to address such situations. The political and strategic ramifications of U.S. forces entering a mosque in a Muslim nation are simply too volatile to risk, so the rules of engagement and basic practice actually took a narrower approach than the law might allow. For example, the rules of engagement during Operation Iraqi Freedom provided:

67. *See* Josh White, *For U.S. Soldiers, A Frustrating and Fulfilling Mission*, WASH. POST, Jan. 2, 2005, at A12.

68. *See* Geoffrey S. Corn, *Snipers in the Minaret—What Is the Rule? The Law of War and the Protection of Cultural Property: A Complex Equation*, 28 ARMY LAW., July 2005, at 40 ("While use of the vantage point offered by such a structure was undoubtedly intended to enhance the effectiveness of the operation, the prohibition against the military use of cultural property absent such a justification does not allow for a general military necessity based exception. Instead, . . . imperative necessity suggests that no other feasible alternative be available for achieving what is presumptively an important military objective.").

3.E.(2) . . . ENTRY AND SEARCH OF MOSQUES OR OTHER RELI-GIOUS STRUCTURES. There are three requirements to enter and search a mosque or other religious structure during TIC [troops in contact]/self-defense:

    3.E.(2)(A) . . . The OSC [on-scene commander] has a reasonable belief that the target contains enemy forces, individuals assisting enemy forces, weapons, ammunition, important information, or any materials, equipment or contraband that may be used by enemy forces during hostilities.

    3.E.(2)(B) . . . US Forces will not enter mosques without the approval of the CDR [commander], MND-B [Multi-National Division — Baghdad], in coordination with MOD [Ministry of Defense] and MOI [Ministry of Interior]. When approval is granted, coordination will be made with ISF to enter the mosques with cordon support from US Forces.

    3.E.(2)(C) . . . The OSC will notify MND-B G3 BTL MAJ before, during, or after the operation as the situation permits. The MND-B G3 BTL MAJ will notify MNC-I C3.

4. In another example, a group of armed Palestinians took control of the Church of the Nativity in Bethlehem in 2002.

> Although the use of the Church by these combatants in support of a military effort turned it *ipso facto* into a military objective, Israel could not ignore the reverence with which Christians the world over view this shrine. As a result, Israel resorted to siege tactics and refrained from storming the site. . . . The case serves as a reminder that there are singular cultural and spiritual places, which cannot be subjected to a mechanical application of the ordinary rules of [LOAC].[69]

5. In the summer of 2012, fighting in Syria spread to Aleppo, one of the oldest cities in the world and considered to be the world's oldest continuously inhabited human settlement. Reports at the time hinted at the potential for extensive destruction of irreplaceable cultural treasures:

> Already the massive iron doors to the city's immense medieval Citadel have been blown up in a missile attack . . . .
>
> President Bashar al-Assad's forces have been shelling the city, and in recent days his army has taken up positions inside the Citadel, trading fire with insurgents through the castle's arrow loops, according to news reports. Built on a massive outcropping of rock, the easily defended Citadel has been an important strategic military point for millenniums and is once again serving that function.
>
> Among the significant archaeological sites endangered is the Temple of the Storm God, which dates from the third to the second millennium B.C. and [is] identified as one of the oldest structures in the world.

---

69. Yoram Dinstein, The Conduct of Hostilities Under the Law of International Armed Conflict 181-182 (2d ed. 2010).

Never opened to the public, the recently discovered temple and its huge carved reliefs are protected only by sandbags and a flimsy corrugated tin roof . . . .

Aleppo's labyrinthine streets reveal a microcosm of human history. Beneath the Citadel are remains of Bronze Age friezes and Roman fortresses. The entire walled Old City, with its 12th-century Great Mosque, thousands of pastel-colored medieval courtyard houses, Arab souks and 17th-century stone madrasas, an Ottoman palace and hammams, is recognized as a World Heritage Site by [UNESCO], the United Nations cultural arm.

Images of the Citadel show rubble in some locations, but it is difficult to verify the extent to which either side is responsible for any damage.

The Syrian National Council, a coalition of antigovernment forces, issued a communiqué saying that the Citadel was damaged on Friday by an army rocket. Al Jazeera filmed rebels last week talking about the need to capture the Citadel.[70]

Unfortunately, much of Aleppo was destroyed over the course of the next several years. What can be done in such situations to preserve and protect this type of cultural heritage? Think about the considerable challenges involved when an entire city is, in essence, a cultural landmark deserving of protection.

6. Is digital art cultural property? Should it be protected as such? What if there are multiple copies? What about digital copies of famous paintings, such as Monet's *Water Lilies* or Da Vinci's *Mona Lisa*?

PRAYER RUGS AND AK-47S

Respecting religious symbols/artifacts is a core ingredient of manifesting respect and dignity for the civilian population. As Commander of the Israel Defense Forces (IDF) School of Military Law, I had command responsibility for the creation of an interactive video teaching "Morality in Armed Conflict" to IDF soldiers and junior commanders. This was a core principle that we identified as essential to the interaction between soldiers and the Palestinian population. However, as the vignette below tragically illustrates, there are costs attendant to the teaching—and implementation—of moral principles and codes.

Two soldiers manning an IDF checkpoint between Bethlehem and Jerusalem were approached by a Palestinian carrying a furled prayer rug; in accordance with the principle above (which I had personally discussed—in addition to the

70. Patricia Cohen, *Syrian Conflict Imperils Cultural Treasures*, N.Y. TIMES (Aug. 15, 2012).

> *video—with their unit), the soldiers did not ask the Palestinian to unfurl the rug. The result was an extraordinary tragedy: inside the prayer rug was an AK-47; needless to say, both soldiers were killed.*
>
> The vignette raises extraordinarily important questions regarding the limits of morality in armed conflict. Where and what are the appropriate limits in balancing powerful competing tensions? While respect for religious symbols/artifacts is, undoubtedly, an absolute obligation, should that obligation be mitigated in the context of "armed conflict short of war" when distinguishing between a combatant and civilian poses extraordinary challenges, in real time, to soldiers? What are the consequences of lessening the obligation?
>
> *— Lieutenant Colonel Amos Guiora, Military Advocate General's Corps (Ret.), Israel Defense Forces*

3.   *Protection of the Environment*

During the first Persian Gulf War, Iraqi troops set fire to hundreds of oil wells during their retreat from Kuwait. They also deliberately pumped millions of gallons of oil into the Persian Gulf to try to thwart any Coalition attempt at a marine assault on Kuwait. The environmental effects of these and other actions continue today, and, in some ways, the magnitude still remains unknown. Destruction of the environment during armed conflict is certainly not a new phenomenon, however; the U.S. use of Agent Orange and other toxic herbicides during the Vietnam War caused massive deforestation and chemical contamination that also has had significant long-term effects. Indeed, these latter tactics led directly to the 1976 UN Convention on the Prohibition of Military or Any Other Use of Environmental Modification Techniques (ENMOD), which prohibits the use of any techniques that turn the environment into a "weapon." Article 1(1) of ENMOD provides that "[e]ach Party to this Convention undertakes not to engage in military or any other hostile use of environmental modification techniques having widespread, long lasting or severe effects as the means of destruction, damage or injury to any other State Party." The first environment-specific LOAC treaty, ENMOD focuses solely on prohibiting modification of environmental processes as a method of warfare—such as defoliation or deforestation. It did not take the broader approach of protecting the environment itself.

Additional Protocol I is therefore the first LOAC treaty to address protection of the environment directly (note that the environment does not appear at all in the four Geneva Conventions of 1949).

> # ARTICLE 35(3) OF ADDITIONAL PROTOCOL I
>
> It is prohibited to employ methods or means of warfare which are intended, or may be expected, to cause widespread, long-term and severe damage to the natural environment.

> # ARTICLE 55 OF ADDITIONAL PROTOCOL I
>
> 1. Care shall be taken in warfare to protect the natural environment against widespread, long-term and severe damage. This protection includes a prohibition of the use of methods or means of warfare which are intended or may be expected to cause such damage to the natural environment and thereby to prejudice the health or survival of the population.
>
> 2. Attacks against the natural environment by way of reprisals are prohibited.

QUESTIONS FOR DISCUSSION

1. Harm to the environment itself is a consideration in any targeting decision, as are the consequences for the civilian population of any damage to the natural environment. The natural environment is thus generally categorized as a civilian object. Should it sometimes be granted special protection? Can it sometimes also be a legitimate military objective, such as a forest used by the enemy for concealment or a strategic mountain pass? In light of this legal framework, consider the Iraqi destruction of Kuwaiti oil wells noted above:

> As a rule, oil wells may be regarded as military objectives, the use of which can legitimately be denied to the enemy. . . . Still, considering that the oil wells set on fire by Iraq were located in an occupied country (Kuwait) being evacuated by a defeated army, their systematic destruction—which could not possibly affect the progress of the war—did not offer a definite military advantage in the circumstances ruling at the time. The only possible military advantage to Iraq (on a purely tactical level) was the creation of thick smoke obscuring its ground forces from view by Coalition aviators, but the measure had little impact on military operations. Even if the oil wells constituted military objectives in the circumstances prevailing at the time, and there was a limited military advantage in the smoke screen reducing visibility, the Iraqi action was subject to the application of the principle of proportionality. The monstrous air pollution throughout Kuwait was tantamount to excessive injury to the environment and to

the civilian population in breach of that principle. On balance, the Iraqis appear to have been motivated not by military considerations but by sheer vindictiveness.[71]

After the war, United Nations Security Council Resolution 687 stated that "Iraq is liable under international law for any . . . damage, including environmental damage and the depletion of natural resources . . . as a result of Iraq's unlawful invasion and occupation of Kuwait." As the United Nations Compensation Commission found, Iraq's actions in destroying oil wells and causing other environmental damage violated Article 23(g) of the Hague Regulations regarding the destruction of enemy property.

2. Looting, plunder and exploitation can also violate LOAC's provisions protecting the environment during armed conflict. In August 1998, Ugandan forces invaded the Democratic Republic of the Congo, occupied territory in Ituri, and provided military, financial, and logistical support to anti-Kabila Congolese rebels for the next few years. The DRC brought Uganda to the ICJ. Among a wide range of issues—prohibition on the use of force, attacks on civilians, child soldiers, and others—the ICJ said the following regarding the exploitation of natural resources:

> the Court considers that it has ample credible and persuasive evidence to conclude that officers and soldiers of the UPDF, including the most high-ranking officers, were involved in the looting, plundering and exploitation of the DRC's natural resources and that the military authorities did not take any measures to put an end to these acts. . . . Thus, whenever members of the UPDF were involved in the looting, plundering and exploitation of natural resources in the territory of the DRC, they acted in violation of the *jus in bello* . . . .[72]

4.   *Objects Indispensable to the Civilian Population*

Residents of Derna, a city in eastern Libya, lived under siege for two years as the Libyan National Army sought to drive out the Derna Mujahideen Shura Council, an Islamist armed group that took control of the city in August 2016. The siege of Sarajevo lasted for three years, longer than the siege of Leningrad. Daraya, Syria, fell to government forces after four years of siege, and Aleppo succumbed to regime control after five long years of battles and several weeks of siege. LOAC allows belligerent parties to besiege enemy forces—that is, "to encircle them with a view towards inducing their

---

71. *See* YORAM DINSTEIN, THE CONDUCT OF HOSTILITIES UNDER THE LAW OF INTERNATIONAL ARMED CONFLICT 184 (2004).

72. Armed Activities on the Territory of the Congo (Dem. Rep. Congo v. Uganda), 2005 I.C.J. 116, ¶¶ 242, 245 (Dec. 19).

surrender by cutting them off from reinforcements, supplies, and communications with the outside world."[73] Siege can be an effective method to force surrender, often less costly than attacks. However, the use of siege tactics in modern warfare, against urban areas with large civilian populations, raises important questions about protections for the basic needs of the civilian population.

As noted at the very start of this chapter, beyond the prohibitions on specific weapons or cruel treatment or other deliberate harms, LOAC also prohibits total warfare and methods used in pursuit of total warfare. As part of this framework, starvation of civilians as a method of warfare is prohibited, as set forth in Article 54(1) of Additional Protocol I. Using starvation as a method of warfare means "to provoke it deliberately, causing the population to suffer hunger, particularly by depriving it of its sources of food or supplies."[74] Article 54(2) of Additional Protocol I further prohibits the most common methods by which a party to armed conflict might seek to cause the starvation of the civilian population:

> It is prohibited to attack, destroy, remove or render useless objects indispensable to the survival of the civilian population, such as foodstuffs, agricultural areas for the production of foodstuffs, crops, livestock, drinking water installations and supplies and irrigation works, for the specific purpose of denying them for their sustenance value to the civilian population or to the adverse Party, whatever the motive, whether in order to starve out civilians, to cause them to move away, or for any other motive.

The focus of this rule is on acts taken with the specific purpose of denying sustenance to the civilian population. Note that attacks on objects used solely as sustenance for the members of the enemy armed forces are allowed, as are attacks that destroy supply routes used for both military supplies and basic civilian food and medical supplies. In essence, incidental civilian suffering caused by destruction of lawful military objects is allowed. For example, it would not be "unlawful to attack or destroy a railroad line simply because the railroad was used to transport food needed to supply the population of a city, if the railroad was otherwise a military objective."[75]

---

73. U.S. Department of Defense, Law of War Manual § 5.19.1 (2015, rev'd Dec. 2016). *See also* United Kingdom Ministry of Defence, JSP 383: The Joint Service Manual of the Law of Armed Conflict ¶ 5.34.1 (2004).

74. Claude Pilloud, Yves Sandoz, Christophe Swinarski & Bruno Zimmerman, Commentary on the Additional Protocols of 8 June 1977 to the Geneva Conventions of 12 August 1949 653 (1987).

75. Michael Bothe et al., New Rules for the Victims of Armed Conflicts 339 (1982).

5.   *Works and Installations Containing Dangerous Forces*

Armies have harnessed natural forces to defend against invasion or to destroy enemy positions and territory throughout history, including attacks on hydroelectric dams in World War II or German troops flooding land in the Netherlands to prevent the advance of Allied forces in 1944, for example. In accordance with general distaste for such practices, the drafters of Additional Protocol I included protections for installations containing dangerous forces. Article 56 of Additional Protocol I thus mandates that "[w]orks or installations containing dangerous forces, namely dams, dykes and nuclear electrical generating stations, shall not be made the object of attack, even where these objects are military objectives, if such attack may cause the release of dangerous forces and consequent severe losses among the civilian population." Unlike the protection for objects indispensable to the civilian population, which prohibits not only damage and destruction but also acts to render them useless or remove them, this rule only protects installations containing dangerous forces from attacks. A state may, therefore, engage in acts to render such an installation useless, as long as it takes steps to ensure that the civilian population is not affected as a result.

As a starting point, dams, dykes, nuclear power plants, and other works containing hazardous forces are civilian objects. If such installations become military objectives, they may lose their protection from attack if they provide regular and direct support to military operations and an attack is the only way of ending such support. In such situations, the attacking party must take particular care to avoid severe losses among the civilian population that could result.

QUESTIONS FOR DISCUSSION

1. Your forces have taken control of an important town and an enemy advance is expected within days. Wheat fields line both sides of the main approach to the town, offering useful cover for enemy forces. Can you order the fields to be destroyed to prevent them from being used as cover?

2. In January 2016, ISIS based senior officials and high-value prisoners at the Taqba Dam, 25 miles outside Raqqa, Syria, where the group had its main headquarters. According to reports, the terrorist group believed that the United States would not "bomb it for fear of unleashing a giant flood."[76] Was the dam a military objective? What options did the United States have in seeking to dislodge ISIS from its temporary headquarters at the dam?

---

76. Damian Paletta, *Islamic State Uses Syria's Biggest Dam as Refuge and Potential Weapon*, WALL ST. J. (Jan. 20, 2016).

3. During the conflict against the FARC, the Colombian armed forces attacked rebel forces that had taken control of and built a base of operations at a dam. Responding to a news article about the attack, the Human Rights Advisor of the Presidency of the Colombian Republic explained that "it is very clear that government troops may attack it in order to dislodge the guerrillas. However, the crux of the matter is how this should be done to ensure that the attack, which is otherwise lawful, does not cause superfluous injury or unnecessary suffering. Obviously, it would not occur to any sensible military officer to bomb the position with high-power explosives which would destroy the dam wall and cause a deluge that would sweep away the inhabitants of the basin of the tributary feeding the dam."[77]

---

77. *See* Int'l Comm. Red Cross, Customary International Humanitarian Law, *Colombia, Practice Relating to Rule 42, Works and Installations Containing Dangerous Forces.*

CHAPTER 9

PLANNING AND LAUNCHING ATTACKS

Legal analysis does not end with identification of a legitimate target. Rather, the attacking party must then assess whether the attack meets the requirements of the principles of proportionality and precautions—key principles focused on operationalizing LOAC's core purpose of minimizing harm to civilians. LOAC flatly prohibits any intentional targeting of civilians, but armed conflict involves an infinite array of circumstances in which civilians may die or suffer grievous injury as a result of attacks launched directly at military targets and combatants. Technical malfunctions, inclement weather, faulty intelligence, and navigation errors can all also cause a bomb to fall short and cause significant unanticipated civilian casualties. Errors and accidents are beyond the control of the parties, but on many occasions, the commander can anticipate that some civilians will suffer harm. In addition, there may be civilians nearby or even at the location that is identified as a legitimate target. The commander planning the attack may have a range of choices in terms of tactics and weapons in attacking the target, which could result in different consequences for civilians in the area; in some situations, there may only be one option. The law of targeting, therefore, is ultimately a methodology to put the principles of distinction, proportionality, and precautions into practice and a comprehensive process to assess the lawfulness of an attack on a target or as part of a more complex mission.

A. PROPORTIONALITY

One of the fundamental goals of LOAC is the protection of civilians from the ravages of war. It thus seeks to minimize incidental civilian casualties. Proportionality in effect operationalizes LOAC's fundamental premise that the means and methods of attacking the enemy are not unlimited. Set forth in Article 35 of Additional Protocol I ("In any armed conflict, the right of the Parties to the conflict to choose methods or means of warfare is not unlimited"), this basic principle dates back at least to the 1907 Hague

Convention. LOAC thus mandates that the only legitimate object of war is to weaken the military forces of the enemy.

Importantly, however, the law does not prohibit all civilian deaths—and, in fact, anticipates and accepts the inevitability of some incidental civilian casualties. At its foundation, therefore, proportionality is a manifestation of LOAC's delicate balance between the military imperative of defeating the enemy as quickly as possible and the humanitarian imperative of mitigating suffering during war as much as possible. To protect innocent civilians from the effects of war and minimize undue suffering, LOAC therefore requires not only that parties to conflict refrain from deliberately attacking civilians and civilian objects, but also that they make extensive efforts to minimize the incidental harm from their attacks on lawful military targets.

Additional Protocol I contains three separate statements of the principle of proportionality.

ARTICLE 51(5) OF ADDITIONAL PROTOCOL I

Among others, the following types of attacks are to be considered as indiscriminate . . . (b) an attack which may be expected to cause incidental loss of civilian life, injury to civilians, damage to civilian objects, or a combination thereof, which would be excessive in relation to the concrete and direct military advantage anticipated.

Article 57, which refers specifically to precautions in attack, uses the same language twice.

ARTICLE 57 OF ADDITIONAL PROTOCOL I

(2) With respect to attacks, the following precautions shall be taken:
   (a) those who plan or decide upon an attack shall: . . .
      (iii) refrain from deciding to launch any attack which may be expected to cause incidental loss of civilian life, injury to civilians, damage to civilian objects, or a combination thereof, which would be excessive in relation to the concrete and direct military advantage anticipated.
      (b) an attack shall be cancelled or suspended if it becomes apparent that the objective is not a military one or is subject to special protection or that the attack may be expected to cause incidental loss of civilian life, injury to civilians, damage to civilian objects, or a combination thereof, which would be excessive in relation to the concrete and direct military advantage anticipated.

The definition of proportionality sets forth how those who are fighting implement the obligation to minimize incidental harm to civilians in the course of lawful military operations. Before launching an attack, commanders must examine whether the expected loss of civilian life or damage to civilian property from an attack will be excessive in relation to the anticipated military advantage gained from the attack. If the attack is likely to cause excessive civilian harm in relation to the military gain, it must be cancelled. As a result, sometimes attacking even a lawful enemy objective is impermissible because the collateral consequences clearly outweigh whatever advantage would result from the attack. Proportionality thus establishes a balance of sorts between two factors — military advantage and civilian casualties — and uses the concept of "excessiveness" rather than measuring one against the other.

1.   *"Excessive"*

Applying proportionality requires a comparison of two dissimilar factors: military advantage and civilian harm. By definition, a lawful military objective offers a concrete and direct military advantage. But that military advantage could be significant or minimal, depending on the circumstances. The other factor involves a now common term: collateral damage. Collateral damage refers to civilians killed in the course of attacks on military objectives — that is, the incidental casualties from an attack. Here it is crucial to understand a fundamental distinction between LOAC and human rights or domestic criminal law. Both legal regimes forbid the deliberate killing of innocent civilians. LOAC, however, anticipates and accepts that parties may knowingly kill civilians without violating the law. Thus, a party attacking a military objective may know for certain that some number of civilians — perhaps janitorial staff working in the building at night — will die when the building is hit. Such knowledge does not mean the party has committed a crime; rather, LOAC allows for such incidental civilian casualties to the extent that they are not *excessive* in relation to the military advantage gained from the attack. The crux of the issue, therefore, is how to interpret "excessive." Some situations raise few if any questions; for example, an obvious breach of proportionality would include destroying an entire residential building with hundreds of civilian residents in order to kill a sniper on the roof who has a military unit pinned down. As the hypothetical changes, however — perhaps to firing rockets at the sniper with the risk of endangering the civilians on the top floor — the analysis grows more complicated.

In practice, to be sure, the application of the principle is rarely clearcut: comparing the destruction of a munitions factory — or, in Gaza, a storage facility for rockets — to the number of civilian deaths or serious injuries is difficult, perhaps impossible. How do parties weigh the loss of innocent life and the military benefit of a given attack? Unfortunately, military commanders are not issued a "proportionometer"[1] to help them make such calculations. The common terminology of proportionality is one of "balance" or "weighing," but the actual provision in Additional Protocol I talks of "excessiveness." Excessive is not equivalent to "greater than," nor is it the same as "extensive." The issue, therefore, is not when one additional civilian death will tip the scale and make an otherwise lawful attack disproportionate. Instead, "focusing on excessiveness avoids the legal fiction that collateral damage, incidental injury, and military advantage can be precisely measured."[2]

2.   *Military Advantage*

Articles 51(5)(b), 57(2)(a)(iii), and 57(2)(b) of Additional Protocol I refer to a "concrete and direct" military advantage. The Commentary states that the phrase "concrete and direct" was intended to show that "advantages which are hardly perceptible and those which would only appear in the long term should be disregarded."[3] Although this explanation reinforces the need for a strong connection between the military operation at issue and its advantage or goals, state practice also demonstrates that "concrete and direct" must not be interpreted too narrowly. For example, in ratifying Additional Protocol I in 1998, the United Kingdom stated that the "military advantage anticipated from an attack is intended to refer to the advantage anticipated from the attack considered as a whole and not only from isolated or particular parts of the attack."[4] Many states also cite the security of the attacking forces as a factor to consider in analyzing military advantage. At the same time, proportionality and military advantage cannot be considered solely in light of the entire war taken as a whole, which would be an extreme approach likely to justify any loss of civilian life.

1. *See* Joseph Holland, *Military Objective and Collateral Damage: Their Relationship and Dynamics*, 2004 Y.B. INT'L HUM. L. 7, 48.

2. Michael N. Schmitt, *Fault Lines in the Law of Attack*, *in* TESTING THE BOUNDARIES OF INTERNATIONAL HUMANITARIAN LAW 277, 293 (Susan Carolyn Breau & Agnieszka Jachec-Neale eds., 2006).

3. CLAUDE PILLOUD, YVES SANDOZ, CHRISTOPHE SWINARSKI & BRUNO ZIMMERMAN, COMMENTARY ON THE ADDITIONAL PROTOCOLS OF 8 JUNE 1977 TO THE GENEVA CONVENTIONS OF 12 AUGUST 1949 684 (1987).

4. Statement Made on Ratification of Additional Protocol I, United Kingdom (Jan. 28, 1998), *reprinted in* DOCUMENTS ON THE LAWS OF WAR 511 (Adam Roberts & Richard Guelff eds., 3d ed. 2000).

Final Report to the Prosecutor by the Committee Established to Review the NATO Bombing Campaign Against the Federal Republic of Yugoslavia

International Criminal Tribunal for the Former Yugoslavia, June 14, 2000

48. The main problem with the principle of proportionality is not whether or not it exists but what it means and how it is to be applied. It is relatively simple to state that there must be an acceptable relation between the legitimate destructive effect and undesirable collateral effects. For example, bombing a refugee camp is obviously prohibited if its only military significance is that people in the camp are knitting socks for soldiers. Conversely, an air strike on an ammunition dump should not be prohibited merely because a farmer is plowing a field in the area. Unfortunately, most applications of the principle of proportionality are not quite so clear cut. It is much easier to formulate the principle of proportionality in general terms than it is to apply it to a particular set of circumstances because the comparison is often between unlike quantities and values. One cannot easily assess the value of innocent human lives as opposed to capturing a particular military objective.

49. The questions which remain unresolved once one decides to apply the principle of proportionality include the following:

(a) What are the relative values to be assigned to the military advantage gained and the injury to non-combatants and or the damage to civilian objects?
(b) What do you include or exclude in totaling your sums?
(c) What is the standard of measurement in time or space? and
(d) To what extent is a military commander obligated to expose his own forces to danger in order to limit civilian casualties or damage to civilian objects?

50. The answers to these questions are not simple. It may be necessary to resolve them on a case by case basis, and the answers may differ depending on the background and values of the decision maker. It is unlikely that a human rights lawyer and an experienced combat commander would assign the same relative values to military advantage and to injury to noncombatants. Further, it is unlikely that military commanders with different doctrinal backgrounds and differing degrees of combat experience or national military histories would always agree in close cases. It is suggested that the determination of relative values must be that of the "reasonable military commander." Although there will be room for argument in close cases, there will be many cases where reasonable military commanders will agree that the injury to noncombatants or the damage to civilian objects was clearly disproportionate to the military advantage gained.

51. Much of the material submitted to the OTP [Office of the Prosecutor] consisted of reports that civilians had been killed, often inviting the conclusion to be drawn that crimes had therefore been committed. Collateral casualties to civilians and collateral damage to civilian objects can occur for a variety of reasons. Despite an obligation to avoid locating military objectives within or near densely populated areas, to remove civilians from the vicinity of military objectives, and to protect their civilians from the dangers of military operations, very little prevention may be feasible in many cases. Today's technological society has given rise to many dual use facilities and resources. City planners rarely pay heed to the possibility of future warfare. Military objectives are often located in densely populated areas and fighting occasionally occurs in such areas. Civilians present within or near military objectives must, however, be taken into account in the proportionality equation even if a party to the conflict has failed to exercise its obligation to remove them.

Screen Shot!

In *A Bridge Too Far* (1977), Allied forces are fighting their way toward Germany in September 1944. Operation Market Garden involved dropping thousands of paratroopers into the Netherlands, behind German lines, to capture and secure a series of bridges near Arnhem in order to gain access over the Rhine into Germany and trap the Germans. Ultimately, the Allied operation failed, and the Allies had to wait until 1945 to cross the Rhine with sufficient manpower.

Think about how you would calculate military advantage in such an operation. Would each bridge be a separate attack? Would a small bridge have less military advantage than another larger one? What about the crucial bridge at Arnhem, the final objective in the operation?

Buildings, strategic locations, combatants, transportation lines—these all come to mind when thinking about military objectives. Assessing the military advantage depends on additional considerations as well: how will destroying, capturing or neutralizing the target contribute to the tactical and operational goals? How will the use of suppressing fire or other fire support for ground forces, for example, contribute to those forces' ability to fulfill the mission? How will any such actions weaken the enemy's forces, and in what way? How will they strengthen the commander's own forces, and in what way? For example, a munitions factory supplying the bulk of the enemy's armaments and munitions would be indispensable to the enemy's war effort. Destroying it offers a significant military advantage, one that could likely justify large numbers of civilian casualties.[5] The military advantage from such an attack differs naturally from the advantage gained from a smaller, less strategic objective. The same might be said in comparing an attack on the leader of the enemy forces or an attack on two mid-level commanders or insurgents. At the start of Operation Iraqi Freedom, U.S. forces targeted Saddam Hussein and his sons in a "decapitation strike," on the assumption that killing them would leave Iraqi forces in disarray and shorten the fighting. At least one of the attempts targeted a restaurant where they were reported to be, along with a number of innocent civilians. In assessing whether such an attack is acceptable under the principle of proportionality, the military advantage is not simply the deaths of three enemy personnel, but rather the military advantage of killing those particular three individuals and the impact on the course of the conflict if successful. How do you determine how many innocent civilian deaths are acceptable—that is, not excessive—in light of that military advantage? What about targeting Osama bin Laden? Before the May 1, 2011, U.S. operation that killed bin Laden at his compound in Abbottabad, Pakistan, would killing him at a cost of ten civilian deaths been acceptable? Fifty? One hundred? What if those civilians were children? In the end, the operation reportedly led to only one innocent civilian death, without a doubt a result that raises no proportionality considerations given the military value of bin Laden as a target.

Proportionality and military advantage questions do not arise only in major attacks on high-value targets, however. Consider one instance of insurgents planting an IED along the road in Afghanistan, for example. In 2009, four Taliban insurgents were spotted by a drone as they dug a hole for a roadside bomb along a main transit route for NATO forces. British forces monitoring the drone feed called for an airstrike and then, just as the two Belgian F-16s approached to attack the insurgents, the British commanders noticed a young Afghan boy with a herd of goats walking toward the very spot where the insurgents were planting the IED, and radioed the pilots to hold their fire. For the next few minutes, the goatherd and goats progressed along their path, the insurgents continued to plant the bomb, the fighter jets circled, and the British commanders watched—and waited. Eventually,

---

5. *See* Yoram Dinstein, The Conduct of Hostilities under the Law of International Armed Conflict 121 (2004) (noting that "even extensive civilian casualties may be acceptable, if they are not excessive in light of the concrete and direct military advantage anticipated. The bombing of an important army or naval installation (like a naval shipyard) where there are hundreds or even thousands of civilian employees need not be abandoned merely because of the risk to those civilians.").

one insurgent rode off in one direction and one began to withdraw from the IED site slowly, holding a wire. Still, the goatherd was too close to the location for the British forces to authorize an attack; once they determined he was sufficiently clear of the area, they gave the pilots the green light. The fighter jets fired at the two remaining insurgents who were nearly finished burying the IED, killing them. The drone followed the third insurgent, the one with the wire, as he headed away from the area, tracking him as he traveled to a known Taliban command center, but he was not targeted.[6]

What is the military advantage here? Preventing the burial of the roadside bomb? Killing the insurgents, and if so, how many of them? What about the civilian loss of life? Did the law require that the British pilot hold fire until the goatherd had passed far enough away? In the complex counterinsurgency environment of Afghanistan, the strategic need to avoid any civilian casualties will often lead to a different analysis than the traditional proportionality analysis.

Consider what type of information commanders need to determine which targets they could attack, given the possible effect on the civilian population. In assessing likely civilian harm, a commander must gather information regarding civilians who live and work in the area, their patterns of movement, whether they would be susceptible to the means and methods of attack under consideration, how many might be present at the time of and within the blast radius of the attack, and any other information relevant to understanding the potential consequences for civilians in the area. How did this information play a role in the decisions in the following situation? How did the commanders determine the military advantage of particular targets and then assess that advantage in light of the likely harm to civilians?

In August 1995, Croatian forces launched a major operation to re-take the Krajina, which Serb forces had captured four years earlier at the start of the conflict in the former Yugoslavia, establishing an autonomous Republic of Serbian Krajina (RSK). In the battle to regain control of Knin, the capital of Krajina and strategically the most important objective of the entire offensive, Croatian forces attacked numerous military targets throughout the city, including the use of suppressing and harassing fire against the residence of the RSK President, Milan Martić, a supply factory, and the police station. Remember that the discussion of military objective in the previous chapter was not limited to destruction, however, but included capture and neutralization. Another common military tactic is to harass and disrupt the enemy so as to undermine their ability to plan attacks, issue orders, communicate with and re-supply military units and so forth. In examining these attacks, the ICTY in *Prosecutor v. Ante Gotovina et al.* highlighted the value of

---

6. *See* Michael Evans, *Wandering Afghan Goatherd Holds Up Lethal Attack on Taleban Roadside Bombers*, SUNDAY TIMES (London) (May 5, 2009).

neutralization and disruption in considering the lawfulness of attacks on military objectives:

> As commander in chief and President of the RSK, Martić was a lawful military objective, and although the probability of killing or disabling Martić by artillery attack was limited, if [the defendant] believed Martić to be an important component in [enemy] decision-making, the potential operational advantage in disrupting the [enemy] command and control structure would be substantial. Further, indirect, harassing fire at the TVIK factory, an apparent logistics supply facility and ammunition components production facility, would degrade the enemy's ability to use the resources stored there to re-supply forces engaged in combat. The Knin police station was also a valuable military objective, because police forces had been mobilized to participate in hostilities and harassing fire could demoralize police forces unaccustomed to combat operations, as well as disrupt the communication capability in the station, which could have been used to augment military communication disrupted by other attacks.[7]

QUESTIONS FOR DISCUSSION

1. As explained above, one component of the targeting plan in the attack on Knin was to harass and disrupt the command and control operations of President Martić, who was operating out of a residential building in Knin. Doing so offers a military advantage — if the enemy forces cannot communicate or re-supply, their ability to fight will be severely compromised — but also endangers civilians in the area. How would you compare that military advantage to the military advantage of killing Martić or destroying or capturing enemy forces, which might lead to operational success sooner? Would a greater number of civilian casualties be justified in the latter cases?

2. Military advantage could also include protecting civilians from attack, either a party's own nationals or, in the case of counterinsurgency for example, nationals of the country where the conflict is taking place. Stopping attacks on your own civilians by destroying the enemy's rocket launchers or artillery batteries — even if no attacks are launched against your own military forces or positions — offers a definite and concrete military advantage, for example. A common issue that arises is how to weigh the protection of the soldiers in the attacking party in the course of a military operation. All military commanders seek to prevent or at least minimize casualties among their own forces, as a simple matter of maximizing resources and capabilities, making this a significant consideration in planning an operation. But should it be a factor in proportionality assessments,

---

7. Prosecutor v. Ante Gotovina et al, Case No. IT-06-90-T, Judgement ¶ 1175 (Int'l Crim. Trib. for the Former Yugoslavia April 15, 2011).

such that greater friendly casualties would justify greater civilian casualties as a balancing measure?

3. Note that proportionality only arises when there is an attack on a military objective that is anticipated to cause some number of civilian casualties. An attack on a warship with no civilians on board would raise no proportionality concerns because there would be no potential civilian casualties. An intentional direct attack on civilians also does not raise proportionality considerations—it is a grave breach and a war crime. So what happens when one party targets a military objective believing no civilians are present but in fact civilians are there and are killed? Is that a disproportionate attack? Such a scenario arose in the 1991 Persian Gulf War. The United States targeted the Al Firdos bunker, located in the outskirts of Baghdad. The bunker, originally used as a civilian air raid shelter during the Iran-Iraq war (1980-1988), was refitted as a command and control post and used by senior Iraqi military officials during the 1991 war. U.S. surveillance reported that it was camouflaged, surrounded by barbed wire and guarded, and regularly transmitted command and control radio traffic. The United States bombed the bunker on February 12, destroying the bunker and—as was discovered the next morning—killing hundreds of civilians using it as shelter. U.S. intelligence had not detected or reported any civilians using the building as a shelter. Beyond the questions about how the U.S. had failed to note the civilian use of the bunker, what are the key issues here? U.S. practice now is to carry out a "pattern of life" assessment before every planned attack, an assessment of who lives in a particular structure or area and a tracking of the daily activities of suspected militants to ensure that innocent civilians are not mistakenly targeted. Given the intelligence the allies possessed, should they have done a "pattern of life" analysis? Was this an indiscriminate attack violating the principle of proportionality? Was the bunker a legitimate military objective? Did the United States violate LOAC in killing hundreds of civilians in the attack? What about Iraq's role in purposefully sheltering civilians in a military command post?

4. The U.S. decision to drop atomic bombs on Hiroshima and Nagasaki resulted in the deaths of nearly 200,000 Japanese civilians, destroyed two cities, and caused untold environmental and economic damage. Did the attack violate the principle of proportionality? The decision to use these weapons is generally viewed as a decision to end the war sooner and therefore save the lives of countless Allied military personnel and Japanese civilians that would have been lost in prolonging the war. More specifically, U.S. strategists estimated it would have cost 500,000 to one million American military deaths in any military campaign to invade and conquer the main islands of Japan. In addition, the Japanese vowed to execute all Allied POWs if such an attack occurred, adding another approximately 300,000 deaths to the anticipated total loss. In preparation for such an invasion, the Allies would have conducted extensive bombing missions consistent

with the practice of destroying cities from the air in World War II, causing countless Japanese casualties. The Japanese government was also preparing women, children, and the elderly to fight the "invading armies" alongside the remainder of the Japanese military. During the battle for Okinawa, the Japanese suffered casualties ninefold to those suffered by the Americans. In the fight for the home islands and the safety of Emperor Hirohito, American decision makers expected the same "fight to the death" and "never surrender" mentality. Taking all these factors together, a reasonable and conservative estimate of at least two million civilian and military deaths would have been the price to take the home islands. Does this change your answer as to whether the attack violated the principle of proportionality? Consider that in 1945, the Fourth Geneva Convention and the Additional Protocols had not yet been written. How would that change your analysis?

5. How does the prohibition on reprisals (see Chapter 7) relate to the arguments made during WWII that the carpet bombing of Dresden and other cities and the dropping of the atomic bombs on Hiroshima and Nagasaki were justified as a way to save the lives of Allied servicemen and even more local civilians by ending the war sooner?

3. Who Decides—The Reasonable Commander

Combat, even a minor fire-fight, involves confusion and uncertainty—the so-called "fog of war." Events rarely turn out as planned, no matter how careful the planning. As an old military adage says, no plan of attack survives first contact with the enemy. Take a look at the language of Article 51 of Additional Protocol I—it refers to "anticipated" military advantage and "expected" civilian casualties. This careful choice of words shows that the analysis must be taken in a prospective manner from the viewpoint of the commander at the time of the attack; that is, did the commander expect, or should he have expected, excessive civilian casualties relative to the military advantage he anticipated gaining, based on what he knew or should have known (based on reasonably available information) at the time of the decision to attack the target. After the fact, the urge to simply count up the casualties and declare a war crime is powerful, as can be seen in the frequent tendency to link civilian deaths automatically with LOAC violations. A retrospective approach falls prey to the challenge of comparing the impact of civilian deaths to military advantage gained or lost. The former are dramatic and emotional and "lend themselves to powerful pictures and strong reactions."[8] Military advantage, in contrast, is abstract, has little or no emotional impact, and is difficult to convey in pictures. It

8. Joseph Holland, *Military Objective and Collateral Damage: Their Relationship and Dynamics*, 2004 Y.B. INT'L HUM. L. 7, 47.

will often prove difficult to fairly assess whether collateral damage is excessive in practice because the military advantage from an attack may not be immediately apparent to an observer. The retrospective approach can therefore lead to departures from the accepted application of the principle of proportionality.

For this reason, numerous countries issued statements upon ratifying Additional Protocol I to emphasize that "military commanders and others responsible for planning, deciding upon, or executing attacks necessarily have to reach decisions on the basis of their assessment of the information from all sources which is reasonably available to them at the relevant time."[9] Military manuals provide the same guidance to commanders regarding how to assess the lawfulness of a potential attack, recognizing that

> [i]t will not always be easy for a commander to evaluate [whether an attack will be disproportionate] with precision. On the one hand, he must take into account the elements *which are available to him*, related to the military necessity necessary to justify an attack, and on the other hand, he must take into account the elements *which are available to him*, related to the possible loss of human life and damage to civilian objects.[10]

The officer's responsibility thus "would be assessed in light of the facts as he believed them to be, on the information reasonably available to him from all sources."[11] In addition, these decisions must also take into account the urgent and difficult circumstances under which such decisions must usually be made—the fog of war.

This prospective analysis depends, at its heart, on what is commonly referred to as "the reasonable commander." Analogous to domestic criminal law's notion of the "reasonable person," the reasonable commander is "the reasonable man in the law of war . . . and is based upon the experience of military men in dealing with basic military problems."[12] Merely adding up the resulting civilian casualties and injuries and assessing the actual value gained from a military operation may be the simpler approach, because "the results of an attack are often tangible and measurable, whereas expectations are not."[13] However, it does not do justice to the complexities inherent in combat; instead, the proportionality of any attack must be viewed from the perspective of the military commander on the ground, taking into account the information he or she had at the time.

9. Jean-Marie Henckaerts & Louise Doswald-Beck, 1 Customary International Humanitarian Law 332 (3d ed. 2009).

10. *Id.* (citing Belgium, Ministry of Defence, Law of War Manual 29 (1983)).

11. United Kingdom Ministry of Defence, JSP 383: The Joint Service Manual of the Law of Armed Conflict 2.4.2 (2004).

12. William V. O'Brien, *The Conduct of Just and Limited War, in* Contemporary Moral Problems: War, Terrorism, and Torture 21, 28 (James E. White ed., 4th ed. 2009).

13. Michael N. Schmitt, *Fault Lines in the Law of Attack, in* Testing the Boundaries of International Humanitarian Law 277, 294 (Susan Carolyn Breau & Agnieszka Jachec-Neale eds., 2006).

This principle is known as the "Rendulic Rule": a commander should be judged based on what he or she knew and expected at the time he or she made the decision, not based on how events actually turned out. The rule stems from the *Hostages Trial*, the prosecution of twelve German generals, including General Lothar Rendulic, the commander of German troops in Finland and Norway in 1944. Addressing the charge of wanton destruction of property not justified by military necessity—for the scorched earth campaign during the German retreat through Norway—the Nuremberg Tribunal stated:

> We are not called upon to determine whether urgent military necessity for the devastation and destruction in the province of Finmark actually existed. We are concerned with the question of whether the defendant at the time of its occurrence acted within the limits of honest judgment on the basis of the conditions prevailing at the time. The course of a military operation by the enemy is loaded with uncertainties, such as the numerical strength of the enemy, the quality of his equipment, his fighting spirit, the efficiency and daring of his commanders, and the uncertainty of his intentions. These things when considered with his own military situation provided the facts or want thereof which furnished the basis for the defendant's decision to carry out the "scorched earth" policy in Finmark as a precautionary measure against an attack by superior forces. It is our considered opinion that the conditions, as they appeared to the defendant at the time were sufficient upon which he could honestly conclude that urgent military necessity warranted the decision made. This being true, the defendant may have erred in the exercise of his judgment but he was guilty of no criminal act.[14]

As noted above, the terminology of the principle of proportionality demonstrates that the decision regarding military advantage and expected harm to civilians is a matter of judgment for the commander. Although few international tribunals and domestic courts have tackled questions of proportionality in depth, those that have done so have hewed carefully to the reasonable commander approach. In *Prosecutor v. Galic*, for example, the ICTY declared that

> [i]n determining whether an attack was proportionate it is necessary to examine whether a reasonably well-informed person in the circumstances of the actual perpetrator, making reasonable use of the information available to him or her, could have expected excessive civilian casualties to result from the attack.[15]

---

14. United States v. Wilhelm List and Others (The Hostages Trial), Case No. 47, Judgment (U.S. Mil. Trib., Nuremberg, Feb. 19, 1948), *in* VIII Law Reports on the Trials of War Criminals 69 (1949).

15. Prosecutor v. Galić, Case No. IT-98-29-T, Judgement ¶ 58 (Int'l Crim. Trib. for the Former Yugoslavia Dec. 5, 2003).

The NATO bombing report by the ICTY Prosecutor also took a prospective approach to proportionality determinations, examining each incident under consideration by looking at the facts at the time of the attack rather than the facts that were known at the time of the investigation.

Domestic courts have adopted the same approach. Most notably, in dismissing the charges against the colonel who ordered the attack on two fuel tankers and the Taliban forces who had captured the tankers in Kunduz, Afghanistan, in September 2009, the Federal Prosecutor General at Germany's Federal Court of Justice examined any proportionality issues from the colonel's perspective at the time of the attack:

> In the present case the bombing pursued [two] military goals, namely the destruction of the fuel tankers robbed by the Taliban and of the fuel as well as the killing of the Taliban, including not least the high-level regional commander of the insurgents. The anticipated military advantage, namely on the one hand the final prevention of using the fuel and the fuel tankers as "driving bombs" or to fuel the insurgents' militarily used vehicles and on the other hand the at least temporary disruption of the Taliban's regional command structure fall within the usual, recognized tactical military advantages. . . . The fact that the goal mentioned in second place was not fully achieved is irrelevant for the legal assessment because the expectations at the time of the military action based on the facts are decisive. . . .
>
> The anticipated civilian collateral damages are also to be assessed from the perspective of the attacker at the time of the attack, rather than with hindsight according to the actual unfolding of events. . . . In view of the circumstances known to Colonel (*Oberst*) Klein (distance to inhabited settlements, night time, presence of armed Taliban) and the informant's statements, he considered the presence of protected civilians unlikely. . . . Further feasible reconnaissance and precautionary measures . . . were not promptly available in the concrete situation. Colonel (*Oberst*) Klein did not have to accept the danger of the fuel tankers or the fuel being retrieved by the Taliban. . . .
>
> Even if the killing of several dozen civilians would have had to be anticipated (which is assumed here for the sake of the argument), from a tactical-military perspective this would not have been out of proportion to the anticipated military advantages. The literature consistently points out that general criteria are not available for the assessment of specific proportionality because unlike legal goods, values and interests are juxtaposed which cannot be "balanced". . . . Therefore, considering the particular pressure at the moment when the decision had to be taken, an infringement is only to be assumed in cases of obvious excess where the commander ignored any considerations of proportionality and refrained from acting "honestly", "reasonably" and "competently". . . . This would apply to the destruction of an entire village with hundreds of civilian inhabitants in order to hit a single enemy fighter, but not if the objective was to destroy artillery positions in the village. . . . There is no such

obvious disproportionality in the present case. Both the destruction of the fuel tankers and the destruction of high-level Taliban had a military importance which is not to be underestimated, not least because of the thereby considerably reduced risk of attacks by the Taliban against own troops and civilians. There is thus no excess.[16]

QUESTIONS FOR DISCUSSION

1. What would be the effect of using a more retrospective approach to proportionality determinations? How would that affect military operations and targeting decisions? What about broader effects on strategic decision making regarding the use of force?

2. At the same time, a commander cannot willfully ignore critical information about the civilian population in the area of an attack. How should determinations be made regarding the information that was feasible in terms of assessing proportionality?

3. Should more technologically advanced countries face a more restrictive proportionality standard because they have significantly greater intelligence gathering capabilities and highly precise weapons?

4. Any targeting decision and proportionality assessment requires information about the target, the likely destruction from different types of weapons or attacks, the inhabitants or employees likely to be present at different times, the blast radius and the nature and population of the surrounding neighborhood, and other information. Until at least August 2010 in Afghanistan, the International Security Assistance Force rules of engagement mandated a 48-hour "pattern of life" assessment before any target could be approved. As a matter of practice, this method should allow for significant knowledge regarding civilians in the area, where they live and work, and when they are present in different buildings or locations. Targets of opportunity—which are targets that arise during operations, including regular patrols—do not offer the same opportunity for intelligence gathering and assessment. How does this impact the proportionality assessment?

5. What are the consequences of information overload? In February 2010, a U.S. helicopter attack in Afghanistan caused twenty-three civilian deaths. Upon investigation, officials discovered that the drone operators gathering and processing images and information from the location of the attack failed to pass along critical information suggesting the presence of children in what looked like an enemy convoy. With mounting pressure to protect U.S. forces in the area, the drone operators incorrectly determined that the village convoy posed an imminent threat to those forces, giving the

---

16. Federal Court of Justice, Federal Prosecutor General, Decision ¶ 3(bb) (Apr. 16, 2010), https://ihl-databases.icrc.org/customary-ihl/eng/docs/v2_cou_de_rule14.

green light to an attack that caused some of the greatest civilian losses in the Afghanistan conflict.

The massive intake and flow of information in real-time offers the military astounding capabilities. "Unprecedented amounts of raw information help the military determine what targets to hit and what to avoid. And drone-based sensors have given rise to a new class of wired warriors who must filter the information sea. But sometimes they are drowning."[17] After this incident, investigators determined that more time to process the information and assess the data would have prevented this error. On a broader level, this incident highlights the challenges produced by the massive information flows the U.S. military now gathers and must process, direct, and analyze.

There is no doubt that intelligence information is critical to any targeting and proportionality analysis. Today, that information flows rapidly across multiple screens, drone feeds, instant-messaging, and real-time voice communication—all happening at once. According to some reports, the amount of intelligence gathered by drones and other surveillance platforms has increased 1,600 percent. Does this multifaceted flow of information pose new questions about how to make these determinations? Could there be too much information?

6. A senior military officer interviewed about the above incident pointed to information overload, stating that "if we had just slowed things down and thought deliberately,"[18] the deaths would have been prevented. This is a common refrain and the consequences of not slowing down can often result in friendly fire casualties. In listening to cockpit recorders during a bombing run that resulted in such casualties, you can often hear the pilot's pace (in breath and voice) speed up as he senses the opportunity to bomb a real target. After the bombs are away and they have found their target, there is often a pause and then a sobering realization that they might have been "friendlies." Does it surprise you that there are not more friendly fire casualties? Why? Why not?

7. Who is responsible for undertaking the proportionality analysis before an attack? The shooter? The pilot? The unit commander? The overall commander? All of them? When does a determination need to be made?

8. U.S. drone strikes are often criticized—apart from reasons relating to the identification of targets and questions regarding self-defense—for the use of unmanned vehicles to deliver the lethal attack. In the context of proportionality, however, drones appear to be particularly well designed for adherence to the need to gather and assess information about the target, the target area, and those persons and objects in the vicinity of the target.

---

17. Thom Shanker & Matt Richtel, *In New Military, Data Overload Can Be Deadly*, N.Y. Times (Jan. 16, 2011).

18. *Id.*

The heart of this comprehensive surveillance and intelligence-gathering process is the "pattern of life" analysis. Using drones, some of which can loiter over a target and the surrounding area for days, commanders can follow a target and gather information about the civilian population in the area and the potential for civilian casualties in possible strike locations and at certain times.

> Because the drones provide high quality information about the target area in real-time (or near real time), for extended periods and without risk to the operators, they [thus] permit more refined assessments of the likely collateral damage to civilians and civilian objects. The ability of armed drones to observe the target area for long periods before attacking means the operators are better able to verify the nature of a proposed target and strike only when the opportunity to minimize collateral damage is at its height.[19]

At a preliminary level, therefore, the capacity that armed drones offer for pre-attack surveillance and at-the-moment awareness of the target and civilians in the area offers great opportunities for compliance with LOAC's proportionality obligations. Drones do introduce additional interesting considerations into the proportionality and precautions calculus as well, however. The very capabilities that make drones an effective weapon with regard to distinction, proportionality, and precautions can also have the effect of actually changing the calculus for assessing a lawful attack. In essence, does the use of drones raise expectations for what a reasonable commander knows or is expected to know?

9. Does civilian harm include second- and third-order effects, often described as reverberating effects? Imagine an attack on a power station that is a military objective. Should the proportionality analysis include loss of civilian life due to power outages at the local hospital? What about civilian deaths caused by a lack of heat or air-conditioning in residential buildings?

10. In its *Targeted Killing* case, the Israeli Supreme Court examined the extent of force that could be used against an insurgent or civilian directly participating in hostilities:

> a civilian taking a direct part in hostilities cannot be attacked at such time as he is doing so, if a less harmful means can be employed. In our domestic law, that rule is called for by the principle of proportionality. Indeed, among the military means, one must choose the means whose harm to the human rights of the harmed person is smallest. Thus, if a terrorist taking a direct part in hostilities can be arrested, interrogated, and tried, those are the means which should be employed. . . . Trial is preferable to use of force. A rule-of-law state employs, to the extent possible, procedures

---

19. Michael N. Schmitt, *Drone Attacks under the* Jus ad Bellum *and* Jus in Bello: *Clearing the "Fog of Law,"* 2010 Y.B. Int'l Hum. L. 311, 314.

of law and not procedures of force. . . . Arrest, investigation, and trial are not means which can always be used. At times the possibility does not exist whatsoever; at times it involves a risk so great to the lives of the soldiers, that it is not required. . . . However, it is a possibility which should always be considered. It might actually be particularly practical under the conditions of belligerent occupation, in which the army controls the area in which the operation takes place, and in which arrest, investigation, and trial are at times realizable possibilities. . . . Of course, given the circumstances of a certain case, that possibility might not exist. At times, its harm to nearby innocent civilians might be greater than that caused by refraining from it. In that state of affairs, it should not be used.[57]

Does this requirement that targeting a legitimate target is only lawful if no less harmful means is available stem from LOAC? From human rights law? What is the effect of conflating LOAC proportionality with human rights proportionality in this way? Consider whether factors unique to the situation in Gaza and the West Bank could have motivated this finding.

11. Proportionality is used in many ways in international law—often creating confusion. Proportionality in LOAC is the principle discussed in this chapter: an attack is disproportionate if the expected civilian casualties will be excessive in light of the anticipated military advantage gained. But proportionality is also a key term in human rights law and in *jus ad bellum*, the law governing the resort to force. In the latter, proportionality refers to one of the parameters of the lawful use of force in self-defense. In particular, the issue is whether the defensive use of force in response to an armed attack is appropriate in relation to the ends sought, measuring the extent of the use of force against the overall military goals, such as fending off an attack or subordinating the enemy. This proportionality focuses not on some measure of symmetry between the original *attack* and the use of force in response, but on whether the measure of counterforce used is proportionate to the needs and goals of *repelling* or *deterring* the original attack.[20] Civilian casualties are not a relevant factor for *jus ad bellum* proportionality—and yet they are the central concern of *jus in bello* proportionality. With regard to human rights law, proportionality is relevant when law enforcement use force as a last resort against a hostile threat. Here, the issue is whether the force used is proportionate to the threat the individual poses; in essence, was the measure of force necessary and proportionate to the threat. The key difference is that in human rights law, proportionality is concerned with the target of the attack or use of force, while in LOAC,

---

57. Public Committee Against Torture in Israel v. Gov't of Israel ¶ 40, HCJ 769/02 [2005].

20. Yoram Dinstein, War, Aggression and Self-Defense 225 (2005). *See also* Michael N. Schmitt, *"Change Direction" 2006: Israeli Operations in Lebanon and the International Law of Self-Defense*, 29 Mich. J. Int'l L. 127 (2008).

proportionality is concerned with the unintended victims of the use of force, the incidental casualties or collateral damage. In many situations, particularly the complex modern conflicts that involve counterterrorism, counterinsurgency, and often a mix of military force and law enforcement, these concepts of proportionality can get conflated and confused. Consider the consequences of uncertainty about the governing legal framework for military or police faced with the need to use force in particular situations. What is the effect of a lack of clarity? Who bears the risk? What about uncertainty after the fact, during an investigation? What are the consequences of applying the incorrect (or perhaps a murky) legal framework? How will that affect future operations?

B. PRECAUTIONS IN ATTACK

A commander wants to attack a particular target. She has identified it as a legitimate military objective and has assessed any expected civilian casualties or damage for purposes of proportionality questions. Is she ready to give the attack order? What other considerations come into play? What about the party about to be attacked? Do they have any obligations under the law?

LOAC mandates that all parties take certain precautionary measures to protect civilians. In many ways, the identification of military objectives and the proportionality considerations are, of course, precautions. But the obligations of the parties to a conflict to take precautionary measures go beyond that. Beginning at the broadest level, Article 57(1) of Additional Protocol I states: "In the conduct of military operations, constant care shall be taken to spare the civilian population, civilians and civilian objects." This provision is a direct outgrowth of and supplement to the Basic Rule in Article 48, which mandates that all parties distinguish between combatants and civilians and between military objects and civilian objects. The Commentary explains that the obligation to take constant care is a general principle, but one that has important ramifications for the conduct of hostilities and the protection of civilians:

> It is quite clear that by respecting this obligation the Parties to the conflict will spare the civilian population, civilians and civilian objects. Even though this is only an enunciation of a general principle which is already recognized in customary law, it is good that it is included at the beginning of this article in black and white, as the other paragraphs are devoted to the practical application of this principle. The term 'military operations' should be understood to mean any movements, manoeuvres and other activities whatsoever carried out by the armed forces with a view to combat.[21]

21. Claude Pilloud, Yves Sandoz, Christophe Swinarski & Bruno Zimmerman, Commentary on the Additional Protocols of 8 June 1977 to the Geneva Conventions of 12 August 1949 680 (1987).

The practical provisions in Article 57 talk of precautions to be taken specifically when launching an attack. Note that paragraph 1 of Article 57 uses the much more general and broader term "military operations," which includes a much larger category of activities than attacks. Rather than simply an inspirational statement, the obligation to take "constant care" creates its own "concrete legal obligations."[22] As you read the rest of this chapter, focusing on the specific precautions that attacking and defending parties must take, consider what other obligations arise as a result of the "constant care" formulation. What consideration must military forces give to civilians and civilian objects in the course of transiting an area? In setting up a forward operating base?

Article 57 of Additional Protocol I sets forth several precautions that attacking parties must take before launching an attack.

ARTICLE 57 OF ADDITIONAL PROTOCOL I

2. With respect to attacks, the following precautions shall be taken:
   (a) those who plan or decide upon an attack shall:
      (i) do everything feasible to verify that the objectives to be attacked are neither civilians nor civilian objects and are not subject to special protection but are military objectives within the meaning of paragraph 2 of Article 52 and that it is not prohibited by the provisions of this Protocol to attack them;
      (ii) take all feasible precautions in the choice of means and methods of attack with a view to avoiding, and in any event to minimizing, incidental loss or civilian life, injury to civilians and damage to civilian objects;
      (iii) refrain from deciding to launch any attack which may be expected to cause incidental loss of civilian life, injury to civilians, damage to civilian objects, or a combination thereof, which would be excessive in relation to the concrete and direct military advantage anticipated;
   (b) an attack shall be cancelled or suspended if it becomes apparent that the objective is not a military one or is subject to special protection or that the attack may be expected to cause incidental loss of civilian life, injury to civilians, damage to civilian objects, or a combination thereof, which would be excessive in relation to the concrete and direct military advantage anticipated;
   (c) effective advance warning shall be given of attacks which may affect the civilian population, unless circumstances do not permit.

---

22. Jean-François Quéguiner, *Precautions Under the Law Governing the Conduct of Hostilities*, 88 INT'L REV. RED CROSS 793, 797 (2006).

3. When a choice is possible between several military objectives for obtaining a similar military advantage, the objective to be selected shall be that the attack on which may be expected to cause the least danger to civilian lives and to civilian objects.

4. In the conduct of military operations at sea or in the air, each Party to the conflict shall, in conformity with its rights and duties under the rules of international law applicable in armed conflict, take all reasonable precautions to avoid losses of civilian lives and damage to civilian objects.

5. No provision of this article may be construed as authorizing any attacks against the civilian population, civilians or civilian objects.

Precautions are, understandably, a critical component of the law's efforts to protect civilians and are of particular importance in densely populated areas or areas where civilians are at risk from the consequences of military operations. For this reason, even if a target is legitimate under the laws of war, failure to take precautions can make an attack on that target unlawful.

1. Planning and Launching Attacks

First, parties must do everything feasible to ensure that targets are military objectives. Doing so helps to protect civilians by limiting attacks to military targets, thus directly implementing the principle of distinction. Second, they must choose the means and methods of attack with the aim of minimizing incidental civilian losses and damage. For example, during the 1991 Persian Gulf War, "pilots were advised to attack bridges in urban areas along a longitudinal axis. This measure was taken so that bombs that missed their targets—because they were dropped either too early or too late—would hopefully fall in the river and not on civilian housing."[23] Another common method of taking precautions is to launch attacks on particular targets at night when the civilian population is not on the streets or at work, thus minimizing potential losses. In addition, when choosing between two possible attacks offering similar military advantage, parties must choose the objective that offers the least likely harm to civilians and civilian objects. Each of these steps requires an attacking party to take affirmative action to preserve civilian immunity and minimize civilian casualties and damage—in effect, to take "constant care." Proportionality considerations are also a major component of the precautions framework. Parties are required to refrain

23. *Id.* at 801 (noting that this angle of attack "also means that damage would tend to be in the middle of the bridge and thus easier to repair").

from any attacks that would be disproportionate and to cancel any attacks where it becomes evident that the civilian losses would be excessive in light of the military advantage. At the same time, it is important to note that, as in other areas, LOAC is at its foundation concerned with practicalities. The obligation is to take precautions that are feasible in the circumstances, given the information available to the commanders and military planners. The Eritrea-Ethiopia Claims Commission explained that, "[b]y 'feasible,' Article 57 means those measures that are practicable or practically possible, taking into account all circumstances ruling at the time."[24] Precautions cannot be judged by whether a certain result obtained after the fact; nonetheless, the obligations do demand that parties gather, analyze, and act on all relevant information in the planning process.

QUESTIONS FOR DISCUSSION

1. On October 3, 2015, U.S. forces misidentified and mistakenly destroyed a Médecins Sans Frontières (MSF) hospital in Kunduz, Afghanistan, killing thirty doctors and patients and wounding over thirty more individuals. According to the investigation report, an AC-130U Gunship flew from Bagram Airfield to support U.S. Special Forces and Afghan Special Security Forces operations in Kunduz. The aircraft launched over an hour early and,

> due to the early launch, the aircrew did not have the typical information it would have on a mission. While en route to Kunduz, one of the aircraft's critical communications systems failed, resulting in the aircraft's inability to receive and transmit certain critical information to multiple command headquarters. While loitering over Kunduz, the aircraft avoided a significant surface to air threat. In response, the Aircraft Commander took defensive measures that decreased the aircrew's ability to precisely locate targets on the ground.[25]

More important, the air crew and ground controllers repeatedly failed or, at a minimum, struggled to coordinate regarding the grid coordinates of the target, a prison with similar physical characteristics to the MSF hospital building and approximately 400 meters away. They also failed to abort the attack once notified of the mistake. The investigation concluded that U.S. forces, from the Ground Force Commander to the Joint Terminal Attack Controller to the navigator and other members of the aircrew, failed to take sufficient precautions before the attack. For example,

> The Navigator failed to obtain positive identification of a lawful military objective. The Navigator failed to transmit critical information about the

24. Eri.-Eth. Cl. Comm'n, Western & Eastern Fronts—Ethiopia's Claims 1 & 3 ¶ 33 (2005).
25. Investigation Report of the Airstrike on the Médecins Sans Frontières/Doctors Without Borders Trauma Center in Kunduz, Afghanistan on 3 October 2015 (Nov. 21, 2015).

aircraft's targeting process to the GFC; failed to seek clarification from the JTAC on critical target descriptions; failed to reconcile inconsistent targeting information and situational awareness; and ignored an accurate target grid location in favor of a vaguely described compound which was later determined to be the MSF Trauma Center.[26]

What happens when systems fail—is that part of the "fog of war" or does an attacking party need to take steps to compensate for the lack of information?

2. During Operation Iraqi Freedom, the United States pursued a strategy of attacking senior Iraqi leaders, a strategy that was also used in Afghanistan against the Taliban and in targeting Slobodan Milošević during the NATO bombing campaign in Serbia and Kosovo. In a report on the conduct of the U.S. air campaign against Iraq, Human Rights Watch made the following criticisms of the U.S. approach:

> In attacking leadership targets in Iraq, the United States used an unsound targeting methodology largely reliant on imprecise coordinates obtained from satellite phones. Leadership targeting was consistently based on unreliable intelligence. It is also likely that Iraqi leaders engaged in successful deception techniques. This combination of factors led directly to dozens of civilian casualties.
>
> The United States identified and targeted some Iraqi leaders based on GPS coordinates derived from intercepts of Thuraya satellite phones. Thuraya satellite phones are used throughout Iraq and the Middle East. They have an internal GPS chip that enabled American intelligence to track the phones. The phone coordinates were used as the locations for attacks on Iraqi leadership.
>
> Targeting based on satellite phone-derived geo-coordinates turned a precision weapon into a potentially indiscriminate weapon. According to the manufacturer, Thuraya's GPS system is accurate only within a one-hundred-meter (328-foot) radius. Thus the United States could not determine from where a call was originating to a degree of accuracy greater than one-hundred meters radius; a caller could have been anywhere within a 31,400-square-meter area. This begs the question, how did CENTCOM know where to direct the strike if the target area was so large? In essence, imprecise target coordinates were used to program precision-guided munitions.
>
> Furthermore, it is not clear how CENTCOM connected a specific phone to a specific user; phones were being tracked, not individuals. It is plausible that CENTCOM developed a database of voices that could be computer matched to a phone user. The Iraqis may have employed deception techniques to thwart the Americans. It was well known that the United States used intercepted Thuraya satellite phone calls in their search for members of al-Qaeda. . . .

26. *Id.*

The United States undoubtedly attempted to use corroborating sources for satellite phone coordinates. Based on the results, however, accurate corroborating information must have been difficult if not impossible to come by and additional methods of tracking the Iraqi leadership just as unreliable as satellite phones.

Satellite imagery and signals intelligence (communications intercepts) apparently yielded little to no useful information in terms of targeting leadership. Detection of common indicators such as increased vehicular activity at particular locations seems not to have been meaningful. Human sources of information were likely the main means of corroborating the satellite phone information in tracking the Iraqi leadership. A human intelligence source was reportedly used to verify the Thuraya data acquired in the attack on Saddam Hussein in al-Mansur, described below. But the source was proven wrong. Human sources were also reportedly used to verify the attack on Ali Hassan al-Majid in Basra, as well as the strike on al-Dura that opened the war. Given the lack of success, it seems human intelligence was completely unreliable.

Without reliable intelligence to identify the location of the Iraqi leadership, it appears the United States fell back upon all it had, namely, inaccurate coordinates based on satellite phones, with no guarantee of the identity of the user. Leadership targets developed by inaccurate data should have never been attacked.

Given the dozens of civilian casualties caused by this profoundly flawed method of warfare, aerial attacks on leadership targets such as those witnessed in Iraq should be abandoned until the intelligence and targeting failures have been corrected. Like all attacks, leadership strikes should not be carried out without an adequate collateral damage estimate; strikes should not be based solely on satellite phone intercepts; and there should be no strikes in densely populated areas unless the intelligence is considered highly reliable. Consideration should also be given to possible alternative methods of attack posing less danger to civilians.[27]

Is it sufficient to take precautions if the methodology for identifying targets and taking precautions is faulty? How does this situation compare to the cases above?

3. The United States and other advanced militaries possess, and often use, precision-guided munitions and other advanced technology. In some situations, such as a small military target of high value in a densely populated area, it is possible that using "smart-bombs" is the only legitimate means of attack. What about in general—does the capacity to use precision-guided munitions mean that a state is legally obligated to use them all the time? What are the consequences of such an obligation? Or of not having such an obligation?

4. Consider a scenario in which the attacking party seeks to target the train system in order to disrupt the enemy's ability to move and supply its

---

27. HUMAN RIGHTS WATCH, OFF TARGET: THE CONDUCT OF THE WAR AND CIVILIAN CASUALTIES IN IRAQ 24-26 (2003).

military personnel. The commander has two primary options: target the main train station in the center of town, surrounded by a residential area, or target the rail lines and the bridges outside the city. Both options offer the military advantage of interrupting the rail lines, but the second option raises the risk of the bombers flying within range of the enemy's surface-to-air missiles. In addition, the rail lines also transport food, medicine and other supplies to the civilian population outside the city, including internally displaced persons in camps on the city outskirts. If both options are legitimate military objectives, how should the commander decide which to attack?

5. What is the extent of an attacking party's obligations to verify a target after it has been initially selected and approved? In September 2010, NATO forces bombed a convoy with a man alleged to be an al Qaeda operative, killing him and wounded approximately ten other insurgents. Human rights groups asserted that NATO had killed the wrong man; NATO stood by its intelligence that it had targeted an al Qaeda operative. However, NATO also "asserted that a Taliban leader in Takhar, whom the man knew, used his name as an alias, adding a further layer of confusion that played a part in NATO's use of flawed intelligence to kill [who some argued was] the wrong man."[28] How should questions of mistaken—or uncertain—identity be viewed in such circumstances? Would the concept of precautions be relevant? That is, if the United States took appropriate precautions to identify and track the person they were seeking, would the attack then be reasonable even if the United States were mistaken? Or does distinction require more precise abilities to identify legitimate targets?

2. *Warnings*

The obligation to warn civilians of impending attacks appears in the law of war dating back to the Lieber Code, which required military commanders to inform the enemy "of their intention to bombard a place, so that non-combatants, and especially the women and children, may be removed before the bombardment commences."[29] The main purpose of warnings is to give civilians an opportunity to leave and find a place of greater safety. Article 26 of the Regulations annexed to the 1907 Hague Convention is the most oft-cited statement of the obligation to warn: "[t]he officer in

28. Alissa J. Rubin, *Murky Identities and Ties Hinder NATO's Hunt for Afghan Insurgents, Report Says*, N.Y. TIMES (May 11, 2011).

29. FRANCIS LIEBER, WAR DEPARTMENT, INSTRUCTIONS FOR THE GOVERNMENT OF ARMIES OF THE UNITED STATES IN THE FIELD art. 19 (1863). *See also* Jean-Francois Quéguiner, *Precautions Under the Law Governing the Conduct of Hostilities*, 88 INT'L REV. RED CROSS 793, 806 n. 42 (2006) (describing the content of this obligation in successive law of war instruments, including the Brussels Declaration (Article 16), the Oxford Manual (Article 33) and the Regulations annexed to the 1899 Hague Convention II (Article 26)).

command of an attacking force must, before commencing a bombardment, except in cases of assault, do all in his power to warn the authorities." Like Article 57(2)(c) of Additional Protocol I, this requirement provides a practical limitation taking into account the circumstances and the feasibility of issuing such a warning. In essence, the obligation to warn is not absolute and can be avoided if issuing a warning would seriously compromise the chances of success, such as in the case of a surprise attack.

LOAC contains no further guidance to help understand what actions make a warning "effective," but state practice supports the Commentary's view that "[w]arnings may also have a general character."[30] Examples in the Commentary, particularly from World War II, include giving notice by radio of attacks on certain types of facilities, dropping pamphlets, providing a list of objectives to be attacked or flying low over targets to give civilians time to seek safety. In the 1991 Gulf War, for example, the United States military dropped leaflets to warn before attacks in Basra, Faw, Zubair, Tannuwa, and Abdul Khasib, among other cities. Responding to ICRC queries, the United States wrote: "a warning need not be specific; it may be a blanket warning, delivered by leaflets and/or radio, advising the civilian population of an enemy nation to avoid remaining in proximity to military objectives."[31]

30. CLAUDE PILLOUD, YVES SANDOZ, CHRISTOPHE SWINARSKI, BRUNO ZIMMERMAN, COMMENTARY ON THE ADDITIONAL PROTOCOLS OF 8 JUNE 1977 TO THE GENEVA CONVENTIONS OF 12 AUGUST 1949 687 (1987).

31. United States, Message from the Department of the Army to the legal advisor of the U.S. Army Forces deployed in the Gulf, 11 January 1991, §8(I).

The Japanese text on the reverse side of the leaflet above carried the following warning:

> Read this carefully as it may save your life or the life of a relative or friend. In the next few days, some or all of the cities named on the reverse side will be destroyed by American bombs. These cities contain military installations and workshops or factories which produce military goods. We are determined to destroy all of the tools of the military clique which they are using to prolong this useless war. But, unfortunately, bombs have no eyes. So, in accordance with America's humanitarian policies, the American Air Force, which does not wish to injure innocent people, now gives you warning to evacuate the cities named and save your lives. America is not fighting the Japanese people but is fighting the military clique which has enslaved the Japanese people. The peace which America will bring will free the people from the oppression of the military clique and mean the emergence of a new and better Japan. You can restore peace by demanding new and good leaders who will end the war. We cannot promise that only these cities will be among those attacked but some or all of them will be, so heed this warning and evacuate these cities immediately.[32]

QUESTIONS FOR DISCUSSION

1. The committee investigating the NATO bombing in Yugoslavia examined the warnings NATO issued before bombing the radio and television station in Belgrade:

> Although NATO alleged that it made "every possible effort to avoid civilian casualties and collateral damage" some doubts have been expressed as to the specificity of the warning given to civilians by NATO of its intended strike, and whether the notice would have constituted "effective warning . . . of attacks which may affect the civilian population, unless circumstances do not permit" as required by Article 57(2) of Additional Protocol I.
>
> Evidence on this point is somewhat contradictory. On the one hand, NATO officials in Brussels are alleged to have told Amnesty International that they did not give a specific warning as it would have endangered the pilots. On this view, it is possible that casualties among civilians working at the RTS may have been heightened because of NATO's apparent failure to provide clear advance warning of the attack, as required by Article 57(2).
>
> On the other hand, foreign media representatives were apparently forewarned of the attack. As Western journalists were reportedly warned

32. Josette H. Williams, *The Information War in the Pacific 1945: Paths to Peace*, CIA.GOV (May 9, 2009).

by their employers to stay away from the television station before the attack, it would also appear that some Yugoslav officials may have expected that the building was about to be struck. Consequently, UK Prime Minister Tony Blair blamed Yugoslav officials for not evacuating the building, claiming that "[t]hey could have moved those people out of the building. They knew it was a target and they didn't. . . . [I]t was probably for . . . very clear propaganda reasons. . . ." Although knowledge on the part of Yugoslav officials of the impending attack would not divest NATO of its obligation to forewarn civilians under Article 57(2), it may nevertheless imply that the Yugoslav authorities may be partially responsible for the civilian casualties resulting from the attack and may suggest that the advance notice given by NATO may have in fact been sufficient under the circumstances.[33]

Could warnings only given to Western journalists—if such an allegation were true—be truly considered warnings under LOAC? What about warnings given to the Yugoslav authorities with the expectation or request that they pass the warnings along? One might argue that warnings from the local authorities would be more effective because they would be considered reliable by the civilian population and more efficient, but can an attacking party pass along obligations in that manner?

2. During Operation Cast Lead, the Israeli military operation in Gaza in 2008-2009, the Israelis issued extensive warnings: according to Israeli records, 165,000 phone calls, 2,500,000 leaflets, and radio broadcasts. They also used a new technology called "roof knocking," in which the military fires a non-explosive missile at the roof of a building as an additional warning to the civilians before launching an attack. The Israeli report on the operation explained:

> In addition to the above, the IDF made specific telephone calls just before an attack was about to take place, informing residents at risk about the upcoming strike and urging them to leave the place. In certain instances, although such warnings were made, the civilians chose to stay. In such cases, the IDF made even greater efforts to avoid civilian casualties and minimise collateral damage by firing *warning shots from light weapons that hit the roofs* of the designated targets, before proceeding with the strike. These warnings were accompanied by real-time surveillance in order to assess the presence of civilians in the designated military target, despite the advance warnings. Accordingly, the commander in charge assessed whether the collateral damage anticipated, including to those who chose to stay at the premises, was not excessive

---

33. REVIEW COMMITTEE, OFFICE OF THE PROSECUTOR, INTERNATIONAL CRIMINAL TRIBUNAL FOR THE FORMER YUGOSLAVIA, FINAL REPORT TO THE PROSECUTOR BY THE COMMITTEE ESTABLISHED TO REVIEW THE NATO BOMBING CAMPAIGN AGAINST THE FEDERAL REPUBLIC OF YUGOSLAVIA ¶ 77 (2000).

in relation to the military advantage anticipated. The specific warnings were generally effective [as described later in the report regarding specific incidents].[34]

Compare the analysis in the U.N. Fact-Finding Mission Report (the Goldstone Report):

> The Mission is doubtful whether roof-knocking should be understood as a warning as such. In the context of a large-scale military operation including aerial attacks, civilians cannot be expected to know whether a small explosion is a warning of an impending attack or part of an actual attack. . . . The legal requirement is for an effective warning to be given. This means that it should not require civilians to guess the meaning of the warning. The technique of using small explosives to frighten civilians into evacuation, even if the intent is to warn, may cause terror and confuse the affected civilians. . . . Finally, apart from the issue of fear and ambiguity, there is the question of danger. The idea that an attack, however limited in itself, can be understood as an effective warning in the meaning of article 57(2)(c) is rejected by the Mission.[35]

Which argument fits better within the general scope of LOAC? Is it reasonable to use a warning shot that will not explode or cause injuries if other warnings have not had the desired effect? At what point can or should the attacking party progress on the belief that it has given all feasible warnings under the circumstances?

3. In April 2016, U.S. forces combating ISIS in Iraq used the roof-knocking tactic for the first time in targeting a building housing an ISIS fighter and cash storage site. The U.S. fired a Hellfire missile to explode above the targeted building to ensure that the woman and children who had been spotted in the building evacuated before the building was hit. The woman and children left the building, but unfortunately the woman ran back in just before the building was destroyed.[36] How can an attacking party communicate that the "roof knock" is a warning and not an attack?

4. If a commander issues warnings and then sees through surveillance that the civilians did not leave, what considerations must she address before launching the attack? Are the civilians who stay after a warning still protected from attack?

---

34. THE OPERATION IN GAZA, 27 DECEMBER 2008-18 JANUARY 2009: FACTUAL AND LEGAL ASPECTS ¶ 264 (2009).

35. Human Rights Council, Report of the United Nations Fact Finding Mission on the Gaza Conflict, ¶¶ 530-533 A/HRC/12/48, Sept. 15, 2009.

36. *In the Fight Against ISIS, U.S. Adopts Israeli "Roof Knocking" Tactic*, NEWSWEEK.COM (Apr. 26, 2016).

5. When U.S. forces attacked ISIS oil tankers (see Chapter 8), they determined that while the oil and the tanker trucks were legitimate military objectives, the drivers were civilians. As a result, U.S. forces dropped leaflets warning the drivers of the impending attacks:

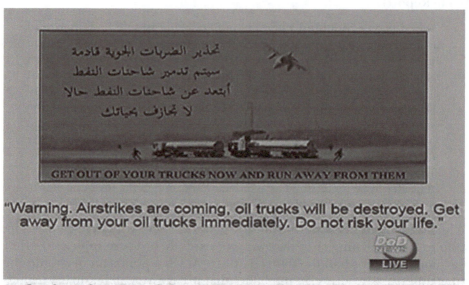

Leaflets dropped 45 minutes before airstrikes targeting ISIL oil tankers. Image credit: US Defense Department

C. DEFENDING PARTY'S PRECAUTIONS

Recognizing that the party in control of the territory where the conflict is taking place is often best situated to protect civilians from the unfortunate consequences of war, Additional Protocol I places obligations on the defending party as well.

ARTICLE 58 OF ADDITIONAL PROTOCOL I

The Parties to the conflict shall, to the maximum extent feasible:

(a) without prejudice to Article 49 of the Fourth Convention, endeavour to remove the civilian population, individual civilians and civilian objects under their control from the vicinity of military objectives;

(b) avoid locating military objectives within or near densely populated areas;

(c) take the other necessary precautions to protect the civilian population, individual civilians and civilian objects under their control against the dangers resulting from military operations.

Although Additional Protocol I emphasizes the attacking party's affirmative obligation to take precautions in planning and launching attacks, this obligation in no way diminishes the defending party's obligations.[37] As the Commentary explains, "[b]elligerents may expect their adversaries to conduct themselves [lawfully] and to respect the civilian population, but they themselves must also cooperate by taking all possible precautions for the benefit of their own population as is in any case in their own interest."[38] Parties therefore have an obligation to protect their own civilians from the consequences of their own offensive actions as well as those of the enemy. Article 58, which expands on pre-existing norms, is considered customary international law.

1. Location of Military Objectives

Recent conflicts in particular have involved extensive co-mingling of civilian and military objects, which poses a grave danger to civilians. The precautions noted in Article 58 involve both peacetime and wartime obligations. As the Commentary explains,

> As regards permanent objectives, governments should endeavour to find places away from densely populated areas to site them. These concerns should already be taken into consideration in peacetime. For example, a barracks or a store of military equipment or ammunition should not be built in the middle of a town. As regards mobile objectives, care should be taken in particular during the conflict to avoid placing troops, equipment or transports in densely populated areas. In both cases, it is likely that governments are sufficiently concerned with sparing their own population and that they will therefore act in the best interests of that population.[39]

It is important to note the preliminary clause — "to the maximum extent feasible" — because there can certainly be situations in which attempting to evacuate the civilian population could actually place them in greater danger, for example. At the same time, violation of these obligations simply involves a failure to take the necessary precautions; intent to endanger

---

37. Although the obligation to take "constant care" appears in Article 57, which addresses the attacking party, the Commentary suggests that both parties have such an obligation: "The term 'military operations' should be understood to mean any movement, manoeuvres, and other activities whatsoever carried out by the armed forces with a view to combat." CLAUDE PILLOUD, YVES SANDOZ, CHRISTOPHE SWINARSKI & BRUNO ZIMMERMAN, COMMENTARY ON THE ADDITIONAL PROTOCOLS OF 8 JUNE 1977 TO THE GENEVA CONVENTIONS OF 12 AUGUST 1949 680 (1987).

38. *Id.* at 692.

39. *Id.* at 694.

the civilian population is not a factor in the analysis. Thus, noncompliance rather than intent is the determining factor.

Although all three obligations in Article 58 play a critical role in protecting the civilian population from the dangers of armed hostilities, the obligation to refrain from locating military objectives in densely populated areas is particularly relevant in today's conflicts. A Human Rights Watch report on Schools and Armed Conflict highlights these dangers. Although many of the incidents detailed therein involve the occupation of schools for headquarters or barracks for soldiers or militants in addition to the positioning of military objectives in schools, the dangers for the civilian population are the same. As one mother in Thailand explained after removing her children from a school occupied by paramilitary forces for two years: "when they moved into the school, I feared there would be an attack on the school, so that is the reason I withdrew my children . . . if there was an attack on the grounds, the children would be hit as well."[40] In the same vein, the United States listed several examples in denouncing Iraq's mingling of military and civilian objects during the first Gulf War:

(a) The Iraqi Government moved significant amounts of military weapons and equipment into civilian areas with the deliberate purpose of using innocent civilians and their homes as shields against attacks on legitimate military targets;

(b) Iraqi fighter and bomber aircraft were dispersed into villages near the military airfields where they were parked between civilian houses and even placed immediately adjacent to important archaeological sites and historic treasures;

(c) Coalition aircraft were fired upon by anti-aircraft weapons in residential neighbourhoods in various cities. In Baghdad, anti-aircraft sites were located on hotel roofs;

(d) In one case, military engineering equipment used to traverse rivers, including mobile bridge sections, was located in several villages near an important crossing point. The Iraqis parked each vehicle adjacent to a civilian house.[41]

Locating military objectives—and weapons, equipment and headquarters for military personnel certainly qualify—within civilian buildings or densely populated civilian areas violates Article 58(b) and undermines efforts to protect civilians.

---

40. Human Rights Watch, Schools and Armed Conflict 5 (2011).

41. United States, Letter Dated 5 March 1991, to the President of the UN Security Council, 2-3, U.N. Doc. 2/22341 (Mar. 8, 1991).

> # ARTICLE 58(b) IN PRACTICE
>
> - In the 2008 conflict between Georgia and Russia over South Osse-tia, many South Ossetian fighters fired at Georgian forces from civilian homes and buildings.
> - During Operation Cast Lead, Palestinian armed groups fired mobile rocket launchers from schoolyards, mosques, hospitals and residential buildings.
> - In Afghanistan, Taliban militants have stored heavy weaponry in mosques and reportedly positioned two large anti-aircraft guns in front of the office of a major international humanitarian aid organization.

Regardless of the conduct of the defending party in locating military objectives in populated areas, the attacking party is in no way absolved of its duty to take precautions and abide by the principles of distinction and proportionality.

QUESTIONS FOR DISCUSSION

1. Does LOAC's focus on the attacking party's obligations create perverse incentives for the defending party to use civilians as a shield?

2. Locating military objectives in densely populated civilian areas has both a tactical purpose and a strategic purpose. The tactical purpose is to protect the rocket launchers, weapons caches or other military objectives—even fighter jets in downtown Baghdad—by deterring attacks. The strategic purpose, which is significantly more insidious, is to use any resulting civilian deaths as a broader strategic tool to accuse the attacking party of war crimes, diminish support for the war effort in that country, or otherwise change the course of the conflict.

3. Who bears responsibility when civilians die during attacks on objectives hidden within the civilian population? How does the international "court" of public opinion match up with the correct application of the law?

4. What about military family housing or schools for military dependents (i.e., the children of service members) on military bases? Are they civilian items co-located near military objects? Are they human shields?

5. The Pentagon, perhaps the world's largest and most recognizable military objective, is located mere minutes from the center of Washington, D.C., a city of more than half a million people. Is the Pentagon's location a violation of Article 58(b)?

6. In recent years, Hezbollah has created hundreds of so-called "rocket villages" in southern Lebanon.

The genesis of this approach could be first observed after the 2006 war, when Hezbollah embarked on a project to rebuild homes for needy Shiite families, with the caveat that at least one rocket launcher and several rockets would be housed there, and would be fired at Israel when the order was given. Hezbollah has also set up camouflaged defense positions in villages, containing Russian-, Iranian-, Chinese-, or even North Korean-made anti-tank missiles, while planting large explosive devices along access roads and converting large village structures into arms caches. In this manner, the organization converted some 180 Shiite villages and towns between the Zahrani River and the Blue Line into fighting zones—both above and below ground.[42]

What are the consequences for the civilian population in southern Lebanon if war breaks out again between Israel and Hezbollah? For the civilian population of Israel? What steps can and should the Israel Defense Forces take to address these challenges?

2. Human Shields

The use of human shields refers to the practice of using civilians to protect military objectives from attack by gathering at the site of the objective and using their civilian immunity to deter attacks. In effect, human shielding directly undermines LOAC's delicate balance between military necessity and humanity by using the protections of the latter principle for military purposes. Multiple provisions of the Geneva Conventions and Additional Protocol I prohibit the use of civilians or the civilian population as a shield.

ARTICLE 51(7) OF ADDITIONAL PROTOCOL I

The presence or movements of the civilian population or individual civilians shall not be used to render certain points or areas immune from military operations, in particular in attempts to shield military objectives from attacks or to shield, favour or impede military operations. The Parties to the conflict shall not direct the movement of the civilian population or individual civilians in order to attempt to shield military objectives from attacks or to shield military operations.

ARTICLE 23 OF THE THIRD GENEVA CONVENTION

No prisoner of war may at any time be sent to, or detained in, areas where he may be exposed to the fire of the combat zone, nor may his presence be used to render certain points or areas immune from military operations. . . .

---

42. JONATHAN SCHANZER ET AL., FOUNDATION FOR THE DEFENSE OF DEMOCRACIES, THE THIRD LEBANON WAR: THE COMING CLASH BETWEEN HEZBOLLAH AND ISRAEL IN THE SHADOW OF THE IRAN NUCLEAR DEAL 28 (July 2016).

ARTICLE 28 OF THE FOURTH GENEVA CONVENTION

The presence of a protected person may not be used to render certain points or areas immune from military operations.

ARTICLE 12(4) OF ADDITIONAL PROTOCOL I

Under no circumstances shall medical units be used in an attempt to shield military objectives from attack. Whenever possible, the Parties to the conflict shall ensure that medical units are so sited that attacks against military objectives do not imperil their safety.

The prohibition on human shielding includes both passive shielding, when the defending party takes advantage of the presence of civilians, and active shielding, when the defending party directs civilians to a location to act as shields. It is part of customary international law, a war crime under the Rome Statute of the International Criminal Court, and included in numerous military manuals of countries around the world. The central element of human shielding is the intent to use civilians as a shield. The fact that military forces are in the same area as civilians does not violate the prohibition—but deliberate co-mingling to shield forces from attack is a violation.

The use of human shields flies directly in the face of a party's basic obligations under the principle of distinction by deliberately mingling civilians with military objects. As a U.N. report investigating an attack on U.N. forces in Somalia in 1993 stated:

> No principle is more central to the humanitarian law of war than the obligation to respect the distinction between combatants and non-combatants. That principle is violated and criminal responsibility thereby incurred when organizations deliberately target civilians or when they use civilians as shields or otherwise demonstrate a wanton indifference to the protection of non-combatants.[43]

Human shielding poses a direct and severe challenge to the principle of distinction and to the protection of civilians during armed conflict. Indeed, those who use human shields exploit the obligation of distinction and upend LOAC's balance between military necessity and humanity by deliberately mingling civilians and military objects and, still worse, using civilians directly to protect military targets.

---

43. *Report Pursuant to Paragraph 5 of Security Council Resolution 837 (1993) on the Investigation into the 5 June 1993 Attack on United Nations Forces in Somalia Conducted on behalf of the Secretary-General*, Annex § 9, U.N. Doc. S/26351 (Aug. 24, 1993).

Unfortunately, human shielding is all too common in a wide variety of armed conflicts around the world and has a long history. British troops placed Boer civilians on trains to prevent Boer commandos from attacking them during the Boer War, and General Sherman marched Confederate prisoners at the head of his forces on his march through Georgia during the U.S. Civil War.[44] More recently, during the 1991 Persian Gulf War, Saddam Hussein seized foreign citizens and used them to shield designated military targets, calling them "special guests."[45] In Liberia, rebel "fighters forced civilians out of the government hospital, where they had taken refuge, and used them as human shields for their positions" during fighting in Tubmanburg.[46] The Security Council has condemned "use by the Taliban and other extremist groups of civilians as human shields" in Afghanistan.[47] In one of the more horrifying and vivid examples of wholesale human shielding, LTTE fighters forcibly prevented civilians from leaving LTTE-controlled areas in the designated No Fire Zones, "ensuring their continued presence as a human buffer."[48] As the U.N. Report on Sri Lanka concludes, the use of civilians "as a strategic human buffer" and "as dispensable 'cannon fodder' . . . added significantly to the total death toll in the conflict."[49]

In her book, *A Long Road Home* (often referred to as the *Black Hawk Down* for Iraq), *Washington Post* reporter Martha Raddatz tells of an Army unit pinned down in Sadr City in Iraq. The unit takes up a defensive position in a residential compound down an alley and positions its vehicles at the entrance of the compound. At one point during the ordeal the insurgents round up approximately 100 local women, children, and elderly and march them down the alley towards the vehicles. Behind this crowd, the insurgents are shooting AK-47s at the soldiers while pushing the civilians towards the Army vehicles. The soldiers fire warning shots from their .50 caliber weapons—first high and then low. The group keeps coming, the insurgents in the back of the civilians keep firing their automatic weapons, and eventually the soldiers are forced to open fire on the civilians in order to protect themselves from being overrun by the insurgents.[50] The battle in Somalia featured in Mark Bowden's *Black Hawk Down* offers another example: women wearing their local African dress were used as human shields (presumably,

44. Robert E. Rodes, Jr., *On Clandestine Warfare*, 39 Wash. & Lee L. Rev. 333, 341 (1982).

45. *See* Michael N. Schmitt, *Human Shields in International Humanitarian Law*, 47 Colum. J. Transnat'l L. 292, 295 (2009) (noting that the U.N. Security Council condemned this conduct in Resolution 664 (1999)).

46. U.N. Secretary General, *Fifteenth Progress Report on UNOMIL*, § 24, U.N. Doc. S/1996/47 (Jan. 23, 1996).

47. S.C. Res. 1776, ¶ 82, U.N. Doc. S/Res/1776 (Sept. 19, 2007).

48. U.N. Secretary-General, Report of the Secretary-General's Panel of Experts on Accountability in Sri Lanka ¶ 98 (Mar. 31, 2004).

49. *Id.* ¶ 177(a).

50. Martha Raddatz, The Long Road Home: A Story of War and Family 130-134 (2007).

against their will) as shooters fired their weapons from between their legs and under their arms:

> Peering out from underneath toward the north now, Nelson saw the Somali with a gun lying prone on the street between two kneeling women. The shooter had the barrel of his weapon between the woman's legs, and there were four children actually *sitting* on him. He was completely shielded in noncombatants, taking full cynical advantage of the Americans' decency. "Check this out, John," he told Waddell, who scooted over for a look. "What do you want to do?" Waddell asked. "I can't get that guy through those people." So Nelson threw a flashbang, and the group fled so fast the man left his gun in the dirt.[51]

ISIS: Human Shields in Mosul

In late March 2017, the United Nations High Commissioner for Human Rights strongly condemned ISIS's use of the civilian population of Mosul as human shields, tactics that caused extensive civilian casualties during the Battle of Mosul.

Bodies continue to be found in buildings where civilians were reportedly held by ISIL as human shields, and were subsequently killed by airstrikes conducted by Iraqi Security Forces and International Coalition forces, as well as by Improvised Explosive Devices (IEDs) allegedly planted in the same buildings by ISIL. Numerous other civilians have been killed by shelling and have been gunned down by ISIL snipers as they tried to flee. . . .

According to information verified by the UN Human Rights Office and the UN Assistance Mission in Iraq, at least 307 people were killed and another 273 wounded between 17 February and 22 March. The most deadly incident occurred on 17 March, when an airstrike—reportedly targeting ISIL snipers and equipment—hit a house in al-Jadida neighbourhood in western Mosul city. Witnesses reported that ISIL had previously forced at least 140 civilians into the house to be used as human shields. They also said that ISIL had booby-trapped the house with IEDs. So far, official figures indicate at least 61 people were killed in this single incident, but the actual figure may be much higher.

In another serious incident, on 22 March, an airstrike hit a residential building in Rajm Hadid neighbourhood in western Mosul city. ISIL reportedly filled the house with people from the surrounding

51. Mark Bowden, Black Hawk Down 46 (1999).

neighbourhood, including children, and then used the house to launch rocket-propelled grenades against the Iraqi Security Forces. The airstrike killed a seven-year-old girl and trapped eight other children under the rubble, seven of whom were later found and taken to hospital. . . .

There are also reports that ISIL has forcibly transferred civilians within western Mosul. On 20 March, ISIL militants allegedly forced 38 families to leave their homes in the Bab al-Beth neighbourhood, as Government forces began operations in the area, and moved them to a west Mosul neighbourhood known as 17 Tamouze, using them to shield their fighters as they relocated, as well as in strategic locations. ISIL has also reportedly forced families to stay in some 15 houses on the frontlines in the Nablis and Risala neighbourhoods and are using those houses to launch attacks on Government forces. There have been numerous reports that ISIL snipers have shot at, and in some cases killed or wounded, civilians attempting to flee towards the Iraqi Security Forces, and that ISIS has also shelled civilians in areas of the city retaken by Government forces. . . .

"ISIL's strategy of using children, men and women to shield themselves from attack is cowardly and disgraceful. It breaches the most basic standards of human dignity and morality. Under international humanitarian law, the use of human shields amounts to a war crime," High Commissioner Zeid said. "And shooting civilians in the back as they flee for their lives is an act of monstrous depravity."[52]

The consequences of human shields for the attacking party are challenging and complex:

First, the attacking side may refrain from conducting an attack based on moral concerns about harming those civilians forced to act as shields. Second, the attacker may abandon a planned strike because of possible negative communicative consequences. After all, images of dead and injured civilians transmitted across a globalized media (which often pays little heed to the military rationale of an operation) can make it appear as if the attacker has mounted inhumane operations. . . . Third, at a certain point, the number of civilians likely to be injured or killed during an attack becomes "excessive" relative to its anticipated "military advantage," such that the international humanitarian law proportionality principle bars attack.[53]

52. U.N. Office of the High Commissioner for Human Rights, *Mosul: Protection of Civilians Paramount as ISIL Intensifies Use of Human Shields* (Mar. 28, 2017).

53. Michael N. Schmitt, *Human Shields in International Humanitarian Law*, 47 COLUM. J. TRANSNAT'L L. 292, 297-98 (2009).

Most important, the use or presence of human shields does not absolve the attacking party of its fundamental obligations under LOAC. Article 51(8) of Additional Protocol I affirms that "[a]ny violation of these prohibitions shall not release the Parties to the conflict from their legal obligations with respect to the civilian population and civilians, including the obligation to take the precautionary measures provided for in Article 57." Regardless of the defending party's conduct, therefore, an attacking party remains bound by the obligations to take all feasible precautions, including an assessment of proportionality, before launching an attack. As the Commentary explains, "[i]t is an attempt to safeguard the population even when the appropriate authorities do not take the required measures of protection with regard to them."[54] Civilians being used as human shields do not lose their protection from attack and must be protected from incidental harm in the same manner as all other civilians. An attacking party that "could feasibly minimize [incidental] harm (without forfeiting military advantage) by employing alternative means or methods of warfare, or striking a different target, would be obliged to do so."[55]

The treaty provisions, and the examples above, address and describe what are generally referred to as involuntary human shields, meaning individuals who are forced to shield military objectives from attack. Voluntary human shields, in contrast, are individuals who willingly protect military objectives. For example, during the NATO bombing of Serbia and Kosovo in 1999, Serbian residents of Belgrade blocked bridges to prevent NATO airstrikes. In 1991, foreigners flew to Iraq to serve as voluntary human shields protecting critical infrastructure sites from U.S. attack. While involuntary human shields are without a doubt victims of one or more LOAC violations,[56] what about voluntary human shields? If the defending party is not actively placing the civilians in those locations, is it violating the law? Does it need to affirmatively prevent such conduct? Voluntary human shields also specifically raise the question of direct participation in hostilities. Some argue that they remain civilians protected from attack at all times. Others argue that by dint of their voluntary action to protect military objectives from attack, they are directly participating in hostilities—indeed, shielding an objective can often be a significantly more effective contribution

54. CLAUDE PILLOUD, YVES SANDOZ, CHRISTOPHE SWINARSKI & BRUNO ZIMMERMAN, COMMENTARY ON THE ADDITIONAL PROTOCOLS OF 8 JUNE 1977 TO THE GENEVA CONVENTIONS OF 12 AUGUST 1949 628 (1987).

55. Michael N. Schmitt, *Human Shields in International Humanitarian Law*, 47 COLUM. J. TRANSNAT'L L. 292, 325 (2009).

56. For example, the ICTY has held that the use of human shields constitutes hostage-taking and cruel and inhuman treatment. *See* Prosecutor v. Blaskić, Case No. IT-95-14-T, Judgement ¶¶ 716, 750 (Int'l Crim. Trib. for the Former Yugoslavia Mar. 3, 2000); Prosecutor v. Kordić, Case No. IT-94-14/2, Judgement ¶ 800 (Int'l Crim. Trib. for the Former Yugoslavia Mar. 3, 2000).

than firing a rocket or other individual weapon. If they are considered to be directly participating in hostilities, they would lose their immunity from attack, which, of course, would undo the effect of the shielding. A middle theory is that voluntary human shields retain their civilian status but no longer factor into the proportionality analysis for an attack on that objective. These considerations are extraordinarily significant for determining the attacker's obligations and appropriate course of action when faced with a military objective protected by human shields.

QUESTIONS FOR DISCUSSION

1. In the 1993 battle in Somalia portrayed in *Black Hawk Down*, another U.S. soldier faced a similar situation:

> "Hey, sir, I can see there's a guy behind this woman with a weapon under her arm," shouted Elliot. Perino told him to shoot. The 60 gun made a low, blatting sound. The men called the gun a "pig." Both the man and woman fell dead.[58]

Is there an obligation to attempt "non-lethal" tactics as displayed in the first scenario in Somalia? Or can one go straight to the lethal tactics used in this second scenario?

2. Contrast that with the following scenario in the HBO documentary *Battle for Marjah* featuring U.S. Marines fighting in Afghanistan. It took weeks for the Marines to finally flush elements of the Taliban out into the open. At one point, some of the Marines have positioned themselves on a rooftop in order to be ready to intercept the Taliban in the kill zone when they attempt to cross a field. One Marine shoots and kills a Taliban and becomes demonstratively excited about how he just "shot that motherfucker!" Yet moments later, the Taliban, realizing what is happening, grab some women in burkas and use them as human shields in order to cross the open ground. The very same Marine who was excited about killing a Taliban is now equally enraged that they are using women to hide behind. But more importantly—he's not firing a shot. Essentially, that Marine went from seemingly out of control about getting his first kill after a very frustrating several weeks to complete restraint in accordance with LOAC. In both scenarios, the Somali fighters and the Taliban are violating LOAC. But when civilians die, who is responsible for the deaths of the civilians in these types of situations? Does it make a difference if those fighters using the human shields are firing their weapons or trying to flee the battlefield?

3. In November 2010, North Korea shelled Yeonpyeong Island, a South Korean island near the maritime border between the two countries. Two

---

58. MARK BOWDEN, BLACK HAWK DOWN 42 (1999).

South Korean civilians and two South Korean marines were killed, eighteen civilians were injured, and over 1,500 civilians evacuated from the island. The shelling was the first time North Korea had shelled South Korean territory and civilian areas since the end of the Korean War in 1953, and led to an exchange of artillery fire between the two nations. In response to claims that the shelling was unlawful, North Korea argued that South Korea is using the civilians on the island as human shields to protect military installations there from attack. How does this claim fit within the understanding of human shields? If one could demonstrate that the civilians were indeed being used as human shields, how would that impact a legal analysis of North Korea's actions? Does the mere fact that civilians live on an island on the front line between the two nations—an island that also houses military installations and personnel—mean that the civilians are human shields?

CIVILIANS AT RISK: AFGHANISTAN

In Now Zad District, Helmand Province, Afghanistan, following clearing operations in an area where insurgents established an illegal bazaar, the Marines started conducting security patrols from a small patrol base. The patrols routinely were met with harassing fire from compounds; however, they did not take any casualties because as soon as the Marines began returning fire, the insurgents retreated. When the Marines searched the compounds where the harassing fire came from, they found the compounds to be abandoned but with evidence that people had been living there very recently (such as cooking items). They also found escape routes that the insurgents used, spent shell casings, and "murder holes" (holes drilled into walls through which the insurgents fired their rifles).

After approximately three weeks of conducting routine security patrols in the area, a patrol came under more intense firing than it had experienced before. The patrol was encircled by an ambush of insurgents firing from compounds. One Marine was shot in the neck and died almost instantly. Still taking fire from the compounds, the patrol leader decided to call for air support. The company commander called for support from the battalion; the battalion authorized two 500-pound bombs to be dropped. The bombs were dropped on one particular compound where a majority of the firing was coming from and the patrol was then able to return safely to the patrol base without suffering any more casualties.

The following morning, the locals brought fourteen dead bodies to the patrol base, several of them women and children, but some of them military aged males who were likely the insurgents firing on the

Marines. Through investigations, the Marines later discovered that the insurgents forced the family whose compound they were firing from to remain in the house while they fired from it. The insurgents threatened to kill the family if they fled the compound, leaving them little choice.

As the insurgents discovered that they could significantly sway public opinion away from the Marines by creating circumstances wherein Marines were blamed for civilian casualties, their tactics became more and more blatant. On a separate occasion, insurgents in the area of a local farm again fired upon Marines in a different area of the district. The Marines returned fire and the insurgents fled. That night, a local family brought the dead body of a young man, approximately thirteen years old, who had suffered a gunshot wound to the head, alleging that Marines shot the young man during the skirmish. From rudimentary examinations performed by law enforcement professionals working as contractors with the infantry battalion, the wound appeared to have not come from a Marine rifle (M4) but rather from a different caliber weapon. Additionally, the family's retelling of the event made it clear that the young man was not near enough to the skirmish to have been struck during the crossfire. It started to become apparent from these incidents that insurgents would shoot the closest civilian present during skirmishes as they retreated in order to make it appear that the Marines had caused the death.

— *U.S. military officer*

CHAPTER 10

MEANS AND METHODS: WEAPONS AND TACTICS

LOAC's key principles also govern the means and methods of warfare—the weapons chosen for a particular attack, and the tactics soldiers and other fighters use in the course of military operations. The regulation of the means and methods of warfare was first enshrined in the Hague Conventions with the goal of rejecting total war in favor of certain fundamental rules applicable during combat. As the Commentary on Additional Protocol I explains, these provisions from the Hague Conventions reinforce the

> principle by which the right of belligerents to adopt means of injuring the enemy is not unlimited [and] contain two types of fundamental rules: on the one hand, humanitarian rules, and on the other hand, rules on good faith. The humanitarian rules prohibit killing or wounding an enemy who has laid down his arms or no longer has the means to defend himself and has therefore surrendered unconditionally; they also prohibit refusing to give quarter and causing superfluous injury or unnecessary suffering. The rules on good faith prohibit killing or wounding the enemy treacherously, as well as deceiving him by the improper use of the flag of truce, of national emblems or of enemy uniforms, and also by the improper use of the red cross emblem.[1]

The term "means of warfare" refers to weapons or physical devices used in combat. "Methods of warfare" are tactics or strategies designed to weaken the enemy and gain an advantage during military operations.

---

1. CLAUDE PILLOUD, YVES SANDOZ, CHRISTOPHE SWINARSKI & BRUNO ZIMMERMAN, COMMENTARY ON THE ADDITIONAL PROTOCOLS OF 8 JUNE 1977 TO THE GENEVA CONVENTIONS OF 12 AUGUST 1949 382 (1987).

> # GUIDING PRINCIPLES FOR THE MEANS AND METHODS OF WARFARE
>
> ## Article 35(1), Additional Protocol I:
>
> - In any armed conflict, the right of the Parties to the conflict to choose methods or means of warfare is not unlimited.
>
> ## Article 35(2), Additional Protocol I:
>
> - It is prohibited to employ weapons, projectiles and material and methods of warfare of a nature to cause superfluous injury or unnecessary suffering.
>
> ## Preamble, St. Petersburg Declaration:
>
> - [T]he only legitimate object which States should endeavour to accomplish during war is to weaken the military forces of the enemy.

A.   WEAPONS

International law prohibits two categories of weapons in armed conflict: indiscriminate weapons and weapons that cause unnecessary suffering. The first prohibition appears in Article 51(4) of Additional Protocol I, which defines indiscriminate attacks as attacks not directed at a specific military objective; attacks "which employ a method or means of combat which cannot be directed at a military objective; or [attacks] which employ a method or means of combat the effects of which cannot be limited as required by this Protocol." Thus, as the ICJ declared in *Legality of the Threat or Use of Nuclear Weapons*, parties to a conflict may not "use weapons that are incapable of distinguishing between civilian and military targets."[2] There is little doubt that any weapon can be used in an indiscriminate way during conflict, such as spraying automatic weapons fire into a crowd with no regard for the presence of civilians or others *hors de combat*. But such illegal use does not make the automatic weapon itself an unlawful weapon. Some weapons are designed in a way that they cannot be used in a discriminating manner, such as rockets with no system for aiming at a particular target, like the rockets that Hamas and Hezbollah have fired into Israel for many years.[3] Similarly,

---

2. Legality of the Threat and Use of Nuclear Weapons in Armed Conflict, Advisory Opinion, 1996 I.C.J. 226, ¶ 78 (July 8).

3. *See, e.g., Gaza/Israel: Hamas Rocket Attacks on Civilians Unlawful*, HUM. RTS. WATCH (Aug. 6, 2009), https://www.hrw.org/news/2009/08/06/gaza/israel-hamas-rocket-attacks-civilians-unlawful (noting that the rockets Hamas has fired on Israel are indiscriminate because "they cannot be aimed with any reliability").

missiles with a faulty guidance system resulting in an inability to aim only at military objectives or biological weapons that can spread contagion among the civilian population when not checked by an antidote, are also indiscriminate.[4] The ban on indiscriminate effects encompasses both these types of indiscriminate weapons and the use of otherwise lawful weapons in an indiscriminate manner.

Second, weapons that cause unnecessary suffering or superfluous injury are prohibited. The goal is to minimize harm that is not justified by military utility, either because of a lack of any utility at all or because the utility gained is considerably outweighed by the suffering caused. The international community's first effort at regulating weapons was the St. Petersburg Declaration Renouncing the Use, in Time of War, of Explosive Projectiles under 400 Grams Weight of 11 December 1868, which sought to outlaw "the employment of arms which uselessly aggravate the sufferings of disabled men, or render their death inevitable." Repeated in Article 23(e) of the Regulations attached to the 1907 Hague Convention IV, this prohibition is recognized as customary international law. The ICJ *Nuclear Weapons* decision emphasized this norm as the second of two cardinal principles of international law, explaining that

> it is prohibited to cause unnecessary suffering to combatants; it is accordingly prohibited to use weapons causing them such harm or uselessly aggravating their suffering. In application of that second principle, States do not have unlimited freedom of choice of means in the weapons they use.[5]

The basic idea behind the prohibition on weapons that cause unnecessary suffering is that weapons that increase suffering—specifically that of combatants—without increasing military advantage in any way are unlawful. Expanding bullets and blinding lasers offer two examples. Certainly, many weapons cause extensive, even horrible suffering and injury, but that in and of itself is not the key issue. The analysis hinges on two primary factors: "whether an alternative weapon is available, causing less injury or suffering; and . . . whether the effects produced by the alternative weapon are sufficiently effective in neutralizing enemy personnel."[6]

Article 36 of Additional Protocol I requires legal review of new weapons. The acquisition and procurement of the weapon must be consistent with all applicable treaties, customary international law, and LOAC. In the United States, the appropriate service judge advocate reviews any weapons before the award of the engineering and development contract and again

---

4. Michael N. Schmitt, *Future War and the Principle of Discrimination*, 28 ISR. Y.B. HUM. RTS. 51, 55 (1998).

5. Legality of the Threat or Use of Nuclear Weapons, Advisory Opinion, 1996 I.C.J. 226, 257 (July 8).

6. YORAM DINSTEIN, THE CONDUCT OF HOSTILITIES UNDER THE LAW OF INTERNATIONAL ARMED CONFLICT 60 (2004).

before the award of the initial production contract. In the reviews, the discussion often focuses on whether the suffering occasioned by the use of the weapon is needless, superfluous, or grossly disproportionate to the advantage gained by its use. Determinations of legality do not mean that states must anticipate any possible unlawful use of a weapon. Rather, as discussed at the 1974-1977 Diplomatic Conference that produced the Additional Protocols,

> the question [was] whether the employment of a weapon for its normal or expected use would be prohibited under some or all circumstances. A State is not required to foresee or analyze all possible misuses of a weapon, for almost any weapon can be misused in ways that would be prohibited.[7]

Finally, some weapons prohibited under LOAC are lawful for use in law enforcement scenarios, such as expanding bullets or tear gas. LOAC prohibits exploding or expanding projectiles (e.g., hollow point rounds) because they cause unnecessary suffering. An enemy soldier is rendered *hors de combat* just as effectively with normal non-expanding bullets. However, expanding bullets have an important and legitimate use in civilian law enforcement situations. Bullets that expand on impact are less likely to go through the target and hit innocent bystanders or cause collateral damage to property (for example, the skin of an aircraft). For this reason, they are especially valuable in hostage and counter-terrorist operations.

QUESTIONS FOR DISCUSSION

1. In some situations, U.S. snipers have authorization from the appropriate authorities to use hollow-point (expanding) rounds because they are more accurate over longer distances and therefore make collateral damage less likely. What is the balance between the unnecessary suffering of an individual combatant and the death of a civilian? How should one balance more than one core LOAC principle in this manner? Do you think the value of hollow-point rounds to the military will increase in operations that are conducted in close proximity to civilians or where human shields are used (such as operations in Somalia in October 1993)?

2. In February 1991, U.S. Army forces used plow-equipped tanks to bury up to 200 Iraqi soldiers alive in their trenches in the early hours of the Allied ground offensive.[8] Commanders chose this tactic to avoid hand-to-hand combat in the trenches, and most of the Iraqi troops in the trenches

---

7. Claude Pilloud, Yves Sandoz, Christophe Swinarski & Bruno Zimmerman, Commentary on the Additional Protocols of 8 June 1977 to the Geneva Conventions of 12 August 1949 424 (1987).

8. Eric Schmitt, *U.S. Army Buried Iraqi Soldiers Alive in Gulf War*, N.Y. Times (Sept. 15, 1991).

had time to jump out of the trenches and surrender. Was this a LOAC violation? Was plowing dirt into the trenches over the soldiers a tactic calculated to cause unnecessary suffering?

1. Nuclear Weapons

At first glance, the basic principles of unnecessary suffering and distinction would appear to outlaw the use of nuclear weapons for what seems to be their inherent inability to meet these two central standards. Nuclear weapons are currently regulated by a number of arms control agreements restricting their development, deployment, and use. During the development of Additional Protocol I, the United States engaged in the negotiations with the understanding that the new protocol was not intended to regulate nuclear, biological, and chemical warfare. In 1996, the U.N. General Assembly requested an advisory opinion from the ICJ on the legality of the use of nuclear weapons. The ICJ first reaffirmed that LOAC applies to the use of nuclear weapons and emphasized two "cardinal principles" of LOAC. First, "[s]tates must never make civilians the object of attack and must consequently never use weapons that are incapable of distinguishing between civilian and military targets." Second, "it is prohibited to cause unnecessary suffering to combatants: it is accordingly prohibited to use weapons causing them such harm or uselessly aggravating their suffering." Notwithstanding the fact that "the unique characteristics of nuclear weapons . . . [make] the use of such weapons . . . scarcely reconcilable with respect for [LOAC's] requirements," the Court concluded that it could not reach a "a definitive conclusion as to the legality or illegality of the use of nuclear weapons by a State in an extreme circumstance of self-defence, in which its very survival would be at stake."[9]

QUESTIONS FOR DISCUSSION

1. Do the Court's conclusions make sense in light of LOAC's key principles? Could there be a situation in which a nuclear weapon meets the requirements of distinction and unnecessary suffering?

2. In a dissenting *Nuclear Weapons* opinion, Judge Weeramantry wrote:

If international law had principles within it strong enough in 1899 to recognize the extraordinary cruelty of the "dum dum" or exploding bullet as going beyond the purposes of war, and projectiles diffusing asphyxiating or deleterious gases as also being extraordinarily cruel, it would cause some bewilderment to the objective observer to learn that in 1996 it is so

9. Legality of the Threat and Use of Nuclear Weapons in Armed Conflict, Advisory Opinion, 1996 I.C.J. 226, ¶¶ 78, 95 (July 8).

weak in principles that, with over a century of humanitarian law behind it, it is still unable to fashion a response to the cruelties of nuclear weapons as going beyond the purposes of war. At the least, it would seem passing strange that the expansion within the body of a single soldier of a single bullet is an excessive cruelty which international law has been unable to tolerate since 1899, and that the incineration in one second of a hundred thousand civilians is not. This astonishment would be compounded when that weapon has the capability, through multiple use, of endangering the entire human species and all civilization with it.[10]

Who has the better argument?

3. The Court seems to rely on an existential self-defense justification as the ultimate reason to not ban nuclear weapons as illegal under LOAC or other international law. What are the consequences of blending *jus ad bellum* and *jus in bello* in that way for other situations and other weapons?

2. *Chemical Weapons*

CHEMICAL WEAPONS ATTACKS IN SYRIA, 2013-2018

Reports document eighty-five chemical weapons attacks in Syria over a five year period. In early 2013, chemical weapons were used multiple times on a small scale. On March 24, 2013, Syrian opposition activists reported that Syrian forces used chemical weapons from multiple rocket launchers at the town of Adra, northeast of Damascus, killing two and injuring twenty-three more. The weapons were believed to be phosphorus bombs that harm the nervous system and cause imbalance and loss of consciousness. The first large-scale attack reportedly occurred on August 21, 2013, in Ghouta, as part of Syrian forces' efforts to expel rebel forces. According to reports, thousands of victims were counted in the Damascus suburbs, with symptoms of body convulsions, foaming at the mouth, blurry vision and suffocation. ISIS is believed to be responsible for the use of sulfur mustard at Umm Hawsh in September 2016. The next major attack was on April 4, 2017, when Syrian regime forces used sarin gas, a nerve agent, in Khan Sheikhoun, killing dozens. Finally, after chlorine gas attacks in Douma in March 2018, regime forces launched a major chemical weapons attack in that same area, killing at least several dozen civilians.[11]

---

10. *Id.* at 485 (dissenting opinion of JUDGE WEERAMANTRY).

11. Yuta Kawashima, *Timeline of Syrian Chemical Weapons Activity, 2012-2018, Arms Control Association*, April 2018, https://www.armscontrol.org/factsheets/Timeline-of-Syrian-Chemical-Weapons-Activity.

The use of chemicals as weapons has a long history in warfare. From their first use in 2000 B.C.E. to the present day, chemical weapons have been used to slow, deter, or eliminate the enemy. Defined as "the wartime use against an enemy of agents having a direct toxic effect on man, animals or plants,"[12] chemical warfare has continued to evolve since its first use.

In ancient India, toxic fumes were used to cause "slumber and yawning."[13] During the Peloponnesian War, wood soaked in sulfur was used to create larger, more destructive fires. During the Middle Ages, rags were dipped in chemicals that, when burned, created toxic smoke clouds. Chemical weapons continued to be a common part of military conflicts well into the nineteenth century. During the U.S. Civil War, for example, various plants and herbs were used to incapacitate enemy forces. Cayenne pepper, black pepper, powdered tobacco, and mustard seeds were among those used to cause violent sneezing and coughing, as well as to irritate the eyes and respiratory passages.

However, by the 1899 Hague Declaration Concerning Asphyxiating Gases, the international community began to abjure the use of chemical weapons. The Hague Declaration signatory states agreed "to abstain from the use of projectiles the sole object of which is the diffusion of asphyxiating or deleterious gases." Nonetheless, the use of chemical weapons in warfare was pervasive through World War I and continued infrequently throughout the twentieth century. The first recorded effective use of chemical weapons in World War I was the German release of 160 tons of chlorine gas in ten minutes, killing 5,000 French soldiers and injuring 100,000 more along the frontline at Ypres on April 22, 1915.[14] Estimates suggest that phosogene, chlorine, and mustard gas caused 91,000 deaths and over one million gas casualties during World War I.

Repulsed by the use and consequences of chemical weapons, states gathered to promulgate the 1925 Protocol for the Prohibition of the Use in War of Asphyxiating, Poisonous or Other Gases, and of Bacteriological Methods of Warfare. The treaty reinforced the prohibition of "the use in war of asphyxiating, poisonous, or other gases, and of all analogous liquids, materials, or devices" and extended the prohibition to the use of bacteriological weapons as well. Fifty years later, the Convention on the Prohibition

---

12. STOCKHOLM INTERNATIONAL PEACE RESEARCH INSTITUTE, 1 THE PROBLEM OF CHEMICAL AND BIOLOGICAL WARFARE: A STUDY OF THE HISTORICAL, TECHNICAL, MILITARY, LEGAL, AND POLITICAL ASPECTS OF CBW, AND POSSIBLE DISARMAMENT MEASURES: THE RISE OF CB WEAPONS 25 (1971). Biological warfare is defined as "the wartime use against an enemy of agents causing disease or death in man, animals, or plants following multiplication within the target organism." *Id.*

13. SEYMOUR M. HERSH, CHEMICAL AND BIOLOGICAL WARFARE: AMERICA'S HIDDEN ARSENAL 3 (1968).

14. Gerard J. Fitzgerald, *Chemical Warfare and Medical Response During World War I*, 98 AM. J. OF PUBLIC HEALTH 631, 631-632 (2008).

of the Development, Production and Stockpiling of Bacteriological (Biological) and Toxin Weapons and on Their Destruction (1972) took an additional step and added a prohibition on even the development, production, and stockpiling of these weapons. The United States unilaterally renounced the use of biological weapons in 1969. The United States and the Soviet Union ratified the Convention in 1975. The treaty permits development of limited quantities for antidotal reasons.

The consequences of chemical weapon use sparked an international discussion on the appropriate limits for the use of chemical weapons. In January 1993, the Chemical Weapons Convention (CWC) opened for signature; within two days, 130 nations had signed this comprehensive treaty banning the use, production, or stockpiling of chemical weapons.

ARTICLE 1 OF THE CHEMICAL WEAPONS CONVENTION: GENERAL OBLIGATIONS

1. Each State Party to this Convention undertakes never under any circumstances:

(a) To develop, produce, otherwise acquire, stockpile or retain chemical weapons, or transfer, directly or indirectly, chemical weapons to anyone;

(b) To use chemical weapons;

(c) To engage in any military preparations to use chemical weapons;

(d) To assist, encourage or induce, in any way, anyone to engage in any activity prohibited to a State Party under this Convention.

2. Each State Party undertakes to destroy chemical weapons it owns or possesses, or that are located in any place under its jurisdiction or control, in accordance with the provisions of this Convention.

3. Each State Party undertakes to destroy all chemical weapons it abandoned on the territory of another State Party, in accordance with the provisions of this Convention.

4. Each State Party undertakes to destroy any chemical weapons production facilities it owns or possesses, or that are located in any place under its jurisdiction or control, in accordance with the provisions of this Convention.

5. Each State Party undertakes not to use riot control agents as a method of warfare.

The treaty also provides for inspection and verification of domestic chemical industries as an additional measure to promote compliance. Pleased with this more expansive approach, commentators considered the

CWC the "most important global agreement in the history of arms control and disarmament."[15]

QUESTIONS FOR DISCUSSION

1. In April 2017 and April 2018, the United States launched missile strikes against airfields and chemical weapons facilities used in the attacks in Syria noted above. Is the use of force a lawful means of enforcing the prohibition on chemical weapons? Should it be?

2. Although comprehensive, the CWC has not resolved significant disagreements among states over the use of riot control agents. The CWC defines riot control agents (RCA) as "any chemical . . . which can produce rapidly in humans sensory irritation or disabling physical effects which disappear within a short time following termination of exposure."[16] Article 1(5) prohibits the use of "riot control agents as a method of warfare" but offers no definition of a "method of warfare." The United States has renounced the use of riot control agents in an offensive manner but reserved the right to use them in "defensive military modes to save lives. . . ."[17] Presidential approval may be given for the use of RCAs in the following situations: (1) to control riots in areas under U.S. control; (2) in situations where civilians are being used as a screen; (3) in rescue missions in remote areas; (4) in rear echelon areas for protection against civil disturbances, terrorists, and paramilitary operations; and (5) for protection and recovery of nuclear weapons. Many agree that the use of RCAs to control prisoners and civilians engaged in civil disturbances is acceptable during an armed conflict. What about protecting combatants—such as downed crew members—from hostile civilians during a rescue mission?

3. Can LOAC or other international law ever keep pace with scientific developments in chemical warfare and other similar areas?

3. Landmines and Booby Traps

Protocol II of the United Nations Convention on Certain Conventional Weapons addresses mines and booby traps and bans any use against civilians and any indiscriminate use. As with other weapons and means of warfare, militaries must take all feasible precautions to prevent injury to

---

15. Thomas Bernauer, *The End of Chemical Warfare*, 24 SECURITY DIALOGUE 97 (1993).

16. Convention on the Prohibition of the Development, Production, Stockpiling and Use of Chemical Weapons and on Their Destruction, art. II (7), Jan. 13, 1993, S. Treaty Doc. No. 103-121, 1974 U.N.T.S. 45.

17. Exec. Order No. 11,850, 3 C.F.R. 980 (1971-1975), 40 Fed. Reg. 16,187 (Apr. 10, 1975).

civilians. Mines may only be used in areas where there are military objectives, and they must either be capable of having their locations accurately recorded or contain a self-actuating or remotely controlled device that renders them harmless when they no longer serve a military purpose. Landmines thus raise significant legal concerns regarding indiscriminate use and the difficulty of ensuring proper dismantling after deployment. Both of these problems pose significant dangers for the civilian population and have far-reaching humanitarian implications.

Although minefields can be laid very easily, they are extremely dangerous and time consuming to defuse. Landmines are estimated to kill as many as 10,000 civilians a year and maim many more. Mines could also be a threat to soldiers, who can be hemmed in or endangered by their own minefield. Even if not illegal *per se*, land mines also raise the issue of proportionality—whether the military value of mines laid in a particular location outweighs the cost in civilian lives and injuries. As one example, General Al Gray, the former Commandant of the Marine Corps, testified before a Senate Committee that he never saw a case in which mines were effectively used to affect enemy troop movement.[18]

A massive public relations campaign in the mid-1990s led to the 1997 Convention on the Prohibition of the Use, Stockpiling, Production, and Transfer of Anti-Personnel Mines and on Their Destruction (Ottawa Convention), which entered into force on March 1, 1999. The United States ultimately refused to sign the Ottawa Convention after failing to secure an exception for the minefields already in place on the Korean peninsula. Landmines are seen as critical to the defense of the Republic of Korea (South Korea) and are designed to slow any advance of the North Korean military southward. The United States did however commit to extensive de-mining in other locations. The fact that many U.S. allies have ratified the Ottawa Convention raises significant issues of interoperability in multinational coalition operations.

A booby trap is "any device or material which is designed, constructed or adapted to kill or injure, and which functions unexpectedly when a person disturbs or approaches an apparently harmless object or performs an apparently safe act."[19] Booby traps may never be directed at civilians and may never be used in an indiscriminate manner. These requirements mean that certain precautions must be taken in their use:

> the method used, or the circumstances, must be such that there is a
> reasonable prospect that only combatants will become victims of the

18. EXPLODING THE LANDMINE MYTH IN KOREA: WHY THE UNITED STATES CAN SIGN THE OTTAWA LANDMINES TREATY AT MINIMAL RISK TO US AND SOUTH KOREAN TROOPS 15-16 (Demilitarization for Democracy 1997).

19. Protocol on Prohibitions or Restrictions on the Use of Mines, Booby-Traps, and Other Devices (Protocol II) as Amended, art. 2(4), May 3, 1996, 35 I.L.M. 1206.

booby-traps and that the risk to civilians does not outweigh the military advantage of laying booby-traps. Care has to be taken to ensure that civilians do not become the unwitting victims of booby-traps.[20]

In particular, booby traps cannot be used in ways that are connected to other protected objects or persons under LOAC. Therefore, it is prohibited in all circumstances to use booby traps and other devices that in any way are attached or associated with sick, wounded, or dead persons; internationally recognized protective emblems or signs; food or drink; objects of a religious nature; or medical facilities, equipment, or transportation. The Amended Mines Protocol also prohibits booby traps designed to cause unnecessary suffering (e.g., "tiger-pits" with pungi sticks covered with human excrement) and those deliberately made in the form of apparently harmless objects such as toys or animals.

Consider this description from the 2008-2009 conflict in Gaza, where "Hamas, with training from Iran and Hezbollah, has used the last two years to turn Gaza into a deadly maze of tunnels, booby traps and sophisticated roadside bombs":

> In one apartment building in Zeitoun, in northern Gaza, Hamas set an inventive, deadly trap. According to an Israeli journalist embedded with Israeli troops, the militants placed a mannequin in a hallway off the building's main entrance. They hoped to draw fired from Israeli soldiers who might, through the blur of night vision goggles and split-second decisions, mistake the figure for a fighter. The mannequin was rigged to explode and bring down the building. In an interview, the reporter, Ron Ben-Yishai, a senior military correspondent for the newspaper *Yediot Aharonot*, said soldiers also found a pile of weapons with a grenade launcher on top. When they moved the launcher, "they saw a detonator light up, but somehow it didn't go off." . . .
>
> To avoid booby traps, the Israelis say, they enter buildings by breaking through side walls, rather than going in the front. Once inside, they move from room to room, battering holes in interior walls to avoid exposure to snipers and suicide bombers dressed as civilians, with explosive belts hidden beneath winter coats. . . .
>
> Last week, Israel captured a hand-drawn Hamas map in a house in Al Atatra, near Beit Lahiya, which showed planned defensive positions for the neighborhood, mine and booby trap placements, including a rigged gasoline station, and directions for snipers to shoot next to a mosque. Numerous tunnels were marked.[21]

---

20. UNITED KINGDOM MINISTRY OF DEFENCE, JSP 383: THE JOINT SERVICE MANUAL OF THE LAW OF ARMED CONFLICT 6.7 (2004).

21. Steven Erlanger, *A Gaza War Full of Traps and Trickery*, N.Y. TIMES (Jan. 10, 2009).

QUESTIONS FOR DISCUSSION

1. Think back to the questions regarding the use of nuclear weapons and whether such weapons could ever be used in a discriminating manner. What about mines and booby traps? Is it actually possible to ensure—as Protocol II requires—that civilians do not become the victims of booby traps? Or are such weapons inherently indiscriminate because it is too hard to know who will encounter them and be harmed as a result?

2. How does the use of booby traps by one party affect the LOAC obligations of the other party to the conflict?

3. During the 2014 Gaza conflict, three Israeli soldiers were killed when they entered a booby-trapped health clinic building bearing the UNRWA (United Nations Relief and Works Agency) sign above its door. The soldiers were attempting to destroy or neutralize a terror tunnel shaft housed under the health clinic. When they entered, the entire building, wired for this purpose, exploded.[22] Use of any protected site, such as a medical facility, in this manner is absolutely prohibited. Booby-trapping a health clinic also offers an obvious example of the dangers of booby traps as inherently indiscriminate—consider the harm that could have befallen civilians who might have innocently entered the health clinic seeking treatment. What if the booby trap were set inside a command post, designed to explode if enemy soldiers entered in an attempt to kill or capture the main command element?

4. The aftermath of the battle for Mosul in late 2016 highlighted the dangers of booby traps. ISIS booby-trapped buildings and streets throughout Mosul "on an industrial scale," with "improvised explosives in buildings . . . wired into household appliances such as fridges, heaters and televisions, primed to explode at the flick of a switch or an opened door."[23] As one demining expert explained, "[t]here are kilometers and kilometers and kilometers of active devices, sensitive enough to be detonated by a child and powerful enough to blow up a truck."[24]

4.   Cluster Munitions

Cluster and fragmentation weapons are currently lawful, but the conditions for their legitimate use remain highly disputed. Protocol I to the U.N. Convention on Certain Conventional Weapons prohibits the use of any weapon whose primary effect is to injure a combatant by fragments

---

22. Mitch Ginsburg, *Militants "Blow Up UNRWA Clinic," Killing 3 Soldiers*, TIMES OF ISRAEL (July 30, 2014).

23. Angus MacSwan, *ISIS Laid Booby-Traps All Over Mosul to Kill, Injure Returning Civilians*, HUFFINGTONPOST.COM (July 26, 2017).

24. *Id.*

that X-rays cannot detect. This Protocol was motivated by concerns over cluster bombs containing plastic components that the United States used in Vietnam. However, most modern weapons contain fusing mechanisms or lightweight plastic shell casings not designed as wounding agents. For this reason, the Protocol prohibits only weapons whose primary effect is to injure by non-detectable fragments. These types of weapons violate the principle of unnecessary suffering because physicians are not able to readily detect the presence of plastic fragments, making it harder to treat the wounded.

Pressure from humanitarian organizations over the last few decades led to the Convention on Cluster Munitions, which opened for signature in December 2008. The Convention completely bans any use, development, production, stockpiling, retention, or transfer to a third party of any type of cluster munitions. In addition, no state party may assist, encourage, or induce any state to engage in the use of cluster munitions, and any current stock of cluster munitions must be destroyed.[25] The Convention also requires states to remove and destroy any cluster munition remnants in foreign countries and to provide victim assistance to those affected by cluster munitions. At present, the United States, China, India, Pakistan, Iran, Israel, and the Russian Federation have not signed the Convention, nor did they participate in the negotiations.

A cluster munition, as defined by the Convention, is "a conventional munition that is designed to disperse or release explosive submunitions each weighing less than twenty kilograms, and includes those explosive submunitions." Cluster munitions·can affect wide areas of land — once deployed, the dozens to hundreds of submunitions inside the weapon can spread over a surface area equivalent to the size of a football field. Even if properly targeted at military targets in accordance with LOAC, submunitions can accidently disperse into nearby civilian areas, including homes, schools, businesses, farms, and other infrastructures necessary for daily life. In addition, cluster munitions are known to have a high failure rate (approximately 10 percent), thereby resulting in many undetonated submunitions, or explosive remnants of war (ERW). Because of these distinct features, cluster munitions result in grave and ongoing threats to civilian populations, even after the conflict ends. It is estimated that there have been more than 100,000 victims of cluster munitions worldwide.

QUESTIONS FOR DISCUSSION

1. Proponents of a ban on cluster munitions argue that they have been shown to cause more harm to civilians than to military targets and have been described as presumptively disproportionate when used in populated

25. Convention on Cluster Munitions, arts. 1(a)-(b), 1(c), 3, Dec. 3, 2008, 48 I.L.M. 357.

areas, particularly when the failure rate and the munitions' long-term effects are considered. During the 2006 Israel-Hezbollah conflict, Israel launched, by some estimates, four million submunitions into southern Lebanon. The U.N. estimated it would take 12 months to clear all of the failed submunitions from the littered backyards and olive groves.[26] Other studies charge that civilians comprise 98 percent of all cluster munition casualties.[27] Since March 2015, the coalition led by Saudi Arabia has been using cluster munitions in air strikes against Houthi forces in Yemen. During this same period, the Syrian-Russian joint military operation used cluster munitions against civilians in Syria. According to a report by the Cluster Munitions Coalition, civilian casualties from landmines doubled during that time.[28] The fundamental question is whether these weapons can ever satisfy LOAC's principles of proportionality and discrimination. The ICRC explains:

> [t]he characteristics of cluster munitions raise serious questions as to whether such weapons can be used in populated areas in accordance with the rule of distinction and the prohibition of indiscriminate attacks. The wide area effects of these weapons and the large number of unguided submunitions released would appear to make it difficult, if not impossible, to distinguish between military objectives and civilians in a populated target area.[29]

Is a complete ban on cluster munitions necessary to implement distinction and proportionality, particularly when conflicts take place in and among civilian populations?

2. Others argue that this type of weapon is often necessary and the only efficient option when needing to attack a large area. If cluster munitions were banned, many more missions would be needed to achieve the same effect and in order to cover the same amount of area. By increasing the number of missions, the attacking force consequently would expose more of its force to a heightened risk. Further, cluster munitions can reduce collateral damage because of their small detonating impact—otherwise, forces would have to use a more highly explosive weapon to accomplish the same military goal, thereby creating more damage. The United States, among other countries, rejects blanket claims that cluster munitions are unlawful, because there is a place for them in the artillery "given the right technology

---

26. Bonnie Docherty, *The Time Is Now: A Historical Argument for a Cluster Munitions Convention*, 20 Harv. Hum. Rts. J. 53, 55 (2007).

27. *Id.* at 62. *See also* Virgil Wiebe, *For Whom the Little Bells Toll: Recent Judgments by International Tribunals on the Legality of Cluster Munitions*, 35 Pepp. L. Rev. 895, 899-903 (2008).

28. Cluster Munition Attacks Spike Casualty Toll as World Shows Steadfast Resolve for Humanitarian Ban, Cluster Munition Monitor 2017, Aug. 31, 2017, https://reliefweb.int/report/world/cluster-munition-monitor-2017.

29. Int'l Comm. of the Red Cross, *Observations on the Legal Issues Related to the Use of Cluster Munitions*, CCW/GGE/2007/WP.8 (June 25, 2007).

as well as the proper rules of engagement."[30] Can LOAC's existing enforcement mechanisms, such as the grave breaches provisions and other prohibitions on unlawful attacks, provide sufficient oversight and guidance for the appropriate use of cluster munitions?

THE CONVENTION ON CLUSTER MUNITIONS AND JOINT MILITARY OPERATIONS

In 2011, a coalition of NATO forces conducted military operations in Libya to enforce U.N. Security Council Resolution 1973 and ultimately helped Libyan rebels oust Colonel Muammar Qaddafi. These joint operations were the first initiated by NATO after the Convention on Cluster Munitions entered into force in August 2010. The convention, which was designed to eliminate cluster munitions and the humanitarian harm they cause, absolutely bans the use, production, transfer, and stockpiling of cluster munitions. Some members of the NATO coalition in Libya, including the United Kingdom, were states parties to the new convention and obligated not to use cluster munitions "under any circumstances." The United States, the largest past user, however, remained outside the convention and was thus not legally bound by its provisions.

The scenario raised questions of interoperability, i.e., how states parties should implement the convention during joint military operations with non-party states. Article 1 of the convention prohibits states parties not only from using cluster munitions but also from assisting, encouraging, or inducing anyone "under any circumstances" to use the weapons. Article 21 obliges states parties to promote the norms of the convention:

> 1. Each State Party shall encourage States not party to this Convention to ratify, accept, approve or accede to this Convention, with the goal of attracting the adherence of all States to this Convention.
>
> 2. Each State Party shall notify the governments of all States not party to this Convention, referred to in paragraph 3 of this Article, of its obligations under this Convention, shall promote the norms it establishes and shall make its best efforts to discourage States not party to this Convention from using cluster munitions.
>
> 3. Notwithstanding the provisions of Article 1 of this Convention and in accordance with international law, States Parties, their military personnel or nationals, may engage in military cooperation and operations

---

30. U.S. Dept. of State Daily Press Briefing (Feb. 23, 2007), at www.state.gov/r/pa/prs/dpb2007/80978.htm.

with States not party to this Convention that might engage in activities prohibited to a State Party.

4. Nothing in paragraph 3 of this Article shall authorise a State Party:

(a) To develop, produce or otherwise acquire cluster munitions;

(b) To itself stockpile or transfer cluster munitions;

(c) To itself use cluster munitions; or

(d) To expressly request the use of cluster munitions in cases where the choice of munitions used is within its exclusive control.

The actions that the Convention on Cluster Munitions allows a state party to take during joint military operations with a state not party have been hotly debated.

You are a U.K. officer working closely with the U.S. military during the Libyan campaign. Your U.S. counterpart wants to use cluster munitions in an airstrike on a convoy leaving the town of Serte and asks for you to be involved in the attack.

Can you participate in such an operation, given that your country is a full party to the Convention on Cluster Munitions? If yes, can you provide any form of assistance with the use of cluster munitions? Can you jointly plan the strike? Can you provide intelligence that will inform the U.S. efforts? Can you order your forces to refuel U.S. aircraft that are carrying cluster bombs and are on their way to drop them on Serte?

What would be reasons for refusing to participate or assist? How would you respond to political pressure to do otherwise?

If you were the U.S. commander, would you seek to use cluster munitions in this situation given that more than half the world has signed the Convention on Cluster Munitions and that many of your allies have obligations thereunder?

In the end, no member of the NATO coalition, including the United States, used cluster munitions during the 2011 operations in Libya. Insiders have reported that the Convention on Cluster Munitions played a role in dictating the U.S. choice of weapons. Qaddafi's forces were the only ones to use cluster munitions in this conflict.

— *Bonnie Docherty, Arms Division, Human Rights Watch*

5.   *White Phosphorus and Other Incendiary Devices*

White phosphorus is a chemical used in artillery shells, bombs, and rockets and is spontaneously flammable. It can be used to illuminate targets and is a highly effective smokescreen agent because it burns very quickly and produces a thick bank of smoke that provides an effective screen to mask military maneuvers or the position of fire. For example, U.S. and coalition forces used white phosphorus during the battle for Mosul in October 2017, creating a smoke screen that enabled nearly 28,000 civilians to escape from ISIS-held territory.[31] White phosphorus also has useful capabilities as an incendiary weapon for offensive purposes. Protocol III to the Conventional Weapons Convention, also called the "Incendiary Protocol," establishes prohibitions on the use of incendiary weapons. The Protocol defines an incendiary weapon as "any weapon or munition which is primarily designed to set fire to objects or to cause burn injury to persons through the action of flame, heat, or combination thereof, produced by a chemical reaction of a substance delivered on the target." Examples include flame-throwers, rockets, grenades or bombs containing incendiary substances. The Protocol prohibits any attack on civilians or civilian objects using incendiary weapons and bans attacks by incendiary weapons on forests except when such forests are being used to conceal military objectives or combatants. Most important, Article 2 states:

> . . . 2. It is prohibited in all circumstances to make any military objective located within a concentration of civilians the object of attack by air-delivered incendiary weapons.
>
> 3. It is further prohibited to make any military objective located within a concentration of civilians the object of attack by means of incendiary weapons other than air-delivered incendiary weapons, except when such military objective is clearly separated from the concentration of civilians and all feasible precautions are taken with a view to limiting the incendiary effects to the military objective and to avoiding, and in any event to minimizing, incidental loss of civilian life, injury to civilians and damage to civilian objects.

Note that the Protocol is fairly limited in scope and does not prohibit the use of incendiary weapons outright, instead allowing for their use against military objectives and combatants.

Recent conflicts have included controversial uses of white phosphorus, including during the Battle of Fallujah and during Operation Cast Lead in Gaza. The United States first denied reports that it had used white phosphorus in Fallujah but then confirmed that it had used it for screening purposes and against military objectives. One description of the battle explained:

> [White phosphorus rounds] proved to be an effective and versatile munition. We used it for screening missions at two breeches and, later in the fight, as a potent psychological weapon against the insurgents in trench lines and spider holes when we could not get effects on them with [high explosive rounds]. We fired 'shake and bake' missions at the insurgents, using [white phosphorus] to flush them out and [high explosive rounds] to take them out.[32]

---

31. Alison Meuse, *U.S.-led Coalition Has Used White Phosphorus in Fight for Mosul, General Says*, NPR (June 13, 2017), https://www.npr.org/sections/parallels/2017/06/13/532809626/u-s-led-coalition-has-used-white-phosphorus-in-fight-for-mosul-general-says.

32. Robert Burns, *Pentagon Used White Phosphorus in Iraq*, WASH. POST (Nov. 16, 2005) (citing James T. Cobb et al., *The Fight for Fallujah*, Field Artillery, Mar./Apr. 2005, at 26).

QUESTIONS FOR DISCUSSION

1. Upon ratification of Protocol III in 2009, the United States issued the following reservation:

> The United States of America, with reference to Article 2, paragraphs 2 and 3, reserves the right to use incendiary weapons against military objectives located in concentrations of civilians where it is judged that such use would cause fewer casualties and/or less collateral damage than alternative weapons, but in so doing will take all feasible precautions with a view to limiting the incendiary effects to the military objective and to avoiding, and in any event to minimizing, incidental loss of civilian life, injury to civilians and damage to civilian objects.[33]

The reservation appears to place incendiary weapons on the same footing as other weapons, subject to the primary LOAC obligations of proportionality and precautions. Does the Protocol seek to create enhanced protections against such weapons? If so, does this reservation uphold the basic goals of the Protocol?

2. Protocol III to the Convention on Certain Conventional Weapons provides that a weapon that can have incidental incendiary effects can otherwise be excluded from the definition of an incendiary device if that same weapon is used "[as] illuminants, tracers, smoke or signaling systems." How can these valid uses be balanced with fundamental concerns for civilian safety and protection?

3. Use of white phosphorus in populated areas for illumination purposes sometimes leads to civilian casualties or injuries due to burning if civilians are hit by the incendiary fragments. Should the use of white phosphorus — even for legitimate military purposes — be banned altogether in civilian areas because of the inability to determine exactly how it will impact the civilian population?

6. *Unmanned Aerial Vehicles*

Unmanned aerial vehicles (UAVs), often called drones or remotely piloted aircraft, are used extensively for surveillance and reconnaissance, a critical piece of modern intelligence gathering and targeting determinations. UAVs are also commonly used to launch aerial attacks on targets within armed conflict and counterterrorism operations. A UAV is defined as:

> [a] powered, aerial vehicle that does not carry a human operator, uses aerodynamic forces to provide vehicle lift, can fly autonomously or be

---

33. *Declarations and Reservations: United States of America*, UNTC: Convention on Prohibitions or Restrictions on the Use of Certain Conventional Weapons Which May Be Deemed to Be Effectively Injurious or to Have Indiscriminate Effects (Jan. 21, 2009).

piloted remotely, can be expendable or recoverable, and . . . carr[ies] a lethal or nonlethal payload. Ballistic or semi ballistic vehicles, cruise missiles, and artillery projectiles are not considered unmanned aerial vehicles.[34]

"Within the current United States inventory, [UAVs] range in size from the Wasp and the Raven, at 38 inches long, both of which are 'launched' by being thrown in the air by hand, to the twenty-seven foot long Predator and the forty-foot long Global Hawk."[35] The most commonly used UAVs in the United States arsenal are the 36-foot-long MQ-9 Reaper and the MQ-1B Predator, both of which are designed for persistent intelligence, reconnaissance, and surveillance, as well as target acquisition and "destroy and disable" capabilities. Both systems are armed with Hellfire missiles. UAVs are not truly "unmanned," but rather remotely piloted. In fact, experts have noted that the operation of UAVs involve more people than F-16s or other piloted fighter planes. For example, beyond the pilot and the sensor operator, who operate the plane from a remote location, recoverable UAVs also involve launch and recovery teams, numerous intelligence analysts, and other legal and operational decision makers.

There is no specific treaty regulating the use of or applying to UAVs. Rather, they are governed by the same LOAC principles that regulate the use of any other weapon: indiscriminate weapons or weapons causing unnecessary suffering are prohibited. By either measure, UAVs pass muster. Armed UAVs fire Hellfire missiles and other similar munitions, all of which are also carried by or are similar to the weapons carried by piloted fighter aircraft. These missiles are not banned by any international agreement and do not manifest any characteristics that cause superfluous injury as understood in international law. In general, the precision-guided munitions UAVs carry and their extensive surveillance capabilities make them particularly discriminate weapons. With regard to distinction, proportionality, and precautions, UAVs now play a major role in the "pattern of life" assessment that is an essential ingredient of all planned targeting determinations. They can loiter over a target for hours, even days, providing a much more refined assessment of who is in the area and at what times—information critical to minimizing collateral damage. "Unmanned systems [therefore] seem to offer several ways of reducing the mistakes and unintended costs of war," such as using "far better sensors and processing power, allow[ing] decisions to be made in a more deliberate manner," and "remov[ing] the anger and

---

34. Joint Chiefs of Staff, Joint Pub. 1-02, Department of Defense Dictionary of Military and Associated Terms 577 (2011).

35. Chris Jenks, *Law from Above: Unmanned Aerial Systems, Use of Force, and the Law of Armed Conflict*, 85 N.D. L. Rev. 650, 653 (2009) (citing P.W. Singer, *Military Robots and the Laws of War*, The New Atlantis, Winter 2009, at 37-39).

emotion from the humans behind them."[36] Therefore, armed UAVs can easily be aimed at only military objectives and have effects that can be limited, as much as possible, to military objects, thus meeting the standards in Article 51(4) of Additional Protocol I.

QUESTIONS FOR DISCUSSION

1. A UAV pilot's life is never in jeopardy; in contrast, a dismounted soldier must make what could be a split-second decision regarding distinction. If the soldier makes the wrong decision it could cost him his life or the life of a civilian. Does this change how we analyze the lawfulness of the use of UAVs? Should it?

2. The combination of counterinsurgency strategy and UAV capabilities in Afghanistan has led to a growing perception that any civilian deaths are unlawful. Could the confluence of these two factors mean that proportionality in the context of UAV strikes will be reconfigured, in effect a recalibration of the relationship between military advantage and civilian casualties—away from "excessive" and towards "none"? Think back to the discussion about the overload of information in Chapter 9. What happens if the notion of "information reasonably available to the commander" becomes "perfect information"? Could proportionality become more of a strict liability standard of targeting analysis in which "zero casualties" is the standard?

3. With regard to the attacking party's obligations to take precautions, the actual choice of weapon is one component of the precautions a commander must take when launching an attack. Could there be situations in which that obligation would require using a weapon other than a UAV?

4. Outside of Afghanistan, most or all U.S. drone strikes were carried out by the CIA for many years, which meant that civilian personnel operated the UAVs. What are the legal consequences of civilians operating UAVs for combat operations? Are the civilian operators now lawful targets? Does this practice affect the legality of the strikes? Are civilian operators violating the law?

5. In the spring of 2018, the Israeli Defense Force (IDF) deployed commercially purchased "small drones" above the crowds of demonstrators and

---

36. P.W. Singer, *Military Robots and the Laws of War*, THE NEW ATLANTIS, Winter 2009, at 25, 37 (2009), *available at* http://www.thenewatlantis.com/publications/military-robots -and-the-laws-of-war. *See also* Anna Mulrine, *A Look Inside the Air Force's Control Center for Iraq and Afghanistan*, U.S. NEWS AND WORLD REPORT, May 29, 2008, http://www.usnews.com/ articles/news/world/2008/05/29/a-look-inside-the-air-forces-control-center-for-iraq-and -afghanistan.html (explaining how UAVs enable commanders to "establish a 'pattern of life' around potential targets—recording such things as the comings and goings of friends, school hours, and market times. Despite the distance, the real-time video feeds often give them a better vantage point than an Army unit has just down the street from a group of insurgents.").

Hamas operatives seeking to breach the border fence in Gaza. Some of the drones were equipped with tear gas canisters that could be dropped in order to disperse crowds. Is this a violation of LOAC? On at least one occasion, Palestinians in Gaza shot down the drones. Were the drones lawful targets of attack? Do these "small drones" need to be distinguishable from other commercially purchased drones used by human rights groups and journalists?

7. Cyber

Computer network attacks are now a dominant feature of any linked society, including distributed denial of service attacks, malware, worms, and many others. For example, in July 2008, a few weeks before the outbreak of hostilities between Russia and Georgia over the breakaway republic of South Ossetia, a series of distributed denial of service attacks overloaded and nearly shut down servers and websites in Georgia, including the website of Georgia's president at the time, Mikheil Saakashvili.[37] Cyber activity—cyber warfare, as often described—has ramifications across the application and implementation of LOAC and international law in general, from the categorization of cyber activity as an armed attack to the classification of armed conflict and identification of organized armed groups, to direct participation in hostilities and much more. As with other capabilities employed during armed conflict, the LOAC rules on lawful and unlawful weapons apply equally to cyber tools that constitute weapons, which requires an understanding of what is a cyber "means of warfare" and what is a cyber "method of warfare."

The word weapon generally refers to something used to cause bodily harm or physical destruction. A cyber weapon can therefore be understood as any cyber means used or designed to cause injury or death to persons or destruction of objects. Malware, for example, is malicious code used to disrupt or even paralyze a web application or even a computer's entire operating system, giving an attacker access to confidential information and the ability to spy through personal computers. Examples of malware include viruses, worms, Trojan horses, rootkits, ransomware, grayware, or keyloggers. A cyber method of warfare refers to how the cyber operation is carried out, in contrast to the specific cyber instrument or tool employed. Thus, in the case of "a botnet [used] to conduct a destructive distributed denial of service attack[,] the botnet is the means of cyber warfare while the distributed denial of service attack is the method of cyber warfare."[38] Perhaps the best-known cyber weapon is Stuxnet:

---

37. John Markoff, *Before the Gunfire, Cyberattacks*, N.Y. TIMES (Aug. 12, 2008).

38. TALLINN MANUAL 2.0 ON THE INTERNATIONAL LAW APPLICABLE TO CYBER OPERATIONS 453 (Michael N. Schmitt ed., 2017).

> Stuxnet is an extremely sophisticated computer worm that exploits multiple previously unknown Windows zero-day vulnerabilities to infect computers and spread. Its purpose was not just to infect PCs but to cause real-world physical effects. Specifically, it targets centrifuges used to produce the enriched uranium that powers nuclear weapons and reactors. . . . Despite its unparalleled ability to spread and its widespread infection rate, Stuxnet does little or no harm to computers not involved in uranium enrichment. When it infects a computer, it checks to see if that computer is connected to specific models of programmable logic controllers (PLCs) manufactured by Siemens. PLCs are how computers interact with and control industrial machinery like uranium centrifuges. The worm then alters the PLCs' programming resulting in the centrifuges being spun too quickly and for too long, damaging or destroying the delicate equipment in the process. While this is happening, the PLCs tell the controller computer that everything is working fine, making it difficult to detect or diagnose what's going wrong until it's too late.[39]

The Stuxnet worm caused the Iranian uranium centrifuges to spin out of control, eventually overheating and exploding.

In most cases, cyber weapons are developed for a single use (because once deployed, a cyber weapon can be detected, reproduced, or countered and therefore loses its value), which means that it can be difficult to offer a general statement about the lawfulness of a particular type of cyber weapon. Nonetheless, the same rules regarding unnecessary suffering and indiscriminate use or effects apply to cyber means and methods of warfare. A virus or other cyber weapon whose effects cannot be limited, but rather spread uncontrollably across civilian computer infrastructure or cause physical injury or harm that cannot be limited to lawful targets of attack, will be indiscriminate in the same manner as a kinetic weapon with the same shortcomings. The fact that most cyber weapons do not cause physical effects at all makes this analysis particularly challenging.

QUESTIONS FOR DISCUSSION

1. Many cyber operations do not involve a particular "thing" that could be considered a weapon at all, but rather "a smart human operator with an intuitive understanding of how the target system works and a knack for social engineering."[40] What should be reviewed for compliance with LOAC in such situations?

---

39. Josh Fruhlinger, *What Is Stuxnet, Who Created It and How Does It Work?*, CSOOnline. com, Aug. 22, 2017, https://www.csoonline.com/article/3218104/malware/what-is-stuxnet -who-created-it-and-how-does-it-work.html.

40. Gary D. Brown and Andrew O. Metcalf, *Easier Said Than Done: Legal Reviews of Cyber Weapons*, 7 J. Nat'l Sec. L & Pol'y 115, 124 (2015).

2. U.S. Air Force Instruction 51-4-2, *Legal Reviews of Weapons and Cyber Capabilities*, requires legal review of cyber weapons and cyber capabilities, thus seeking to address some of the challenges in identifying a cyber weapon. According to the Instruction, a "cyber capability requiring a legal review prior to employment is any device or software payload intended to disrupt, deny, degrade, negate, impair or destroy adversarial computer systems, data, activities or capabilities. Cyber capabilities do not include a device or software that is solely intended to provide access to an adversarial computer system for data exploitation."[41] Does this create greater clarity? Why might it be impractical?

3. What degree of knowledge about the likely effects of a cyber weapon does the commander need to have in order to assess whether it is lawful? Given the specialized technical knowledge required for cyber operations, is a commander equipped to make those decisions?

8. Autonomous Weapons

Autonomous weapons are weapons or weapons systems that have the capability to identify, select, and engage targets without intervention by humans in that decision-making process. The U.S. Department of Defense defines an autonomous weapons system as "a weapon system that, once activated, can select and engage targets without further intervention by a human operator. This includes human-supervised autonomous weapon systems that are designed to allow human operators to override operation of the weapon system, but can select and engage targets without further human input after activation."[42] Similarly, the ICRC explains that autonomous weapons are weapons that can "independently select and attack targets, i.e. with autonomy in the 'critical functions' of acquiring, tracking, selecting and attacking targets."[43] The development and potential use of such weapons—which some call "killer robots"—has sparked a heated debate about the legal, ethical and policy issues involved.

Weapons systems and weapons with some degree of autonomy have been in use for decades. For example, the United States and other countries have been deploying Patriot surface-to-air missile systems, "a missile defense system that automatically detects, and tracks targets before firing

---

41. Dep't of the Air Force, Air Force Instruction 51-402, Legal Reviews of Weapons and Cyber Capabilities 5 (2011).

42. U.S. Dep't of Defense Directive 3000.09, Autonomy in Weapons Systems 13-14 (2012).

43. Int'l Comm. Red Cross, Autonomous Weapons Systems: Technical, Military, Legal and Humanitarian Aspects 5 (2014).

interceptor missiles,"[44] since the 1970s. The Aegis Weapon System is a "ship-based system combining radar to automatically detect and track targets with various missile and gun systems."[45] Israel regularly deploys its Iron Dome missile defense, a ground-based air defense system that detects, assesses the trajectory and threat of, and intercepts incoming rockets, mortars, and artillery.[46]

The particular challenge that autonomous weapons systems pose lies not in the types of munitions they deliver (which also need to be lawful), but in the fact that such systems can select and engage targets without human involvement in an unstructured environment. Can weapons that act independently and do not have a human "in the loop" be lawful? Should they be? The three main types of autonomous weapons systems are generally described as:

- Human-in-the-loop or semi-autonomous systems: require a human to direct the system to select a target and attack it (an "open loop" system); examples are Predator or Reaper UAVs.
- Human-on-the-loop or human-supervised autonomous systems: select targets and attack them with human operator oversight; examples are the U.S. Navy's Phalanx Close-In Weapons System (CIWS) or Israel's Iron Dome.
- Human-out-of-the-loop or fully autonomous weapons systems: can attack without any human interface (a "closed loop" system); at present there are no examples in use.

Another way to characterize autonomous weapons is in terms of mission complexity. "Supervised" weapons have human operators making the decisions; "scripted" weapons carry out a "pre-planned script of the 'point, fire and forget' variety"; and "intelligent" systems are fully autonomous.[47]

Autonomous weapons systems do not appear to raise any specific questions regarding the prohibition on weapons calculated or of a nature to cause unnecessary suffering. Of course, if an autonomous weapons system deployed chemical weapons or blinding lasers or other prohibited weapons, the entire system would be unlawful as a result. But autonomy itself does not present any concerns regarding unnecessary suffering. With regard to the prohibition on weapons or weapons systems that cannot be directed at a specific military objective—that is, they are *per se* indiscriminate—autonomous

---

44. *Global Patriot Solutions*, RAYTHEON, http://www.raytheon.com/capabilities/products/patriot/.

45. *Aegis Weapon System*, AM.'S NAVY, http://www.navy.mil/navydata/fact_display.asp?cid=2100&tid=200&ct=2.

46. *Iron Dome Weapon System*, RAYTHEON, https://www.raytheon.com/capabilities/products/irondome.

47. Noel Sharkey, *Saying 'No!' to Lethal Autonomous Targeting*, 9 J. OF MIL. ETHICS 369, 377 (2010).

weapons have triggered intense debate. Those calling for a ban on the development and future use of such weapons systems argue that "[f]ully autonomous weapons would not have the ability to sense or interpret the difference between soldiers and civilians, especially in contemporary combat environments."[48] However, the inability to distinguish does not automatically render a weapons system unlawful. "Not every battlespace contains civilians or civilian objects. When they do not, a system devoid of any capacity to distinguish protected persons and objects from lawful military targets can be used without endangering the former."[49] Consider also the nature of modern technology, which has advanced to enable highly specific identification of objects and individuals through visual, audio, and other data analysis.

As with all other weapons, autonomous weapons must be used lawfully, that is, in accordance with the fundamental obligations of distinction, proportionality, and precautions. An autonomous weapons system must therefore be able to identify combatants or other fighters, and civilians directly participating in hostilities, and distinguish them from civilians who are protected from attack. It must be able to assess the military advantage from an attack and the expected civilian casualties likely to result and determine whether the civilian harm will be excessive. This application of the proportionality rule is where the greatest doubt lies regarding the ability of autonomous weapons systems to comply with LOAC. Although an autonomous system could likely engage in the same type of collateral damage estimation methodology (CDEM) that is used now to determine harm to civilians, assessing military advantage in a dynamic and rapidly changing conflict environment is much more difficult. "Given the complexity and fluidity of the modern battlespace, it is unlikely in the near future that, despite impressive advances in artificial intelligence, 'machines' will be programmable to perform robust assessments of a strike's likely military advantage."[50] The obligation to take precautions raises two issues: can an autonomous weapons system engage in the necessary precautions, and would the choice to deploy an autonomous weapons system at all need to be considered as part of the obligation to choose the means or method of attack likely to cause the least harm to civilians.

Finally, autonomous weapons introduce challenging questions about accountability, questions that simply do not arise with other weapons or weapons systems. The fact that a machine made the actual decision to identify and engage the target should not leave an accountability gap—enforcement and accountability for violations is an essential component of LOAC

---

48. Human Rights Watch, Losing Humanity: The Case Against Killer Robots 30 (2012).

49. Michael N. Schmitt, *Autonomous Weapons Systems and International Humanitarian Law: A Reply to the Critics*, Harv. Nat'l Sec. J. Features 11 (2013).

50. *Id.* at 20.

and ensuring effective implementation of the law and protection of persons, as discussed in greater detail in Chapter 11. But in the absence of a human being pulling the trigger or issuing an attack order, consider who should or could be held accountable if an autonomous weapons system violates LOAC. The commander who deploys the weapons system? The system programmer? The manufacturer?

QUESTIONS FOR DISCUSSION

1. One of the themes in the debate over autonomous weapons systems is the notion of "meaningful human control." Human Rights Watch and other organizations calling for a total ban on autonomous weapons systems interpret "meaningful human control" to mean that humans identify, select, and engage targets—meaning that there will be no fully autonomous weapons. The U.S. Department of Defense has directed that "[a]utonomous and semi-autonomous weapon systems shall be designed to allow commanders and operators to exercise appropriate levels of human judgment over the use of force."[51] Can you envision an autonomous weapons system that acts independently in target selection and engagement but nonetheless allows commanders to exercise appropriate levels of human judgment over the use of force? What might such "appropriate levels of human judgment" look like?

2. Should an autonomous weapons system be expected to perform better than humans? Soldiers and commanders are judged based on a standard of reasonableness, but is that a sufficient standard for examining the actions of a machine? What does reasonableness mean for a machine?

3. How should the decision to deploy an autonomous weapon or a post-hoc accountability process consider malfunctions, errors, breakdown, glitches, or other problems? What about the dangers of an adversary hacking into the weapons system?

4. Many argue that only a human should be allowed to take another human being's life, that "decisions to kill, injure, and destroy must not be delegated to machines, and that humans must be present in this decision-making process sufficiently to preserve a direct link between the intention of the human and the eventual operation of the weapon system."[52] In contrast, others advance an ethical argument for the use of autonomous weapons systems, asserting that "their potential precision and reliability might enable better respect for both international law and human ethical values, resulting in fewer adverse humanitarian consequences."[53]

---

51. U.S. Dep't of Defense Directive 3000.09, Autonomy in Weapons Systems 2 (2012).

52. Int'l Comm. Red Cross, *Ethics and Autonomous Weapon Systems: An Ethical Basis for Human Control?* 1-2 (Apr. 3, 2018).

53. *Id.* at 1.

5. The debate around unmanned aerial vehicles has raised important questions about whether the availability of unmanned weapons systems has made it "easier" for leaders to use force by removing or decreasing concerns about boots on the ground and casualties. Do autonomous weapons exacerbate those concerns? What about at the individual level?

6. As you think about the implementation of LOAC's fundamental principles and obligations of distinction, proportionality, and precautions, what do you see as the greatest challenges in programming an autonomous weapon system to comply with the law and fulfill LOAC's basic goals?

B. TACTICS

Warfare is the Way (Tao) of deception. Thus, although [you are] capable, display incapability to them. When committed to employing your forces, feign inactivity. When [your objective] is nearby, make it appear as if it is distant; when far away, create the illusion of being nearby.[54]

Rick Beyer

Freddy Fox Goes to War

Princeton Alumni Weekly, Mar. 21, 2012

Three U.S. Army jeeps roared through the small Luxembourg village, just a few miles from the front lines near the German border. It was early September 1944, three months after D-Day. The vehicles in front and back bristled with guards and machine guns. The one in the middle bore the distinctive red license plate of a major general. In the backseat sat a ramrod figure sporting a magnificent military moustache and general's stars. All three jeeps were clearly identified by their markings as belonging to the 6th Armored Division. The convoy pulled up to a tavern run by a suspected Nazi collaborator. The general and his lanky, bespectacled aide strode inside. With the help of their bodyguards, they "liberated" six cases of fine wine, loading them onto the general's jeep. The little convoy then took off, leaving the seething proprietor plenty of incentive to get word to the Germans about what he had just witnessed: that the American 6th Armored was moving in.

But in fact, the whole bit was a carefully choreographed flim-flam. The 6th Armored Division was far away. The commanding presence in the back seat was no general, but a mustachioed major playing king for a day. . . . The unit to which [Freddy] Fox was assigned in January 1944 was unique in the history of the U.S. Army. Officially, it was called the 23rd

54. Sun-Tzu, The Art of War 79 (Ralph D. Sawyer trans., 1994) (220 B.C.).

Headquarters Special Troops, but eventually it became known as the Ghost Army. Its mission was to stage frontline deceptions designed to dupe Hitler's legions — and avoid getting killed by the audience while doing so. Instead of artillery and heavy weapons, it was equipped with truckloads of inflatable tanks, a world-class collection of sound-effects records, and a corps of radio operators trained in the art of impersonation. "Its complement was more theatrical than military. . . . It was like a traveling road show that went up and down the front lines impersonating the real fighting outfits. . . ."

Once they landed in France, the men of the 23rd would be expected to conjure up phony convoys and phantom divisions to mislead the enemy about the strength and location of American units. To pull this off, they were equipped with truckloads of inflatable tanks, trucks, artillery, jeeps, and even airplanes — enough to simulate two divisions. Each lightweight dummy could be set up and taken down in about 20 minutes, and from several hundred yards away looked indistinguishable from the real thing. The men also had specially outfitted halftracks, carrying speakers with a range of 15 miles, that could project the sounds of armored columns moving in the darkness. Dozens of radio trucks could create faux networks that sounded utterly like the real thing to eavesdropping enemy officers. In theory, they could impersonate a division of 15,000 soldiers holding a spot in the line, while the fighting division was moving someplace else to launch a surprise attack. . . .

From June 1944 to March 1945, the Ghost Army ranged across Europe, staging more than 20 full-scale deceptions, each choreographed down to the smallest detail. The men frequently operated within earshot of the front lines, and took casualties when they succeeded too well in drawing enemy fire to their position. Three men were killed and nearly two dozen wounded over the course of the war. In September 1944, they helped hold a critical part of Gen. George Patton's line along the Moselle River. That December, they barely escaped capture by the Germans in the Battle of the Bulge. In March 1945 the unit executed its most dazzling deception, misleading the Germans about where two American divisions would cross the Rhine River.

This was the Ghost Army's grand finale, and the men of the 23d went all out, puffing themselves up to look like 30,000. Radio operators following a minute-by-minute script set the stage, creating the illusion that a convoy was moving to the point of the fake attack. Hundreds of fake tanks were inflated overnight and clustered around farmhouses in the villages of Anrath and Dülken. Enclosed farmyards were turned into phony repair depots, and a grove converted into a decoy motor pool. A phony airstrip complete with dummy aircraft was laid out in a farmer's field. Sonic trucks projected the sounds of bridge-building all night, as if engineering battalions behind the line were assembling the pontoon structures needed to bridge the Rhine.

On March 24, 1945, with Winston Churchill and Dwight Eisenhower among those looking on, two divisions of the 9th Army crossed the Rhine with few casualties. The 23d earned a special commendation from the 9th Army commander, Lt. Gen. William Simpson—a glowing review of the final performance of the Ghost Army.

---

1. Ruses

Good faith is an essential component of LOAC and LOAC compliance. As a result, LOAC prohibits fighting in the enemy's uniform, feigning surrender or willingness to parley, or misusing protected emblems. Not all deception is prohibited, however. Ruses, for example, are legitimate tools of warfare; the Lieber Code states that "deception in war is admitted as a just and necessary means of hostility . . . consistent with honorable warfare."[55] The Trojan Horse is, of course, a classic ancient example of a successful ruse. The Hague Regulations affirmed the legality of ruses, and Article 37(2) of Additional Protocol I explains that "Ruses of war are not prohibited. Such ruses are acts which are intended to mislead an adversary or to induce him to act recklessly but which infringe no rule of international law applicable in armed conflict and which are not perfidious because they do not invite the confidence of an adversary with respect to protection under that law." Ruses can be an integral part of any military strategy and success; indeed, "in the period after the first world war[,] ruse as manifested in mimicry tactics, camouflaging, deception and psychological combat were regarded as an essential feature of modern warfare."[56] Examples of ruses include camouflaging a tank so that the enemy does not see it, using disinformation to lead the enemy to believe that the attack will take place at a different time or a different place, faking retreat, or faking communications to suggest the presence of multiple units or a larger force. Indeed, military deception is an essential part of military strategy and tactics.

The U.S. defines military deception (MILDEC) as "those actions executed to deliberately mislead adversary decision makers as to friendly military capabilities, intentions, and operations, thereby causing the adversary to take specific actions (or inactions) that will contribute to the accomplishment of the friendly mission."[57] The four basic MILDEC techniques are:

---

55. Francis Lieber, War Department, Instructions for the Government of Armies of the United States in the Field art. 101 (1863).

56. Dieter Fleck, *Ruses of War and Prohibition of Perfidy*, 13 Mil. L. & L. War Rev. 269, 270 (1974).

57. Joint Chiefs of Staff, Joint Publication 3-14.3: Joint Doctrine for Military Deception I-1 (2006).

- *Feints:* an offensive action involving contact with the adversary conducted for the purpose of deceiving the adversary as to the location and/or time of the actual main offensive action.
- *Demonstrations:* a show of force where a decision is not sought and no contact with the adversary is intended. A demonstration's intent is to cause the adversary to select an unfavorable course of action.
- *Ruses:* a cunning trick designed to deceive the adversary to obtain friendly advantage. It is characterized by deliberately exposing false or confusing information for collection and interpretation by the adversary.
- *Displays:* the simulation, disguising, and/or portrayal of friendly objects, units, or capabilities in the projection of the MILDEC story. Such capabilities may not exist, but are made to appear so (simulations).

Perhaps one of the most successful ruses in modern history was the deception and disinformation operation that preceded the Allied invasion of Normandy on D-Day in June 1944.

> "The greatest hoax in military history" was the description officially applied to the scheme of deception used to induce the Germans to believe that the invasion of the Continent in June, 1944, was coming in the Pas de Calais and not in Normandy. It was carried out by a force of 105 aircraft of the R.A.F., by 34 ships of the Royal Navy, and by 'R.C.M.' (Radio Counter-Measures). On the night of 5 June, 18 small ships of the Navy steamed towards Cap d'Antifer to give the impression of an intended landing, while a bomber squadron, No. 617, under G/Capt. G.L. Chesire, V.C., circled over them, dropping bundles of "Window," the thin metallised strips which produce false echoes on the enemy's radar screens and so confuse their plotting. Another squadron, No. 218, with 16 ships, made a similar feint towards Boulogne, and other methods of deception were practiced elsewhere along the Channel. The result was that the enemy were led to believe that convoys were moving to points other than that at which the landing was in fact made with complete success and without opposition by air or sea.[58]

U.S. forces engaged in a similar deception operation in advance of the 1991 Persian Gulf war, using "[a]ggressive ground force patrolling, artillery raids, amphibious feints and ship movements, and air operations" as part of a coordinated effort "to convince Iraq that the main attack would be directly into Kuwait, supported by an amphibious assault."[59]

---

58. J.M. Spaight, Air Power and War Rights 185 (1947).
59. Conduct of the Persian Gulf War: Final Report to Congress 344 (1992).

> ## SCREEN SHOT!
>
> In *The Eagle Has Landed,* Oberst (Colonel) Kurt Steiner is sent to England on a covert mission to kidnap Prime Minister Winston Churchill and bring him to Germany. He and his men arrive in the small English town where Churchill is to attend a meeting. Dressed as Polish soldiers to avoid detection, they ostensibly engage in training maneuvers while they await Churchill's arrival and the decisive moment. When one of the soldiers rescues a young girl from death under a water wheel, he is killed and his Polish uniform gets pulled off, revealing the German uniform he wore underneath. The operation is foiled, and a firefight ensues.
>
> 1. Was wearing the Polish uniforms to conceal their true identity a violation of LOAC? Did wearing the German uniforms under the Polish uniforms change the nature of the violation?
> 2. What if the German soldiers had engaged in hostilities while wearing the Polish uniforms?

QUESTIONS FOR DISCUSSION

1. Operation Mincemeat was another brilliant and critically important Allied deception operation during World War II.

> [It] was designed to convince the enemy high command that the objectives of the impending Allied offensive in the Mediterranean were Sardinia and the Peloponnesus rather than Sicily. The plan itself was simply but highly imaginative. With painstaking care a counterfeit letter from "Archie Nye" of the British War Office in London was drawn up . . . [i]ndicating that a feint against Sicily would be a deception maneuver to screen an invasion of Sardinia. . . . To get this letter into Axis hands, British intelligence obtained with great difficulty the body of a service man who had been a victim of pneumonia. . . . With a courier's briefcase realistically chained to the wrist, the body was cast adrift at a predesignated spot where tide and current would carry it to [the Axis-controlled] shore. . . . The information reached the Germans who accepted it as authentic.[60]

2. In September 2001, the first U.S. Special Forces in Afghanistan dressed in the indigenous attire of the Northern Alliance forces they supported. Is dressing in the uniform of friendly forces an acceptable ruse of war?

3. Part of the D-Day deception operation involved actual bombing raids on Pas de Calais and surrounding areas. Can kinetic force be used as a

---

60. Albert N. Garland & Howard M. Smyth, Sicily and the Surrender of Italy 64-65 (1993).

disinformation campaign? How would you consider the basic obligations of distinction, proportionality, and precautions?

4. Consider how modern technology affects the use of ruses. Could the Allies have disseminated a fake video of their landing force at Pas de Calais? Imagine that you are trying to defend two key bridges from enemy attack. Could you disseminate photos showing civilians on one of the bridges for the purpose of diverting the enemy's attack to a different bridge where you have concentrated your anti-aircraft capabilities?

2. *Perfidy*

Perfidy, in contrast, is a particularly insidious violation of LOAC and contravenes the very notions of honor and chivalry on which much of LOAC is based. The traditional definition of perfidy is "[t]o kill or wound treacherously individuals belonging to the hostile nation or army," as set forth in Article 23(b) of the 1907 Hague Convention (IV). Suicide bombers disguising themselves as civilians to gain closer access to military checkpoints or other locations are a prime example of killing "treacherously." Article 37(1) of Additional Protocol I offers a more comprehensive formulation, forbidding killing, capturing, or injuring the enemy "by resort to perfidy." In particular, the Protocol states that "[a]cts inviting the confidence of an adversary to lead him to believe that he is entitled to, or is obliged to accord, protection under the rules of international law applicable in armed conflict, with intent to betray that confidence, shall constitute perfidy." Additional Protocol I thus added capture to the existing prohibitions against killing or wounding by perfidious means.[61]

The Commentary to the Additional Protocols explains that "[t]he central element of the definition of perfidy is the deliberate claim to legal protection for hostile purposes. The enemy attacks under cover of the protection accorded by humanitarian law of which he has usurped the signs."[62] Thus, when fighters intentionally disguise themselves as civilians in order to lead soldiers on the opposing side to believe they need not take defensive action to guard against attack, they commit perfidy. The indirect consequence of such actions is that civilians are placed at greater risk, since soldiers previously attacked by fighters disguised as civilians may be more

---

61. The United States, which is not a party to Additional Protocol I, does not accept capture as part of the customary international law definition of perfidy. *See* UNITED STATES DEPARTMENT OF DEFENSE LAW OF WAR MANUAL § 5.22.2.1 (2015 rev'd 2016).

62. CLAUDE PILLOUD, YVES SANDOZ, CHRISTOPHE SWINARSKI & BRUNO ZIMMERMAN, COMMENTARY ON THE ADDITIONAL PROTOCOLS OF 8 JUNE 1977 TO THE GENEVA CONVENTIONS OF 12 AUGUST 1949 435 (1987) (explaining that the "definition is based on three elements: inviting the confidence of an adversary, the intent to betray that confidence (subjective element) and to betray it on a specific point, the existence of the protection afforded by international law applicable in armed conflict (objective element).").

likely to view those who appear to be civilians as dangerous and respond accordingly. Another example is feigning death or injury in order to stage an ambush or attack. In each of these scenarios, perfidy directly undermines the very essence of LOAC:

> Perfidy degrades the protections and mutual restraints developed in the interest of all Parties, combatants, and civilians. In practice, combatants find it difficult to respect protected persons and objects if experience causes them to believe or suspect that the adversaries are abusing their claim to protection under the [law of war] to gain a military advantage.[63]

Additional Protocol I also prohibits as perfidy the use of distinctive emblems — whether the Red Cross, Red Crescent, or Red Crystal, or the United Nations emblem — to invite the adversary's confidence and then launch an attack. The key difference between a ruse and perfidy is that the latter must involve a deliberate attempt to benefit from the protections of LOAC by inducing the other side to believe that one is protected under LOAC. As a result, it is not the act of hiding from the enemy or making oneself less noticeable that is the essence of perfidy, but the use of what appears to be protected status.

SCREEN SHOT!

The movie *Hacksaw Ridge* (2016) depicts the heroism of U.S. Army combat medic, and conscientious objector, Corporal Desmond Doss on the Maeda Escarpment during the battle for Okinawa. After U.S. forces were pushed off the ridge in a counterattack that forced them to retreat, Corporal Doss stayed behind and saved seventy-five soldiers in one day. In the movie, Corporal Doss (Andrew Garfield) is moving from soldier to soldier looking for wounded to help when the Japanese soldiers start patrolling amongst the dead and dying looking to kill any survivors. In one scene, the Japanese are closing in on Doss after he finds a partially buried wounded soldier. Doss covers the wounded man with dirt to hide him and then rolls a dead soldier on top of himself and holds still. After the Japanese soldiers pass by Doss gets up, uncovers the wounded man, and pulls him to safety.

- Is this a ruse or perfidy?
- Is this allowed under LOAC?
- What, if any, limitations are there to such actions? Could Doss shoot the Japanese soldier from his hiding place under the dead soldier?

---

63. INTERNATIONAL AND OPERATIONAL LAW DEPARTMENT, THE JUDGE ADVOCATE GENERAL'S SCHOOL, OPERATIONAL LAW HANDBOOK 24 (2010).

David Rohde

Perfidy and Treachery

CRIMES OF WAR (Roy Gutman & David Rieff eds., 1999)

The Dutch UN peacekeepers and the NATO jets the UN Security Council had promised would protect Srebrenica had put up scant resistance. The men knew that they were earmarked for death and they had fled, joining a three-mile-long, single-file column of fifteen thousand mostly unarmed men trying to make their way across thirty miles of enemy territory to reach Bosnian government lines. Over and over again along the line of march, hundreds had been killed in a series of well-planned ambushes by Bosnian Serb forces. After that, Bosnian Serb soldiers wearing stolen UN uniforms and driving stolen UN vehicles announced over megaphones that that they were UN peacekeepers and that they were prepared to oversee the Bosnian Muslims' surrender and guarantee they would not be harmed. Disoriented and exhausted, many Bosnian Muslims fell for the lie. It was only after they had surrendered that they discovered their fatal mistake. For in surrendering, they were going to their deaths. Those whom the Serbs got their hands on were killed by firing squad.

QUESTIONS FOR DISCUSSION

1. Are there occasions when the components of military deception could overlap with perfidy? On Iwo Jima, when the Japanese "often yelled 'Corpsman!' in order to shoot them, 1st Battalion was told to yell 'Tallulah!' if they needed medical attention. Most of the Marines would have recognized that the code word (with all the difficult to pronounce L's for the Japanese) was the first name of a popular actress, Ms. Tallulah Bankhead."[64] Could it be argued that the Japanese were merely engaging in another form of military deception equivalent to what the 23d Headquarters Special Troops conducted?

2. Colonel Otto Skorzeny of the Germany Army was prosecuted by a U.S. Military Court after World War II for improper use of American military uniforms — his unit had a special mission to infiltrate behind Allied lines and wore American uniforms. The court acquitted the defendants of all charges, most likely because they did not fight in the enemy uniforms. At the time, it was not a violation of LOAC to wear an enemy uniform; the violation occurred if one fought in the enemy uniform. That changed with Additional Protocol I, which states in Article 39, "it is prohibited to make use of the flags or military emblems, insignia or uniforms of adverse Parties

---

64. HUGH AMBROSE, THE PACIFIC 379 (2010).

while engaging in attacks or in order to shield, favour, protect or impede military operations." Would it be a violation to dress as a civilian to pass through the enemy lines to escape without engaging the enemy?

3. Abd al-Rahmin al-Nashiri, the mastermind behind the U.S.S. *Cole* bombing in October 2000, was charged with perfidy (in addition to murder and a number of other crimes) before the military commissions tasked with prosecuting some of the detainees at Guantanamo Bay. The charge sheet in al-Nashiri's case reads:

> Specification: In that Abd al Rahim Hussayn Muhammad al NASHIRI . . . , an alien unprivileged enemy belligerent subject to trial by military commission, did, in or around Aden, Yemen, on or about 12 October 2000, in the context of and associated with hostilities, invite the confidence and belief of one or more persons onboard USS COLE (DDG 67), including but not limited to then FN Raymond Mooney, USN, that two men dressed in civilian clothing, waving at the crewmembers onboard USS COLE (DDG 67), and operating a civilian boat, were entitled to protection under the law of war, and intending to betray that confidence and belief, did thereafter make use of that confidence and belief to detonate explosives hidden on said civilian boat alongside USS COLE (DDG 67), killing 17 Sailors of the United States Navy . . . and injuring one or more persons, all crewmembers onboard USS COLE (DDG 67). . . .[65]

The charge rests, at base, on the existence of an armed conflict at the time of the attack. What if you determine that there was no armed conflict at the time?

4. What happens when perfidy is used for what appears to be humanitarian purposes?

In July 2008, Colombian military personnel posing as members of an international aid organization rescued fifteen hostages from their FARC captors who had imprisoned the group in jungle camps for more than five years—with some held for as long as ten years. The hostages included three U.S. contactors, Marc Gonsalves, Thomas Howes, and Keith Stansell (employees of Northrop Grumman Corp.), who were captured in February 2003 after their single engine drug-surveillance plane crashed in the jungles of southern Colombia. A former Colombian presidential candidate, Ingrid Betancourt, was also among the fifteen rescued. The other eleven hostages were Colombian police and soldiers. Operation Jaque was the result of Colombian military intelligence's successful infiltration of the communications network of the FARC. The plan was designed to trick the local commander, Gerardo Antonio Aguilar, who was responsible for the hostages' captivity, into believing that the FARC's supreme leader, Alfonso Cano, had

---

65. Charges and Specifications in the case of United States of America v. Abd Al Rahim Hussayn Muhammad Al Nashiri, Charge 1: Violation of 10 U.S.C. §950t(17), Using Treachery or Perfidy, September 15, 2011.

ordered that these high-value hostages be sent to him. Aguilar, who was known as Cesar, had been told—through fake radio communications and courier messages—that an aid organization would transport the hostages. At the appointed time and place, two helicopters loaded with Colombian military personnel disguised as civilians arrived to pick up the hostages. Two of the military personnel pretended to be a reporter and his cameraman, others reportedly wore Che Guevara t-shirts, and one wore a bib over his jacket that had a red cross displayed on it with the French words "Comité International Genève"—translated as "International Committee Geneva." Cesar and his lieutenant, Alexander Farfan, also known as Enrique Gafas, decided that they would like to present the hostages personally to their leader, and they boarded the helicopter. Shortly after takeoff, both rebels were overpowered and subdued and the hostages were then told that they were free. Initially, the Colombians denied the reports that any Red Cross insignia were used, but when faced with video evidence (the soldier posing as a news cameraman was indeed filming the entire rescue as it unfolded), the government apologized for the "last minute" action of one rescuer.

The misuse of the Red Cross emblem provoked little criticism. Would the goal of rescuing hostages provide an excuse for an otherwise unlawful use of the emblem? Does perfidy apply only in international armed conflict? The rescue team that planned the mission later stated that they felt it was important to include someone from the "Red Cross" as part of their deception because previous missions run by real aid groups always included a Red Cross representative. Does the fact that they felt the use of the Red Cross emblem was critical to achieving their mission change any of your answers above? The Colombian government routinely denounces LOAC violations by the FARC, and by the smaller guerrilla army known as the National Liberation Army, for abusing the Red Cross symbols (e.g., using ambulances to transport fighters). Should that impact the analysis?

5. When a military unit sends its medevac helicopter to rescue wounded members of the unit who are pinned down under enemy fire, could the helicopter carry other members of the combat unit and drop them off first to provide backup for another unit in trouble? What if it covers up the Red Cross on the side of the helicopter? Is doing so a violation of LOAC? If not, what are the consequences of doing so?

6. Another area in which perfidy questions arise is the practice of naval deceptive lighting. Deceptive lighting has been described as the practice of "changing the configuration of lights aboard a warship so that—to a casual or distant viewer—the ship appears to be something other than it really is."[66] Different classes and sizes of ships at sea carry different lights, which help make them identifiable at night. If a warship changes its normal

---

66. Matthew G. Morris, *"Hiding Amongst a Crowd" and the Illegality of Deceptive Lighting*, 54 NAVAL L. REV. 235, 236 (2007).

lighting configuration, it may be able to deceive an enemy regarding its location, identity, status, and intentions. Consider different ways and reasons a military vessel might use deceptive lighting. What if a warship deceptively lights itself to appear as a fishing vessel? What about rigging the lighting to pass through a blockade unchallenged? Or if the vessel uses deceptive lighting to pass through a blockade or hostile checkpoint only to then attack the enemy forces?

PART V

IMPLEMENTATION AND ENFORCEMENT

CHAPTER 11

ACCOUNTABILITY FOR VIOLATIONS OF LOAC

As in other legal regimes, enforcement and accountability for violations of the law of armed conflict are key to effective implementation of and adherence to the law. LOAC—as discussed earlier—involves obligations between states, obligations between individuals, and obligations of states to individuals. As a result, responsibility for violations rests on more than one level. The international law of state responsibility governs the identification of and response to LOAC violations by states. As a general principle, any breach of international law by a state creates an obligation for that state to make reparations for the wrong. The International Court of Justice has held that states are responsible for making reparations—through compensation or other means—for violations of LOAC. But merely relying on state responsibility is not sufficient to punish or deter crimes, especially LOAC violations, committed by individuals. LOAC thus provides for individual criminal responsibility for violations—and was one of the first branches of international law to do so. Criminal prosecution, whether at the national or international level, plays a critical deterrent role, but will not be sufficient on its own, of course, to ensure protection of civilians. Enhanced implementation, training, and other mechanisms to ensure compliance with the law before and during armed conflict is essential to promote LOAC's key objectives: protect civilians, minimize unnecessary suffering, and enable effective military operations.

A fair and just system of military discipline has historically been viewed as the best way to achieve these goals. The literally "life and death" need to complete the mission successfully while controlling soldiers in battlefield operations and at the same time protecting noncombatants and minimizing property damage relies on discipline as the essential complement to effective training. The Romans had one of the first formalized military justice codes. Special military magistrates were charged with enforcing rules governing acts such as cowardice, desertion, mutiny, and committing a violent act against a superior officer. Even after the breakup of the Roman Empire, successor nations often followed its system of military justice. As the early Middle Ages evolved in Europe, military codes were used to dispense justice during war and peace. For example, William the Conqueror invaded

England in 1066 with formal, written rules for his Norman army operating on English soil. In 1621, King Gustavus of Sweden, often referred to as the "Father of Military Justice," issued 167 articles for the maintenance of order in an attempt to change the contemporary image of soldiers as barbarians and opportunists. Gustavus' written military code combined ideals of chivalry with the need to maintain order and discipline in his army. As modern warfare evolved, large armies were required to fight and be stationed in distant locations for longer periods of time. The greater destructive capacity of modern armies also demanded greater discipline.

Every code of military justice faces the complex task of balancing the need to maintain good order and discipline with the need to preserve the rights of the soldier. A military justice system that is perceived as unjust by military members or the non-military citizens of a country will ultimately hurt the morale of any military unit, significantly detract from the operational readiness of that unit, and undermine the confidence that the voting public has in the military and its leaders.

FORUM: COURTS-MARTIAL

In the United States, the court-martial is the oldest system of justice, even pre-dating the Declaration of Independence and the Constitution. During World War II, the number of courts-martial increased dramatically and alleged abuses of individual rights were widespread, setting the stage for major federal law reform and the passage of the Uniform Code of Military Justice (UCMJ) in 1951.

Under the UCMJ, any offense committed by a service member on active duty, regardless of location, is triable by court-martial. UCMJ jurisdiction is thus worldwide, on and off duty, on and off base. This approach is markedly different from many other nations, whose jurisdiction does not go beyond their national borders, making prosecutions of alleged overseas wrongdoing significantly more difficult. The UCMJ is a complete set of criminal laws, covering many crimes punishable under civilian law (such as murder, rape, assault, and larceny), as well as military offenses that affect good order and discipline (such as dereliction of duty and disobeying a lawful order). U.S. military courts-martial are the preferred forum for LOAC prosecutions of U.S. service members. Article 18 of the UCMJ vests general courts-martial with jurisdiction to try "any person who by the law of war is subject to trial by military tribunal."[1] However, the accused will be charged with

---

1. Uniform Code of Military Justice, art. 818(a), *reprinted in* MANUAL FOR COURTS-MARTIAL UNITED STATES, at A2-1 (2019).

the common law crimes under the UCMJ (e.g., several counts of murder), not for war crimes or crimes against humanity. Courts-martial are also used for trying enemy prisoners of war for pre-capture LOAC violations or crimes committed during captivity; Article 102 of the Third Geneva Convention mandates that POWs be tried in the same or comparable forum as members of the detaining power's armed forces.

Three types of courts-martial can be convened by a commanding officer: general, special, or summary. The higher the level of court-martial, the greater the authority needed to convene it. A summary court-martial consists of one commissioned officer and may only try enlisted persons for minor offenses with a maximum punishment of one-month confinement. A special court-martial (SPCM) consists of a military judge, defense counsel, prosecutor, and at least three panel members as the jury. A SPCM is for crimes with a maximum punishment of one-year confinement, forfeitures of pay, a reduction in rank, and bad conduct discharge. A general court-martial (GCM) has the same participants as a SPCM but must have at least five panel members as the jury. A GCM's maximum punishment is based upon the maximum allowed by the law for each offense charged, up to and including the possibility (for only the most severe offenses) of death as a punishment. A violation of LOAC involving "grave breaches" would most likely be prosecuted at a GCM and violations of "simple breaches" could potentially be prosecuted at a SPCM.

The twentieth century has brought a focus on international criminal responsibility for atrocities, to fill the gap left by inadequate or nonexistent national prosecutions in far too many conflict situations. The notion of responsibility for violations of international law is not a new one; arguably the first recorded international war crimes trial was the trial of Peter von Hagenbach in 1474 for rape, murder, and illegal taxation. War crimes, crimes against humanity and genocide are the major violations of LOAC that demand accountability. War crimes are often considered "retail" or "one-offs" because usually an individual or a small group commits these violations against another individual or small group. In contrast, crimes against humanity are more "wholesale"; the perpetrators commit such crimes in a widespread or systematic manner as part of a broader policy of attacking the civilian population. Genocide involves the specific intent to eliminate members of a group *because* of their race, religion, ethnicity, or nationality. It is important to note that crimes against humanity and genocide can be committed during peacetime—they do not require a nexus to armed conflict. All parties to the 1948 Genocide Convention and the 1949 Geneva Conventions have an obligation to suppress all acts of genocide and war crimes. In many cases, violations of LOAC will be prosecuted under domestic law rather than international law; for example, as noted above, the U.S. prosecutes military personnel for any substantive offense under the UCMJ rather than try them for war crimes.

In the past few decades, there has been an extraordinary development in international criminal jurisprudence and options for holding perpetrators accountable for atrocities — tribunals for Yugoslavia, Rwanda, Sierra Leone, East Timor, Cambodia, and the International Criminal Court. The aftermath of the September 11th attacks also brought the resurgence of military commissions as a tool for the United States to try captured enemies in the course of the conflict with al Qaeda and other terrorist groups. The choice of forum can affect the implementation and enforcement of LOAC in a variety of ways: the types of crimes, who to prosecute, and the balance of international and domestic law. This chapter addresses individual criminal responsibility for violations of LOAC, in particular for the major international crimes of war crimes, crimes against humanity, and genocide.

A.   PURPOSES

At the most basic level, prosecution of LOAC violations accomplishes the same retributive and deterrent effect as prosecution for ordinary domestic crimes: the perpetrator is punished and, in most cases, removed from society through incarceration, thus unable to repeat his or her crimes. In the arena of armed conflict and mass atrocities (as discussed below, genocide and crimes against humanity can be committed outside of an armed conflict), there are several broader thematic purposes, just as domestic criminal law has multiple purposes.

> The regular prosecution of war crimes would have an important preventive effect, deterring violations and making it clear even to those who think in categories of national law that [LOAC] is law. It would also have a stigmatizing effect, and would individualize guilt and repression, thus avoiding the vicious circle of collective responsibility and of responsibility and punishment at the level of the individual. It shows that the abominable crimes of the twentieth century were not committed by nations but by individuals. By contrast, as long as the responsibility was attributed to States and nations, each violation carried within it the seed of the next war. That is the civilizing and peace-seeking mission of international criminal law favouring the implementation of [LOAC].[2]

2. Marco Sassoli et al., How Does Law Protect in War? Cases, Documents and Teaching Materials on Contemporary Practice in International Humanitarian Law 396 (3d ed. 2011).

Individual criminal responsibility thus completes the continuum of efforts to regulate the conduct of war and provide protection for both civilians and combatants or fighters during armed conflict: dissemination, implementation, and enforcement.

In 1945, the prosecution of captured German military and civilian leaders at Nuremberg was the first modern effort to impose international criminal responsibility on those responsible for massive and horrific violations of international law. Justice Robert Jackson of the United States, who took leave from the U.S. Supreme Court to serve as the lead prosecutor at Nuremberg, opened the trial with these now-famous words.

> The privilege of opening the first trial in history for crimes against the peace of the world imposes a grave responsibility. The wrongs which we seek to condemn and punish have been so calculated, so malignant, and so devastating, that civilization cannot tolerate their being ignored, because it cannot survive their being repeated. That four great nations, flushed with victory and stung with injury stay the hand of vengeance and voluntarily submit their captive enemies to the judgment of the law is one of the most significant tributes that Power has ever paid to Reason. . . .
>
> This principle of personal liability is a necessary as well as logical one if international law is to render real help to the maintenance of peace. An international law which operates only on states can be enforced only by war because the most practicable method of coercing a state is warfare. . . . Hence, the principle of the criminality of aggressive war is implemented by the [London] Charter with the principle of personal responsibility. . . . Crimes are always committed only by persons. While it is quite proper to employ the fiction of responsibility of a state or corporation for the purpose of imposing a collective liability, it is quite intolerable to let such a legalism become the basis of personal immunity. . . . Modern civilization puts unlimited weapons of destruction in the hands of men. It cannot tolerate so vast an area of legal irresponsibility. . . .
>
> The real complaining party at your bar is Civilization. . . . Civilization asks whether law is so laggard as to be utterly helpless to deal with crimes of this magnitude by criminals of this order of importance. It does not expect that you can make war impossible. It does expect that your juridical action will put the forces of international law, its precepts, its prohibitions and, most of all, its sanctions, on the side of peace, so that men and women of good will, in all countries, may have "leave to live by no man's leave, underneath the law."[3]

International criminal prosecutions also seek the truth in order to assign criminal responsibility and promote accountability, much like domestic prosecutions. The truth has significantly broader purposes, such as to contribute to the healing of societies in the transition to peace. Upon

3. Proceedings, Second Day, Wednesday, 21 November 1945, *in* II Trial of Major War Criminals before the International Military Tribunal 98, 98-99, 149-150, 153-155 (1947).

establishment of the ICTY, then–U.S. Secretary of State Madeleine Albright stated, "Truth is the cornerstone of the rule of law, and it will point towards individuals, not peoples, as perpetrators of war crimes. And it is only the truth that can cleanse the ethnic and religious hatreds and begin the healing process."[4] Most judgments issued by international tribunals—whether the *ad hoc* tribunals, the hybrid tribunals or the ICC—thus take on a storytelling role as well, as part of the truth-seeking aspect of international criminal accountability. One central purpose of the ICTY's founding, therefore, was to promote reconciliation through justice, by using the unimpeachable factual record of a trial, an authoritative record of the origins and nature of the violence.

INVESTIGATING MASS ATROCITIES IN IRAQ—THE ROAD TO JUSTICE

As our convoy turned off the highway, the scene in front of us was devastating. People were streaming in by the thousands on foot to a large field in the distance. As we approached, we could see fathers and sons digging up the ground with shovels and their bare hands. Old clothing and bones were littered about, and a stench was in the air. Mothers, grandmothers and daughters, dressed in black, traditional attire, were sobbing and moaning by gravesites, many of them hugging old, dirty clothes they believed were the last remnants of their missing loved ones. This was the Mahawil mass grave site in May 2003, where thousands of Iraqi Shi'a from Hillah region were massacred in the spring of 1991 by Saddam Hussein's regime as part of the 1991 Shi'a Uprising. It was the first major mass grave uncovered in Iraq after the overthrow of the regime, but we all knew there were hundreds, if not thousands, more of these sites waiting to be uncovered throughout the country.

As the senior U.S. official addressing human rights issues in Iraq, I found it difficult to know how best to approach these grieving Iraqis. They had waited for decades to say a final goodbye and ensure a proper Muslim burial for family members who were taken away to this field where they were shot in a firing squad or buried alive. Some were dead on arrival, after torture or killing somewhere else. The locals recall the sound of bulldozers, which were digging large pits in the sandstone to create mass graves.

4. Madeleine K. Albright, U.S. Perm. Rep. U.N., *UN Security Council Adopts Resolution 827 on War Crimes Tribunal* (May 25, 1993), *in* 4 Dep't St. Dispatch 417, 417-418 (1993).

Several media reports described the situation at Mahawil as chaotic, and some international advocates were urging the U.S. military to seize control of the site and secure it to preserve evidence of atrocities for future accountability. But I could tell quickly that it was too late to secure this site or to remove grieving families from a place where they were seeking much-needed closure. Instead, I spoke to the young Iraqi man who appeared to be in charge, Dr. Rafid al-Husseini. He was providing death certificates and Muslim burials for those remains that could be identified using the rudimentary methods available, such as identity cards, unique clothing, or objects near the bones.

While Dr. al-Husseini's methodology does not ensure 100% accuracy in identification, the local Iraqis were satisfied. Many international advocates, however, were not. They continued to press for full DNA accountability for all of the mass graves in Iraq to ensure accuracy in the identification of remains. An expensive, high caliber DNA program in Bosnia had reached a certain level of success in both identifying remains and ensuring adequate forensic evidence for war crimes trials. The Bosnia program was based on a much smaller population with identified next of kin, and still took years to complete the forensic exhumations and match the remains to family members in a computer database. In contrast, Iraq's estimated mass graves would outnumber Bosnia's by tenfold. Remains were scattered around the country, with few records, and in many cases, no living next of kin from whom to take samples. The Iraqi crimes also dated back decades. But most importantly, the Iraqis we encountered had one thing in common — they believed that they had waited long enough under Saddam's regime for this day to come. Now was the time to say a final goodbye to their missing loved ones and ensure that they were buried according to their faith. Even with proper donor funding, the Iraqis did not have a decade longer to wait.

So, instead of seeking large-scale military assistance to secure sites throughout the country, I began to work closely with Dr. Rafid, as he was known, who had become inspirational for his efforts at Mahawil and had started his own nongovernmental organization (NGO) for the Preservation of Mass Grave Sites in Iraq. He helped design a methodological "Iraqi" way to balance this need for large-scale rapid exhumation of mass gravesites around the country with the need to preserve critical evidence for future war crimes trials. Our Office of Human Rights and Transitional Justice (OHRTJ) at the Coalition Provisional Authority (CPA) had already been working closely with Iraqi lawyers and members of the interim Governing Council on the establishment of a tribunal to hold members of the regime accountable for their atrocities. The documentary and physical evidence collected to date, coupled with the well-known history of brutality under Saddam's regime, showed at least eight major campaigns or periods involving atrocities, including Halabjah, the Anfal Campaign, the Shi'a Uprising, the Marsh Arabs, Torture and Killing of Political Actors or Religious Minorities (including Iraqi Christians and Jews, etc.), the Iran-Iraq War, the Invasion of Kuwait, and the 1999 Shi'a Uprisings. For every one of these atrocities where mass graves were believed to exist, we wanted to ensure that one to three mass gravesites were forensically exhumed to the highest international standard for possible use in a war crimes tribunal. This would total around 16-24 mass gravesites for full forensic exhumation, in contrast with hundreds if we had followed the plan some international advocates were endorsing. This was a number that was achievable, could be funded by existing donors and could occur quickly.

Accordingly, the United Kingdom seconded to our office a team of forensic experts who traveled the country identifying mass grave sites that would meet the criteria for full forensic exhumation (e.g., they were not previously overrun, the remains appeared completely intact, and they were representative in nature of the major atrocity that had occurred). The remaining mass gravesites around the country were to be handled in a similar manner as Mahawil, providing closure and proper Muslim burials for the maximum number of Iraqis as quickly as possible. Dr. Rafid, and later the newly established Iraqi Ministry of Human Rights, worked to ensure that the local communities had the assistance they needed to conduct these local exhumations.

Later that year, the Iraq High Tribunal, a domestic Iraqi war crimes tribunal, was established to hold members of the regime accountable for war crimes and violations of Iraqi law. Mass grave site evidence collected according to this plan was ultimately used in 2007 and 2008 to secure convictions against Ali Hassan al Majid ("Chemical Ali") and other regime officials for the genocide of approximately 182,000 Kurdish people during the Anfal Campaign, and for the 1991 Shi'a Uprising massacres, which had resulted in the Mahawil mass grave site. Chemical Ali was hanged for these crimes in January 2010. Saddam Hussein would also have been tried for these events if he had not previously been sentenced to death and executed for ordering the Dujail massacre.

—*Sandra Hodgkinson, Senior Advisor to the Ministry of Human Rights and Co-Director of the Office of Human Rights and Transitional Justice, Iraq, 2003-2004*

B.   GRAVE BREACHES REGIME

The 1949 Geneva Conventions establish an extensive catalog of obligations under LOAC. Some are fundamental to the protection of civilians during armed conflict, such as the prohibition on deliberate or indiscriminate attacks, the prohibition against torture, and many others. Others occupy a more technical arena, such as the obligation in Article 59 of the Third Geneva Convention to keep cash taken from POWs in separate accounts, for example. As the Commentary explains, "there are violations of certain detailed provisions of the Geneva Convention which would constitute minor offences or mere disciplinary faults which as such could not be punished to the same degree."[5] For the most serious crimes, the Geneva Conventions created the category of grave breaches, which mandate a comprehensive system of prevention, investigation, and enforcement. In comparable provisions, each of the four Geneva Conventions of 1949 establishes a three-part obligation for states with regard to grave breaches (First Geneva Convention, art. 49, Second Geneva Convention, art. 50, Third Geneva Convention, art. 129, and Fourth Geneva Convention, art. 146).

1.   Aut Dedere Aut Judicare

The central components of the grave breaches regime, in terms of state obligations, are: (1) suppress, (2) search for, and (3) prosecute or extradite. In effect, the grave breaches regime is based on the principle of *aut dedere aut judicare*, which means extradite or punish, and the notion that some crimes are so heinous as to grant all states the right to punish them. Grotius first formulated this concept in 1625, writing:

> The fact must be recognized that kings, and those who possess rights equal to those kings, have the right of demanding punishment not only on account of injuries committed against themselves or their subjects, but also on account of injuries which do not directly affect them but excessively violate the law of nature or of nations in regard to any persons whatsoever.[6]

Some crimes, such as piracy and slavery, were historically considered to be crimes against mankind that triggered universal jurisdiction. In 1949, the drafters of the Geneva Conventions, recognizing the need to have a system of enforcement that would transcend domestic and interstate political

---

5. INT'L COMM. RED CROSS, COMMENTARY ON THE GENEVA CONVENTION (IV) RELATIVE TO THE PROTECTION OF CIVILIAN PERSONS IN TIME OF WAR 597 (Oscar M. Uhler & Henri Coursier eds., 1958).

6. HUGO GROTIUS, THE LAW OF WAR AND PEACE: DE JURI BELLI AC PACIS LIBRI TRES 526-528 (James B. Scott ed., Francis W. Kelsy trans., 1925) (1625).

challenges, sought to create a system of enforcement that would be as robust as possible. This enforcement system thus stretches from the obligation to pass legislation criminalizing all grave breaches, to the active duty to search for perpetrators, to the obligation to arrest and prosecute wrongdoers.

Jurisdiction over grave breaches is universal jurisdiction: a state exercising jurisdiction over an individual accused of a grave breach need not have any connection to the defendant, the victim, the conflict, the territory on which the crime occurred, or any other aspects of the crime. The essence of universal jurisdiction is that the most serious crimes are ultimately offenses against the international community and all states, providing the requisite justification and interest for all states to prosecute alleged offenders. Each of the four Geneva Conventions sets forth crimes against persons protected in those conventions that constitute grave breaches, including, for example, willful killing, torture, or inhuman treatment; hostage-taking; compelling a POW or protected person to serve in the forces of a hostile power; unlawful confinement; or willfully depriving a POW or protected person free and fair trial rights set forth in the Conventions.[7]

The grave breaches regime in the four Geneva Conventions focused almost exclusively on the treatment of persons protected in those conventions: wounded, sick, shipwrecked, prisoners of war, and protected persons. In 1977, Additional Protocol I added to the list of grave breaches in two ways—it expanded the category of persons protected against grave breaches and it added an extensive list of grave breaches drawn directly from the Protocol's provisions governing the conduct of hostilities and the protection of the civilian population during conflict. Article 85(2) of Additional Protocol I thus adds the following new categories of persons or objects protected under the Protocol: persons who have taken part in hostilities and have fallen into the power of an adverse party under Article 44; persons who have taken part in hostilities under Article 45; refugees and stateless persons under Article 73; wounded, sick, and shipwrecked as expanded under Article 8; and medical and religious personnel, medical units and medical transports as categorized in Article 8. Article 85(3) and (4) then provide a list of additional acts that constitute grave breaches.

QUESTIONS FOR DISCUSSION

1. Some additional crimes not listed in the grave breaches provisions of the Conventions or the Additional Protocols are considered to be serious violations of LOAC based on customary international law or other conventional law, such as the conscription or enlistment of children under the age of 15 or the use of such children in hostilities.

---

7. *See* First Geneva Convention, art. 50; Second Geneva Convention, art. 51; Third Geneva Convention, art. 130; Fourth Geneva Convention, art. 147.

2. Consider the distinction between grave breaches and other violations of LOAC (often termed "simple breaches"). What is the value of having certain acts bear the additional opprobrium of being labeled "grave breaches"? Does the fact that technical and other seemingly lesser violations of LOAC merit less attention and less criminal responsibility detract from efforts to enforce those obligations? Here, think about the role of LOAC during conflict, as a tool for regulating conduct during hostilities, in addition to after conflict, when accountability is the primary consideration.

FORUM: THE *AD HOC* TRIBUNALS

U.N. Security Council Resolution 827 established the **International Criminal Tribunal for the Former Yugoslavia** on May 25, 1993. Under Chapter VII of the U.N. Charter, the Resolution "establish[ed] an international tribunal for the sole purpose of prosecuting persons responsible for serious violations of international humanitarian law committed in the territory of the former Yugoslavia." The ICTY's core purposes include bringing perpetrators to justice and providing justice to the victims; deterring further crimes; and contributing to the restoration of peace by promoting reconciliation. The ICTY Statute provides jurisdiction over four groups of crimes committed on or after January 1, 1991 in the territory of the former Yugoslavia: grave breaches of the Geneva Conventions of 1949, violations of the laws or customs of war, genocide, and crimes against humanity. When the ICTY ceased operations on December 31, 2017, it had indicted 161 people and completed 130 cases. Of the concluded proceedings, eighteen individuals were acquitted, ninety-one have been sentenced, five are in custody at the detention unit, thirteen have been transferred to a national jurisdiction for trial, and thirty-seven defendants either had their indictments withdrawn or died before or during trial.[8] In 2010, in preparation for the ICTY's closure at the end of 2017, the United Nations Security Council created the International Residual Mechanism for Criminal Tribunals (MICT) to perform essential functions of the ad hoc tribunals, including appeals, reviews, tracking fugitives, protection of witnesses, contempt proceedings, and supervision of sentences. There are currently two retrials pending before the MICT.

In 1994, genocide exploded in Rwanda, leading to the deaths of approximately 800,000 people, mostly ethnic Tutsis. On November 8, 1994, acting under Chapter VII of the U.N. Charter, the U.N. Security

---

8. U.N. Comm'n Serv., *Key Figures of ICTY Cases, available at* https://www.icty.org/en/cases/key-figures-cases.

Council enacted Resolution 955 establishing the *International Criminal Tribunal for Rwanda* "for the sole purpose of prosecuting persons responsible for genocide and other serious violations of International Humanitarian Law committed in the territory of Rwanda and Rwandan citizens responsible for genocide and other such violations committed in the territory of neighbouring States, between 1 January 1994 and 31 December 1994." Like the ICTY Statute, the ICTR Statute provides for jurisdiction over genocide, crimes against humanity, and violations of Common Article 3 of the Geneva Conventions. The ICTR ultimately indicted ninety-three individuals and completed proceedings for eighty-two accused. Of the concluded proceedings, fourteen were acquitted, sixty-one were sentenced, and four cases were referred to national jurisdictions. Six accused are still at large.[9] The ICTR closed on December 31, 2015.

2. Accountability in Non-International Armed Conflict

The grave breaches regimes in the four Geneva Conventions and Additional Protocol I only apply during international armed conflict, because only international armed conflict triggers the application of the full panoply of the Geneva Conventions and Additional Protocol I. Neither Common Article 3 nor Additional Protocol II contains any statements regarding grave breaches. Over the past few decades, however, a general consensus has developed recognizing that 1) violations of the fundamental protections in Common Article 3 entail individual criminal responsibility, and 2) other serious violations of the law of internal armed conflict are also similar to serious violations of the laws and customs of international armed conflict. In particular, both *ad hoc* tribunals faced challenges to jurisdiction over atrocities committed during internal conflict. Where gaps exist in the law related to such internal, or non-international, armed conflict, both the ICTR and ICTY have drawn directly from customary international law related to international armed conflict and applied this to internal armed conflict. In its first case, the ICTY faced the question of whether the jurisdiction to prosecute violations of the laws or customs of war, set forth in Article 3 of the ICTY Statute, applied equally in non-international armed conflicts. After an exhaustive analysis of the customary rules of LOAC applicable to non-international armed conflicts and the historical development of the regulation of hostilities in such conflicts, the ICTY held that individual criminal responsibility attaches for violations of LOAC in non-international armed conflicts. The Tribunal affirmed that the "[p]rinciples and rules of

9. *Key Figures of Cases*, INTERNATIONAL CRIMINAL TRIBUNAL FOR RWANDA, https://unictr .irmct.org/en/cases/key-figures-cases.

humanitarian law reflect 'elementary considerations of humanity' widely recognized as the mandatory minimum for conduct in armed conflicts of any kind. No one can doubt the gravity of the acts at issue, nor the interest of the international community in their prohibition."[10]

The establishment of the ICTR in 1994 — to prosecute genocide and other atrocities in an entirely internal conflict — formed an important backdrop to the ICTY's deliberations in the *Tadić* case. A few years after the *Tadić* jurisdiction decision, the Appeals Chamber of the ICTY reaffirmed in another case that violations of Common Article 3 entail individual criminal responsibility, solidifying the international community's efforts to hold perpetrators of atrocities accountable, regardless of the type of conflict. As the Appeals Chamber in that case stated, "in light of the fact that the majority of the conflicts in the contemporary world are internal, to maintain a distinction between the two legal regimes and their criminal consequences in respect of similarly egregious acts because of the difference in nature of the conflicts would ignore the very purpose of the Geneva Conventions, which is to protect the dignity of the human person."[11]

QUESTIONS FOR DISCUSSION

1. One essential question regarding accountability for LOAC violations in non-international armed conflict involves the obligations of non-state parties under LOAC. Such groups have not signed the Geneva Conventions, the Additional Protocols, or any other treaties. The strongest answer is that LOAC not only creates obligations for states, but also creates both rights and obligations for individuals. Thus, "[t]reaty norms applicable in internal armed conflicts create rights and obligations for rebels, as for any other citizen of the states which have ratified international humanitarian law treaties."[12] Customary international law principles have the same force.

2. International tribunals have enforced international accountability for non-state actors as a result. The Special Court for Sierra Leone held that "it is well settled that all parties to an armed conflict, whether States or non-State actors, are bound by international humanitarian law, even though only States may become parties to international treaties."[13]

3. Very few internal conflicts — as a percentage of all the recent or ongoing conflicts — ultimately involve international prosecutions for atrocities.

10. Prosecutor v. Tadić, Case No. IT-94-1, Decision on Defence Motion for Interlocutory Appeal on Jurisdiction ¶ 129 (Int'l Crim. Trib. for the Former Yugoslavia Oct. 2, 1995).

11. Prosecutor v. Delalić, Case No. IT-96-21-A, Appeals Judgment ¶ 172 (Int'l Crim. Trib. for the Former Yugoslavia Feb 20, 2001).

12. Eve La Haye, War Crimes in Internal Armed Conflicts 120 (2008).

13. Prosecutor v. Sam Hinga Norman, Case No. SCSL-2004-14-AR72(E), Decision on Preliminary Motion Based on Lack of Jurisdiction (child recruitment) ¶ 22 (May 31, 2004).

However, this proportion is slowly increasing due to the ICC's investigations and prosecutions of crimes committed during internal conflicts. Some States have established courts or other accountability mechanisms to try perpetrators from internal conflicts. Is there a value for international criminalization of atrocities when prosecutions occur domestically?

4. The conflict in Syria poses one of the most intractable challenges in the international system — and at present offers little prospect for accountability for any of the parties. The United Nations Security Council has attempted, and failed, to refer the situation in Syria to the International Criminal Court. In December 2016, the U.N. General Assembly established the International, Impartial and Independent Mechanism to Assist in the Investigation and Prosecution of Persons Responsible for the Most Serious Crimes Under International Law Committed in the Syrian Arab Republic since March 2011 (commonly referred to as the IIIM). The Mechanism is not a tribunal and does not have authority to prosecute crimes. Its purpose is to collect and analyze evidence received from states or gathered through its own missions. What impact do you think the Mechanism can or will have? What is the value of documentation and evidence gathering if there is a possibility that few, if any, prosecutions will ever take place?

5. Two other significant investigative mechanisms created recently are the United Nations Investigative Team to Promote Accountability for Crimes Committed by Da'esh/ISIL (UNITAD) and the Independent Investigative Mechanism for Myanmar (IIMM). In 2017, the U.N. Security Council created UNITAD to establish an investigative team to support domestic accountability efforts by collecting, preserving, and storing evidence of acts that might amount to war crimes, crimes against humanity, and genocide committed by ISIL (ISIS) in Iraq between June 2014 and December 2017. With respect to atrocities committed in Myanmar, the United Nations Human Rights Council established the IIMM (also called the "Myanmar Mechanism") in September 2018 to collect evidence and prepare files for criminal prosecution. The Human Rights Council routinely establishes Fact Finding Missions (FFMs) and Commissions of Inquiry (COI) to gather pertinent evidence of significant human rights violations.

C. PROSECUTING WAR CRIMES

War crimes are reprehensible on moral, ethical, or religious grounds, on the grounds that they constitute violations of legal norms, result in injury to the innocent and defenseless, degrade a belligerent's purposes and principles, weaken discipline in one's own military forces, leave the violators with a sense of guilt or . . . social sanction, injure one's relations with other nations, and may provoke reprisals by one's opponents. The laws governing the conduct of armies in the field have both practical and ethical roots. They are both reasonable and humane.[14]

War crimes are acts that violate LOAC and trigger penal accountability. One of the key distinctions between "wartime" and "peacetime" is that certain acts that would be criminal during peace are not criminal during armed conflict, such as the killing of a lawful combatant or the destruction of a legitimate military objective. Nonetheless, as discussed throughout earlier chapters, LOAC provides extensive regulation of the treatment of persons and the conduct of hostilities—war crimes are those acts that continue to be criminal during armed conflict. As noted above, there are some technical violations of LOAC that do not constitute war crimes, such as the failure to comport with notification requirements regarding prisoners of war, for example. States need to take action to ensure that their personnel comply with such legal obligations, but the violation thereof does not constitute a crime with individual accountability. The most frequently cited definition of war crimes appears in the 1945 London Charter establishing the International Military Tribunal at Nuremberg:

> War crimes: namely violations of the laws and customs of war. Such violations shall include, but not be limited to, murder, ill-treatment or deportation to slave labour or for any other purpose of civilian population of or in occupied territory, murder or ill-treatment of prisoners of war or persons on the seas, killing of hostages, plunder of public or private property, wanton destruction of cities, towns or villages, or devastation not justified by military necessity.

As the International Military Tribunal stated, these crimes "were already recognized as War Crimes under International Law. They were covered by Articles 46, 50, 52, and 56 of the Hague Convention of 1907, and Articles 2, 3, 4, 46, and 51 of the Geneva Convention of 1929. That violations of these provisions constituted crimes for which the guilty individuals were punishable is too well determined to admit of argument."[15]

FORUM: INTERNATIONAL CRIMINAL COURT

The movement to create the **International Criminal Court** began in earnest in the 1990s and in July 1998, 160 countries and numerous NGOs participated in the Rome Conference negotiations to establish the ICC. 120 nations voted in favor of the Rome Statute of the ICC and the treaty entered into force upon the 60th ratification on July 1, 2002.

---

14. PETER KARSTEN, LAW, SOLDIERS, AND COMBAT xv (1978).

15. *International Military Tribunal (Nuremberg), Judgment and Sentences, 1946*, 41 AM. J. INT'L L. 172, 248 (1947).

123 countries are now States Parties to the Rome Statute. One of the ICC's central—and unique—features is the system of *complementarity*, according to which the ICC only has jurisdiction if states with jurisdiction over the relevant crimes are unwilling or unable to exercise such jurisdiction. The ICC itself makes the "unwilling or unable" determination when required.

The ICC has jurisdiction over genocide, crimes against humanity, war crimes, and the crime of aggression. Among international tribunals, the crime of aggression is unique to the Rome Statute. Although the Rome Statute does not define the crime of aggression, the Review Conference at Kampala in June 2010 established a definition of the crime; in December 2017, the Assembly of State Parties adopted a resolution to activate the ICC's jurisdiction over the crime of aggression as of July 17, 2018. For all crimes, the ICC can only exercise jurisdiction if:

- the accused is a national of a State Party or other state accepting the jurisdiction of the court;
- the crimes took place on the territory of a State Party or other state accepting jurisdiction of the court; or
- the U.N. Security Council refers the situation to the court, regardless of the nationality of the accused or the location of the crimes.

In all situations, the ICC's jurisdiction begins on July 1, 2002, when the Rome Statute entered into force, or on the date the Statute entered into force for the state in question if it ratified the Statute later.

As of May 2021, the ICC has thirty cases arising out of fourteen situations (Uganda, Kenya, Mali, Democratic Republic of the Congo, Darfur, Central African Republic I and II, Libya, Georgia, Burundi, Bangladesh/Myanmar, Palestine, Afghanistan, and Côte d'Ivoire), and eight preliminary examinations. The court has issued thirty-five arrest warrants and nine summonses to appear, and seventeen individuals have been detained and appeared before the court. The court has issued verdicts in eight cases, with ten defendants convicted (five for contempt) and four acquitted. Thirteen accused remain at large and charges against three accused were dropped due to their deaths.[16]

The Rome Statute of the ICC is the first international instrument to set forth a detailed and exhaustive list of specific war crimes for both international and non-international armed conflict. Article 8 separates the list of war crimes into several categories. The first category, applicable in international armed conflict, is grave breaches of the four Geneva Conventions. The Rome

---

16. *Facts and Figures*, International Criminal Court, https://www.icc-cpi.int/about.

Statute then provides a list of twenty-six additional war crimes, described as "[o]ther serious violations of the laws and customs applicable in international armed conflict, within the established framework of international law," including deliberate attacks against civilians or civilian objects; destruction of property not justified by military necessity; perfidy; attacks on United Nations peacekeeping personnel; use of unlawful weapons; attacks on religious, cultural, or historic objects or hospitals; rape and other sexual violence; use of child soldiers; or subjecting individuals to humiliating and degrading treatment. The framework of Article 8 thus differentiates between grave breaches and "other serious violations" of LOAC. Although all of the crimes listed constitute war crimes, not all war crimes are grave breaches, a "distinction [that] is not important in the context of the ICC Statute because the Statute does not stipulate different consequences for the two categories, [but] is relevant for the national implementation of international humanitarian law."[17] The grave breaches provisions of the Geneva Conventions and Additional Protocol I provide for mandatory universal jurisdiction over grave breaches—states must fulfill their obligations to suppress, search for, and extradite or prosecute perpetrators of such abuses. For other serious violations of LOAC, states can exercise universal jurisdiction but are not obligated to do so.

Building directly on the jurisprudence of the *ad hoc* tribunals with regard to individual criminal responsibility for LOAC violations in non-international armed conflicts, the Rome Statute sets forth two additional lists of war crimes specific to such conflicts. The first list, in Article 8(2)(c), covers "serious violations of article 3 common to the four Geneva Conventions of 12 August 1949, namely, any of the following acts committed against persons taking no active part in the hostilities, including members of armed forces who have laid down their arms and those placed *hors de combat* by sickness, wounds, detention or any other cause":

(i) Violence to life and person, in particular murder of all kinds, mutilation, cruel treatment and torture;

(ii) Committing outrages upon personal dignity, in particular humiliating and degrading treatment;

(iii) Taking of hostages;

(iv) The passing of sentences and the carrying out of executions without previous judgement pronounced by a regularly constituted court, affording all judicial guarantees which are generally recognized as indispensable.

Although slightly more limited in number than the war crimes codified in Article 8(2)(b)—other serious violations in international armed conflict—Article 8(2)(e) provides a nearly identical list of "[o]ther serious

---

17. Knut Dörmann, Elements of War Crimes Under the Rome Statute of the International Criminal Court 128 (2003).

violations of the laws and customs applicable in armed conflicts not of an international character, within the established framework of international law. . . .”

QUESTIONS FOR DISCUSSION

1. Why might some crimes appear in the Rome Statute with regard to international armed conflicts but not non-international ones?

2. Article 8(2)(d) of the Rome Statute specifically states that the previous provision, setting forth war crimes that are violations of Common Article 3, “does not apply to situations of internal disturbances and tensions, such as riots, isolated and sporadic acts of violence or other acts of a similar nature.” Interestingly, Article 8(2)(f), which follows the second non-international armed conflict list of war crimes, adds the additional caveat that Article 8(2)(e) “applies to armed conflicts that take place in the territory of a State when there is protracted armed conflict between governmental authorities and organized armed groups or between such groups.” Does the addition of the second sentence with regard to “other serious violations” of LOAC in non-international armed conflicts restrict the range of conflicts in which the ICC has jurisdiction over those crimes?

The ICC Elements of Crimes delineates four foundational elements describing the subject-matter jurisdiction for war crimes: the victims were protected under one or more of the Geneva Conventions, including Common Article 3; the perpetrator was aware of the factual circumstances that established that protected status; the conduct took place in the context of and was associated with either an international or non-international armed conflict (depending on the situation and the crime charged); and the perpetrator was aware of factual circumstances that established the existence of an armed conflict.[18] These foundational elements raise two questions: did the crime occur within the context of an armed conflict, and was the victim a person protected under the applicable LOAC? Another relevant question involves the status of the perpetrator; that is, whether war crimes can be committed only by members of the armed forces or by civilians as well.

The ICC has generally followed the jurisprudence of the ICTY with regard to the nexus required between the crimes charged and the underlying armed conflict:

> In determining whether or not the act in question is sufficiently related to the armed conflict, the Trial Chamber may take into account, *inter alia,* the following factors: the fact that the perpetrator is a combatant; the fact

18. *See id.*

that the victim is a non-combatant; the fact that the victim is a member of the opposing party; the fact that the act may be said to serve the ultimate goal of a military campaign; and the fact that the crime is committed as part of or in the context of the perpetrator's official duties.[19]

Armed conflict produces chaos, a shortage of law enforcement in many cases, and other ingredients that facilitate the growth of crime. But not all crimes are necessarily war crimes—imagine a bank robbery or other "ordinary crime" that happens to take place during an armed conflict. At the same time, the crime does not have to be explicitly linked to a particular battle or military operation either, a point the ICC emphasized in its first case, *Prosecutor v. Lubanga*. In the Decision on Confirmation of Charges, the ICC followed the same approach as above, finding that "the armed conflict must play a substantial role in the perpetrator's decision, in his or her ability to commit the crime or in the manner in which the conduct was ultimately committed."[20]

Beyond the nexus to the armed conflict, questions may remain regarding the status of both the victims and the perpetrators. The underlying components of the war crimes listed in Article 8(2)(a) and Article 8(2)(c) depend on the victim being a person protected in some way under the Geneva Conventions or Common Article 3. For the former, the person must therefore be a protected person under the Fourth Geneva Convention or fall into the protected categories of one of the first three Geneva Conventions (wounded, sick, shipwrecked, or POW). For the latter, the victim or victims must be *hors de combat* as understood in Common Article 3—that is, not actively participating in hostilities. As a result, the foundational questions of whether there was an international armed conflict, which would trigger the protected persons regime of the Fourth Geneva Convention, and the nature of the victims, specifically whether they fit within the category of protected persons set forth in Article 4 of the Fourth Geneva Convention, are essential.

The Rome Statute, the Geneva Conventions or other treaties do not set forth a list or class of perpetrators of war crimes. Anyone can commit war crimes during an armed conflict. Indeed, as the ICTY Prosecutor stated in one of the ICTY's early cases, "it is not even necessary that the perpetrator be part of the armed forces, or be entitled to combatant status in terms of the Geneva Conventions, to be capable of committing war crimes during international armed conflict."[21] The ICTR Appeals Chamber similarly

19. Prosecutor v. Germain Katanga and Mathieu Ngudjolo Chui, Case No. ICC-01/04-01/07, Decision on the Confirmation of Charges ¶ 382 (Sept. 30, 2008).

20. Prosecutor v. Thomas Lubanga Dyilo, Case No. ICC-01/04-01/06, Decision on Confirmation of Charges ¶ 287 (Jan. 29, 2007).

21. Kurt Dörmann, Elements of War Crimes Under the Rome Statute of the International Criminal Court 22 (citing Prosecutor v. Delalić, IT-96-21-T, Prosecution's Response to Defendant's Motion, ¶3.25).

rejected any such requirement in the *Akayesu* case, emphasizing that "international humanitarian law would be lessened and called into question if it were to be admitted that certain persons be exonerated from individual criminal responsibility for a violation of common Article 3 under the pretext that they did not belong to a specific category."[22]

In both international and non-international armed conflict, war crimes fall into three main categories: offenses against persons requiring particular protection; crimes against property and other rights; and prohibited methods of warfare. Another approach to the types of war crimes is to focus on the nature of the conduct, broadly speaking. Thus, the ICRC highlights two categories of war crimes: first, conduct that endangers protected persons or objects, which is a thematic approach that mirrors the first two categories above; and second, conduct that breaches important values, such as desecration of the dead, humiliating treatment, or recruitment of child soldiers.[23] The idea of criminalizing conduct that breaches important values is a direct outgrowth of the central importance of the principle of humanity and the role that it plays in the application of LOAC and the regulation of combat. Some war crimes that fit within the notion of a breach of important values are those that involve conduct that is only criminal during armed conflict, like perfidy or other acts of treachery.

QUESTIONS FOR DISCUSSION

1. In the summer of 2012, Ansar Dine, an al Qaeda-linked militant group in northern Mali, destroyed several ancient shrines and mausoleums in Timbuktu, declaring them un-Islamic. The sites were long identified as UNESCO World Heritage sites. Prior to the shrines' destruction, the long-simmering conflict in Mali between the government and the Tuareg rebels (Azawad National Liberation Movement, or MNLA) exploded into renewed fighting after several years of intermittent violence and peace negotiations. In March 2012, disaffected Malian military officers overthrew the government in an accidental coup. Tuareg rebels then captured portions of northern Mali and declared an independent state of Azawad in April 2012. At the same time, during the spring and summer of 2012, Ansar Dine also launched attacks against Malian government installations. In 2016, Ahmad al Faqi al Mahdi, a leader of Ansar Dine, pleaded guilty to the war crime of intentionally destroying religious or cultural objects (Article 8(2)(e)(iv)). Does it matter that, unlike the MNLA, Ansar Dine was not fighting for the secession of northern Mali but instead for the institution

---

22. Prosecutor v. Akayesu, Case No. ICTR-96-4-A, Appeals Judgement ¶ 443 (Int'l Crim. Trib. for Rwanda June 1, 2001).

23. Jean-Marie Henckaerts & Louise Doswald-Beck, 1 Customary International Humanitarian Law 569-570 (2005).

of Sharia law throughout Mali? Was the fact that the destruction took place during the armed conflict a sufficient nexus?[24]

2. How should the nexus requirement be applied in situations where extensive violent crime occurs either as part of or alongside an armed conflict? In some situations, such as Mexico, governments engage in long-running and comprehensive campaigns against organized crime. Where such violence creates an armed conflict, would any murder or unlawful act committed by members of the criminal enterprise constitute a war crime? Would it need to be committed in furtherance of the armed conflict? How should such determinations be made? Now consider a situation in which organized crime flourishes during an armed conflict, but the criminal organization is not directly a party to the conflict. How would your analysis change regarding international criminal accountability for acts by members of that organization?

3. After World War II, both the Nuremberg tribunals and the International Military Tribunal for the Far East addressed a wide range of perpetrators. In addition to military officers and government leaders, the tribunals convicted cabinet members and other government officials; party officials; industrialists and businessmen; judges; prosecutors; doctors and nurses; and executioners. As you consider current conflicts, what other categories might pose challenging questions about who can be prosecuted as a perpetrator of war crimes?

4. Consider the difference between the war crime of willful killing of civilians and the war crime of wanton destruction of property not justified by military necessity. The former has no qualification for military necessity or other exigency. In *Prosecutor v. Blaškić*, the Trial Chamber stated that targeting civilians is an offense "when not justified by military necessity."[25] The Appeals Chamber quickly rectified that statement, clarifying that "there is an absolute prohibition on the targeting of civilians in customary international law."[26] Why would the war crime of wanton destruction of property provide a qualification for military necessity?

5. Torture is a grave breach of the Geneva Conventions and a war crime under Common Article 3 in non-international armed conflict. As defined in *Prosecutor v. Furundžija*, torture "consists of the infliction, by act or omission, of severe pain or suffering, whether physical or mental." In

---

24. Prosecutor v. Ahmad al Faqi Al Mahdi, Case No. ICC-01/12-01/15, Judgment and Sentence ¶ 18 (Sept. 27, 2016) (finding that the nexus to armed conflict element requires "only an association with the non-international armed conflict more generally" and "not a link to any particular hostilities").

25. Prosecutor v. Blaškić, Case No. IT-95-14-T, Judgement ¶ 180 (Int'l Crim. Trib. for the Former Yugoslavia Mar. 3, 2000).

26. Prosecutor v. Blaškić, Case No. IT-95-14-A, Judgement ¶ 109 (Int'l Crim. Trib. for the Former Yugoslavia July 29, 2004).

addition, the act or omission must be intentional and be aimed at "obtaining information or a confession, or at punishing, intimidating, humiliating or coercing the victim or a third person, or at discriminating, on any ground, against the victim or a third person." Finally, the act must be linked to an armed conflict and "at least one of the persons involved in the torture process must be a public official or must at any rate act in a non-private capacity, e.g. as a *de facto* organ of a State or any other authority-wielding entity."[27]

6. Can a state or armed group commit war crimes against members of its own forces? In the *Ntaganda* case, the ICC rejected a challenge from Bosco Ntaganda, the former deputy chief of staff of the Union of Congolese Patriots (UPC), asserting that the Court did not have jurisdiction over rape and sexual slavery committed against child soldiers who served in the UPC. Finding that Articles 8(2)(b)(xxii) and 8(2)(e)(vi) of the Rome Statute do not expressly require that the crimes be committed against protected persons, the Court declared that "there is never a justification to engage in sexual violence against any person; irrespective of whether or not this person may be liable to be targeted and killed under international humanitarian law."[28] Does the Court's ruling make sense under LOAC? Does it fulfill Common Article 3's basic goals or is it a problematic expansion of LOAC's protections?

D.　CRIMES AGAINST HUMANITY

Crimes against humanity are crimes that are an international concern because they exceed any limits tolerated by civilized societies. First used to describe the Young Turks' brutal and systematic slaughter of Armenians during World War I, the term "crimes against humanity" appeared in positive international law for the first time in the 1945 London Charter that established the Nuremberg International Military Tribunal. Article 6(c) defined crimes against humanity as:

> namely, murder, extermination, enslavement, deportation, and other inhumane acts committed against any civilian population, before or during the war, or persecutions on political, racial or religious grounds in execution of or in connection with any crime . . . whether or not in violation of the domestic law of the country where perpetrated.

---

27. Prosecutor v. Furundžija, Case No. IT-95-17/1-T, Judgement ¶ 162 (Int'l Crim. Trib. for the Former Yugoslavia Dec. 10, 1998).

28. Prosecutor v. Bosco Ntaganda, Case No. ICC-01/04-02/06, Second Decision on the Defence's Challenge to the Jurisdiction of the Court in Respect of Counts 6 and 9 ¶ 49 (Jan. 4, 2017).

At Nuremberg, General Telford Taylor, Chief Prosecutor for the Nuremberg Subsequent Proceedings, defined crimes against humanity in the following words:

> These crimes cover the vast and terrible world of the Nuremberg laws, yellow arm bands, "aryanization," concentration camps, medical experiments, extermination squads, and so on. . . . Actually, when committed in the course of belligerent occupation (whether in the occupied country or elsewhere), these were also "war crimes." But the concept of crimes against humanity comprises atrocities which are part of a campaign of discrimination or persecution, and which are crimes against international law even when committed by nationals of one country against their fellow nationals or against those of other nations irrespective of belligerent status.[29]

In many situations, the component acts of crimes against humanity might technically not be "war crimes" because they do not violate the law of war (e.g., killing one's own citizens). As the Nuremberg Tribunal stated in *The Justice Case*, "it can no longer be said that violations of the laws and customs of war are the only offenses recognized by common international law."[30] Instead, the tribunal continued, "[t]he force of circumstance, the grim fact of world-wide interdependence, and the moral pressure of public opinion have resulted in international recognition that certain crimes against humanity committed by Nazi authority against German nationals constituted violations not alone of statute but also of common international law."[31] Unlike war crimes, crimes against humanity can be committed wholly outside of armed conflict—a key foundational distinction between crimes against humanity and war crimes. In addition, many acts that constitute war crimes also serve as the predicate acts for a finding of crimes against humanity.

Article 7 of the Rome Statute defines crimes against humanity as any of the component acts "when committed as part of a widespread or systematic attack directed against any civilian population, with knowledge of the attack." Those acts include murder, extermination, enslavement, deportation or forcible transfer of population, imprisonment, torture, rape and other sexual violence, persecution, enforced disappearance, apartheid, or other inhumane acts. Crimes against humanity thus contain two critical elements: they are committed against a civilian population and the crimes constitute a widespread or systematic attack. To constitute an attack on the civilian population, the crimes must be more than simply isolated attacks, but they do not need to be directed at all members of the population. The

29. Telford Taylor, Final Report to the Secretary of the Army on the Nuremberg War Crimes Trials Under Control Council Law No. 10 64-65 (1949).

30. USA v. Altstötter et al., *in* VI Law Reports of Trials of War Criminals 45 (1948).

31. *Id.*

notion of widespread seems to suggest a large number of victims and crimes committed across more than a small area. As the ICC has stated, "the term 'widespread' has also been explained as encompassing an attack carried out over a large geographical area or an attack in a small geographical area, but directed against a large number of civilians."[32] Systematic generally refers to the nature of the planning and organization—the policy behind the attack on the civilian population: "either an organised plan in furtherance of a common policy, which follows a regular pattern and results in a continuous commission of acts or as 'patterns of crimes' such that the crimes constitute a 'non-accidental repetition of similar criminal conduct on a regular basis.'"[33] The ICTY and the ICTR have issued numerous and extensive decisions on crimes against humanity over the past two decades. Crimes against humanity also feature prominently in the jurisprudence of the Special Court for Sierra Leone, one of two hybrid tribunals prosecuting perpetrators of atrocities.

FORUM: HYBRID TRIBUNALS

The *Special Court for Sierra Leone* (SCSL) was an independent judicial body established as a "hybrid" tribunal by the United Nations and the Government of Sierra Leone in January 2002. The SCSL's task was to prosecute those who bear the greatest responsibility for the atrocities committed during the civil war in Sierra Leone in the second half of the 1990s. The SCSL had a few unique features: 1) it had concurrent jurisdiction with the national courts of Sierra Leone, but statutory primacy in which the Court had the power to formally request that the national courts hand over cases to the Special Court; 2) it was the first international tribunal to be located in the country where the crimes occurred; and 3) its mandate was limited to those who "bear the greatest responsibility" for the crimes. The Special Court also had no jurisdiction over persons who at the time of an alleged crime were under fifteen years of age, an important qualification in a conflict where all sides forced thousands of children to fight and commit atrocities. Before its closure in 2013, the Special Court convicted and sentenced nine individuals in four cases for offenses including murder, rape, extermination, acts of terror, enslavement, looting and burning of property, sexual enslavement, forced conscription of children, forced marriage, and attacks upon humanitarian aid workers.

---

32. Prosecutor v. Germain Katanga & Mathieu Ngudjolo Chui, Case No. ICC-01/04-01/07, Decision on Confirmation of Charges ¶ 395 (Sept. 30, 2008).

33. *Id.* ¶ 397.

In April 2012, the SCSL convicted Charles Taylor, the President of Liberia from 1997-2003 and the first African President to face trial for war crimes, of aiding and abetting war crimes and crimes against humanity.

After several years of negotiations, the United Nations and the Cambodian National Assembly created the *Extraordinary Chambers in the Courts of Cambodia* (ECCC) based on a 2003 U.N. General Assembly Resolution and a 2004 Cambodian trial law. The purpose of the Court is to try those most responsible for the crimes committed during the 1975-1979 Khmer Rouge regime. The ECCC is a Cambodian court with international participation and operating in accordance with international standards. To that end, each component of the court—prosecutors, defense, and judges—is staffed with national and international personnel. At present, the ECCC has completed two cases, convicting three defendants. One other defendant died before trial, and another was found unfit to stand trial. In the first case, Kaing Guek Eav, former Chief of the Phom Phen Prison, was convicted and sentenced to life imprisonment for grave breaches of the Geneva Convention of 1949, including crimes against humanity, on the grounds of political persecution, extermination, enslavement, imprisonment, torture, and other inhumane acts. In August 2014, the Trial Chamber rendered a second guilty verdict for crimes against humanity, against Nuon Chea and Khieu Samphan, who have appealed the convictions. Four additional defendants have been charged in Cases 003 and 004.

Nearly all of the international jurisprudence on crimes against humanity stems from situations of conflict—certainly it is most likely that these types of crimes will be committed in a highly militarized context. Like genocide, however, crimes against humanity can be committed in a non-conflict situation. For example, on September 28, 2009, tens of thousands gathered in the main stadium in Conakry, Guinea, to protest against continued military rule. After blocking the exits, security forces burst into the stadium and opened fire on the crowd, killing, injuring, or disappearing more than 150 people. As the United Nations International Commission of Inquiry established to examine the incident concluded,

> The red berets and gendarmes surrounded the stadium, blocked the exits, stormed through the main gates, fired tear gas and set about killing or wounding the demonstrators or subjecting them to sexual assault. In under two hours, hundreds of civilians had died or been seriously wounded, stripped in public and subjected to widespread sexual abuse, being unable to flee as the exits from the stadium had been blocked. The

authorities then began an organized attempt to cover up the crimes and, as a result, at least 89 persons have been reported missing, some are suffering from permanent injuries, while others will be afflicted with long-term physical and mental suffering. . . . These acts constitute a general and systematic attack against the civilian population in the implementation or pursuit of a strategy aimed at quelling, through this attack, political opposition movements and especially targeting women, who, according to the aggressors, should not have been there.[34]

QUESTIONS FOR DISCUSSION

1. One category of crimes against humanity is persecution. The London Charter codified persecution as a crime against humanity for the first time. Criminalizing persecution was aimed specifically at establishing accountability for acts against civilians within the domestic population that did not fit within the existing law of war (which only protected enemy populations during times of war). The ICTY Statute and jurisprudence then significantly developed the elements of the offense of persecution, defining persecution as "the gross or blatant denial, on discriminatory grounds, of a fundamental right, laid down in international customary or treaty law, reaching the same level of gravity as the other acts prohibited in Article 5."[35] The discrimination component of persecution means that the *mens rea* element of persecution is higher than that of ordinary crimes against humanity (which do not require discriminatory intent), but still lower than that required for genocide. In *Prosecutor v. Kupreskić* the ICTY explained that persecution falls within the same category of crimes as genocide and elaborated on the difference between the two crimes:

> persecution as a crime against humanity is an offence belonging to the same genus as genocide . . . In both categories what matters is the intent to discriminate: to attack persons on account of their ethnic, racial, or religious characteristics. . . . While in the case of persecution the discriminatory intent can take multifarious inhumane forms and manifest itself in a plurality of actions including murder, in the case of genocide that intent must be accompanied by the intention to destroy, in whole or in part, the group to which the victims of the genocide belong. Thus, it can be said that, from the viewpoint of *mens rea*, genocide is an extreme and most inhuman form of persecution.[36]

34. Report of the International Commission of Inquiry Mandated to Establish the Facts and Circumstances of the Events of 28 September 2009 in Guinea, U.N. Doc. S/2009/693 ¶ 198, December 18, 2009.

35. Prosecutor v. Kupreskić, Case No. IT-95-16-T, Judgement ¶ 621 (Int'l Crim. Trib. for the Former Yugoslavia Jan. 14, 2000).

36. *Id.* ¶ 636.

2. The prosecution of crimes against humanity committed during armed conflict also raises the question of who are victims of crimes against humanity. In *Prosecutor v. Martić,* the ICTY considered whether combatants who were *hors de combat* could be victims of crimes against humanity. In rejecting the Trial Chamber's finding that *hors de combat* combatants could not be the victims of crimes against humanity, the Appeals Chamber highlighted the difference between the definition of civilian (found in Article 50 of Additional Protocol I) and the notion of the civilian population. Persons who are *hors de combat* do not become civilians — such a conclusion would fundamentally affect the distinction between civilians and combatants that forms a core part of LOAC. However, the Appeals Chamber held that combatants or other fighters (such as the French resistance fighters in the post-WWII *Barbie* case[37]) who are *hors de combat* can be the victims of crimes against humanity. The issue is whether persons are targeted in the course of a widespread or systematic attack on the civilian population, not whether individual victims were civilians.[38]

3. Note that the individual acts that form part of crimes against humanity can also constitute war crimes, if committed during an armed conflict. What is the added value of charging an accused with both war crimes and crimes against humanity for the same underlying acts? Could there be a detrimental aspect to such duplicative charges?

4. If crimes against humanity can be committed during peacetime, does the requirement that the attacks be committed against the civilian population make sense? Would there be any persons or groups that did not belong to the civilian population in a peacetime situation?

E. GENOCIDE

Genocide is considered the "quintessential" crime against humanity and the most heinous international crime. The Nuremberg Tribunals did not use the term genocide; rather, the crimes inherent in genocide were viewed as a subset or component of crimes against humanity. The term "genocide" comes from Raphael Lemkin, a Polish scholar who immigrated to the United States in 1941. Writing in the last years of World War II, Lemkin believed that there were no existing words that could sufficiently describe the horrors of the Holocaust and so created the term "genocide."

---

37. Klaus Barbie Case, Chambre Criminelle de la Cour de Cassation, judgment of 20 Dec., 1985, 78 I.L.R. 125, 140.

38. Prosecutor v. Milan Martić, Case No. IT-95-11-A, Judgement ¶¶ 308-311 (Int'l Crim. Trib. for the Former Yugoslavia Oct. 8, 2008).

Raphael Lemkin

Axis Rule in Occupied Europe

(1944)

New conceptions require new terms. By "genocide" we mean the destruction of a nation or of an ethnic group. This new word, coined by the author to denote an old practice in its modern development, is made from the ancient Greek word *genos* (race, tribe) and the Latin *cide* (killing), thus corresponding in its formations to such words as tyrannicide, homicide, infanticide, etc. Generally speaking, genocide does not necessarily mean the immediate destruction of a nation, except when accomplished by mass killings of all members of a nation. It is intended rather to signify a coordinated plan of different actions aiming at the destruction of essential foundations of the life of national groups, with the aim of annihilating the groups themselves. The objectives of such a plan would be disintegration of the political and social institutions, of culture, language, national feelings, religion, and the economic existence of national groups, and the destruction of the personal security, liberty, health, dignity, and even the lives of the individuals belonging to such groups. Genocide is directed against the national group as an entity, and the actions involved are directed against individuals, not in their individual capacity, but as members of the national group. . . .

Genocide has two phases: one, destruction of the national pattern of the oppressed group; the other, the imposition of the national pattern of the oppressor. This imposition, in turn, may be made upon the oppressed population which is allowed to remain, or upon the territory alone, after removal of the population and the colonization of the area by the oppressor's own nationals. Denationalization was the word used in the past to describe the destruction of a national pattern. The author believes, however, that this word is inadequate because: (1) it does not connote the destruction of the biological structure; (2) in connoting the destruction of one national pattern, it does not connote the imposition of the national pattern of the oppressor; and (3) denationalization is used by some authors to mean only deprivation of citizenship.

In 1948, the U.N. General Assembly adopted the Convention on the Prevention and Punishment of the Crime of Genocide, providing the foundation for genocide's place as a specific—in fact the most heinous—international crime. The Convention criminalizes genocide, in peacetime or during conflict, and obligates States parties to prevent and punish genocide. Articles 2 and 3 of the Convention define the crime and its constituent parts:

Article II: In the present Convention, genocide means any of the following acts committed with intent to destroy, in whole or in part, a
national, ethnical, racial or religious group, as such:

(a) Killing members of the group;
(b) Causing serious bodily or mental harm to members of the group;
(c) Deliberately inflicting on the group conditions of life calculated
to bring about its physical destruction in whole or in part;
(d) Imposing measures intended to prevent births within the group;
(e) Forcibly transferring children of the group to another group.

Article III: The following acts shall be punishable:

(a) Genocide;
(b) Conspiracy to commit genocide;
(c) Direct and public incitement to commit genocide;
(d) Attempt to commit genocide;
(e) Complicity in genocide.

The statutes of the international tribunals reproduce this definition
of genocide verbatim. First, the crime of genocide rests on the commission of one or more of the component acts listed in Article II. Second,
as the Convention sets forth, genocide is a specific intent crime. Thus, in
committing one or more of the underlying acts, the accused must either
intend to destroy, in whole or in part, a national, ethnic, racial, or religious group, or the accused must have clear knowledge that he or she
is participating in genocide. This specific intent to annihilate the group
to which the targeted individuals belong is the distinguishing feature of
genocide and differentiates genocide from war crimes or crimes against
humanity. The particular nature of the target group is also carefully specified in the definition of genocide: national, ethnical, racial or religious.
Political, economic or other categories are not included within the definition, primarily because under customary international law, such groups
are not considered to be distinct from the rest of the population in the
same immutable fashion, but rather are "unstable" or "fluctuating" in
nature.[39] The Convention also criminalizes other acts connected with
genocide, such as complicity, conspiracy, and incitement to commit genocide. Finally, genocide is not necessarily linked to armed conflict but is
prohibited in both times of war or times of peace.

In the first conviction for genocide, the ICTR convicted Jean Paul
Akayesu, the Mayor of Taba commune in Rwanda, of genocide and crimes
against humanity and sentenced him to life imprisonment. In particular,
Akayesu was accused of ordering, facilitating, and supervising the killing
of Tutsis in Taba. The ICTR found that "there is no doubt that considering
their undeniable scale, their systematic nature and their atrociousness, the

39. Marco Sassoli et al., How Does Law Protect in War? Cases, Documents and
Teaching Materials on Contemporary Practice in International Humanitarian
Law 405 (3d ed. 2011).

massacres were aimed at exterminating the group that was targeted."[40] With regard to the requirement of specific intent, the ICTR held:

> On the issue of determining the offender's specific intent, the Chamber considers that intent is a mental factor which is difficult, even impossible, to determine. This is the reason why, in the absence of a confession from the accused, his intent can be inferred from a certain number of presumptions of fact. The Chamber considers that it is possible to deduce the genocidal intent inherent in a particular act charged from the general context of the perpetration of other culpable acts systematically directed against the same group, whether these acts were committed by the same offender or by others. Other factors, such as the scale of the atrocities committed, their general nature, in a region or a country, or furthermore, the fact of deliberately and systematically targeting victims on account of their membership of a particular group, while excluding the members of other groups, can enable the Chamber to infer the genocidal intent of a particular act.[41]

The genocide in Rwanda was, by all accounts, an attempt to destroy the Tutsi population entirely—the classic image of genocide. But the definition of genocide includes equally efforts to destroy a group "in part." "In whole or in part" does not mean a single individual or a few persons, but an important part of the group, such as a large proportion or key part of the targeted group. This term is also designed to prevent a technical legal defense of "we only intended to kill some but not all." The ICTY addressed this specific issue in the prosecutions arising out of the massacre in Srebrenica just one year after the genocide in Rwanda. In July 1995, Bosnian Serb forces launched a sustained assault on the United Nations safe areas of Srebrenica and Žepa. When Bosnian Muslims in Srebrenica fled the fighting, the men were separated from the women and children and ultimately massacred by the Bosnian Serb forces. Over 8,000 Bosnian Muslims were killed. In upholding the conviction of General Radislav Krstić for genocide, the Appeals Chamber stated:

> Among the grievous crimes this Tribunal has the duty to punish, the crime of genocide is singled out for special condemnation and opprobrium. The crime is horrific in its scope; its perpetrators identify entire human groups for extinction. Those who devise and implement genocide seek to deprive humanity of the manifold richness its nationalities, races, ethnicities and religions provide. This is a crime against all of humankind, its harm being felt not only by the group targeted for destruction, but by all of humanity.
>
> The gravity of genocide is reflected in the stringent requirements which must be satisfied before this conviction is imposed. These requirements—the demanding proof of specific intent and the showing that

40. Prosecutor v. Akayesu, Case No. ICTR-96-4-T, Judgement ¶ 118 (Int'l Crim. Trib. for Rwanda Sept. 2, 1998).

41. *Id.* ¶ 523.

the group was targeted for destruction in its entirety or in substantial part—guard against a danger that convictions for this crime will be imposed lightly. Where these requirements are satisfied, however, the law must not shy away from referring to the crime committed by its proper name. By seeking to eliminate a part of the Bosnian Muslims, the Bosnian Serb forces committed genocide. They targeted for extinction the forty thousand Bosnian Muslims living in Srebrenica, a group which was emblematic of the Bosnian Muslims in general. They stripped all the male Muslim prisoners, military and civilian, elderly and young, of their personal belongings and identification, and deliberately and methodically killed them solely on the basis of their identity. The Bosnian Serb forces were aware, when they embarked on this genocidal venture, that the harm they caused would continue to plague the Bosnian Muslims. The Appeals Chamber states unequivocally that the law condemns, in appropriate terms, the deep and lasting injury inflicted, and calls the massacre at Srebrenica by its proper name: genocide. Those responsible will bear this stigma, and it will serve as a warning to those who may in future contemplate the commission of such a heinous act.[42]

On August 3, 2014, ISIS swept out of Mosul, which it captured two months earlier, and attacked the region around Mount Sinjar in northwestern Iraq, home to approximately 400,000 Yazidis. Within a few hours, ISIS fighters had killed or kidnapped tens of thousands of Yazidis who could not flee; it besieged those who fled on Mount Sinjar for days without food, water, or medical care. In June 2016, the United Nations–established Independent International Commission of Inquiry on the Syrian Arab Republic determined that ISIS had committed genocide. After categorizing the Yazidis as a religious group and therefore protected under the Genocide Convention, the Commission detailed the crimes falling within the definition of genocide that ISIS committed against the Yazidis:

- *Killing members of the group*: including hundreds of Yazidis killed in the attack on Mt. Sinjar, Yazidis executed upon capture, and hundreds of Yazidi men and adolescent boys "summarily executed . . . when [they] refused to convert to Islam."
- *Causing serious bodily or mental harm to members of the group*: including "acts of torture, rape, sexual violence or inhuman or degrading treatment."
- *Rape and sexual violence, including sexual slavery*: including systematic rape of Yazidi women and girls as young as nine, sexual violence and sexual slavery. "Once captured by ISIS, Yazidi women and girls are deemed to be the property of the terrorist group, and later the individual fighters who purchase them. [Organized] sales

---

42. Prosecutor v. Krstić, Case No. IT-98-33-A, Judgement ¶¶ 36-37 (Int'l Crim. Trib. for the Former Yugoslavia April 19, 2004).

are conducted with individual fighters coming to holding sites, at slave markets where groups of ISIS men inspect and select women and girls, and in online auctions. Once sold, the Yazidi females are the sole property of their fighter-owner, who can re-sell, gift, or will them to other ISIS fighters. ISIS fighters threaten to kill women and girls who resist rape. Resistance is also routinely met with beatings and threats against any children the Yazidi woman has with her. ISIS fighters block escape attempts by refusing to provide Yazidi women and girls with clothing that would allow them to move unnoticed in the streets. Escape attempts have been met with extreme violence including the killing of the women's children, gang rape, rape, and beatings. Yazidi women and girls are also forced to work for the ISIS fighters and their families, including being made to cook, clean and wash clothes. Throughout their captivity, captured Yazidi women and children are treated as less than human and undeserving of respect and dignity, due to their status as 'dirty infidels.'"

- *Enslavement:* including "forc[ing] Yazidi women and girls to cook, clean, and wash clothes for [fighters], and sometimes for their families"; forcing "Yazidi men and boys over the age of puberty . . . to labour on ISIS projects in Tel Afar and Mosul [including] construction and cleaning work, digging trenches, and looking after cattle."

- *Torture and inhuman and degrading treatment:* including severe mental harm due to being separated from their families and being forced to bear witness to their murders, severe physical harm from beatings for attempts to escape or failure to follow orders, and degradation from being treated as chattel and sex slaves.

- *Forcible transfer:* including "forcibly transferr[ing] Yazidi men, women and children from the point of capture to various primary and then to secondary holding sites in Syria and Iraq." Yazidi women and children were then sold and re-sold.

- *Deliberately inflicting on the group conditions of life calculated to bring about its physical destruction in whole or in part:* including "deliberately cut[ting] those on the mountain off from food, water, and medical care" and "attack[ing] planes seeking to ai[r] drop water and food supplies, and helicopters which attempted to rescue those in need [of] medical attention or who were otherwise particularly vulnerable."

- *Imposing measures to prevent births within the group:* including by "separating Yazidi men and women, by killing hundreds of Yazidi men, and by forcing conversions to Islam." Yazidi religious tradition dictates that "both parents must be Yazidi for the child to be of Yazidi faith." As a result, ISIS "imposed measures intended to prevent births within the group."

- *Forcibly transferring children to another group:* including by taking girls age nine and older from their mothers and selling them as sex slaves, and by taking Yazidi boys, "once they reach the age of seven . . . from their mothers and [sending] them to ISIS training bases in Syria and Iraq where they are instructed on how to follow Islam as interpreted by ISIS, and on how to fight."

The Commission then determined that ISIS committed these acts with the intent to destroy, in whole or in part, the Yazidis, based on ISIS's explicit statements that the Yazidis were "a *mushrik* group, judged not to believe in God as worshipped by *Ahl Al-Kitab*, or the People of the Book," and therefore must be killed or enslaved because "it is impermissible for [them] to live as Yazidis inside its so-called caliphate because they are not People of the Book."[43]

QUESTIONS FOR DISCUSSION

1. In March 2016, the Obama Administration first used the term "genocide" to describe ISIS's crimes against the Yazidis. The magnitude of ISIS's atrocities had been clear for some time—why do you think the U.S. waited so long?[44] What obligations did the statement trigger? What about the horror and brutality ISIS visited on tens of thousands of other civilians in Iraq and Syria—why was the finding of genocide specific only to the Yazidis? And does that pronouncement diminish the crimes committed against others?

2. Incitement to genocide is also a serious crime under international law. Jean-Paul Akayesu was convicted of direct and public incitement to genocide for the speeches and exhortations to genocide he gave in April 1994, which contributed to and facilitated the commission of genocide by others. Rwandan radio broadcaster Georges Ruggiu pled guilty to incitement to genocide before the ICTR and was sentenced to twenty-four years in prison in June 2000:

> In *Akayesu*, the Tribunal also noted that "at the time the Convention on Genocide was adopted, the delegates agreed to expressly spell out direct and public incitement to commit genocide as a specific crime, in particular, because of its critical role in the planning of a genocide." In this regard, the delegate from the USSR stated that, "It was impossible that hundreds of thousands of people should commit so many crimes unless

---

43. Independent International Commission of Inquiry on the Syrian Arab Republic, *They Came to Destroy: Human Rights Crimes Against the Yazidis,* June 16, 2016. In May 2021, the United Nations Investigative Team to Promote Accountability for Crimes Committed by Da'esh/ISIL announced that it had found "clear and convincing evidence" that ISIS committed genocide against the Yazidis. Edith M. Lederer, *UN experts: Islamic State committed genocide against Yazidis,* Assoc. Press (May 10, 2021).

44. Laurie Blank & Geoffrey S. Corn, *ISIS Committed Genocide: Are the Gloves Off?*, CNN. com (March 18, 2016).

they had been incited to do so and unless the crimes had been premeditated and carefully organized. He asked how in those circumstances, the inciters and organizers of the crime could be allowed to escape punishment, when they were the ones really responsible for the atrocities committed."

The Tribunal held, in the same case, that the crime of genocide is so serious that the direct and public incitement to commit genocide must be punished as such, even if the incitement failed to produce the result expected by the perpetrator. . . .

The Trial Chamber considers that when examining the acts of persecution which have been admitted by the accused, it is possible to discern a common element. Those acts were direct and public radio broadcasts all aimed at singling out and attacking the Tutsi ethnic group and Belgians on discriminatory grounds, by depriving them of the fundamental rights to life, liberty and basic humanity enjoyed by members of wider society. The deprivation of these rights can be said to have as its aim the death and removal of those persons from the society in which they live alongside the perpetrators, or eventually even from humanity itself.[45]

Consider what facts would be necessary to prove direct and public incitement to commit genocide. What about crimes against humanity? Could the Qaddafi regime's public call for violence in Libya in 2011 amount to direct and public incitement of crimes against humanity? Is such a charge possible?

3. In Case No. 002, the ECCC charged the four defendants with crimes against humanity, war crimes, and genocide, but only charged genocide with regard to acts against certain minorities. Why would the genocide charge not encompass all of the killings in Cambodia between 1975 and 1979?

4. In 2016 and 2017, the Government of Myanmar (formerly Burma) began a campaign against the Rohingya, a distinct ethnic group who practice Islam. The military surrounded Rohingya villages and proceed to beat, torture, rape, dismember, and kill the inhabitants. The military told the Rohingya that "This is not your country—you're Bengali!" This is a derogatory term and rooted in the long-held idea among the Burmese that the Rohingya are foreigners and are actually from Bangladesh, despite the fact that the Rohingya have always been in Myanmar. During this period of violence, nearly 800,000 Rohingya fled Myanmar and entered Bangladesh, where they have temporarily settled in massive refugee camps. There is little doubt that the Myanmar military's widespread and systematic assault on the Rohingya qualifies as crimes against humanity. Is it genocide? Are the acts committed against the Rohingya war crimes?

45. Prosecutor v. Ruggiu, Case No. ICTR-97-32-I, Judgement and Sentence ¶¶ 15-22 (Int'l Crim. Trib. for Rwanda June 1, 2000).

5. Despite all the ambiguities, contradictions, and difficulties discussed above, the international community is more united now than it has ever been in its condemnation of genocide and war crimes. There has been increased international support for trying the perpetrators of such crimes under the Genocide Convention and the law of war. Nevertheless, given the history of the international community's decidedly mixed success in actually bringing such cases to the indictment stage, much less to trial, what is the best advice an international lawyer could give the leaders of any country afflicted by such crimes? Is it that if you want justice done, do it yourself? Will the international community support nations in investigating and prosecuting perpetrators of atrocity crimes in domestic tribunals?

F. SEXUAL VIOLENCE

Sexual crimes during wartime, particularly rape, are unfortunately not new. Although Cicero implored soldiers to observe the rules of war, women were considered the property of the man who had lawful ownership over her. As the law of war became increasingly systemized throughout the Middle Ages, the focus of the crime of *rapine* shifted from a crime against property to an offense against a woman's purity.[46] Slowly, the protections for civilians during times of war expanded, including protections for violent crimes against women, but rape was still generally treated as an attack on a woman's honor or dignity rather than an inherently violent act that results in physical, psychological, and emotional harm. Brutal acts of sexual violence were a feature of both World Wars, and these crimes were not charged at the Leipzig Trials, listed in the Nuremberg or Tokyo Charters, or mentioned during the Nuremberg Trials. The International Military Tribunal for the Far East, however, did prosecute crimes of sexual violence and found that approximately 20,000 cases of rape occurred in Nanking. The U.S. military commission prosecuting General Yamashita also established rape as a war crime, stating that "where murder and rape and vicious, revengeful actions are widespread offences, and there is no effective attempt by a commander to discover and control the criminal acts, such a commander may be held responsible, even criminally liable, for the lawless acts of his troops."[47]

During the Rwandan genocide, roughly 250,000 to 500,000 Tutsi women were raped and subjected to a wide variety of sexual violence and torture, including gang rape, rape with objects such as sharpened sticks

46. Kelly Dawn Askin, War Crimes Against Women 23-29 (1997).

47. Trial of General Tomoyaki Yamashita, Case No. 21, Judgment (U.S. Mil. Comm'n, Manila Oct. 8, 1945-Dec. 7, 1945), *reprinted in* IV U.N. War Crimes Comm'n, Law Reports of Trials of War Criminals 1, 35 (1945).

or gun barrels, sexual slavery (either collectively or through forced "marriage"), or sexual mutilation. As with other crimes committed during the genocide, these sexual attacks were the result of a well-executed Hutu propaganda campaign, promoting the stereotype that Tutsi women were beautiful and considered themselves "too good" for Hutu men. Rape became a means of exerting power over Tutsi women by humiliating, degrading, and ultimately destroying them.

Similarly, rape and other acts of sexual violence were often used as propaganda to incite violence within various armed groups during the conflict in the former Yugoslavia. Women in combat zones, detention camps, and even areas of relative peace were subjected to brutal acts of individual rape, gang rape, forced or coerced prostitution, sexual slavery, sexual mutilation, invasive interrogation procedures, and forced impregnation. Young girls and elderly women were not spared, and victims were often targeted to punish the men or ethnicity with which they were associated. And yet, in the face of this brutality, no authoritative definition of rape existed within international law before the ICTY and the ICTR. Nearly thirty years after the establishment of the ICTY, international criminal jurisprudence on sexual crimes has expanded dramatically into a robust and extensive body of law, in which rape and other sexual crimes have been found to be war crimes, crimes against humanity, and even genocide. In *Prosecutor v. Akayesu*, a case in which rape was not even originally charged but added in response to witness testimony, the court unequivocally stated:

> With regard [to] rape and sexual violence, the Chamber wishes to underscore the fact that in its opinion, they constitute genocide in the same way as any other act as long as they were committed with the specific intent to destroy, in whole or in part, a particular group, targeted as such.[48]

Sexual crimes during armed conflict also extend beyond rape and violent sexual crimes. Sexual slavery was common practice during the conflict in Sierra Leone, as was the practice of "bush wives." Fighters on all sides of the conflict abducted women and young girls and forced them to become their wives, an insidious form of domestic and sexual slavery. Advocacy groups estimate that over 60,000 women were victims of forced marriage, sexual slavery, and other forms of sexual abuse during the civil war in Sierra Leone.[49] Early efforts to prosecute forced marriage as a separate crime—within the paradigm of crimes against humanity—fell short; the Trial Chamber in the first case, *Prosecutor v. Brima*, ruled that forced marriage was a redundant charge falling within existing categories of sexual

---

48. Prosecutor v. Akayesu, Case No. ICTR-96-4-T, Judgement ¶ 731 (Int'l Crim. Trib. for Rwanda Sept. 2, 1998).

49. Jina Moore, *In Africa, Justice for 'Bush Wives,'* CHRISTIAN SCI. MON. (June 10, 2008).

violence and sexual slavery. In 2008, the Appeals Chamber judgment in *Brima* overturned the trial judgment and held that forced marriage is a crime against humanity in its own right:

> Based on the evidence on record, the Appeals Chamber finds that no tribunal could reasonably have found that forced marriage was subsumed in the crime against humanity of sexual slavery. While forced marriage shares certain elements with sexual slavery such as non-consensual sex and deprivation of liberty, there are also distinguishing factors. First, forced marriage involves a perpetrator compelling a person by force or threat of force, through the words or conduct of the perpetrator or those associated with him, into a forced conjugal association with another person resulting in great suffering, or serious physical or mental injury on the part of the victim. Second, unlike sexual slavery, forced marriage implies a relationship of exclusivity between the "husband" and "wife," which could lead to disciplinary consequences for breach of this exclusive arrangement. . . .
>
> In light of the distinctions between forced marriage and sexual slavery, the Appeals Chamber finds that in the context of the Sierra Leone conflict, forced marriage describes a situation in which the perpetrator through his words or conduct, or those of someone for whose actions he is responsible, compels a person by force, threat of force, or coercion to serve as a conjugal partner resulting in severe suffering, or physical, mental or psychological injury to the victim.[50]

QUESTIONS FOR DISCUSSION

1. The Rome Statute specifically includes sexual violence within the categories of acts that can form the constituent crimes for crimes against humanity, listing "[r]ape, sexual slavery, enforced prostitution, forced pregnancy, enforced sterilization, or any other form of sexual violence of comparable gravity" in Article 7(g). Under the categories of war crimes in Article 8, rape and other forms of sexual violence are not included within the grave breaches in Article 8(2)(a), but rather within other serious violations of law applicable in international armed conflict in Article 8(2)(b) and other serious violations of law applicable in non-international armed conflicts in Article 8(2)(e). Should rape and sexual violence be considered a serious violation of Common Article 3? Can the prohibition against violence to life and person, including cruel treatment, encompass rape and sexual violence?

2. What is the significance of treating forced marriage as a separate crime, not encompassed within sexual slavery or other crimes of sexual violence? How restrictive—or innovative—should a tribunal be in assessing the appropriate categories of crimes?

50. Prosecutor v. Brima, Kamara, and Kanu, Case No. SCSL-2004-16-A, Judgment ¶¶ 195-196 (Special Court for Sierra Leone Feb. 22, 2008).

G.   COMMAND RESPONSIBILITY

Command (or superior) responsibility is a form of liability used in military and international law to hold an individual in a leadership position accountable for the actions of his subordinates. In essence, command responsibility refers to the commander's liability for the criminal conduct of his underling. The concept of command responsibility is critical to LOAC: If the commander knew or should have known of unlawful actions committed by his or her troops, the commander can be held accountable for such actions. LOAC entrusts commanders with ensuring their subordinates respect and comply with LOAC, including by taking necessary measures to prevent or punish subordinates committing violations. The commander is thus held responsible for a sin of omission—the failure to properly supervise and control his or her subordinates who have committed war crimes or other violations. A disciplined fighting force must be the goal of every commander for numerous reasons. First and foremost, a disciplined force will be more effective in accomplishing the mission while adhering to LOAC. Secondly, a disciplined force will have fewer "friendly fire" casualties (i.e., the forces are more deliberate and less likely to shoot at "anything," which often could be their fellow countryman). As if those two reasons were not enough—international law may hold the commander personally responsible for acts he or she did not commit.

Often the most horrific perpetrators of atrocities are the military and civilian leadership of a unit, government organization, or state. These leaders use the cloak of authority to condone and direct heinous crimes. The legal theory of command responsibility holds such individuals accountable for the actions of their subordinates. As the Nuremberg Military Tribunal stated, "under basic principles of command authority and responsibility, an officer who merely stands by while his subordinates execute a criminal order of his superiors which he knows is criminal violates a moral obligation under international law. By doing nothing he cannot wash his hands of international responsibility."[51] Although command responsibility is most often applied to military commanders, civilian leaders can also be held responsible if they have the requisite authority—authority equivalent to that of a military commander over military or civilian subordinates.

Military commanders and civilian leaders may be convicted for crimes committed by their subordinates if: (1) the commander or leader ordered or knowingly permitted the crime; or (2) the commander knew or should have known of the crime, and the commander or leader had the capability to prevent the crime but failed to do so. Difficult proof issues arise when there is no direct evidence of involvement by the commander. Circumstantial evidence must be used to establish actual or constructive knowledge of subordinates' acts. Examples of such evidence include the regularity and accuracy of the

---

51. United States v. Wilhelm von Leeb et al., XI TRIALS OF WAR CRIMINALS BEFORE THE NUREMBERG MILITARY TRIBUNALS UNDER CONTROL COUNCIL LAW NO. 10 1230, 1303 (US Govt. Printing Office, Washington, 1950).

reports from the field, the proximity of the headquarters to the action, and the level of control the commander exerts over his troops, to name a few.

FORUM: MILITARY COMMISSIONS

Before the enactment of the UCMJ and the growth of the U.S. court-martial system into a well-respected judicial paradigm, the U.S. military often relied on the use of *Military Commissions*. "A military commission is a military criminal court historically created out of a necessity to fill a jurisdictional gap or to provide battlefield commanders a forum to hold captured enemy personnel accountable for pre-capture violations of the laws and customs of war."[52] Military commissions have historically been used for three purposes: to substitute for civilian criminal courts during martial law when those courts are not functioning; to prosecute crimes committed by the local inhabitants of territory under U.S. belligerent occupation; and to prosecute LOAC violations by both U.S. personnel and enemy personnel during armed conflict.[53]

President George W. Bush created the current military commissions in November 2001, establishing a mechanism to try suspected terrorists in the aftermath of the 9/11 attacks. After several years of court challenges and debates as to the constitutionality of the commissions, Congress enacted the Military Commissions Act (MCA) of 2006, which codified military commission procedures and jurisdiction. Congress then passed an updated Military Commissions Act of 2009, providing some additional procedural protections and rules for the use and treatment of classified evidence. As of May 2021, the military commissions have obtained six guilty pleas and convicted two defendants after trial; the conviction of Salim Hamdan was then overturned by the D.C. Court of Appeals, and al Bahlul's conviction for material support and solicitation was vacated and resentencing for his conspiracy conviction is pending. Four cases with ten defendants are currently active, as well as one appeal.[54]

The concept of command responsibility dates back to the fifteenth century.[55] As time progressed, the concept appeared in different forms

---

52. JIMMY GURULÉ & GEOFFREY S. CORN, PRINCIPLES OF COUNTER-TERRORISM LAW 151 (2011).

53. Hamdan v. Rumsfeld, 548 U.S. 557, 595 (2006).

54. *Military Commission Cases*, OFFICE OF MILITARY COMMISSIONS, http://www.mc.mil/cases.aspx.

55. Victor Hansen, *What's Good for the Goose Is Good for the Gander: Lessons from Abu Ghraib: Time for the United States to Adopt a Standard of Command Responsibility Towards Its Own*, 42 GONZ. L. REV. 335, 337 (2007) (citing the Ordinance of Orléans issued in 1439 by Charles the VII of France, which states: "The King orders that each Captain or lieutenant be held responsible for the abuses, ills, and offences committed by members of his company.").

throughout history, most notably at the war crimes trial of General Tomoyuki Yamashita, which was held by a U.S. Military Commission in Manila, Philippines. The prosecution alleged that Yamashita, the commander of Japanese armed forces in the Philippines, allowed his forces to commit brutal atrocities against Americans in violation of the law of war.

JAPANESE TACTICS IN THE PHILIPPINES

Where was Joe Kramer? Joe Kramer was a hulking, happy-go-lucky football player from Scranton . . . during the fighting he gave "mean" new meaning. . . . Kramer in action was a fighter possessed. But where was he? He had not been seen since the attack on the nest. He was not among the body bags or the stretchers. None of the men could account for him. For the moment, at least, Kramer was missing in action.

"What the hell is that?" The question came from Murphy of Pickens' squad. "What is that up on the side of the hill? It looks like a statue." Pickens reached for his field glasses. He spotted the object of Murphy's inquiry. It was some sort of structure. A body had been propped in front of it . . . dead bodies exposed to searing heat bloated to abnormal size very quickly. The dead body was already larger than life. "The bastards," muttered Pickens. "It's got to be Kramer. They've killed him. They're tempting us to come for the body[.]" . . . Pickens peered through his field glasses again. "It can only be Kramer. And some of the machine gun fire seems to be coming from that area. If we're going to get him, we'll have to fight for him." . . . Extreme caution was used, given the possibility of booby traps. Grenades were thrown at the entrance of the cave . . . some came out with guns firing. . . . No one escaped. Company anger had been translated into expert marksmanship.

A close-up view of Kramer revealed . . . signs of torture and stab wounds on Kramer's body. It looked as if Kramer died slowly, painfully, and cruelly. "The miserable, goddamned, lousy, rotten bastards," was the best anyone could offer. It was so inadequate.

— *Henry Zabierek, U.S. Army, World War II* [56]

---

56. HENRY C. ZABIEREK, BEYOND PEARL HARBOR: I COMPANY IN THE PACIFIC OF WWII 18-20 (2010). Zabierek participated in seventeen landings in the Pacific as part of the U.S. Army's 32nd Division's I Company. He fought from New Guinea to the Philippines and served in the occupying force in Japan.

General Yamashita was charged with "unlawfully disregarding and failing to discharge his duty as a commander to control the acts of members of his command by permitting them to commit war crimes."[57] Upon appeal challenging the level of knowledge required to impose command responsibility, the Supreme Court upheld the conviction and Yamashita was executed shortly thereafter. Affirming the importance of command responsibility to the entire fabric of LOAC and the regulation of hostilities, the Supreme Court stated:

> It is evident that the conduct of military operations by troops whose excesses are unrestrained by the orders or efforts of their commander would almost certainly result in violations which it is the purpose of the law of war to prevent. Its purpose to protect civilian populations and prisoners of war from brutality would largely be defeated if the commander of an invading army could with impunity neglect to take reasonable measures for their protection. Hence the law of war presupposes that its violation is to be avoided through the control of the operations of war by commanders who are to some extent responsible for their subordinates. . . .
>
> These [treaty] provisions plainly imposed on petitioner, who at the time specified was military governor of the Philippines, as well as commander of the Japanese forces, an affirmative duty to take such measures as were within his power and appropriate in the circumstances to protect prisoners of war and the civilian population. This duty of a commanding officer has heretofore been recognized, and its breach penalized by our own military tribunals.[58]

Since its modern inception in *Yamashita*, command responsibility has developed into an accepted principle of international law. Although command responsibility does not appear directly in the Geneva Conventions, it is codified in Article 86 of Additional Protocol I:

> The fact that a breach of the Conventions or of this Protocol was committed by a subordinate does not absolve his superiors from penal or disciplinary responsibility, as the case may be, if they knew, or had information which should have enabled them to conclude in the circumstances at the time, that he was committing or was going to commit such a breach and if they did not take all feasible measures within their power to prevent or repress the breach.

The international tribunals have all incorporated command responsibility into their respective statutes, and into their jurisprudence. The Rome Statute's provision is the most comprehensive:

> (a) A military commander or person effectively acting as a military commander shall be criminally responsible for crimes within the jurisdiction of the Court committed by forces under his or her effective command and

---

57. Trial of General Tomoyuki Yamashita, U.S. Military Commission, Manila (8 October – 7 December 1945), *in* IV Law Reports of Trials of War Criminals 1 (1948).

58. Application of Yamashita, 327 U.S. 1, 15-16 (1946).

control, or effective authority and control as the case may be, as a result of his or her failure to exercise control properly over such forces, where:

   i.   That military commander or person either knew or, owing to the circumstances at the time, should have known that the forces were committing or about to commit such crimes; and

  ii.   That military commander or person failed to take all necessary and reasonable measures within his or her power to prevent or repress their commission or to submit the matter to the competent authorities for investigation and prosecution.

(b) With respect to superior and subordinate relationships not described in paragraph (a), a superior shall be criminally responsible for crimes within the jurisdiction of the Court committed by subordinates under his or her effective authority and control, as a result of his or her failure to exercise control properly over such subordinates, where:

   i.   The superior either knew, or consciously disregarded information which clearly indicated, that the subordinates were committing or about to commit such crimes;

  ii.   The crimes concerned activities that were within the effective responsibility and control of the superior; and

 iii.   The superior failed to take all necessary and reasonable measures within his or her power to prevent or repress their commission or to submit the matter to the competent authorities for investigation and prosecution.

QUESTIONS FOR DISCUSSION

1. Article 28 of the Rome Statute establishes a higher standard of knowledge for civilian superiors, requiring that a civilian leader knew or "consciously disregarded" information which clearly indicated that subordinates were committing or were about to commit LOAC violations. A civilian leader thus does not necessarily bear the same duty to actively seek out information about subordinates' activities but cannot turn a blind eye to such information.

2. Can a commander be held liable for the actions of civilians—such as contractors—operating in her area of authority or in coordination with her unit? Is it reasonable to hold a military commander criminally responsible for the actions of another person when she cannot discipline or train that individual? How would that comport with basic notions of military discipline?

3. What happens if a commander takes over after subordinates have committed violations of LOAC? Can he be liable for those crimes under command responsibility? In *Prosecutor v. Hadžihasanović*, the Appeals Chamber stated that "no practice can be found . . . that would sustain the proposition that a commander can be held responsible for crimes committed by a subordinate prior to the commander's assumption of command over

that subordinate."[59] With regard to crimes committed after a commander changes command, the SCSL Trial Chamber in *Prosecutor v. Sesay* did impose command responsibility, holding that a commander who had ceded control remained liable for actions by his troops even after he had relinquished command. However, the Appeals Chamber rejected that theory and reversed the Trial Chamber's findings in that respect.[60]

4. The Uniform Code of Military Justice (UCMJ) does not expressly affix responsibility to a military leader for violations of the law of war by their subordinates. Are the My Lai Massacre and Abu Ghraib evidence that the United States should incorporate command responsibility into its military law? Does the lack of a clear standard in the UCMJ adversely impact discipline within the military, negatively impact senior leaders, or impact the credibility of the United States?

In 1985, Jean Pictet (considered one of the "fathers" of humanitarian law) wrote the following in *Development and Principles of International Humanitarian Law*, his reflection on the law after many years as a legal advisor at the ICRC:

> To protect man against the evils of war and arbitrary treatment is not a new idea. Springing up long before the dawn of history, it has grown steadily more powerful, and today has become a tidal wave.
>
> The efforts which it has engendered keep pace with the rise of civilization, to which it is inseparably bound. Like civilization itself, it has gone through periods of sudden acceleration, of stagnation, and of setbacks, marking like milestones its journey through history.
>
> Let us be clear that all these successes and reverses are no more than episodes in the formidable struggle which has been carried on from the very beginning of human society between those who wish to preserve, unite and liberate mankind and those who seek to dominate, destroy or enslave it—a manifestation of the eternal opposition between "eros" and "thanatos," complementary and closely bound as they were to one another.
>
> The review we propose to make will demonstrate that violence can be bridled, suffering attenuated and unnecessary death vanquished.

The very same underlying notions appear in the words of Brigadier General Mark Martins, commander of the Rule of Law Field Force in Afghanistan in

---

59. Prosecutor v. Hadžihasanović, & Kubura, Case No. IT-01-47-AR72, Decision on Interlocutory Appeal Challenging Jurisdiction in Relation to Command Responsibility ¶ 45 (Int'l Crim. Trib. for the Former Yugoslavia July 16, 2003).

60. *See* Prosecutor v. Sesay Kallon and Gbao (RUF) case), Case No. SCSL-04-15-T, Judgement ¶¶ 2146, 2151 (Mar. 2, 2009); Prosecutor v. Sesay Kallon and Gbao (RUF) case), Case No. SCSL-04-15-A, Judgement ¶¶ 873-876 (Oct. 26, 2009).

2011, describing the essential role of LOAC in U.S. military operations: "your armed forces heed and will continue to heed the law, take it seriously and in fact respect it for the legitimacy it bestows upon their often violent and lethal—necessarily violent and lethal—actions in the field."[61]

---

61. Brigadier General Mark J. Martins, Harvard Law School Dean's Distinguished Lecture (July 5, 2011), http://harvardnsj.org/wp-content/uploads/2011/04/Forum_Martins _.pdf.